DATE			

THE
DECADE
MATRIX

T H E
DECADE
MATRIX

J A M E S   O.   G O L L U B

ADDISON-WESLEY PUBLISHING COMPANY, INC.

Reading, Massachusetts   Menlo Park, California   New York
Don Mills, Ontario   Wokingham, England   Amsterdam   Bonn
Sydney   Singapore   Tokyo   Madrid   San Juan   Paris
Seoul   Milan   Mexico City   Taipei

Library of Congress Cataloging-in-Publication Data
Gollub, James O.
    The decade matrix / by James O. Gollub.
        p.   cm.
    Includes index.
    ISBN 0-201-15788-8
    1. United States—Social conditions—20th century. 2. Life
cycle, Human. 3. Social values. I. Title.
HN57.G585 1991
306'.0973—dc20   90-22180
                                                   CIP

Jacket design by Richard Rossiter
Text design by Patricia G. Dunbar
Set in 11-point Janson by Compset, Inc., Beverly, MA.

123456789-MW-9594939291
First printing, March 1991

To my late parents who stimulated and confused me,
to Charlotte who soothed me,
and to the eclectic dialectic—
long may it reign

CONTENTS

P A R T   T W O

FOUR: CHILDREN OF THE AMERICAN DREAM:
1920–1929 • 80

FIVE: THE BRIDGE GENERATION: 1930–1939 • 113

SIX: THE GAP GENERATION: 1940–1949 • 144

EPILOGUE: WE HAVE MET THE DECADES AND THEY ARE US • 314

INDEX • 327

PREFACE

This book is not so much an effort at scholarly work as it is an intuitive attempt to articulate and explore the hypothesis that who we are and what we believe is given unique shape in each cohort or generation by the times we have lived through. The inspiration for this theme came from many sources and experiences over many years.

My own mother's point-blank question "What are your values?" started the process when I was a vulnerable eighteen years old. Her typically intellectual question precipitated an inner dilemma that I have only recently made any progress in resolving. For, as my parents' child, raised in the 1950s, I had never truly been clear about the values I held, or with whom I shared them. As I reflected on my beliefs, the dynamic process itself through which those views were forged became a major concern. Why did I share some beliefs with my family and friends and not other beliefs? Why were neighbors' outlooks so different from one another? What type of community did we live in that shared so few values or did so little to cultivate and define them? In our highly pluralistic society, were values so widely separated that there was only a thin veneer of civility that gave our world social coherence on any issue? While I was reassured by discovering those values that I shared with many, I was equally frightened by the lack of mutually shared perspectives among a far greater number.

My years in university did little to help me identify what my values were. However, they did enable me to make progress in learning the tools needed to understand how others perceived values. From studying rhetoric, the psychology of attitudes and problem solving, and both Western and Marxist aesthetics, I became at first highly confused but eventually better prepared to undertake some hybridized thinking about beliefs, though not until after many awkward starts and stops. As one professor in a graduate seminar pointed out: "My dear Jimmy, your paper is very annoying. Should you really be in this seminar?"

In graduate school I had the good fortune to be guided in two parallel directions that fostered my development on the question of the study of preferences and values. First, as a research fellow, I had the opportunity to perform research on how people perceive visual quality and how to use this information in making public policy. The professor with whom I worked introduced me to a world of analysts from urban planners to psychobiologists. Second, as a graduate student in gerontology in a newly formed program, I had the opportunity to integrate concepts in life span development (the longitudinal dimension) into my work through contact with several faculty and through entering the work of professional gerontologists in the clinical, social, and behavioral science fields.

However, it was not until after many years working as a research analyst at SRI International (formerly the Stanford Research Institute) that I began to realize the need for a more systematic manner of linking gerontological perspectives and psychological dimensions underlying the expression of values with practical applications. The more I worked on social and economic issues in different communities around the United States and the world, and the more I worked with business and government on helping them understand American consumer change over time, the more I worried that America was at risk. I felt increasingly that America was at risk of losing its identity—if indeed it has one—as the globalization of the economy continued and America became less a coherent political and social entity and more a place to do business—not a culture, not a country of shared values.

Perhaps, in late twentieth-century America the issue of shared values is important only to those who feel threatened by variety—the pluralism of a globalizing economy that includes diverse ethnic populations and their accompanying languages and cultural norms. For others the issue may be moot—some people share values and others don't and that's that. Among some people, worry about the issue may be unnecessary in that technology will now allow the development of individuality to expand, and decentralization of government functions to the community level will enable the reconstruction of shared community values. For still others, values may be perceived as a hostile political agenda, in which expression of arbitrarily defined "good values" is allowed, while "bad values" are suppressed.

America has always been tolerant and accommodating, but dynamic. If this is true, the question of how values are formed and expressed in our rapidly changing society may be only of practical interest to politicians and marketers, and of academic interest to sociologists scrutinizing that odd species, *homo Americanus.*

I have become clearer about my values through the intervening years and could probably give my mother a decent answer now were she still around. Yet, traveling as much as I do to continents east and west, I am constantly reminded of how much different we are from the rest of the world, despite our roots. Perched here in our North American sanctuary, our own social contours are being constantly re-shaped by the tides not only of immigration, but by the very raw and continuous undulating cultural foundations that constitute our composite world, America.

Knowing what we believe and finding those who share our values is no simple task. Given our changing country, can we reinforce our own identities as both individuals and members of a nation? Is this an absurd notion that violates the premise of America, land of the free? If it does not, this book offers one window through which we may catch a glimpse of who we are and where we are going.

ACKNOWLEDGMENTS

The inspiration for this book has a long developmental history. The initial seed can be traced to the late Professor Richard Crutchfield of the psychology department at the University of California, Berkeley, who introduced me to the framework for understanding creativity, problem solving, and personality.

Irish poet Seamus Heaney also made his contribution one spring by helping me to sense how language, place, and time combine to sculpt the context of our lives.

The techniques I have adapted for studying people's preferences and perspectives derive from work with my friend and professor, Tridib Banerjee, Ph.D., at the University of Southern California. The gerontological perspective used was brought to my attention through my instructor and friend Victor Regnier on the faculty of the Leonard Davis School of Gerontology, at the University of Southern California, and Neil Cutler, Ph.D., then of the same faculty, now executive director of the Boetner Center at Bryn Mawr University.

Three people greatly contributed to this work. First and foremost, Shirley Weinland Hentzell provided historical content that gives life to the chapters on the Children of the Century, those of the Dream Deferred, and Children of the American Dream. Moreover, Ms. Hentzell, a gifted science fiction author in her own right and senior technical writer and editor at SRI International, has edited other professional work of mine at SRI for more than 14 years.

Second, David Gollub, Ph.D., my cousin, provided detailed background for the chapters on the Gap Generations and Baby Boom. David, a scholar of 18th-century literature and puns and a government documents specialist at SRI during working hours, is also a writer and publisher of the poetry of the San Francisco region.

Third, Sarah M. Corse, Ph.D., provided background material for the chapters on the Baby Boom and Techno-Kid Generations. Ms. Corse, now an assistant professor of sociology at the University of Virginia, was able to carry out her work while beginning her doctoral thesis.

The editing of this book was no easy matter. A number of editors worked on the document during its completion. In California, both Shirley Hentzell and Mary Tasner took several passes. In Massachusetts, Cyrisse Jaffee, a consulting editor, as well as Diana Gibney and Stephanie Argeros-Magean, brought the final manuscript together.

While my colleagues at SRI in the Center for Economic Competitiveness (CEC) were not involved in the development of this book, I owe them a debt of thanks for their enduring patience with my moods and tolerance for my interest in fields that often seem to range outside of our normal terrain—political economics and institutional change. We have worked together for a long time and I feel it is a unique privilege to pursue with them what I like to call "the eclectic dialectic," which links the study of values, industry dynamics, the new economic foundations, and development of strategic vision into a cohesive, action-focused consultative practice.

Addison-Wesley and Jane Isay, senior editor, in particular, have been patient and enthusiastic during the production of this work in ways that I have deeply appreciated. No author likes to face the dread of meeting deadlines, and Jane and her associates made the process as painless as my own conscience would let it be.

Finally, I thank my wife, Charlotte Grossman Gollub, a film and video editor who understands the challenge of weaving an integrated story, for her love.

THE RASHOMON QUANDARY

*The storyteller's own experience of men and things,
whether for good or ill—not only what he has passed
through himself, but even events which he has only
witnessed or been told of—has moved him to an emotion
so passionate that he can no longer keep it shut up in his
heart. Again and again something in his own life or in
that around him will seem to the writer so important he
cannot bear to let it pass into oblivion. There must never
come a time, he feels, when men do not know about it.*

—LADY MURASAKI, SHIKIBU, *TALE OF GENJI*
(A.D. 1000)

THE LIFE SPAN PERSPECTIVE

Hang on to your metaphorical hats! You are about to embark on a journey through *terra incognita*, through one of the last remaining jungles on earth—the values and beliefs of 20th-century Americans. By exploring our values and characteristics and how they evolved, this book explains where we came from, where we are, and where we're headed. It is *your* story, and the story of those around you.

Perhaps you want to know yourself better, or perhaps you want to influence, or simply understand, someone in your life. You may have acquired a new client, or you may want to target a new market for your product. How can you find out what might appeal to them? What attitudes do they share? Traditional market research is one way, but the results are not enduring; sociological, anthropological, and ethnological studies are another. But you might retire before scientists agreed on a theory and knew enough to answer your questions. Life span analysis, which combines the convenience of market research with a more scientific perspective, is simple and faster, and it costs less. Moreover, it will hold true for a lifetime.

We are all travelers in time. The values we bring with us on our journey have been formed by our interaction with the world around us—specific historical events, cultural norms, family expectations—and by how we view that world. We are each shaped by key learning experiences, seen through the lens of our past and our genetic foundation. Fed the materials of our times we thus spin out the web of our lives. But we are not freestanding souls, spontaneously creating new outlooks all our own. Instead, we hear our parents' moral, political, and spiritual beliefs and measure them against our world view. We are thus captives of our own individual history, but also of our shared history.

Each person reading this page has come to this moment from a different past and has entered time at a different point—the moment of his or her birth—in the continuum of history. Since each of us made our entrance at different intervals in the same, ongoing play, our experiences and beliefs are not the same.

Who are we? What do we believe? What kind of order can we impose on the diverse identities of a quarter billion individuals to help us see ourselves—and others—in a clearer light? To answer these questions, this book presents a series of life stories and personality profiles of seven "generations" of Americans, born in each decade from 1900 through 1969. (We use the term *generation* for simplicity. We mean, for example, everyone born in the 1920s, or 1930s, and living contemporaneously; not in the usual sense of the 50-year age span between grandparents and grandchildren, or of "the older generation.")

Each decade is described from the standpoint of what was going on in the United States at the time—economically, politically, socially. The story of each 10-year age group, or cohort, tells what happened to make them who they are today. You will find yourself in this book, as well as your parents, grandparents, friends, customers, and clients. The insights you gain here will help you understand the values, attitudes, and behavior of yourself and those around you. This is the *Life Span Perspective*.

Seven generations of Americans are studied:

Children of the Century (1900–1909)—14.2 million people

The Dream-Deferred Generation (1910–1919)—16.8 million people

Children of the American Dream (1920–1929)—22.5 million people
The Bridge Generation (1930–1939)—22.5 million people
The Gap Generation (1940–1949)—32.1 million people
The Baby Boom (1950–1959)—40.5 million people
The Techno-Kids (1960–1969)—39.9 million people

THE RASHOMON QUANDARY

In *Rashomon*, a film by Akira Kurosawa, a samurai and his lady are assaulted in a forest by a robber. The samurai is killed and the lady's honor stolen. The robber is apprehended. During the trial the lady, the robber, and the ghost of the samurai each tell the story from their own viewpoint. The audience does not know what actually happened; the "truth" will never be known. Yet the outcome of the events—the death of the samurai, the ravished lady, the sentencing of the robber—cannot be undone.

This is the Rashomon quandary: how to understand why people behave as they do when we have not seen the world as they see it. Understanding events and the meaning of those events becomes even harder when we must rely on different vantage points. If only we could have experienced the events ourselves! But we each live within the limits of our own world view, forgetting how different life appears to each of us: "Where you stand depends on where you sit."

This book allows you to stand—so to speak—in the footsteps of those who have come before you, or of those of your own age who stand next to you. Unlike many other books, it does not assume the traditional perspective of the omniscient historian who views our lives from a plane far removed from our own. Instead, it assumes a new Life Span Perspective of what is actually a relativistic universe, a changing world in which what you see and how you see it depends on where, and when, and who (your gender, ethnic origin, socioeconomic class) you are. Our values evolve and synthesize new expressions of material, moral, political, and spiritual belief in a kind of feedback loop from those who precede and coexist. They do not simply recapitulate the views of bygone eras.

For instance, being a child during a particular time can significantly alter the formation of personal values. Major events, such as a war, depression, epidemic, political scandal, or changing morals, are not dramatic to someone born in the middle of them. To a child, a shell casing can be a toy like any other, and war may simply be the world outside the door. For adults, however, these events have profound effects on fears, dreams, desires, and expectations.

Gender, race, and socioeconomic status are important for us as we shape our value system, since they often determine how outside events become meaningful. A logical example is the importance of gender in determining the impact of historical-social events such as feminism or the Vietnam War. Our gender also affects how we view role models. Although we generally assume that female role models are more important in a girl's development, they may also have a distinct effect on boys, causing them to be more aware of—if not more accepting of—changing roles for women.

A person who is African-American or Hispanic faces the clear consequence of growing up in a period when racism is high and role models are often martyred. Nonetheless, shared ethnicity does not mean experiencing external events in the same manner. Antiblack or anti-Hispanic sentiment will be felt, however painfully, in a wide variety of ways—from a hated but expected part of everyday life to the acting out of apparently incomprehensible deviancy.

THE LIFE SPAN FRAMEWORK

To describe how events, attitudes, and values have influenced and directed our decisions, choices, and life styles, a method of analysis called the *Life Span Framework* (LSF), based on themes from the study of aging, was created. This approach integrates concepts in gerontology (i.e., cohort and life stage changes), sociology (i.e., consumer and social behavior), and psychology.

The LSF consists of four elements. *Time Signatures* identify the historic events that influenced the formation of our values and outlook; *Birthmarks* tell us how the personality types of each generation developed; *Rites of Passage* show us how people change in the way they express their values; and the *Weather Report* describes the external factors that affect our life styles now and in the future.

The LSF has typically been used in helping business and government understand different consumer groups, in order to plan and formulate public policy, product development, advertising, and so on. The LSF identifies what groups have in common, how they differ within and across age and attitudinal groups, what they prefer, and how this might change over time, as values are expressed through life styles.

The life span idea began as an effort to bring gerontological principles out of the academic cloisters and into the practical world. In

SRI projects prior to 1984 the impact of social change was generalized at the level of aging; for example, in some projects, all people over 65 were treated as being the same—old. In a 1984 report for the Values and Life Styles (VALS) program, *Not the Same Old Story*, segmentation of consumers not only by age but also by psychological types was applied for the first time. Subsequently, a variety of research projects was carried out for both business and government to demonstrate how age-based segmentation could be useful for better understanding today's consumers and also for predicting the structure of future markets and social change.

Past studies examined how age-based psychological and social types could be used to define current and changing health care markets, for creating new types of housing and community designs, for designing new types of financial services products, even for creating new models of food purchasing, preparation, and consumption. This framework has also been used to examine individual motivation to work and retire, to avoid or take on risk, and generally to help organizations plan and operate services for consumers (and voters) in a more sensitive and responsive way. Life span is an effort to help us see the "trees" despite the "forest" of overgeneralization about consumers—about ourselves.

The findings in this book reflect research and observations from a variety of sources, including:

- Gerontological and personality assessment literature on life span behavior and theories of continuity and exchange.
- Historical materials on the experiences of each generation, from contemporary history books; analysis of the books, magazines, newspapers, music, and media of each era.
- Biographical materials, including a nonstatistical sample of personal interviews with representatives of each age group, taped autobiographies, and biographies—published and unpublished— already written for other purposes.

This book is not a scientific treatise, although it aspires to change popular conceptions of how we express our values. The Life Span Framework, such as it is, integrates several important principles in gerontology and psychology, without pretending to be academic. Nonetheless, the book is based on primary empirical insights drawn from prior work at SRI. The ideas used came primarily from studies of adults born between 1900 and 1930. Much of the material for those groups born in 1930 and beyond is based on application of the framework in interviews (rather than surveys), on biographical material (autobiographies by people of many age groups), and on extensive use of historical materials on U.S. economic and political, social, and cultural history.

While the book offers readers a "lens" through which they can view themselves, the stories told should be viewed as synoptic, illustrative, and, at worst, what might pass for expedient profiles of thus far unknown faces of American time travelers.

Part I presents the Life Span Framework and tells how this book was developed. Part II describes the generations born in each decade between 1900 and 1969. Each generation is described by means of the four elements of the Life Span Framework as its members pass through the decades of their lives. Following these descriptions are four composite personality portraits representative of each generation. Each personality type has been given a name indicative of the most salient feature of that type of person. Part III, a reflection on the future, concludes the book. In it we see who we are likely to become over the next decade. The Epilogue asks what this journey through the "decade matrix" means for the American identity and offers a possible answer. So, read on, and prepare to meet yourself coming and going.

PART
ONE

O N E

THE LIFE SPAN FRAMEWORK

There are four elements of the Life Span Framework, used to develop the life stories of each generation and their personality profiles:

- *Time Signatures*—the significant events in the rhythm of history that leave their imprint on each age group, or cohort, during the development of the group's values, such as a stock market crash or a presidential assassination. Those born in 1920–1929, for instance, share different Time Signatures from those born in 1930–1939, since the two groups are at different points in their development when key events occur.
- *Birthmarks*—the personality styles of each cohort that distinguish them from their peers. Each Birthmark is a composite of many individual psychological traits, such as autonomy or self-indulgence.
- *Rites of Passage*—stages of value development that individuals pass through from childhood to late adulthood. Each stage helps the individual define or reaffirm his or her values, which are then expressed through his or her life style.
- *Weather Report*—how the external environment affects the way in which individuals express (or do not express) their values. These include current economic factors, technological changes, political shifts, and cultural attitudes.

3

TIME SIGNATURES: THE RHYTHM OF HISTORY

Traditionally, where we came from was often the best indicator of who we would become. Were we immigrants or Yankees, from the north or south, city or country, one side of the tracks or the other? But today, as the world becomes more complex, *when* we were raised and *what* we have experienced are more important in determining who we become. Events, after all, are not just hazy news headlines; they shape our lives, because they teach us—and sometimes force us—to change how we think.

The impact of historic events may be direct because of their tremendous consequences, such as the stock market crash of 1929, and the Great Depression that followed. Events may also affect us indirectly, such as the assassination of John F. Kennedy and Martin Luther King, Jr. Even when events do not directly touch our lives, they may still have a pervasive effect on us; you or a family member may not have been a victim of the influenza pandemic of 1918 to 1919, the polio epidemic of the 1940s, or the AIDS epidemic of the 1980s, but these events nevertheless influence your life. Some events, seen as independent of those experiencing them, may appear as a natural progression. It may appear inevitable that the depression was followed by the buildup of international tension during the 1930s, World War II, postwar reconstruction, and the cold war. But for each individual, the meaning and impact of important events are determined by his or her age and stage of development when the event occurs.

There is no rigid way in which to label events as good or bad. For each member of a family, the same event could be traumatic, hardly felt, or even beneficial. For instance, during the depression a father may have suffered from being out of work. But a young woman whose fiancé couldn't afford to marry might have learned to type and gone to work outside the home, changing her life pattern forever. A teenage son may have had to drop out of high school to help support his family, missing out on college or a professional career. A younger child may have had to take on more responsibilities but may have been allowed more independence. Each person, therefore, would describe the effect of the same event differently, almost as if they had not experienced the same event.

A personality type within one generation might resemble that of another generation. However, by understanding that type of person's Time Signatures, events that correspond with his or her stage of development, we can better understand the dreams, desires, and motivation of that person. Moreover, we can compare the similarities and differences across generations and observe why there are distinct traits that relate to the life experiences of one period of time and not another. We see this in the generation gap, for example. Those adults born in the 1920s are today so often at odds with those born in the 1940s.

In each generation, younger people do not merely learn from what is around them; they evolve their own social settings and modes of self-expression. This helps explain why children do not often sympathize much with or completely endorse their parents' views of how things were in "the good old days." It is this lack of shared experiences that leads children and teenagers to use their imagination to reconstruct—within their own limits of comprehension—what they have never known, through, for example, fads and nostalgia crazes. This synthesizing is a basic part of the process of social change. A whole generation's Time Signature, therefore, is the set of selected events that were meaningful and significant for that generation. They are composed of

- *Economic Outlook*—shifts in existing industrial structures, employment patterns, generational roles, age groups, and worker skill levels.
- *Technological Conditions*—evolution of new technologies that introduce or alter products and production methods; transformation of transactions between people (i.e., communication) due to the evolution of media—from newspapers to radio to movies to television, and now to computer networks and bulletin boards; the ability of the media to determine what events we will experience and to shape how we will experience them.
- *Social and Political Environment*—changes or unusual features of local institutions, such as public schools (crowding, crime, curriculum, teaching methods), health services (immunization, contraception availability, and affordability of acute and long-term care), government agencies (the military, public services, welfare), and neighborhoods (cities, towns, suburbs); changes in political institutions, including the collapse or growth of credibility and respect for governing institutions and political leaders.
- *Cultural Climate*—changes in family structure and human relations, including immigration, migrations, divorce, family size, demographics, and life expectancy.

BIRTHMARKS: OUR DISTINGUISHING TRAITS

In order to understand what Americans share as a group, we must understand each generation's Time Signatures, since they form the foundation for values. But we must also understand that for all generations there are certain personality dimensions that are timeless, and that each individual has a personality structure that is also timeless, on which can be hung the unique traits evolved during a lifetime. The personalities peculiar to a generation work with this internal foundation, but they are uniquely molded by experience, which distinguishes one generation from another. We could say that the neuroses of one generation are not the same as another. (For example, people have always had eating disorders, but increased anorexia and bulimia are probably more characteristic of young women today.)

Our internal psychological parts work in different ways, as shaped by the world in which we develop. There is nothing very surprising in that; yet we tend to think of our psychosocial trends as just news items, rather than products of a changing world of self, self-image, and social role.

Throughout history individuals have always been aggressive or passive, generous or stingy, flexible or rigid. We are used to thinking of these qualities as describing our "personality," and that it is our "personality" that determines how we "choose" our life paths. But this is only partly true. Take, for example, two 15-year-old boys in the year 1937. One is passive, the other aggressive. But this difference in their personalities, although likely to persist throughout their lives, is of less importance to their future than that both will be of draft age in 1941.

Psychological constructs, the building blocks of personality "types," are those personality traits that can be consistently measured, usually in conjunction with actions that express them, such as voting tendencies, shopping habits, even marriage. A Birthmark is a set of those psychological constructs that are helpful in describing individual values. Through statistical analysis each set provides a composite picture of a "type" of person.

For example, one construct that is used in building a "type" is a measure of openness to change. This construct is based on several individual measures—well-being, anxiety, adaptability, sensation-seeking, and so on. Taken together, these measures describe a strong behavior pattern (openness to change) that affects how a person makes choices. A person who is open is generally more willing to accept others and to change his or her own behavior, with a lower level of anxiety. A person who is not open to change is usually less adaptive, with higher levels of anxiety.

Other constructs that have been used include measures of compulsiveness, such as self-indulgence and self-denial, and of autonomy and dependence, which help define the extent to which individuals are driven to take care of themselves, or to do things a certain way, or to rely on others.

Our Birthmark is our core psychological identity. This core is shaped through childhood relationships with mother, father, siblings, other family members, and teachers. These early and least self-conscious interactions give us our sense of self. We develop ways of interacting with the world—expressing our values—that include:

- *Intrapersonal*—how do we relate to ourselves? Are we open or closed to our innermost feelings? Are we driven by impulses, constrained by anxieties, or balanced in meeting our personal needs?
- *Interpersonal*—how do we relate to family, friends, lovers, spouses? Are we able to build and sustain relationships that are meaningful and adapt to challenges, or do our relationships become extensions of our problems? How do we balance ethics and material well-being in our relationships?
- *Societal*—how do we relate to groups, such as neighbors, coworkers, employers, peers? What do we believe in and practice as members of a social group or club? Is our participation mutually beneficial or exploitive?
- *Global*—how do we relate to larger value systems and world concepts, such as those embraced by national, ethnic, or religious groups? Do we have commitments that drive our actions beyond our immediate priorities? Are we disenfranchised, cynical, or despairing of the future?

Birthmarks help us draw a brief, more intimate portrait of each generation. However, because each Birthmark is a composite, it is necessarily limited in detail and differentiation. Readers may find something they recognize—themselves or someone they know—in one or more Birthmarks. Of course, most of us are inclined to deny that our unique personalities can be reduced to a stereotype. But these Birthmarks are not stereotypes, but generalizations intended to illuminate and amuse, helping us see ourselves and others more clearly.

The LSF views the individual as a time traveler, bringing values formed in his or her early years to the present day. Time Signatures give us a special but shared experience with members of our own generation. Our unique personalities—Birthmarks—distinguish us from our age peers. Although we may have traits that are similar to those of different age groups, our Time Signatures and Birthmarks combine to give each of us a special, *time-based* personality. The fundamental values that define our individuality do not change dramatically during our lives. However, how we express those values can and does change over the years.

RITES OF PASSAGE: VALUES EXPRESSION IN OUR LIFE STAGES

Most of us believe that we acquired our values when we were young—from parents and siblings, perhaps teachers or clergy. These values supposedly serve us well the rest of our days. But what our parents think they taught us may be far different from what we learned. Those born between World War I and World War II had parents trying to fit their own horse-and-buggy values into a world of cars, planes, electricity, and Sigmund Freud. Authoritarian but fair, these parents wanted to teach their children how to tell right from wrong, but they were bewildered sometimes by changes they didn't understand, like no jobs in the 1930s. These children watched their parents listening to national leaders exhorting the American people to tackle the task of rebuilding the collapsed economy, or fighting the "good fight."

Certainly, childhood is the time when our outlook is shaped, but the clay is still wet, the mold not hardened. While the imprint of formal or informal instruction may be strong, the lessons are often untested and sometimes unclear. Our abilities to adapt, to learn, and to use tools to solve problems are characteristic of our species. This adaptability and malleability allows us to reconfirm and perhaps alter the impressions of our earliest, often unremembered, or subconscious, learnings through subsequent experience.

As we pass from childhood into and through adulthood, we reach and enter a series of life stages where our values are challenged by new life choices at each juncture. These junctures are not necessarily determined in any explicit way, but we tend to measure them by the social norms of our times, such as marriage, jobs, and family development. These stages, which generally follow the decades of our lives, are critical thresholds of development, in our inner (intrapersonal) life; in our relationships with significant others, such as spouses, lovers, friends, and children (interpersonal); in our involvement with groups (jobs, careers, clubs); and in our world view.

As we reach these thresholds, we find we need to make choices that will enable us to adapt to the challenges at hand. At each key point we either refine or redefine how we express our values, or we muddle through until the next.

Rarely do we abandon our fundamental values. For example, studies of voting behavior over time tell us that most people vote for the same party their entire lives. However, people will abandon a party when its values no longer reflect their own. Some will insist that values do change over time, but they are confusing change with what is actually consolidation, or clarification of fundamental beliefs.

When actions taken to express values prove to be personally unworkable, "healthy" or "normal" individuals may often choose a new course of action to achieve a better result—a better "fit" between their beliefs and their actions. For instance, a woman who finds herself in an abusive marriage and believes divorce is wrong may choose divorce, despite her initial belief.

When *do* people change values? They rarely do, which is why *how* we develop is so important. Calls for society to change people's behavior usually don't work: "Say No to Drugs" has little chance of causing fundamental value change, but it does allow those whose values have been muffled or intimidated to recognize them and express them better. People rarely change values, but they often express them poorly. By learning to recognize values better, beliefs that may express themselves in racism or hostility to women or even crime can sometimes find modes of expression that are less antisocial. But this is by no means easy. The evidence speaks for itself. Our society is struggling with its own ambiguity of values—a condition that results in considerable social confusion, pain, and indictments by various religious, political, and social factions.

Individually, we can still find better ways to identify and express our beliefs. But not always, and sometimes never. If we are helped, or are able to help ourselves, we may recognize that we are not getting what we want out of life. We may try to change course, but the "ruts" are sometimes deep.

Major trauma causes some but not all people to shift values. The unexpected death of a child of religious parents may cause them either to abandon religion or to become increasingly religious. When expectations are raised and then abruptly altered by events, some people will make radical changes; others will persevere. At the core of life span analysis is the notion that we all try to find the most adaptable, successful method of optimizing our quality of life.

It is our Birthmark that determines if we will be more likely to, seemingly, change from one outlook to another. Our Time Signatures set the stage for our choices, putting more or less pressure on us, or giving us greater or fewer options. Our Rites of Passage are simply periods of development in which the achievements of an earlier stage have enabled us, or required us, to take an additional step in how we relate to ourselves and others. If we succeed at one stage, we stand a better chance of pulling through the next in a positive way. Many people never succeed, but seem to us to be trapped in an ongoing adolescence at age 40, or lost in work, with no signs of balancing external responsibilities with more personal requirements. The life stages through which we pass are called, here, "rites of passage": *rites*, because they are important challenges to our current status, each a consequence of past choices (to seek education or not, to marry or not, to work or not); and *passages*, because they also represent developmental transitions, perhaps not involving clear social ceremonies in every case, but at least inner celebrations, or acknowledgments of transition (coming to terms with career, family, retirement, or mortality). For this book, Rites of Passage are a convenient device for tracking our social development—seeing the patterns, and how they vary from generation to generation as a result of the dynamic character of our world.

Rites of Passage, then, are a series of personal developmental stages that lead us to examine how our actions match our beliefs, and how we can express those beliefs in our life choices and life styles. Rites of Passage are not absolute, nor can they be measured or proved. They are simply junctions, forks in the road, where we must choose the best road to take.

There are ten Rites of Passage; each, with the exception of two—Diversion and Expansion—spans about 10 years of a person's life, and approximately corresponds to the decades since 1900.

Immersion (Birth to Age 12)

Beginning at birth, major imprinting of values takes place during a period in which young children are "immersed" in stimuli they cannot critically evaluate. In medieval times developmental processes were not acknowledged; children were treated as small adults. Today, this first stage of development is recognized as a time when basic values are acquired and learning skills are developed.

Young children are subject to a flow of information controlled by family, peers, teachers, and the media. They absorb a tremendous amount of it from the world around them, yet rarely have sufficient external points of reference for questioning and ordering the information they receive, particularly from television and friends. Children may seem technically more worldly these days, what with media, electronic games, divorced multiparent households, and explicit communications about crime, abuse, sex, and disease. Despite this, the meaning of this bounty of information is still subject to a process of assimilation and application. To assume that children have clearly defined values is not necessarily incorrect, but in reality these beliefs are "prototype" views of life, not yet formalized; or if they are they may be an exaggerated response to a difficult situation. Establishing values is a process of trial and error, and adolescence is where this process begins.

Diversion (Ages 13–18)

Diversion is a period of testing and articulating values. Typically, adults see adolescence as a difficult time (for both parents and teenagers!). Their children are seeking out new sources of information and are forming new values, contrasting them with those of their parents. Friends and the media are especially important sources of values for teenagers, who begin to shift away from the family and toward ambiguous adulthood, with all of its risks and opportunities. At this stage tools for implementing values may be crude; the adolescent's sense of the consequences of actions is inconsistent. If a child learns ineffective ways of expressing values at home, these may be carried into adulthood. Experimentation with drugs, sex, and petty crime—as well as other dramatic means of separating self from family and establishing the rudiments of a personal identity—is common, but not universal. There are no easy roads to adulthood, or through adulthood for that matter. "Good models" are not always what they appear to be. We find our way with the working materials we have.

It is interesting that the concept of the "teenage" years did not exist before mandatory high school education became the widely accepted norm in the United States right after World War I. Children born in the 1930s were the first teen generation to be labeled as such.

Expansion (Ages 19–24)

The perspective of the adolescent expands through the practice of autonomous decision making. At this stage young adults role-play many tough adult choices with greater, although not complete, seriousness than before. They make and remake important life choices, such as going to college or taking a job; getting married or staying single; voting or remaining uninvolved; committing or not (to work, family, etc.).

The expansion of choices often makes it difficult for young, relatively inexperienced adults to balance their priorities. Many lack sufficient role models, since expectations and career choices may have changed significantly since parents or grandparents were young. The period of expansion has varied from era to era. In the United States in the 1950s, expansion involved fulfilling military obligations (for young men) and emulating adult social activities (work, dating, dances). In the 1960s, expansion was an explosive process of questioning the values of the past 50 years and seeking alternatives, many of which were abandoned later on.

The challenge for a young adult at this stage is not so much making the right choices—which cannot be forecast—but in learning to make the choices flexibly, so that choices can be adapted or amended as the individual becomes increasingly informed and better able to consolidate personal values. Flexibility and adaptiveness are hard qualities to acquire. Essentially they require an open outlook that reflects a tolerance of change and yet an ability to remain committed to the completion of tasks. A second challenge is learning how to plan for the future, to allow for achievements that require greater commitment and investment. Both skills require experiences where adapting, planning, and persevering are rewarded.

Conversion (Ages 25–34)

This stage focuses on the negotiation and implementation of critical decisions pertaining to career and family, when adults convert their diverse objectives into tangible actualities—marriage, divorce, children, renting or buying a home, choosing a career.

The level of personal energy expended to attain and achieve these objectives is very high, as are the expectations. Often people initially make enthusiastic or optimistic commitments that are not accurate reflections of their beliefs. As a result, conversion may be a time of dramatic change, as first marriages end and jobs or career expectations change. Disappointment, as well as success, is common.

The challenges at this stage are to make choices that are true to personal values, and then to sustain the commitment to those choices, persevering long enough to work out problems at home and at work.

Submersion (Ages 35–44)

Submersion is the "work" and "commitment" stage, an energy-intensive period in which the individual is driven by what appear to be high-level priorities, started in the Conversion stage. Fundamental personal needs may be ignored, or integrated, as the individual attends to the needs of family and workplace. (The process works in reverse, too—e.g., neglecting family for work or for personal needs.)

There may not be as much similarity among members of the same generation during the Submersion stage today as there was for past generations, due to today's far greater uncertainties and unclear family models (high divorce rates). The 1990s offer far more room for variation. Some may make more job and marriage changes during this time, preventing their lives from becoming predictable, and forcing them to reexamine their values. Others may recapitulate the patterns of past generations, seeking to immerse themselves in work or family, either because they are happy with the status quo, or because they do not wish to question their innermost feelings.

The challenge facing individuals during the Submersion stage is to keep from losing track of what they are doing and why—and not to let life's tasks become the objectives, or to become routine or meaningless. The negative outcome is "drowning" while in the Submersion stage—becoming overwhelmed without knowing or wanting the consequences.

Reversion (Ages 45–54)

This is the period of what is often called "mid-life crisis." Reversion typically occurs as a reaction to a prolonged period of Submersion. If, during the preceding stage, the individual used work or married life as a device to avoid, rather than realize his or her values, the contradictions may emerge in the Reversion stage. A man suddenly "wakes up," and discovers that he can no longer stand his job (after years of ignoring his dissatisfaction or not acting on it); a woman realizes that she is dissatisfied with her marriage (after years of not seriously thinking about it or discussing problems). A crisis may occur—of faith in oneself and in one's investment in career and family so long taken for granted.

At this time, adults often revert to a more adolescent mode of behavior, acting as if they are seeing the world for the first time. This may include rejecting now-unworkable values expression (e.g., work), rebellion due to pent-up anger reaching the "boiling point," and new exploratory actions in an effort to compensate for frustration. Precipitated by the loss of focus during years of being "tuned out," individuals may act out their anger and frustration through divorce, quitting a job, having a nervous breakdown, or making dramatic life style changes.

The challenge during this stage is to rediscover one's own basic values, and to make the needed changes early enough to reduce further negative consequences, or to be able to live with the consequences of choices made in good faith. Reversion may not necessarily occur in the form of rebellion; it might simply be a return to original sound principles—for example, pulling out of the Submersion stage.

Revision (Ages 55–64)

This stage is the period when plans and options for the future are often reevaluated like it or not, when uncertainty is felt about personal priorities (with or without a major upheaval in the Reversion stage). This uncertainty is often caused by the differences between what an individual believes his or her situation in life to be, and what the outside world says it actually is. For example, workers, both blue- and white-collar professionals, typically find themselves being passed over for promotions or laid off. Underskilled employed women are also likely to find themselves in this predicament if they are divorced at this stage. Individuals may find that they are no longer viewed as vital contributors to the workplace, or that the external environment has changed and they haven't (the current "life" of engineers' skills is 4 to 12 years before obsolescence). At this stage individuals must reappraise what they want from work, and what a realistic plan for future work (e.g., changing jobs, upgrading skills) or retirement might be.

Revision is also a period of change for parents. The term "empty nest" does not adequately convey the seriousness of their dilemma. For many, this stage means coping with family needs of older children (housing those that are college-age or unemployed, financing their first home or a business start-up). Adults try to adjust their household to their own needs while still facing pressure from their children. This can be a painful, or mournful task.

Furthermore, this stage brings many adults, barely finished rearing their children, to the role of caring for their own aging parents. Many of the burdens of this stage fall on women who, at this time, are often in the midst of pursuing new career or personal development objectives.

The challenge of the Revision stage is balancing past achievements and goals with the current realities of life. This is a subtle stage, where there is often a need to refresh one's sense of mission and direction, shaking off the stereotypes of aging that society encourages. The direction that is most characteristic of today is a hard career change. This is true for both men and women. Women have typically had to cope with more change and do the balancing both economically and socially.

Transition (Ages 65–74)

This stage centers on the transition between expectations and realities of work and family life and the option of retirement. Revision, while focusing on fundamental conflicts in economic reality, extends into transition in many areas. This stage can encompass the "third-quarter crisis." Here it is the inner dilemma that creates a need for a new game plan. This crisis is the clash between what individuals who have retired think they are—vital and competent people—and how society treats them—disengaged and irrelevant "senior citizens."

The crisis is experienced when expectations for the future do not turn out as planned, usually within a brief time (one to two years after retirement). The Transition stage is made especially difficult when people's plans for the future prove to be shortsighted and inadequate to accommodate their need for engagement and continuity, which has been typical among the first generations to have the option of retirement. Often people feel shocked and depressed as they experience themselves to be unwanted in the economic or social marketplace—a little different from Revision, where the challenge is in adapting to a current condition, rather than a less well defined state of affairs. Of course, as labor demand shifts up or down this process of adapting may become easier or harder.

Not all individuals in transition experience a third-quarter crisis. Transition does not require trauma—those who have been effective in maintaining their life style independent of work or family may find the Transition stage relatively easy. They may be able to refocus their personal priorities and take on a new enterprise, hobby, or recreational activity such as travel.

The challenge of the Transition stage is to reach it prepared, male or female. This is no easy task. Feminist author Betty Friedan once gave a speech with the theme "Why Can't Men Age More Like Women." She pointed out that (so far) women have had to be better at adapting to change than men, since women's lives have been so contingent on others (spouse, children, parents). Men, in contrast, often cannot handle change very well and become frustrated or angry and a general nuisance in retirement.

Emergence (Ages 75–84)

This stage is experienced by some as exhilarating. The individual may clarify or refocus his or her values without the oppressive sense of obligation he or she had during previous life stages. "Wisdom" may emerge, since beliefs are no longer overwhelmed by competing priorities. In a successful period of Emergence, an adult may be able to refine skills and knowledge, and focus, with fewer distractions and clearer vision, on accomplishment (e.g., our senior thinkers, from John Gardner to Peter Drucker). Integrity and quality, not performance, are the focus. Mastery—an efficiency of motion and grace of practice that less experienced individuals cannot achieve—may be reached. Contrary to popular myth, new directions in development can arise in this stage with great strength and purpose of mind. (An individual may learn a new language or technical skill, or become a teacher of others.)

Many find that Emergence is elusive. Religious people become more religious, the politically dogmatic become more passionately entrenched. Those who are poor and in poor health cannot easily move away from the primacy of their needs and remain trapped in those daily realities—a product of our broader social failings.

The challenge of Emergence depends on the individual gaining an honest appraisal of his or her fundamental capabilities and reinvesting in them—hopeful of continuation of a lifelong process, but realizing it is never too late to start. Emergence between ages 75 to 84 is more feasible than ever today.

Transcendence (85 and Beyond)

This stage represents the achievement of a broader vision of life, beyond the pressing priorities of flesh and bone. Transcendence is a stage where, despite probable physical limitations, the individual is able to fully engage in the lives of family or in national events, and consider how the beliefs he or she has maintained for a lifetime stand up to the test of time.

The challenge of the Transcendence stage is to achieve an understanding of how well a person has done in establishing and implementing values. In doing so, the individual can take satisfaction from achievement, or acknowledge failures and vulnerabilities from the vantage point of an experienced time traveler. Clearly, those driven by fundamental needs of the body, as well as by undeveloped potentials and unhealed wounds of a lifetime, will find that Transcendence is hard. Even so, achieving this stage is not like passing a college exam—the potential for discovery is not gone, only buried under the weight of years. If the Transcendence stage is marked by losses in health and social status, the result may be a turning inward, and a lack of concern about the world.

Given increased vitality over the life span, many will have the opportunity to combine the achievements of previous stages over longer periods of time. Thus, careers will evolve and change with insight until the end of life, an additive, interpretive process.

WEATHER REPORT: BUTTON UP YOUR OVERCOAT

"Weather Report" is a term we use to describe how external environmental factors affect the way we make our choices, given the values we already have. They are characteristics of a period in history that influence the expression of social behavior. Time Signatures are past events that have influenced us; the Weather Report consists of factors that affect our decisions today and our life styles in the future. Weather Reports are Time Signatures turned inside out.

Consider how our individual experiences and outlook on life—our Time Signatures and Birthmarks—play a role in how we react to some circumstances in which we find ourselves in the future. What is important to us today may not be tomorrow, and vice versa. Knowing Weather Report factors helps us take into consideration influences outside of our own individual values that might constrain, or enable us to express what we believe.

For example, the economic outlook is a Weather Report factor that might help us predict the impact of the country's economy on different families. Future high interest rates and inflation will cause different problems for young and old. A new family, ready to buy a home and have children, might have few savings and end up moving to a less expensive region, staying in a small apartment longer, or having fewer children. Older adults, who may have owned their homes for some time, might find their retirement incomes significantly eroded; they may be unable to pursue new leisure interests, or may visit children and grandchildren who live far away less often.

Consider the consequences of technologically induced industrial change on the problems of skills obsolescence, such as a switch to computer-aided design in product development, or computer-controlled machine tools in manufacturing. An individual, educated in the 1940s or 1950s, who has worked 20 years in a business doing the same thing, may be less familiar with using a new tool than a person just finishing school who has no experience but has studied current techniques. The education a person brings to his or her work can provide an important competitive advantage, if it allows flexibility and adaptability; but it is a disadvantage if it does not lead the worker to upgrade skills over time.

Political changes can also create polarities. People born in different time periods, with different concerns—such as retirement versus child care and public school education—may experience different levels of satisfaction and have different problems in daily life as a result of policy changes.

Evolving cultural attitudes in business and the community also have different consequences for people with various backgrounds. For example, prejudice against older workers is particularly critical to those who want to continue to work as they age, as is promotion of women to single parents and displaced homemakers. Who we are today will be significantly affected by popular attitudes in the future.

The Weather Report is useful in thinking about how external factors influence us today and might influence us tomorrow. For most of this book, the Weather Report provides primarily background information. However, in Part III, where we reflect on the future, Weather Report factors are essential. There we imagine how economic, technological, political, and cultural systems might affect future American beliefs and values.

The Weather Report, as an inside-out version of a generation's Time Signatures, consists of the same four elements.

Economic Outlook

How the economy makes it harder, or easier, for us to live our lives is on our minds all the time. For individuals on fixed incomes, high inflation means less money to spend, as prices rise. A recession causes higher unemployment, as companies reduce their work force; those looking for work have to look harder and wait longer. No matter what your values are, you cannot express them as easily when economic conditions restrict your ability to purchase consumer goods and services. When money is limited, a person with one set of values will target a certain kind of expenditures as a priority; a person with another set of values will spend his or her money differently.

Technological Conditions

How people express their values has continually been influenced by technological advances. Improvements in health care, for instance, have made it possible for people to survive diseases that would have killed them in the past; as a result there is a *compression of mortality* (fewer people dying at the younger ages compared with the past), as well as an *expansion of morbidity* (more frail, sick people surviving in ill health). Preventive medicine, from good nutrition and healthy behavior to diagnostics that monitor blood pressure or cholesterol levels, is now saving lives. Treatments, such as noninvasive surgery performed on an outpatient basis, and new drug delivery systems, such as skin patches, internal implants, and time-release capsules, make it possible for more individuals to be treated at lower costs. Other, more dramatic skilled labor- and equipment-intensive treatments—from advanced prostheses and complex breathing machines to transplant operations—may make care more expensive.

Other technologies also play an important role in determining how people express their values, often in far more subtle yet significant ways. Consider the telephone and how it allows communication between families living great distances from each other. Cellular phones, phone answering machines, home computers, and fax machines are just a few innovations that have had a profound effect on how people do business, and on the resulting accelerated pace of life. Even cable television and VCRs enable a wider range of individuals—those who might not usually venture out to a movie theater—to enjoy contemporary entertainment and share in a national, popular culture. These media are also a way of transmitting new knowledge—how to speak French or Japanese, how to make a mortise and tenon, how to program, how to read.

The development of new technologies based on microprocessors and advanced manufacturing has had a large-scale impact on the increasing pace of skills obsolescence. Because technology is changing products *and* how they are produced, there is a continual displacement of workers, particularly workers just below the retirement age. There is also a greater need for technological skills in a labor force where jobs and skills are often mismatched.

Advances in health, communication, and workplace technologies will have different consequences for people with different outlooks and backgrounds. For some, such advances will be taken in stride; for others, improvements may be life-saving; still others may reject or fear such changes, particularly when they represent an unsolicited adversary in employment.

Social and Political Environment

The quality of life in the United States is in no small way influenced by national, state, and local government policies and institutions. Any changes in major public programs and social institutions—schools, hospitals, labor laws—will inevitably influence how we live tomor-

row. Consider, for example, the shift toward more environmental leg-
islation and efforts (however fragmented) to improve the education
system.

The average citizen may not always be acutely aware of the direct
effects of federal regulations or other state or local public policies; this
may explain, in part, low voter turnout. Yet shifts in Social Security,
catastrophic and long-term health care coverage (or absence thereof),
civil rights law, child care, education, and other social concerns will
all have dramatic effects on our lives.

Cultural Climate

The mood of the country is not a single state of mind, although the
media likes to characterize it as such. What we read, watch, or listen
to merely reflects a diluted or average summary of the opinions of our
highly pluralistic country. In many ways America is less a country
than a nation. Because it is so varied in its culture, it is less consistent
in the expression of its beliefs than smaller or more culturally homogeneous countries, such as Japan or Denmark. A nation is more of an
administrative system. While ours is large, it is far less centralized or
pervasive than European nations. The region in which we live, or in
which we had our beginnings, will often be a factor in the formation
of our values.

The ability of individuals to pursue their own interests is highly
tempered by cultural values. For example, women were treated as
second-class citizens in the workplace for years; divorced women and
single mothers had least-favored status. Now, although there is still
much progress to be made, women are becoming an accepted and
viable force in business and the professions, and the needs of parents
are slowly being acknowledged.

Our social definitions of family are adapting to change, trailing
along behind the fundamental restructuring of the family that has
taken place in the last 50 years. Divorced adults, single-parent households, stepparents, single teenage parents, are now an undeniable fact
of life. Yet day care and schools are still organized to meet only the
needs of the nuclear family. Older adults no longer live just past age
55, as they did when the first social security system was founded in
Prussia, by Otto von Bismarck in 1889. Still, popular views of older
adults are limited to stereotypically feeble "elderly" or feisty "senior
citizens."

Our society, like it or not, is dynamic—more so than any other.
Social change is constant. The future into which we will eventually

arrive will be a different world, perhaps modestly so, or perhaps dramatically. Therefore, to understand what America and American values will be like, we need to examine who we have been and who we are now. The Life Span Framework begins this journey to the future by reviewing our beginnings. But keep in mind: our beginnings never know our end.

PART

TWO

CHILDREN OF THE CENTURY: 1900–1909

W e begin our exploration of the American Time Travelers with a portrait of the children of this century. Those born between 1900 and 1909 represent the smallest number of the living members of today's world. They have traveled so far in time that there is little doubt that the Time Signatures of their lives have been dramatically different from those born later. The forces they have contended with—or not contended with—helped forge their characters in unique ways that we can only replay today in movies and novels. Born in an era when America was barely connected by roads or rail, when states were fewer in number, and when the promise of technology was still at the threshold between steam and internal combustion. What can this backdrop have meant for the shaping of American values, values that are still with us today?

IMMERSION—CHILDHOOD IN THE 1900S

The Children of the Century came into a world of promise. With a new century, there was a new beginning, free of the decadence of the old world. Progress was rapid, particularly in the North, because it had the resources: energy, technology (a word coined 50 years earlier), and a spirit of self-reliance. You could see proof all around you: towns were getting bigger, railroads were spreading, cables under the sea brought messages in the twinkling of an eye. The 1876 Centennial Exposition in Philadelphia had shown the world how far America had come—it boasted the biggest steam engine in the world, among other achievements. Thomas Edison not only had invented a light that burned without gas or kerosene but had put a power station on Pearl Street in lower Manhattan, and had invented a talking machine as well. You could talk on the telephone in many big cities, and even in smaller cities like Dayton, Ohio, and Portsmouth, New Hampshire, electric railways were being built.

When President William McKinley was assassinated in 1901 by an anarchist, the event made newspaper headlines, but it affected very few people directly. For most, the important result was that Theodore Roosevelt became president. A man who wasn't afraid of danger, he had led the charge up San Juan Hill in 1898. Roosevelt believed in God *and* progress. He was a vigorous man who had overcome by his own exertions the sickly constitution he had inherited. People approved of that; they believed things could change by vigorous action, and if something didn't change it was because they hadn't tried hard enough—hadn't moved far enough west, saved enough money, worked hard enough, or prayed hard enough.

Americans saw no shame in being poor, but they also saw no reason to stay that way. Industrial production grew by over 3000 percent between 1859 and 1919, and the number of workers increased 700 percent, from 1.3 to 9.1 million. America was a rich country, not only in resources but in labor. Europe was sending over millions of workers, and America hadn't had to pay a cent for rearing, educating, or training them. A man who couldn't make a living in America was either lazy or a farmer having a bad year.

People were religious, as were their forebears in Europe, but in America people worshipped God in churches. Organized religion thus served as a necessary social support system in new towns. Spiritualism, each person's personal belief system, was another matter. People were also deistic—they believed in the laws of nature and the universe, with an emphasis on morality. For example, illness was not simply "God's will." If you contracted cholera it was because you had eaten contaminated pork, or you lived in filthy conditions and had damaged your body, probably by drink. "A suffering body is simply the penalty of violated law," the hygiene textbooks declared. Doctors advised people to eat better food, get more rest, and move to a house with better ventilation, but few could afford to. There wasn't much one could do about illness anyway, despite all the theorizing about it.

If you were born to a family of native-born Americans you heard a lot about not violating natural law, and being strong and vigorous.

You heard a lot about the evils of drink and saw a lot of them, too. You heard people say, "Men must work and women must weep," and you understood that women wore out and died sooner than men. You were taught that you were responsible for your own life, but what you saw around you often told a different story. Your horse, for example, might be startled by a piece of paper or a barking dog, and bolt and throw you. Ships could sink, coal mines explode, and trains crash. In 1906 San Francisco was destroyed by an earthquake. People said it should have been expected—San Francisco was so wicked it had a divorce rate 55 times that of London. As told in *The Damnedest Finest Ruins* by Monica Sutherland (New York: Coward-McCann, 1959, p. 182), San Franciscans wrote a verse about it:

> *If, as they say, God spanked the town*
> *For being over-frisky,*
> *Why did he burn the churches down*
> *And save Hotaling's whiskey?*

How could a farmer bring on himself the devastation caused by grasshoppers, or no rain, or buyers setting too low a price in faraway Chicago? How could a man save enough money or start over when he was working a 10- or 12-hour day and half a day on Saturday, mostly on a piecework basis? What could a factory or mine worker do if he was injured because there was no guard on a saw, or no brake on a cable, and the owners and bosses claimed he was careless or drunk? If illness was a violation of natural law, what violation could a two-year-old have committed to die of diphtheria or typhoid? How was a person to tell the difference between a good investment and ruinous speculation? The most improbable things turned out to be true—like electricity and X-rays—giving rise to exaggerated hopes and often unrealized expectations. If such magic could be real, why not put your life savings into belts that could stimulate the nervous system or into a wind-turbine system that could generate all the electricity you'd ever need—and only fourteen miles from the nearest electric light.

Atheism was a subject of considerable debate. There were many views held on it at the time. For example, many scorned the "superstition" of Catholicism and Judaism, which resulted in a great deal of deism and secularism. Atheist lecturers, such as Robert Ingersoll, drew large crowds, and magazines were full of articles denying that atheism was the "logical end of progress" in religion (a popular Marxist tenet), in the way that the transatlantic steamer was considered state-of-the-art in steam technology.

Spiritualism—which was in vogue in London as well—was most often used as a kind of self-stimulation, to add excitement to lives controlled by relatives and neighbors, or as a form of self-aggrandizement. If it became excessive, it was often looked on as an aberration reflecting inappropriate grieving, and was condemned, but not heavily punished. Occult practices, on the other hand, were punished. It was clear to the general community that the practitioners—usually the powerless, such as old women, blacks, and gypsies—stood outside the common social order. The occult was seen as the antithesis of science and thus just as powerful.

When the Children of the Century were born, government was not in Washington, D.C., or even the state capital, but in the county seat. It was there that deeds were recorded, taxes collected, orphans and paupers disposed of, wills probated, and lawsuits tried. Towns were not necessarily made up of fixed populations, as they tended to be in Europe. Families were always moving in, or moving out to start over somewhere else.

Other institutions of social organization were the church, the school, and the fraternal organization. Most turn-of-the-century churches were Protestant. In 1885, there were 27,000 Baptist churches, 23,000 Methodist churches, 10,000 Presbyterian churches, and 5,500 Lutheran churches, among others—and only 6,200 Catholic churches and 269 synagogues. In general, although the churches were differentiated by region and class, they were linked in tight sectarian networks all across the country. An important part of moving to a new town to start over was presenting the pastor with a "transfer letter" from the pastor in the old town. With this, a family could be accepted into a new congregation immediately, without a long period of proving themselves as good citizens. For immigrants, of course, churches and synagogues served a different purpose, providing kinship in a strange land.

Fraternal organizations offered men a further instrument for building community and providing mutual support. Their main function was to give men safe access to one another, particularly when they were new in town. Men belonged to the Elks, the Odd Fellows, the Freemasons, the Foresters, or the Red Men. The Catholic Church often frowned upon secret fraternal organizations, although it had them, too. To give allegiance to a secular organization such as the Masons was to deny to God that portion of your allegiance. Factory workers were a natural segment of society to organize. These groups—or *gemeinschafts*—would evolve into labor unions later on.

Magazines, newspapers, and lectures were the instruments of social communication. Farmers read newspapers for the useful hints they provided: an herb that cured scours in sheep; a strain of watermelon with half the usual number of seeds. Townspeople read *The Ladies*

Home Journal, Harper's, The Atlantic Monthly, and *Youth's Companion* for insight, and confirmation that they were right to believe that honesty and hard work would win over cunning. Women in particular read magazines for a standard against which to measure themselves, for new ideas and new dreams, and for how-to advice (how to pay your maid, knit shawls, make extra money). Men needed practical knowledge related to earning a living.

Reform movements were everywhere. People tried to match their ideals with reality, and their actions laid the foundation for unions, women's rights, child labor laws, compulsory schooling, strong public health laws, sanitary sewers, and municipal water systems.

Because medicines were often almost as dangerous as the illnesses they were supposed to treat, the Pure Food and Drug Act was passed in 1906. Many of the medicines offered in the 1900 Sears catalogue were poisonous or addictive: strychnine was sold as a cure for impotence; opium preparations were sold for teething pain and diarrhea (politely called "summer complaint"); a mercury compound called calomel was sold for children's stomachaches; and arsenic pills were offered to clear up a bad complexion. The White Star Liquor Cure, advertised in 1906, contained enough morphine to put Papa out for the evening. A decade later, most of the poisons and all the addictive drugs were gone from open commerce, although they remained available by prescription or illegally.

Education was not always considered desirable. There were, after all, some ideas that were so corrupting that a mind could be destroyed just by reading about them, such as birth control, witchcraft, anarchy, or atheism. Too much science education could, in fact, *cause* atheism! Whites often condemned the education of Indians and blacks because it made them dissatisfied with their lives, and other Indians and blacks often said it made the educated ones think they were better than them. Attending college was likely to separate a man forever from his family. A western traditional folk song called "Old Paint" included a verse about it:

> *Now, old Bill Jones, he had a daughter and a son.*
> *Son went to college and the daughter went wrong,*
> *Wife got killed in a pool room fight,*
> *Still he keeps singing from morning till night.*

At the same time, a man needed a considerable amount of practical knowledge—how to compute compound interest, the pitch of a roof, the weight of iron pipe. He also needed to read the government bulletins about soil and fertilizer, since he could no longer just move on when his land began to yield less, now that the frontier was gone.

A woman could be educated—up to a point, that is. Her role in life was to be a good wife and mother, to provide a gentle, civilized refuge from the harsh world of business and work. To fulfill this role, ordained by God, she needed to be able to read, write, and cipher; an uneducated woman might not be a fit helpmate to an educated man. But too much education could make a woman "unnatural"; hard study carried the risk of "brain fever"—a condition probably brought on by anxiety, insomnia, and low resistance to infection. A few women with independent ideas and means managed to develop careers. They wrote novels, as did Edith Wharton, or designed buildings, as did Julia Morgan, or trained to be doctors, as did Gertrude Stein.

The French had established the Ecole Polytechnique in the 1790s. Germany had established five Polytechnisches Institutes between 1825 and 1831. But the United States lagged behind in technology education. Although the Rensselaer Institute was established in 1824, it trained teachers and mechanics, not engineers. Higher education, modeled after the English system, had been established early on—it comprised the classics, for gentlemen. Then, in the 1860s, the federal government established land-grant universities and schools of agriculture. But until the Germans showed us otherwise, we didn't think much of education for engineers. "Professional engineer" was a contradiction in terms. The Massachusetts Institute of Technology (MIT) wasn't established until 1859, Georgia Tech wasn't established until 1885, CalTech until 1891, and Carnegie Tech (now Carnegie-Mellon University) until 1900. A few business colleges existed, along with colleges of dentistry, mortuary science, and homeopathic medicine.

The best chance to learn a skill that would pay well was to join the Navy, which was the most technologically advanced service at the time; it was beginning to use diesel engines, electricity, and (by World War I) radio transmitters. For the native-born, opportunity was everywhere—if you knew where to look for it. From 1880 to 1910 nearly 18 million immigrants entered the United States; most stayed. There were jobs for them, too, but many struggled to learn a new language and took jobs that their skills, education, or training made them overqualified for.

Child labor was still legal. Boys often started work at age 8 or 10, girls usually at 12. Social reformers added child labor to their list of causes. The following verse, by Sarah N. Cleghorn, appeared in the *New York Tribune* on January 1, 1915.

> *The golf links lie so near the mill*
> *That almost any day*

> *The laboring children at their work*
> *Can see the men at play.*

Children worked from 6 a.m. to 6 p.m. and half a day on Saturday in the Amoskeag cotton mills in New Hampshire. Many young people worked as servants. In 1902, *Mrs. Seeley's Cook-Book* cautioned the mistress that the scullery maid should be at work by 6 a.m. and the parlor maid by 6:30 a.m. The author adds, "Don't think your mistress is unbearable because she may sometimes be a little short in her manner; ladies often have worries and responsibilities of which servants have no idea."

Skyscrapers were going up in cities, made possible by the innovation of a new inexpensive construction material—steel. All kinds of new occupations were available, although some were limited to the European technicians who accompanied the new machinery, such as the diesel engine or electroplating equipment. Draftsmen were in great demand. However, a man could learn drafting only in particular places—Scotland, one of the polytechnic institutes, or West Point.

In a 1908 book called *Girls of Today*, a young man with a pipe is shown facing a young woman smoking a cigarette. Another young woman is pictured fixing the wheel of a horseless carriage, while a man in driving goggles watches apprehensively. The young women have clear and steady gazes, swanlike necks, improbably long-waisted bosoms, tiny waists, and sweeps of skirt—ankle-length for street wear (to protect from horse manure), and floor-length for evening.

Most girls, however, were not quite so independent, nor was that ideal figure achieved without considerable discomfort, the result of corsets that had stays of steel or whalebone. Women's clothing served some important functions in addition to protection. The tiny waist assured a young man that the girl didn't have unsuitable (i.e., suffragette) notions, since feminists didn't wear corsets, and that she could not be pregnant. The prohibition against makeup assured a potential husband that he was seeing her real complexion. Too much color in the cheeks, for example, could mean tuberculosis; too pale a face might mean anemia or a heart with rheumatic fever damage. Either condition could interfere with a woman's ability to bear healthy children and perform her duties as a wife. Breast size was thought to be related to the ability to nurse children.

Because only wealthy women had a chance at a life outside of marriage, the temptation to mask any infirmity or potential defect was strong. Women were concerned about their potential husbands, too. A girl's father and brothers, and the elders of the community, kept a watchful eye to make sure that eligible young women met only eligible men. This kind of protection, which was one of the aspects of small-town and neighborhood life the young found stifling, was another function of church and fraternal organizations, and of pastoral transfer letters.

Marriage was often delayed long past the age of male sexual initiation; 10 percent of the men inducted into the Army in World War I already had syphilis, for which there was no easy cure. Syphilis, and the fear of it, propelled many campaigns against prostitution, couched not in terms of disease but morality.

There was a convenient double standard: men were supposed to come to the marriage bed experienced, and women were supposed to remain pure. Given the lack of contraception and the harsh realities of childbirth (high maternal and infant mortality rates), it's not surprising that women feared sexual intercourse and its consequences. In fact, fear was so widespread that a popular home doctoring book included a whole chapter on how to deal with it. Only women rich enough to have a doctor could request ether during childbirth, and a doctor with religious objections might refuse. Women were not taught to expect sex to be pleasurable. For men, whose sexual techniques were limited (early experiences were often with prostitutes), a woman's sexual pleasure was not the first priority anyway—procreation was.

Only about half of the adult men married. In many cases men were too poor, or too occupied with their own survival. A man had to provide his wife with a home—if not his own, then at least a rented one—and that required land, an income, or a good job "with prospects."

A woman's trousseau was expected to include three dozen sheets and pillow slips, feather pillows with good ticking, two dozen kitchen towels (minimum), two dozen bath towels, two dozen facecloths, dresser scarves, tablecloths, doilies, antimacassars, and enough personal nightclothes, underclothes, dresses, and coats for two years, as well as china, silver, glassware, and kitchen utensils. For most brides, however, a cast-iron skillet and a blue enamel pot, floursack kitchen towels (carefully hemmed), half a dozen sheets and pillowcases, and rough huck bath towels (not Turkish towels) was what they started with. Women's attractiveness diminished earlier, and those who did not marry by the time they were 20 were at a disadvantage. The best they could hope for—unless they were wealthy—was to marry a widower with small children.

Meals were eaten together, as a family, because it took considerable work and effort to produce a hot meal, and to do so for one or two was too difficult. Cooking on wood and coal stoves provided meat that was baked, fried, boiled, or broiled—never roasted, despite the term "roast" beef or "roast" chicken. Vegetables were overcooked, but the long boiling minimized enteric diseases that might result from unsanitary conditions and a lack of adequate refrigeration. In poorer households, meat was rare except for salt pork or bacon. The man of the house got what meat there was, because his work depended on his strength and good health.

Even in well-off families, clothes for children were likely to be hand-me-downs, at least for the first dozen years. Home-manufactured clothes were for women and children, and took a significant investment of a woman's time. Store-bought clothes were only for men. Thus, a boy's first long-pants suit, from the Sears catalogue or the country store, was a significant event. Women bought corsets, winter coats, and hats, but generally made all other clothes. The treadle sewing machine in the dining room was an important sign of prudence and thrift.

The survival of infants was not assured, especially if the family was very poor. Some families could afford mourning, but it was considered an imposition on one's friends and family to mourn a dead infant for longer than a few days, or a child under 12 for more than three months. We tend to think of birth defects as a modern phenomenon, but they were common in the early 20th century, due to poor prenatal care as well as common pollutants such as heavy metals and hydrocarbons.

Children were welcomed if they were healthy, left unattended to if they were not. Europeans complained that American children were spoiled and undisciplined. Certainly many of them had freedoms that European children would have envied, including the freedom of boys and girls to go to school together. But most children were expected to work hard at their chores, and contribute to the household early on.

Children had homemade toys, and occasionally store-bought ones, such as mechanical banks, toy fire engines, lead soldiers and tin warships, porcelain dolls, kites, jacks, and marbles. A mother might spend time helping a son make a baseball or a catcher's mitt, or helping a daughter make doll clothes. For winter evenings, most families had at least one board game (besides "Checkers"), such as "Snakes and Ladders" or "Parcheesi," and stereopticons. They traded cards with relatives or friends so that the children could see the pyramids in Egypt (with a lady in a white dress being helped onto a camel in the foreground) or the actual Mount of Calvary in the Holy Land. Children had to learn recitation pieces for school, and often had to recite them at home when company came. Poems and stories about orphans dying and going to heaven were popular. Such pathetic pieces were thought to make children more aware of how lucky they were to have parents.

Books were an important diversion. School readers included works by Robert Louis Stevenson, Jules Verne, Louisa May Alcott, and Mark Twain. There were books about elves and fairies, missionaries and explorers.

In general, books and toys were only given on birthdays or at Christmastime; children did not have money to buy things for themselves, even in wealthy families. A father might help one child to make a jigsaw puzzle to give to another. Large presents, like a wagon or a sled, were often given to children collectively, rather than to one child. An exception was often made for sick children. The parent— often at the urging of the doctor—would promise the child a longed-for toy, to be awarded only on recovery, to arouse "the will to live."

It's a common misconception that small-town life in 1900–1910 was idyllic—safe, secure, and comfortable. The truth is that it was often hellishly confining. People were taught and expected to be self-reliant, but in reality there were too many areas of daily life in which they were powerless. Education, and the belief system of the time, was ahead of technology. The result was a kind of personal stress that was often overwhelming. Women developed melancholia and hysterical illnesses as coping mechanisms; men generally drank or fought—or did both. Narcotics were common. The emotional release provided by hellfire preachers was sometimes so extreme that they were forbidden to enter a town or hold a meeting there.

Because guns were so common, they were often used to win an argument. The 1900 Sears catalogue contained 22 pages of guns and ammunition, in contrast to one page of typewriters (all with different keyboards). The extent to which people used guns in America amazed and dismayed European visitors. Rudyard Kipling, in his *American Notes* (1889), reports a soldier saying, "In England, a man aren't allowed to play with no firearms. He's got to be taught all that when he enlists." Later Kipling further noted that Americans tended to kill each other with guns at a rate that would astonish the residents of India and China, where life was held cheap.

DIVERSION—THE ADOLESCENT EXPERIENCE 1910–1920

In rapid succession the promises of the first decade seemed to come to life in this decade. The first airplane flight at Kitty Hawk, North Carolina, had taken place in 1903. By 1910 there was an air meet near Los Angeles, at Dominguez Hills. Those in the grandstands watched the Bleriot monoplane, the Curtiss biplane, and the Farnam airplane compete. A year later the Farnam completed the first transcontinental flight in 41 days, accompanied by a railroad car of spare parts.

Electric lights went on in the smaller cities and towns; people took trolleys in Exeter, New Hampshire, and Palo Alto, California; and ordinary folk had telephones. Trucks became more common, although it still took dray horses to pull heavy loads; and Henry Ford's Model T could now be seen coast to coast.

In the cities, people moved farther from their work so their children could have better air and more space. Dinner became the evening, not afternoon, meal (except on farms and in the smallest towns), because a working man couldn't afford 5 cents for the trolley ride home to eat lunch.

The rise of industry brought men to the cities, but the prospect of war had slowed down European immigration, since those who were old enough to emigrate were also old enough to be conscripted. Women began to work as shop clerks, office "typewriters" (the new word "typist" was considered fancified), and telephone operators. Increasingly, as fewer girls entered domestic service, only the wealthy could afford servants.

As the hired girls left and young aunts took jobs, families tried to make do with their daughters and a cleaning woman who came in two or three days a week to help with the washing, ironing, and housework. But daughters were going to high school now, and some even to college—not just wealthy girls, but daughters of dentists and doctors, preachers and teachers, bankers and merchants. As the supply of domestic workers decreased, the demand for labor-saving devices grew: for washing machines (wringers that turned with a crank), gas stoves that could be regulated, and patented carpet sweepers. Moving farther from work also meant being far from shops. The woman of the house no longer had a hired girl to send to the butcher's, and no time to go herself, so she telephoned her order and waited for the bread man, iceman, milkman, and the vegetable man to deliver. Even the Jewel Tea man came, with his tea, coffee, flavorings, and spices (girls used vanilla extract as perfume).

The Children of the Century were still too young to be profoundly affected by World War I, and although they lost relatives in the influenza pandemic that followed, it was not as catastrophic for them as for the cohort that followed. They learned that raw effort and energy were not enough to overcome all obstacles; individual effort was less effective than community or national effort. They learned that the social function of religion was equally well served by membership in a peer group that centered around the local school, usually small. As for entertainment, more fun could be had at the movies. They learned that "tinkering" with new inventions was not enough; inventions had no economic justification, and investing in them could mean ruin as easily as fortune. The 33-foot solar dish that powered a 10-HP steam pump, lifting 1400 gallons of water 12 feet a minute, the vertically rising aircraft in Fruitdale, California, the moving sidewalks and horizontal elevators—these were marvels, but they were foolish investments. You had to have a real company with real sales before you could risk your labor or your money.

They learned about specialization in education. Doctors, for example, who had specialized in a proper medical school really could save lives—take out an appendix before it burst, find typhoid germs in the well water and have the well filled in, isolate a scarlet fever case so the disease didn't spread, diagnose syphilis. Their parents and grandparents, who had never expected much from physicians and thought one person's opinions were as good as another's, were proven wrong.

The Children of the Century, now entering adulthood, created new social norms. Their immigrant parents thought the boy with the nice manners was a good marriage prospect because he was so like the good prospects in the old country. But his classmates knew he got drunk out behind the gym, before the high school dance. Happiness in marriage? The older generation hadn't expected it, what with Mother worn out before her time from having so many children, and Papa working 10- to 12-hour days, six days a week. They told the younger generation that a man should wait until he could afford to buy a house before he got married. "But the two of you could start out in a rooming house, and then rent something while you save your money; after all, if you pick a growing field and a good solid company, you are bound to advance."

Most of the older generation were understandably ignorant. There wasn't much time for school. They knew about horses but not motors, how to load the stove firebox to bake a cake but not how to use a regulator to judge the time in a gas oven. (More than one girl had to hurry home after school every day because her mother was afraid to light the gas stove.) An old man, forgetting how to use the brakes, might confuse his car with his horse, yelling, "Whoa! Whoa!" and pulling back the steering wheel until it almost came off.

Many of the older people didn't like movies. For one thing, the picture still flickered a lot. For another, those who had gotten along for years with poor vision (they didn't have to read much, anyway) found that they couldn't follow the silent pictures and the subtitles. As for photoengraving and rotogravure, the photographs reproduced in magazines and newspapers were just pictures to the older generation, perhaps a little more detailed than the drawings magazines and newspapers used to have, but just pictures. But to young people, these photographs showed how cities and people really looked. Photography, and news photography in particular, was *real*.

EXPANSION—EARLY ADULTHOOD IN THE 1920S

Insulin was discovered in 1920—a triumph of medical science. People could now take care of themselves, by doing what the doctor or dentist told them. They could stay young and vigorous all their lives, not like their parents. Women would have their babies in hospitals, and the babies would not only live, but be healthy. Men and women would work hard, but they would also go to the movies, take trips into the country on weekends, spend time in the summer camping, or get a vacation cottage by a lake.

The Children of the Century were now in their late 20s and early 30s. They played "Dardanella," and "Whispering," and "Japanese Sandman" on their Victrolas, and they rolled up the rug to dance. They did the foxtrot, and later the Charleston, and they tried to tango like Rudolph Valentino, although the tango was considered really too suggestive for middle-class respectability. Many of them attended Broadway plays. In the 1923–1924 season alone there were 232 performances of *Cyrano de Bergerac*, 257 of *White Cargo*, and 333 of *Ziegfeld Follies*, but only eight performances of Ibsen's drearier *Hedda Gabler*. Eugene O'Neill got three Pulitzer prizes during the decade, for *Beyond the Horizon* (1921), *Anna Christie* (1922), and *Strange Interlude* (1928), but none of them ran more than a total of 500 performances on Broadway during their lives.

Most people never got to see a play on Broadway. Instead, they went to the movies, to see *Wings*, *The Jazz Singer*, *All Quiet on the Western Front*, and *The Gold Rush*. They read Pulitzer-prize-winning books like *So Big* by Edna Ferber and *Arrowsmith* by Sinclair Lewis, as well as Edgar Rice Burroughs's Tarzan stories, Zane Grey's westerns, romantic novels by Ethel M. Dell, and Erle Stanley Gardner's detective stories.

Men played bridge and tennis, but unlike their fathers—who played on the hometown baseball team—they watched baseball games instead of playing them. Some women embroidered, others had bridge parties. For the most part, women gave up sports after they became mothers.

This was the decade when family formation and growth became paramount. It was the decade of the installment plan, when young families in rented houses bought cars, vacuum cleaners, Victrolas, and, especially, electric refrigerators. The refrigerator not only could make ice cream by itself, it also made it possible for people to shop at the new, cheaper, cash-and-carry grocery stores. "Every day, in every way," people thought, things got "better and better."

Despite their optimism, they saw hardship all around them. Four million veterans had come home from World War I, some shell-shocked, some gassed, some missing an arm or a leg. Some never did recover. Many moved restlessly around the country for years, riding the rails, living as hobos, before settling down. Men still wept when they sang "My Buddy," or "There's a Long, Long Trail a-Winding." Sometimes they were able to recover and talk about their war experiences in weekly meetings with their buddies in the local American Legion halls.

Those born in America believed they would succeed, naturally. They had learned about scientific progress, specialization, banks, finance companies, and the installment plan. Others, however, feared the new ideas, and the folks who set science above the Bible. They believed their simple schools were good enough, and if they couldn't afford a doctor, well, Mama had never seen a doctor and had raised 10 kids—almost raised them—before she died. Bankers and finance companies were viewed with suspicion—they could take away your property. Farm foreclosures were increasing, from 12 per thousand farms in 1921 to 26 per thousand in 1929. Poor farmers thrown off their farms went to work in textile mills and in city factories, where they were paid for their stamina and not for what they knew. Some rebelled and robbed banks, some joined the Ku Klux Klan and tried to turn the world back to the way it had been when they were successful.

Most children of immigrants, however, had no such fears. They would succeed naturally because they had gone to school, had learned the language the way everybody else spoke it—not like their parents. Their parents couldn't understand that a poor young man just starting out in an advertising office might be a better husband for a girl than someone at the factory whose family Papa had known in the old country. The older generation didn't understand that you had to have an American name and let your daughters go to school and dress a certain way.

Whether they had come from American or immigrant stock, the Children of the Century who had gone to high school or commercial school went to work in the 1920s, married, rented a house or took out a mortgage (for as long as 10 or 12 years!), and bought a car.

One survey of college-educated couples in the late 1920s showed that 90 percent of them practiced contraception. They raised their children—fewer than their mothers had had—according to schedules.

They took them to the doctor when they got sick or for shots to prevent diphtheria, to the hospital to have their tonsils out, and to kindergarten to get them ready for school.

CONVERSION—ADULTHOOD IN THE 1930S

They couldn't believe it when it happened: in October, 1929, the stock market crashed. It wasn't just that the whole country lost money, but that the economy had been so dependent on the money that had been lost. Businesses that had used stocks as collateral for loans had their loans called in; banks that had issued loans based on stocks faced ruin. Consumers waited to see what would happen; they decided not to buy the Chevy coupe with a rumble seat or the little bungalow at the end of the streetcar line. And because they didn't buy, the companies' workers were laid off or put on short weeks of two or three days. By 1931, people were grateful that they could stay on for half the salary they got in 1929. Some families had to go back to the old farmstead for a while. In 1932, there were more people living on farms than ever before, or since.

Men left home to look for work, and some never came back. In other families, unemployed men got day work cutting lawns or cleaning ashes out of furnaces in homes where they had once been dinner guests. Some men scrounged packing crates and made toys or lawn ornaments to sell. Others cut down somebody else's saplings to make rustic lawn furniture, while the owners pretended not to notice. Often landlords agreed to forgo rent until things got better, as long as the family "kept the place up." Some men got out books that they'd bought years ago, like *Henley's Twentieth Century Home and Workshop Formulas, Recipes and Processes*, published in 1919, and made up cosmetics or colognes to sell door to door.

Everybody who could gardened. People who had started eating vegetables in the 1920s because it was healthy ate them in the 1930s because sometimes it was all there was, except for macaroni and cheese, or bread and lard. Women learned to cook the wheat for the chickens, to make hot cereal, or even to grow popcorn and pop it for cereal.

In the early 1920s they had sung, "Lord, How the Money Rolls In." Now they sang, "Oh, we ain't got a barrel of money, sometimes we're ragged and funny, but we travel along, singing our song, side by side." Movies starred Shirley Temple and Andy Hardy and Clark Gable and Claudette Colbert. On Broadway, *Of Thee I Sing* made fun of Washington corruption, and *You Can't Take It with You* spoofed the worship of money. Little Orphan Annie and Dick Tracy were big hits in the Sunday funnies.

It took a long time for things to get better. In 1935, thanks to the Work Projects Administration (WPA), nearly a quarter of a million people had jobs—building roads and public buildings, painting post office murals, and writing books about rivers. The WPA employed a million and a half people every year until 1941. The money at least helped them buy bacon and coffee and pay their grocery bills. Perhaps the grocer could buy a panel truck. And as folks became better able to buy shoes for their children, shoe stores might invest in X-ray machines to show parents that the shoes fit correctly.

Industry recovered slowly from 1936 on. Then, when war broke out in Europe in 1939, recovery was rapid. Now there were new jobs, building lend-lease destroyers, merchant ships, and tin cans for the fruit that was being sent overseas, and for that new treat of American ingenuity—Spam. The Children of the Century, most of whom were too old for the armed services, were able to move into these jobs. Many men who had gone into the Army or Navy in the early 1930s (because they couldn't get jobs) signed on again and rose in rank. These were the noncommissioned officers caught on the ships at Pearl Harbor and at Bataan and Corregidor.

In 1937 everybody read *Gone with the Wind*, and waited for the movie. They also read *Reader's Digest*, and *Life* magazine. The first issues of *Life* came out in 1936. With its striking photographs, *Life* made Americans believe in the rest of the world, and brought the horrors—and glories—of World War II home.

SUBMERSION IN THE 1940S

For the Children of the Century, the 1940s were a period of fulfillment and tragedy. Unless they were career military, most of the men did not have to go to war, although some did anyway. Others were at last rewarded for decades of hard labor. Farmers had unlimited markets. Factory workers with experience taught women and blacks, who had replaced the young men on the line, and got better wages than they had before. Their wives ran Civil Defense auxiliaries, Red Cross units, and drives of various kinds, collecting cans of bacon grease, flattening tin cans, and tying up newspapers. Tragedy, however, came in the form of casualty and injured lists—the news that a son was dead or wounded.

Because the war made more people mobile, by attracting them from areas of unemployment to defense-plant cities, the Children of the

Century often found themselves living and working with people from other parts of the country. It is easy to forget that the United States was still a country of regions; even the gulf between New York's lower East Side and New Jersey's East Orange was as profound as the Marianas Trench. People from small settlements bypassed by industrial progress didn't always feel accepted when they arrived at the new war plant communities. But their more sophisticated neighbors worked with them, shared food and theater lines with them, and knew that their sons were fighting together. A Red Cross unit in 1939 was typically WASP, but one in 1942 might be composed of an assortment of Catholic, Protestant, and Jewish mothers and wives. The color bar, however, was rarely broken; even the military was segregated.

The myth is that when men returned home from the war, women went back to the kitchen—and stayed there. While it is true that many women returned to being housewives, the organizational and decision-making skills that they had learned during the war stayed with them. The bridge club was no longer the only outside activity for middle-class women. Some became active in community service, hospital auxiliaries, and church groups. Others went to Eastern Star or American Legion auxiliaries, or garden clubs, or civic groups. Some became involved in politics. By the late 1940s there was the atomic bomb to worry about, displaced persons to provide for, and UNICEF.

The men who had worked in war plants instead of going into the service hadn't learned organizational skills as much as they had learned about teaching and leadership. Most never went back to being just factory workers. They had war bonds saved up, unions, and seniority, even if they didn't have formal supervisory or management assignments. For many the war had provided a chance to buy a house—a summer place. They thought about retirement plans. They wanted a house at the lake, maybe, or a little place somewhere they wouldn't have to shovel snow.

REVERSION TO TRANSCENDANCE—1950 AND BEYOND

The Children of the Century entered their mid-life and older years as the first survivors of a new century. By having survived a time of change, these older adults became the harbingers of a new future, where men and women lived beyond their childbearing and working years. Unfortunately, their aging corresponded with a period of unprecedented mobility in the family, and a poorly conceived social welfare system. Few men went into their retirement with significant pensions. Fewer women, particularly those who had not held jobs, received benefits, other than what their husbands had earned and what they had scraped together over the years. Despite the creation of Social Security, the major social achievement of the 1930s, this first generation of modern Americans were not to experience its full potential, even though they were the models for whom it was designed.

Were it not for their families, their own astuteness in saving, or their good fortune in having an employer who paid a modest pension, many would have drowned in poverty as they aged; in fact, they were poor in comparison to the next cohort. By the time they reached their 60s, in the early 1960s, and retired (voluntarily or not), over 5.5 million older adults were living in poverty. Older people, who were 10 percent of the population in the 1960s, comprised 30 percent of the population with incomes lower than $3200 in the 1970s. By the time they reached their 70s, less than half a million were able to support themselves on their earnings alone, and 16 million of all those over 65 (75%) had no earnings from employment.

Most depended on Social Security, Supplementary Security Income (SSI), veterans' pensions, and other public or private programs. In 1964, when the majority turned 65, there were 18 million beneficiaries of the Old Age and Survivors Insurance Program; in 1976 the number had increased to 28.4 million. In 1977 almost 22 million older adults received Social Security benefits.

It is not surprising that this generation, the first to witness such turmoil and survive it, would also comprise the first generation of older adults to begin to assert the legitimacy of their identity as older persons. In 1965 the first White House Conference on Aging was convened. The passage of the Older Americans Act that same year led to the development of thousands of older adult service agencies, specific organizations representing minority aged, and a number of associations representing the interests of older persons, including the American Association of Retired Persons (AARP), and the Gray Panthers.

Did this movement to address the needs of older persons have its roots in the values of older adults born in the early days of this century, or did it reflect how younger groups wished to see the aging of their parents, and their own selves in the future? There were leaders and rebels from all age groups who allied to mandate change. While the Children of the Century are hardy and independent, they are not unified in their political and social outlook; nonetheless, the majority had embraced the recognition of their needs and strongly supported their position of "entitlement" to Social Security and related programs.

The political upheavals of the 1960s that gave impetus to social changes for the poor and deprived also inspired older adults who might never have considered their own predicament as an issue for social justice. The experience of these adults, now in their 60s, was surprise that they had survived and an expectation to bear down and tough out their later years, with whatever resources they had. Despite the efforts made by reformers in the 1960s, the programs and resources eventually implemented, including Medicare and Medicaid, were no panacea, only signs of improvement. By the time this generation was in its 70s, programs had expanded and conditions had improved. The benefits that had been so hard won are now taken for granted, but the 10 million Children of the Century living today are still wrestling with the challenge of survival.

BIRTHMARKS

Preservers

Preservers are, for the most part, European (sometimes Asian) immigrants who have always defined themselves by their country of origin and seek to maintain the culture and ways they were born to. Preservers want to maintain old values and social patterns that may not apply to the world around them. They are highly dependent on personal communications and family support in all aspects of life. At first, when they were growing up, their parents spoke their native language, as did relatives. The old country ways continued. As they grew up, they became strongly wedded to these ways, and realized that they did not easily fit in to the mainstream. For Preservers, expectations, and a world view, are not well defined.

Life is often a struggle for Preservers, but they would rather struggle than change. They never learned to speak English as well as their children would have liked. Many never became U.S. citizens because they were afraid to learn English, and afraid to deal with the seemingly awesome authority of the immigration bureaucracy. They wanted to be Americans, but they also wanted to maintain their ethnic heritage. They wanted their children to be Americans, too, but they also wanted them to marry members of their own religion and ethnic background. The assimilation of their children was a source of unhappiness for them.

Preservers often passed down their dogmatic views to their children. Their children, exposed to a far more diverse world of values and experiences, maintained their parents' values to a certain extent, such as religious affiliation or marrying someone of the same nationality.

Preservers sought ways to share vicariously the status and glamour of America, and so mythologized certain Americans as symbols of legitimacy and status. Middle-class women, less familiar with the media than their children, admired movie stars, but expressed their interest in a distant way for fear of giving the impression that they actually respected them. (Admiration, even appreciation, would be inappropriate to their real, or aspired-to, social position.) Men could admire boxers because they embodied traditional values of manliness, but not baseball or football players. Those were frivolous pastimes and went against the old-world values of hard work.

Preservers tend to be very suspicious, because they are intimidated by a system they cannot understand, and because, educated or not, virtually all of them had negative experiences with authority in their childhoods (or heard tales of mistreatment from their parents). Their suspicion is directed at those who are wealthy, empowered by their position (i.e., police, lawyers, public officials), or not of the same ethnic heritage. Everyone is potentially an abuser of power and not to be trusted.

Despite their accents and cultural agoraphobia, Preservers wanted to improve their lives. They worked hard, but generally were not upwardly mobile, unless there was some windfall or other unusual opportunity. Typically, this might be some fruitful venture where the Preserver was paired with an entrepreneurial partner or family member who was bold enough to reach out into the world.

Higher social status was something they hoped their children, not they, would achieve. They recognized that their children's upward mobility, if it happened, might mean severing links with the family, or at least the neighborhood and family traditions. Knowing this, most Preservers were not able to consciously encourage their children to move away from their own culture. Many Preservers opposed their children going to college or graduate school, or pursuing careers that would take them away from them. In the end, most Preservers lost their children to the new country, secretly pleased at their accomplishments, but feeling betrayed by their success.

Preservers never became mainstream consumers and often resisted opportunities to adopt new products. They would demur, claiming that they did not need this or that; if they had gotten along before without it, they could certainly do so now.

Preservers are generally very anxious people, afraid of change, and uncomfortable communicating their true feelings to others. They value caution, word-of-mouth, and learn more from neighbors, family, and friends than from the media, unless it is a newspaper in their native language. Because the family is the center of life, aspirations are kept simple and achievable.

Preservers have always maintained very strong points of view. This is part of their adaptive stoicism. They are more likely to deny health problems, or define health problems in old-world terms that they can understand. For example, disease is thought of in terms of what were considered "unscientific" causes, such as the "evil eye," or eating the wrong foods at the wrong time, although some of these are now considered valid. The Preserver tends to look for medicines that can be made at home, or for guaranteed cure-alls. As suspicious as they are, Preservers also tend to harbor secret hopes about miraculous cures, which makes them susceptible to "snake oil cures." They are for the most part uneducated, "unscientific," and used to old-world medicines. When they have problems, Preservers tend to take care of them themselves or not acknowledge them. However, compared to others in their age group, Preservers tend to be more seriously ill and more dependent on others, both physically and psychologically, in their later years.

When Preservers face retirement, their attitudes toward housing are survival-oriented. Most Preservers would prefer to work until they die; working beyond age 65 is characteristic, because of the financial realities as well as an inability to comprehend a retired life style. Despite their children's pleas to slow down or retire, they often drag out their employment years until they are truly unable to work, and then begin an awkward post-employment life style. For many, retirement is a confirmation of prior modest expectations: an old person waits alone, gardens to pass the time, thinks about each meal past and the one yet to come, occasionally takes care of grandchildren, and prepares for the inevitable.

The Preserver tends to remain in his or her own home as long as possible. For some, particularly widowed women without family, public or church-sponsored older adult housing might be considered. Some Preservers have close family ties that help keep them alert and active, but many live lonely and isolated lives.

Preservers exist, in one way or another, in virtually every age group. However, Preservers are the largest group in this cohort because it contains so many immigrants.

Adaptors

Unlike the Preservers, there were other immigrants who sought to become as American as possible, in order to participate fully in the economic and social wealth of the nation. These are the Adaptors.

The Adaptor is characterized by a flexible attitude, an extroverted spirit, and a tendency to take risks. Adaptors left behind a world that was neither kind nor nurturing; they had not left the old world to bring it to the new.

Adaptors have a spirit that is often praised in America. The Adaptor looks outward, shyly or boldly, and tries to find a way to join the crowd. Initially, this may have meant going to night classes to learn English after working a 12-hour shift. Or it may have meant borrowing money from family and friends to start a dry cleaning business, learning English by doing business with others.

Adaptors do not reject their cultural heritage, but keep it as a special and intimate aspect of their lives. They work hard for their families and respect their parents' culture, but don't let it prevent them from moving ahead. They are not frightened of new people or new ideas. They also tend to share their feelings with their spouse. However, they often experience stress-related diseases that reflect their efforts to maintain an outwardly calm and positive attitude when they are having a hard time coping.

The Adaptor has strong family bonds. Less autocratic or dogmatic than Preservers, the Adaptor is a keen observer of the world, and tries, to the best of his or her ability, to learn what is going on and what it takes to succeed. They fully expect their children to do better than they did. They encourage experimentation, but expect serious dedication. The Adaptor might push his or her children to do well in school. The Adaptor is proud and sad when children leave to go to college, or take a job far away, and views this as a sign of hard-won success.

The Adaptor loves role models from the media, and success stories of those who have beaten the odds; these reinforce stressful risk-taking: "If he could do it, so can I," the Adaptor thinks. The Adaptor rapidly adopts mainstream culture, from clothing to sports to music. Adaptors have a lifelong fascination with things American, and this makes them strong mainstream consumers. They buy encyclopedias for their children and labor-saving devices for their homes.

Adaptors try to emulate what they believe are healthy behaviors. This includes modern views of sanitation and eating well. They have a high respect for professionals and people in authority, and are less intimidated by them than Preservers. After all, they or their children aspire to achieving the same rank and privilege. Adaptors use the "system" as much as they are able and associate new and modern with quality and improvement. Adaptors accept and enjoy technology, such as "gadgets," but are not particularly mechanical.

Adaptors like the idea of moving up, and although they might only move from one urban neighborhood to another during their lifetime, even this would be considered an important improvement. When Adaptors reach retirement, they are likely to make choices that reflect their preference for independence and autonomy. They like to know they have someone to look after them, whether it is a spouse or service professional. Adaptors like to live in their homes as long as they are able but are not so attached to their neighborhoods that they will not move. In some cases, if they have friends in another state, such as Florida, they will join them.

Pragmatists

Pragmatists are likely to be American-born, primarily in rural areas or small towns. Pragmatists have a self-image and life style that is based on strong concepts of duty and clearly defined principles of right and wrong. They were raised in the Lutheran and Protestant traditions of discipline, hard work, practicality, thrift, and earned trust—values they still maintain.

Pragmatists, unlike Preservers, have a highly defined view of the world, both good and bad. They know what to do or not to do, and they practice what they preach, keeping within the boundaries of what is known and accepted. But their view of the world, although well-defined, is a narrow one, and as a result, they are generally not adventurous. They listen closely to what neighbors and fellow church members say. Although they are very sensitive to how they appear to others and feel very self-conscious, this is in part because they fear they do not truly live up to community standards. Avoiding embarrassment is very important. The usual scope of activities is confined to the world they are familiar with: a cake-baking competition, a 4-H hog-raising contest, a church raffle.

Pragmatist men tend to overcompensate for their strong sense of duty and morality through a kind of rebellion, not necessarily expressed coherently, but rather ritualistically, such as an occasional drunken night out with the boys, a wild card game with fellow lodge members, or a weekend fishing at the lake with buddies. Their escape from the world of upstanding correctness often produces an almost childlike sense of release. The temporary remorse, the sheepish and contrite behavior that accompanies the flight from the rigors of the workaday world, is all part of the pattern of coping with extremes of duty and frustration.

For Pragmatist women, who also come from a tradition of hard work and repressed feelings, release is harder to come by. They depend on the comfort and counsel of other women, and of religion.

The community of the church gives women strength, since their husbands tend to be distant and taciturn. Pragmatist women often rule the roost and dominate their children. Some become schoolteachers, and enjoy instructing and influencing others.

Pragmatists come from a long line of down-to-earth people who take life seriously and are driven by a strong sense of duty and conformity. Like Garrison Keillor's Norwegian bachelor farmers of "A Prairie Home Companion" radio show fame, they will follow their overwrought conscience and not their hearts. Their rural and small-town upbringing, more narrow in its range of options and more consistent than urban life, gives the Pragmatist a calm and serious demeanor. Pragmatists seek to maintain the status quo. They read *Reader's Digest* and order from the Sears catalogue. Afraid of seeming vain, they may, in fact, harbor a secret desire for excitement and prestige, which they believe is unattainable or inappropriate. This makes them vulnerable to unrealistic sales pitches, such as insurance schemes or publishers' clearinghouse sweepstakes.

Pragmatists' health attitudes are based on an understanding of nature and common sense. Complaining is frowned upon, although sometimes an understatement (i.e., "can't complain") can communicate a great deal about pain and anxiety. They take care of themselves and fear being a burden to others. They like home remedies. They do not make a big fuss over illness, yet usually enjoy a long relationship with their doctor. There is a philosophical fatalism about the Pragmatist; life offers few surprises.

Many Pragmatists see aging as a period of appropriate withdrawal—the "Golden Years." They are proud to have survived. The Pragmatist view of aging is often very businesslike. Their choices are driven by practical considerations. They will remain at home as long as "appropriate," and one or more children living nearby often help make this possible. However, Pragmatists are quick to make changes if they sense they are becoming a burden. For example, Pragmatists who are farmers may turn the land over to their kids, and move into a second home on the property. Sometimes they will lease the land and move into a smaller apartment in a nearby town. Most of the time they avoid taking what might appear to be charity, and may find themselves without an adequate informal support structure if family members leave the region.

Pragmatists often prefer older adult housing that is sponsored by a church organization. In this way they can avoid being a financial liability. This is particularly true of older widows. Most Pragmatists want to remain in their own region, and will only move to retirement communities if they exist nearby. Many will move to cabins in small lakeside communities near where they used to live, possibly keeping their homes for winter use. A few will move to Florida—or to Arizona (Pragmatists were the first to join active retirement communities like Sun City because it offered a good deal—sun and a house—at a good price, thus meeting their concerns for stability, and modest indulgence). Pragmatists live all over America, but tend to be found in New Hampshire, Vermont, Pennsylvania, Michigan, Minnesota, and Alabama.

Explorers

The Explorer is the stubborn and often resourceful older American who knows what he or she does or does not want. Explorers possess a gritty individualism. They have a high degree of regard for autonomy, independence, and control. In many ways, the Explorer is a seeker, not of material gain or status, but of a psychologically comfortable fit with life: a fit between their need for autonomy and a nonobtrusive, tolerant world. Explorers are generally averse to authority. They do not necessarily conflict with it, but can be relatively indifferent to it. They are typically easygoing; not particularly extraverted, but not reclusive either (e.g., they want quiet neighbors who mind their own business).

Explorers feel a strong sense of obligation to no one except the immediate family; they are not tied to their neighborhood or ethnic background. Explorers are often entrepreneurial and risk-oriented, but not always. An Explorer may be more individualistic than entrepreneurial. He or she might choose a nine-to-five job on an assembly line, if it provided the time or funds to live the way he or she wanted. Rich or poor, an Explorer may appear financially conservative, denying pleasures that others might assume, such as owning a big house or a new car.

The Explorer is part of a long tradition of Yankees, southerners, and do-it-yourself Americans. The most salient traits of Explorers are autonomy and self-reliance. They want to do things their way. Consumed with a passion to build or achieve something that is not measurable in terms of salary or position, the Explorer takes risks and works to create a legacy, sometimes for him or herself, sometimes for the family. This may be a hidden investment in real estate, for example. This legacy is more often not monetary but a reputation of having done a job right in their previous career. The Explorer is open to change and willing to sacrifice stability for something more meaningful. He or she might change jobs often, seeking new avenues for expression of ideas. Some Explorers are tinkerers. They helped invent the new products that brought technology to the 20th century. Others worked on the Hoover Dam, started their own repair businesses, worked for the gas company, or raised five children.

Explorers are stubborn, dedicated, introverted, sometimes highly abstract, individuals. Often not well educated, Explorers solve life's riddles through trial and error. This quality of perseverance—a virtual stubbornness—sometimes results in a neglect of their own welfare (and sometimes their family's), usually in the interest of what the Explorer believes to be a higher calling. This might be their view of what's right and natural and what's not—be it a question of business ethics or simply a desire to preserve personal freedom and minimize obligations to others. A spouse or child might not heed or like that same calling, however, and end up packing up and moving out. Explorers themselves may pick up and move—to express contempt for the government or an employer. They might decide on a return to nature and settle in a mountain cabin, abandoning work to pursue their convictions.

Explorers are an interesting mixture of introversion and exploration, often engaging with the world their entire lives. At the same time they have the ability to dream. Whether the Explorer is an absent-minded professor or the proprietor of a small hardware store, his or her mind is generally elsewhere.

Explorers may become involved in projects—building a cabinet or landscaping the yard—but these are often left unfinished. Some projects are odd and impractical—a fountain that doesn't work, an unusual color for the bedroom. Often Explorers do not want to be bothered with the details of everyday life; a leak in the ceiling, a car repair, a clogged drain may go unattended. This means that their spouse or other family may be called in when they have deferred decisions for too long.

Explorers frequently ignore health problems until a crisis arises, then make little of it. Sometimes they will ignore problems; other times they might experiment on themselves with home remedies before turning to a professional. The family of an Explorer might have to intervene when problems arise. When it comes to personal matters, the Explorer questions authority and rejects *ex cathedra* views, often contradicting orders or suggestions. An Explorer man or woman might be labeled "peculiar," or a "tough old bird."

Frequently, Explorers choose simple housing options, delaying purchasing a home for a while. Later in life, the Explorer may again choose, at an earlier stage than most, a simple retirement living arrangement. If he or she chooses more than a cabin, convenient trailer park, or apartment, it will be because of a very persistent salesperson or family member, or the fact that the Explorer decides that going along with another's decision is the least annoying alternative.

THE DREAM-DEFERRED GENERATION: 1910–1919

Born in the infancy of this century, raised in the frenzied promise of the 1920s, and chastened by the depression of the 1930s, the Dream-Deferred Generation are a cohort angry about the past and suspicious of the future. Somehow out of sync with the cycles of exuberance in this century's development, through no fault of their own, the journey of the Dream Deferred has often been in the shadow of those both older and younger. Born too late for the opening of the century, young victims of the crash of '29, too established for wartime fervor, and too old to parent the Baby Boom, this cohort was to become the leader of reforms to meet the needs of older adults in the 1960s. Their lives are a trail of events whose tales are often told and constitute a distinctive generational time signature—the Dream Deferred.

IMMERSION—CHILDHOOD IN 1910–1919

Those born in 1910–1920 came into a world quite different from that of the preceding cohort. Cleaner water, enforced quarantine for infectious diseases, a 10-hour work day (except at U.S. Steel, which kept the 12-hour day until 1921), and better nutrition increased life expectancy from 55 in 1900 to 60 in 1910. The improvement in nutrition was not just a result of a better standard of living, but of increased knowledge about health care.

The good-government and reform movements had been somewhat effective in reducing civic corruption and providing more government services like meat inspection. In addition to organized groups, women's magazines were also a powerful instrument of change. Articles covered not only fashions and manners but infant care; how women's clubs could work for better government and beautify the city; how women could earn money at home by updating magazine subscription lists, running news clipping services, engrossing (writing names in fancy script on certificates and diplomas); and how to cope with family problems. Some young women, protected from knowing about money, thought that a good provider should by age 22 earn as much as their fathers had after two decades of work, but columnists explained gently that the world didn't work that way. There were articles about job-related stress in men, why romance didn't last, and what could replace it.

Wages were rising all the time—not in the older industries, like textiles, but in the newer ones, to attract more skilled workers. Henry Ford's lesson, that high wages will cut employee turnover, was not lost on those making new products such as vacuum cleaners, electric light bulbs, motion picture projectors, and radio sets, who needed a stable work force.

Families had fewer servants or hired girls and more labor-saving devices. They attended church less and movies more. Churches, still primarily Protestant, were important in towns, but in the cities a family could get by with going only a few times a year. There was, in general, less hellfire and brimstone in religion, although there were still vivid exceptions, such as evangelists "Soapy" Smith and Billy Sunday. The focus of popular religion was more on psychology and even business; a book was written on Christ as a businessman. Elbert Hubbard, a writer of the period, said, "If we would fix our hearts on good tenements here and let slide all claims to mansions in the skies; drop Adam and take up Macadam; work for good roads now instead of talking about pavements of gold in heaven, we might then have Paradise here in place of waiting and taking chances of finding it after death." (*Concerning Slang and Other Droll Stories*, East Aurora, N.Y.: The Roycrofters, 1920, p. 58.)

Mothers began to sterilize baby bottles and boil water for formula. Public health departments organized well-baby contests and "Baby Weeks" where mothers were instructed in how to prepare baby foods and keep the nursery sanitary. Hospital births, better sanitation, and fewer servants who believed in old-world remedies improved infant survival rates. Maternal survival rates also improved, and as women had fewer babies and began to eat more fruits and vegetables, they were able to recover more completely after childbirth.

The American diet also benefited from additions such as canned salmon, which was cheap, easy to make into a loaf with stale bread-crumbs and egg, and still had enough protein to nourish a working man. It made a nice change from "that everlasting hominy," or toasted cheese ("Welsh rabbit" in some parts of the country, "rarebit" in others), or creamed chipped beef on toast.

It was an increasingly dry world. Although Prohibition failed, 23 states were already dry by 1914, and in many others local option laws meant that towns or whole counties were dry. Some, such as Palo Alto and Menlo Park, California, were still dry in the 1950s, despite their proximity to San Francisco; Wellesley, Massachusetts, remains dry today.

In general, few children lost fathers to, or were much affected by World War I, but many lost a parent to the influenza pandemic of 1918; it killed five times as many Americans as the 126,000 killed in the war. Many had fathers who were sick so long they lost their jobs. These children, who were much less likely to be born on farms than the previous cohort, were also more likely to have a father injured or killed on the job, and less likely to lose a parent to tuberculosis.

Immigration peaked at the beginning of the decade, then dropped off sharply. There were, however, influxes of refugees from Eastern European pogroms, and later, from the devastation of World War I.

Two political changes affected people's lives. First, direct election of senators by the people had finally been ratified. This was an example of government's greater responsiveness to the media, which attempted not only to mold the will of the people but to control the senators by interpreting it for them. When state senates did the electing, senators running for office had only a few people to please, not a whole state of constituents.

Second, the individual income tax was introduced in 1911. Although it directly affected very few people, because only the rich had enough income to be liable for it, the income tax ended a long-standing controversy over whether or not the accumulation of great fortunes ought to be prevented by the introduction of a personal income tax or inheritance tax. Now laws such as the Pure Food and Drug Act could be enforced more vigorously, using some of the wealth that the rich had to give to Washington, D.C. As a result, the federal government seemed more important and closer to people's daily lives.

DIVERSION—THE ADOLESCENT EXPERIENCE IN THE 1920S

The Dream-Deferred Generation watched as towns struggled to get their high schools accredited. There had been high schools before, but only in cities and large towns. Now towns as small as 3000 people were building them. Some children went to high school and others went to work, but there was little doubt as to which was preferable. Young people began to expect to go to high school.

Schools considered Americanization and raising the expectations of their students to be their main goals. Civics was an important subject, partly as a result of the good-government movement, and partly because immigrants now lived all around the country, in smaller cities and rural states as well as industrial cities. To keep students interested and involved, interschool rivalries were fostered.

Fathers worked in the war industries, made money, and bought Liberty Bonds. Women worked in stores, offices, and schools. The number of horses had peaked in 1912. Now they were used mostly on farms, estates, and the outlying residential areas of cities, where each horse knew its delivery route as well as it knew its driver. Mostly families bought new cars; highways, repair shops, and a garage behind every house became more prevalent.

By 1920 only a third of Americans had indoor plumbing, electric lights and appliances, gas stoves, and central heating. But this cohort was far more urban than the preceding one. Farms were the last to receive modern conveniences. Even when running water and electricity were available, it was likely that the barn would get both while the house got neither.

The parents of the Dream-Deferred Generation read and saw different things than their grandparents had. Fiction in the popular magazines was less likely to be about plucky orphans than about uncovering fraud and wickedness. Young heroines learned, in the nick of time, that the smooth suitor was a snake, and found a way to unmask him in public, just like in the movie, *The Perils of Pauline*. Men who appeared to be criminals might turn out instead to be heroes; often it was the pursuing police who were corrupt—or only pretending to be police. Although the classic film *The Birth of a Nation*—about the Civil War period in the South—was released in 1915, few had seen it the year it came out. But toward the end of the decade there were so many movie theaters that the older children even in small towns could go to the movies and see a western.

Eleanor Porter's book, *Pollyanna*, published in 1913, told about a cheerful young orphan girl who had come to live with an embittered maiden aunt. Her incessant good nature was mocked, but everyone read the book. Cheerfulness and enthusiasm were important qualities, with so many people of different backgrounds mixing in schools, and at work. Later, Dale Carnegie's manifesto, *How to Win Friends and Influence People* (1937), would also be very popular. Both books expressed the value Americans placed on persistence and optimism.

EXPANSION—EARLY ADULTHOOD IN THE 1930S

Quite a few found their lives profoundly changed by the Great Depression. There was no hope of a job, so many of those born in 1913–1916 stayed on to finish high school and even go on to college. Those born in 1917–1919 weren't so lucky. They had watched older siblings, parents, and neighbors go jobless despite a high school or even a college diploma. They knew that a wage meant more than education. When recovery began in 1935 there were jobs—like building dams and post offices—that did not require a diploma, so they went to work and never went back to school.

The recovery of 1935–1939 left many of those young people feeling cheated—a feeling that lasted many years. They knew the preciousness of a job too well to let go of one freely, but they began to see that they had been mistaken about the futility of study. They had been betrayed by prudence and suspected they were being conned again to keep dead-end jobs. They recognized, many years later, their own bitterness as clearly portrayed by Jackie Gleason in "The Honeymooners." He knew the pain of sacrificing personal plans to meet family needs during those hard times.

For some boys born in 1916–1920, there was the Civilian Conservation Corps, or CCC. They signed up for six-month hitches and got good food, clean clothes, hard work, and pay sent home to their families. The $30 a month often made the difference between malnutrition and health for parents and younger brothers and sisters. The boys cleared trails, planted trees, put out fires, cleared streams, and built bridges. They also got to meet boys from other parts of the country.

The shift from bravado to a kind of baffled "the-hell-with-it" feeling was reflected in popular music. Early in the decade people listened to "Ain't We Got Fun," and "Side by Side." The middle of the decade brought wistful songs such as "Red Sails in the Sunset" and "High on a Windy Hill." As a reaction to frustration, misery, and uncertainty, there were in the last half of the decade such nonsense songs as "Three

Little Fishies," "Hut Sut Ralson," "Mairzie Doats," and "Tippitippi-tin" or songs of wishful thinking, "Pennies from Heaven," "South of the Border," "Little Grass Shack," and "A Tisket a Tasket."

The Dream-Deferred Generation knew their parents hadn't brought on the crash, but some felt they should have been better prepared or protected. Some thought their immigrant parents should have learned more. This generation later popularized Freud and childhood traumas, dethroned Mother, and loathed the Babbitry of the bourgeoisie. Educated or not, everyone had a grievance with the world they inhabited.

Many blamed capitalism and Wall Street and linked themselves firmly with the opposition, supporting the struggle for unions and learning the songs in the International Workers of the World (IWW) songbook ("There'll be pie in the sky when you die"). Others favored communism or socialism. Quakers, socialists, anarchists, communists, world federalists, pacifists, and the YMCA pursued social reforms that would prevent the agony of another Great Depression, while evangelists and the Ku Klux Klan pursued those they believed had corrupted the pure glories of the past.

It may seem that, considering the importance of the union struggle during the 1930s, union songs such as "Solidarity Forever" should have been widely known, but the radio was dominated by advertisers. Even in the late 1940s, songs like "Bread and Roses" and "There Once Was a Union Maid" were considered sufficiently inflammatory to serve as a kind of underground code: if you suggested singing one and someone else knew it, you were among friends.

Many felt frightened and confused, and moved from place to place looking for work. Some found construction jobs on the Boulder Dam, building the new aqueduct to Los Angeles from the Colorado River, the highway they called Route 66, or a new federal building being constructed by the PWA. Some studied drafting, scientific detection, and bookkeeping by correspondence. Night schools flourished; men and women stuck in boring jobs were determined to achieve success by self-improvement. Those who found work settled down, married, and had a child or two.

Some were "saved" by Jesus. Fundamentalist religion, which had developed during the 1920s, rejected science and replaced it with personal faith in a personal savior. The Holy Rollers, radio evangelists, and the Pentecostals all won large followings that still exist today.

A few sought protection with the rich or powerful. Sometimes they worked in a hotel or resort rich people came to. Perhaps they managed to open an antique shop or art gallery, or they became interior decorators or fashion designers. Others faithfully read *Vogue, Fortune, Time,* Walter Winchell, or the movie magazines. Many believed that they, too, could have been rich and glamorous if only something— God, Wall Street, Mom, polio—hadn't dealt them a bad hand.

Many read movie magazines just to be reminded of the fantasy life they enjoyed on their weekly outing to the movies—on Wednesday, which was "dish night," if they were married or collecting dishes for a relative or friend, Friday or Saturday if they were dating. To watch Fred Astaire and Ginger Rogers waltz by in tuxedo and shimmering gown was to live vicariously in a world most people, still working long hours and getting short rations, could not afford.

CONVERSION—ADULTHOOD IN THE 1940S

For the Dream-Deferred Generation, World War II was another de-tour. Although it helped to end the depression, the war once again took control out of the hands of this generation. Once again they had to put their personal lives and choices on indefinite hold: men had to fight and the women had to cope.

Because many had already formed their families by 1941, wives often followed husbands to Army camps or Navy bases and stayed when he went overseas. Other wives went to work in war plants, offices, schools, and stores. Their children stayed in the war plant nursery or went home to an empty house, or next door to play with the neighbor's kids. Men who had worked their way through three years of college at night fixed trucks or operated radios at the front line, or repaired radar sets because they could read the instructions. Women who had had to put off marriage had to cope with ration stamps and coworkers who thought they should double-date, and de-spaired of hearing from their fiancés while they listened to the war news every night.

Women who were single went on blind dates with lonely service-men, or dated men they met in church, or on the plant bowling team. (Bowling was a popular sport because bowling alleys could be kept open all night for plants running three shifts of workers.) Just as com-pulsory school attendance had liberated girls whose parents saw no need to educate a woman, World War II allowed them new freedoms: to go to bars unescorted, to go out bowling with their coworkers, to accept rides to and from work with men they did not know. But their work was the most liberating of all—not only were they doing useful work, they got a paycheck every week.

Men who were classified as 4-F, or had too many dependents, or were the sole surviving son were always having to explain why they weren't in the service, to those who suspected them of cowardice or of using influence. Men who had a deferment because they had an essential war job were often subjected to harassment by those who disagreed about the essential nature of the job. Those who were not in the service soon learned to stay out of bars that catered to servicemen.

SUBMERSION IN THE 1950S

Unlike the next generation, this generation was bewildered by their postwar experiences. This group had dreamed long, worked hard, had fewer illusions, and trusted less in the postwar promises. Their cautious choices—the modest house in suburbia, a secure corporate job, marriage—had unexpected results: isolation, expense, unhappy marriages. Overall, they were not comfortable with the homogeneity of the postwar world they helped to create, because they had not been children during the years of depression propaganda.

Once out of service, now in their 30s and 40s, members of the Dream-Deferred Generation began working in big corporations. Many sought the protection a solid company could offer against the threat of another depression; others had learned the power of large organizations, including government, through prior, often painful prewar experience.

Personal relationships underwent many dramatic changes. More people met and married across broad geographic and social boundaries. Couples did not necessarily share a similar culture; their methods of communication differed, as did their role models and expectations. The possibility of divorce was a great threat, because of its destabilizing effect. The harbingers of divorce were a failure to fulfill one's obligations: a woman's sloppy housekeeping, or a man's refusal to mow the lawn.

Science—and religion—indicated that sexual desire was what caused people to marry; popular psychology claimed that it was what kept a marriage together. But it is doubtful that any generation ever concentrated so anxiously on sex while pretending to ignore it. People nervously reassured one another that sex was natural and normal, while sanitizing sex education, movies, and books.

Women who had "played the field" often found that when the GI bill sent servicemen back to college, the campuses had plenty of "nice girls" who were considered more eligible wives. When men and women finally did marry and get their little house in the suburbs, there were so many new essentials: a washing machine (there was no laundry nearby to pick up and deliver); a refrigerator (with only one car and young children, they couldn't get to the store whenever they wanted); and a vacuum cleaner (sweeping took too long and the suburban dust was stirred by continuous construction).

Not all women returned home after the war. Although the war plant might have closed down, those who had gone to work on newspapers, in civil service, or as corporate secretaries and clerks remained in the work force. War widows and women whose wartime marriages had not lasted also continued to work outside the home. Many women kept working to help send their husbands through school; sometimes "hubby" watched the baby, too. But the majority of women found themselves stranded in the suburbs, without the family support systems that had helped previous cohorts to cope with child rearing and noncommunicative husbands. When they complained, psychiatrists (overwhelmingly male), who had studied Freud but not culture clashes, prescribed sleeping pills and tranquilizers. Men often withdrew from the family under stress, their lack of participation exacerbated by long commutes.

For already established families, suburbia meant less access to grandparents or aunts or to the familiar ties of hometowns. The new neighborhoods were not united by ethnic background or similarity of belief or occupation. To keep cultural differences insignificant, there was pressure for everyone to look and behave alike: neat lawns, fresh paint, picket fences, blinds drawn to the same level all along the street so that everything "looked nice." Fitting in was essential, increasing the emphasis on what was measurable, such as material possessions and the appearance of one's house. What their children saw—the emphasis on material possessions and keeping up with the neighbors—as narrow-minded and hypocritical was due to a fundamental difference between the two generations. The younger generation had shared a bland suburban culture, solidified by television, since birth. The older generation had to put together a culture from scraps taken from their few shared experiences (mass media and military service).

There were new social rules and methods of interactions. The woman of the house was now truly a housewife—that is, married to her house. Although there were so many helpful appliances and convenience foods, the standards were higher, too. The 11 a.m. coffee visit was an inspection: Were the breakfast dishes done? The beds made? The living room picked up?

New attention was paid to child rearing. This was the generation that made Dr. Benjamin Spock's *Baby and Child Care* a best-seller. "For the children's sake"—that was the rallying cry. The adults had for so long laid aside their own needs and desires that it no longer seemed strange to do so, as long as it was for a good cause. Having sacrificed nearly everything to fight "the good fight," however, now the good cause was familial, not global. Instead of featuring articles on social action, women's magazines now focused on purely domestic issues: a regular column called "Can This Marriage Be Saved?"; how to dress properly; how to decorate on a budget.

Senator Joseph McCarthy successfully played on the mood of the times—protecting hearth and home; fearing those who were "different"—with his hunt for communists. He "unmasked" enemies we didn't know we had. Now there were penalties—in the neighborhood, church, at work—for the wrong attitude or the wrong answer. Even *Consumer Reports* was denounced as a communist-front magazine.

REVERSION TO EMERGENCE—1960 AND BEYOND

The Dream-Deferred life in the 1960s was for the most part a time of adjustment to the changes that the times had wrought in others— spouses, children, neighborhoods, jobs. It was a decade of both joy and confusion. The joy, while not discussed much for fear of having it taken away, came from the solid progress that they had made in consolidating their economic position in life, in raising their daughters and sons to, and through, high school, and now into work and college. The confusion arose as the world around their personal achievements began to show signs of giving way—represented not only by the loss of leadership in the nation (post-Kennedy), but the encroaching furies of civil unrest occurring in the nation's communities (from Newark to Watts) and by the particular transformation that often overtook their own children. For, after a decade of gaining a hard-earned "purchase" on job and home, the Dream-Deferred parents saw their children shift from solid, healthy, earnest students from the old neighborhood to distressed, rejectionist youth. Imagine the horror of parents who had worked so hard to overcome their own difficult beginnings to provide a middle-class life for their children, who went into debt to finance their education, being confronted by a young adult who says, "I love you ma and pa, but I cannot live with the hypocrisy of our lives" and proceeds to grow long hair, wear second-hand clothes, drop in and out of college, experiment with drugs, sex, and so on.

Those of the Dream-Deferred Generation had hoped for their children a life less unstable than their own had been. They had sown the seeds of modest prosperity, with great difficulty, keeping their nose to the proverbial grindstone, and they reaped the whirlwind of their children's discontent (the old "how sharper than a serpent's tooth" syndrome from King Lear). While the anger of their children was not always aimed at their parents, their children chanted back at their parents' dismay: "You just don't understand; how can you? You are prisoners and victims of The System." The poor parents, having had to sweat for what they had earned—modest as it was—were neither impressed by these claims, nor always self-recriminating for the results. Some asked themselves, "Where did we go wrong?" Others said, "The hell with them if they don't respect our accomplishments." Where circumstances permitted, parents and children had a rough truce. The parents hoped that the mania would wear off, and the children hoped against their better judgment (such as it was) that their parents would wise up.

At home, the Dream-Deferred's children were now leaving high school and entering the work force or college. For those living in maturing suburbs of communities such as Philadelphia or St. Louis and communities in the plains states and Southwest (Wichita, Phoenix), the emerging urban conflicts were, for the most part, far off, and not easy to believe or make any sense out of. For the white urban population, many neighborhoods, on the other hand, had been undergoing change for decades. The difference was that now, in the early and mid-1960s, the tensions in these areas were growing as economic disparities were increasing. Fear of crime became a real facet of life—where earlier the changing ethnic pattern was part of a process of immigration and outmigration that had been going on for over a century. One population moved in, and eventually it moved out and another replaced it—German, Irish, Italian, Eastern European, black, Hispanic, and so on, whether it was in Queens, South Chicago, or Boyle Heights. Neighborhoods were "staging areas" from which integration into the nation's economy was launched. When that launching did not take place and when the consequences of paralysis in social progress accumulated in the form of discontent and mutually abusive practices (absentee landlords letting buildings run down, chain stores being moved out, banks refusing to lend to areas), the urban imbalance accelerated into decay which, itself, promoted further decline of families and broke the chain of social and economic integration.

Many 40- to 50-year old middle-class homeowners, who were living in urban neighborhoods in Detroit, Chicago, St. Louis, New York, Cleveland, and other centers, found themselves victims of exploitative tactics by real estate firms. These schemers used "block busting" techniques, in which established residents were intimidated into selling their homes at marginal prices for fear they would lose everything as the neighborhood became increasingly black. These residents unwittingly believed and became part of a strategy that exploited both black families hoping to move into better communities and the fearful (as well as prejudiced) white families. The result was the beginning of an urban exodus of Dream-Deferred families—"white flight." Worse, these people—black and white—became pawns in the decline of communities, which banks eventually "redlined" or refused to lend to, creating a catch-22 that communities, to this day, have only started to recover from. Ironically, this recovery has been led by the children of the Dream-Deferred cohort—the Gap Generation—who now are the new force in the "gentrification" process taking place in urban neighborhoods, from Boston and Washington to downtown Los Angeles. Unfortunately, as the word implies, the new generation coming in is, generally, displacing the old generation that preceded them—urban minorities and lower-income families.

The 1960s witnessed quite a few people in their 40s and 50s moving out of the neighborhoods where they had helped develop schools, playgrounds, and community centers during the 1950s. Many, of course, clung tenaciously to their once-familiar haunts as they were transformed, becoming strangers in their own neighborhoods as younger and very different ethnic populations arrived. The outmigrants, however, left due to their own fears, or direct experience of muggings and burglaries. These people moved to smaller, newer, outlying suburban areas, "upstate" towns, and to entirely new regions, such as Florida.

Those who were most able to move were either near retirement or able to find employment in a field similar to their previous occupation or profession. Professionals had it easiest, as there were many growing communities in the South and West to which they could move.

Those living in less troubled cities and towns had lives filled with other dilemmas of everyday life. Many of the Dream-Deferred Generation had become widowed or divorced in the late 40s and 50s. This cohort, while less prone to marriage breakup than the next younger generation, or their own children, did have their share of divorce. This created a generation of parents who later struggled with the awkwardness of being parent and grandparent alone. They had to live, in the case of divorced couples, with the knowledge of the other, former partner, having access to the children and grandchildren and, of course, the difficulties of sorting out which parent visits which child on which holiday occasion.

The 1960s placed the Dream-Deferred Generation in a variety of awkward situations that caused them uncertainty and anxiety. Their jobs had been relatively secure at the beginning of the decade, but now they were facing new financial demands—not all bad, just more money out of pocket to a financially frugal cohort. One source of new demand was a positive one—the opportunity to move from an apartment into a house or cooperative apartment (since this cohort had become financially established later than others, they had often delayed home purchase). For those who had owned their own homes—and those who did not—the 1960s meant putting the kids through school, or at least helping with college and everyday living expenses. The increasing social change in the lives of the Dream-Deferred Generation's children resulted in surprises, however, if not heart-wrenching conflicts between parent and child. This did not always mean that the children rejected their parents and values, but that the children rejected the social norms they saw around them. These values just happened to be many of the norms that the Dream-Deferred Generation had fought so long to achieve or emulate.

These parents were often stung by their children's dropping out of school or by their refusal to adopt more pragmatic habits, such as working to help with family expenses. Most kids in the 1960s did their share of work, as waiters, clerks, and gas station attendants, or working with their father in the store, or as an apprentice in the plant. But the parents increasingly found themselves left behind, emotionally or physically, by their Gap Generation children, for a variety of reasons. The 1960s were a period of separation between parent and child, of many kinds.

One source of pain and separation for the Dream-Deferred Generation, beyond the range of emotional assaults from their college-age children was from having a child go into military service. Fewer Dream Deferred had served in World War II than the next younger cohort and had a different view of the military than those who were younger. The previous wars had been "good wars" to stop and punish evildoers who had massacred innocents. Moreover, for the Dream Deferred, the war had also been an opportunity for civilian employment or military assignments usually out of the direct line of fire, since they were often older and had a family. In the hiatus between Korea and Vietnam, the Dream Deferred had not lost their view that wartime can be a period of opportunity. Children of working-class and middle-class Dream Deferred were sometimes enlisted, were drafted, or served in the reserves and national guard. Some found the military service a means for developing a technical or administrative skill.

They went along and reassured their parents that they were getting along well. The realities by the mid- to late 1960s were beginning to horrify everyone. The Dream-Deferred families were among the first and most frequent to suffer losses. As they watched the evening news they came to realize that the body counts on television were of their children's friends, and possibly, their own flesh and blood.

The period of Reversion for the Dream-Deferred Generation was characterized by a turning inward to defend themselves from the range of threats and losses in their lives at a time when they were still trying to move their lives forward. Their lives were at a stage where widowhood or divorce was increasing, their neighborhoods were unstable or at risk, their children were often leaving home, militantly rebelling or joining the military (voluntarily as well as drafted). The 1960s could only remind this age group of their own difficulties in their earlier stages of life—the 1930s and 1940s where they had to adapt to the tough conditions of the world at a high personal cost—the deferral of their own development. The times called out from the Dream Deferred a sigh of dismay and the bitter side comment, "So this is what I get for all my effort." The Dream Deferred acquired a distrusting, cynical view that built on their history of discouragement in their lives.

These events, which resulted in a strong conservative vote among many of this age group for the Nixon administration, carried over into the 1970s with a strong trend toward self-concern—a concern that was, on the face of it, primarily reactive and defensive. Disappointed with the era of the 1960s—moon walk and the passage of Medicare and the Older Americans Act aside—the Dream-Deferred Generation faced its final years of work and retirement with enthusiasm for the most part.

With little encouragement the Dream-Deferred Generation began to take their retirement from work, or at least look forward to it with relief. Now that they had Medicare and a small nest egg saved up, they could (some of them) leave the colder northern regions for the sun of Florida and Arizona, and sometimes the towns of their youth (Appalachia, for example).

Those who were neither motivated nor financially able to move away began to compensate for their lack of residential mobility by building up their post–working years life style through expanding hobbies—gardening, carpentry, art, mechanics, and travel.

There was, however, a large group in this cohort who were in their late 50s during the late 1960s who were forcibly retired from their jobs. These people had been workers in the major heavy industries that were now collapsing of their own rusted weight, often taking the workers' pensions with them as they collapsed. Among these were the machine-tool industries in Cleveland, Cincinnati, and Buffalo; the steel industry in Pittsburgh and the surrounding steel valleys; the textile industry in North and South Carolina and Georgia; as well as other sectors, such as chemicals, furniture, and appliances. These factories were the early victims of America's declining competitiveness in the world economy, and changing world trade patterns. The Dream-Deferred Generation was not the only one hurt, by any means. However, their lives had coincided with the development and decline of these plants. This demise of the old manufacturing world, which started in the late 1960s and continued through the 1970s and 1980s, coincided with the aging and retirement of this cohort, making the process of change painful at a very personal level, at least for those in the industries.

The early retirees from these declining manufacturing industry enclaves contrast starkly with the large population of workers with modestly well-paying and more stable civil servant (school, city and state government) and public utility (electric, gas, water) and banking jobs of those times, who had literally worked "womb to tomb," if it was feasible for them. This variation among the Dream-Deferred cohort created a unique composite of people still working, retired with modest pensions, and retired poor, or marginally able to get by.

Urban centers now began to show two categories of older adults among their citizenry. One category comprises the Children of the Century, the other, the younger Dream-Deferred cohort. The Dream-Deferred Generation began to become associated not with the older "Miami" clusters of aging, who sought the cheap housing and warmth of Florida, but with the booming condominium complexes of the Fort Lauderdale and Tampa, Florida, regions, and the active adult communities of Phoenix, Arizona, and southern California.

While the outmigrants, or "Sunbirds," represent only 10–20 percent of the overall Dream-Deferred Generation at most, they created a new image for the older adult that stood out as a harbinger of the future of aging in America—the golden old. This image was far from being true, although it certainly represented one segment of this population.

During the 1970s and 1980s, this group turned their attention and pocketbooks to establishing, for the first time in their lives, a life style centered on their own needs—for the most part. While having modest means, this group was able to begin to travel actively—frequently in groups—going to destinations across Europe and the Middle East, as well as the Far East. The image of the American tourist in Bermuda shorts, loud shirts, and swinging cameras across portly midsections had its origin in the blast of Dream-Deferred Generation travelers revisiting the scenes of World War II, their lost family members, or the glamorous European capitals.

The Dream Deferred purchased their new cars (this was, they swore, the last one), their new homes or second homes, remodeled their first ones, and sometimes helped their children finance their first home. Having reconciled with their parents somewhat during the 1970s, the Gap Generation were also helping their families, where they could (although slower in their economic development due to their 1960s experiments).

The 1970s and 1980s were, in most respects, a period of repositioning for the Dream-Deferred Generation. They had to face their retirement as it became a fact of their lives—good or bad, elected or involuntary. They had to begin to organize their lives, wealthy or poor, around their own priorities—a challenge for this self-denying group. They had the opportunity to have a rapprochement with their children who had affronted them and finish their grieving for lost spouses, divorces, and for their children who had perished in Vietnam. And, most of all, they could now cultivate their lives, focusing on the immediate—no longer waiting or deferring. Some would do this, others never, continuing to hold at arm's length what life had once kept out of reach.

BIRTHMARKS

Martyrs

Martyrs can come from any cultural background, but tend to come from immigrant families. Martyrs have a poor sense of their own self-worth and a fatalistic view of life. They grew up during the Roaring Twenties and had great expectations for the future. Their authority figures—parents, supervisors, leaders—equated effort with success: if you worked hard, you would succeed. But this generation's traumatic Time Signatures, the depression and World War II, made it impossible for them to attain the standards or goals of their family. They also internalized their family's problems. They took personally their father's anger at losing his job, or their mother's pent-up frustration as she tried to cope with the stress of a disgruntled husband and hungry children. When the landlord broke the lease, when they had to drop out of school to get a job, they felt ashamed. Their experience parallels that of children of divorce, who believe they have somehow caused their parents' unhappiness.

The Martyr tried to relieve his or her parents, to make them happy, and to retrieve their love. Yet the Martyr could help only by denying his or her own needs and desires. To even think of nice toys or pretty clothes or a college education when your family is in crisis instills a sense of guilt. They know that anything that you can build (savings, careers, families) can be torn down. As a result Martyrs are cautious and conservative. Don't wish for too much, don't expect too much, don't even talk about your desires. If you do you will be disappointed and perhaps even punished for your selfishness.

Martyrs are compulsive savers of odds and ends, closet savers of money (to hide the fact they are worried, although they are admittedly fiscally prudent). They are protective of the interests of others, verging on being, if not being, deliberately meddlesome. They tend to compensate for their feelings of frustration and guilt by pushing others to enjoy what they could not: "I couldn't have it but you should," they tell their children; or, "It's OK, I don't want it. You take it." They live vicariously, and have a strong tendency to displace their self-denial onto others.

The Martyr tries to improve his or her poor self-image by awkward attempts at self-redemption throughout life. Martyrs criticize and reward in rapid succession, and carry the weight of the world on their shoulders and want everyone to know it. The Martyr is also a soft touch for anyone with a cause, whether it is a door-to-door salesperson or a charity, and will often take on a cause of a group with whom they have psychologically strong ties, such as oppressed people. The Martyr is eager to "buy" the good graces of their children and grandchildren through material gifts, as well as affection verging on the insensitive (or even inane). But a Martyr never feels good about his or her own actions, and is strongly motivated to repeat them again and again.

Martyrs want very badly to receive, but cannot accept easily; they fight and complain at every attempt, and when a gift is accepted, it is always deprecated, as if by reducing its worth they can deny that they are being given anything of value. They undermine themselves by their rituals of inflicting guilt and refusing to be placated. When giving a gift, which may be received lovingly, the Martyr sighs and sends out the message that no matter the extent of the thanks, it cannot assuage the deep pain that underlies the Martyr's life. The Martyr generates guilt in the gift recipient, passing on a mixed message. The Martyr drives spouses, children, and relatives crazy with aggravation.

Martyrs rarely buy anything for themselves. However, if a sales-man suggests that if he does not make his quota, he will be fired, the Martyrs will buy, incorporating the salesman's theoretical anxiety into their own fears of abandonment. They fear being left uncared for and will purchase insurance and other financial products to reduce their potential liability to others.

Martyrs thrive on attention, but will never admit to it. For this reason, they will spend time creating situations—a card game, a wed-ding shower, a family dinner—where they are essential participants. Martyrs are also self-centered and very conscious of their own health. They know they hurt, and maybe the sinus, or the arthritis, or the insomnia, is the reason. Illness—suffering—is a legitimate excuse for asking to be attended to, something they cannot do ordinarily. They develop psychosomatic illnesses that tell them they are alive, and by seeking health care, they have a legitimate reason for the attention they so badly want but cannot directly ask for. Martyrs have strong ties to their doctor, but may actually go to more than one, because they tend to be suspicious and anxious. They are uncomfortable with technology, and place more emphasis on personal relationships and trust than on skill. They will listen to each others' views on the quality of a physician or treatment and use them in making decisions. Nevertheless, they tend to be tough and healthy, despite their com-plaints.

Although Martyrs are generally independent, family and friends are essential—often because the Martyr, for sympathy, can then point to the common problems they cause: "My son never calls me."

Martyrs tend to remain in their own homes as long as they are able to, even if they are widowed. Often, children will put pressure on a mother to move into a smaller apartment or senior citizen project, thinking that is best for her. But most Martyrs are very attached to the world they know, and like their own neighborhood, even if it has become run down over the years. They won't move voluntarily; typ-ically, other family members have to make all the arrangements. Mar-tyrs like to defer decisions to others, partly because they feel they don't deserve anything, and partly because they want demonstrations of the affection and concern of others.

Only by convincing themselves that moving is in the family's inter-est will a Martyr and spouse pack up and go. A Martyr may agree to leave the old neighborhood, often in an urban area (Queens, New York, or St. Louis, Missouri), because his or her spouse wants to. Typically, they will move to a condominium in Florida, or near their children. Martyrs feel very guilty spending the home equity on anything other than their children ("I want to leave you something when I go").

Self-Compensators

The previous cohort, the Children of the Century, were better prepared to deal with the depression than any of the Dream-Deferred Generation. They had already achieved whatever educational goals they were likely to. Most were already married and settled. They knew about hard times from World War I; the Roaring Twenties were something they created, not something they were born into.

The Self-Compensator reacted very differently than the Martyr to early life experiences—in fact, in reverse. Like the Martyr, the young adult Self-Compensator was deprived of many opportunities for personal development. But instead of feeling guilty or ashamed, the Self-Compensator was angry, although the anger was not always explicit. Self-Compensators felt "at war" with "them" from childhood, when the depression robbed them of the American dream. They were bitter, and felt betrayed by their parents. They recognized that no one was going to make it easy for them: you had to make money the old way—by earning it. Self-Compensators don't forgive those who are better off, and they don't trust many people, either.

Business and government were blamed for the pain and humiliation of economic disenfranchisement. The first 100 days of Franklin Delano Roosevelt's administration, the WPA, the CCC—these were stopgap efforts of government. Government projects paid little and despite their romanticism did not solve the economic problems (war did; which required more sacrifice or deferral). Self-Compensators saw their parents floundering; at first they despaired, then became cynical. Their cynicism (about the possibility of things improving) was a reaction not only to the failure of institutions but to the humiliation their families suffered. Some didn't hide their bitterness about the past: "My old man was broken and became a drunk." "My mother spent her days on her hands and knees, scrubbing, just to bring home a few bucks."

Many Self-Compensators saw organized labor as the solution to their problems—unions promised a fairer deal than did greedy employers. Others did go to work for the government but never vested their trust in the institutions that employed them. Other Self-Compensators resisted affiliation with any institution, public or private, and prided themselves on being able to put in their day's work wherever it had to be. Many worked at menial labor and sales jobs, and changed jobs often.

For almost a third of the Self-Compensators, World War II was a means of regaining some of the losses sustained in their youth. Because they were slightly too old for active military duty during World War II, or were in and out of military service before the war overseas heated up, they were able to take advantage of new job and career opportunities. Those who stayed in the armed forces frequently found themselves in desk jobs, and were more able to sustain a "normal" life style.

This respite did not appear as a reward to Self-Compensators, however. The fact that there was an implied loss of status to men who did not see combat during the war made many Self-Compensators feel even more discouraged. They felt as if they were born out of synch, always too late for the party—too young for the Roaring Twenties, too late for the honor and glory of the war.

Self-Compensators complain, criticize, envy, and are always suspicious of others. If someone else succeeds, they grumble, "She must have had an 'in' with the boss." They tend to be parsimonious. Receiving gifts is a dramatic ritual. A small boy, for instance, is made to beg for the gift or favor that he wants, or even to humiliate himself in some small way by having to ply the parent with sickly sweet niceties and promises. If the Self-Compensator can't have something, it's not worth having. Typically, the Self-Compensator will say to a son or daughter who wants money to go to college, "You don't know how easy you have it! I had to work for everything I own. You have to earn what you want." The Self-Compensator is not implacable, however, and will usually give in when children are sufficiently humble. Underlying it all is an intense desire for recognition, compensation, and reward.

The central theme of Self-Compensators is getting what was denied them. Although they might complain of being too poor to buy anything, they will buy things for themselves. Often, they will not only spend their money freely, but use it to buy luxury items, because they crave reward more than anything. They tend to be ostentatious about their wealth whenever possible. A Self-Compensator buys the gaudiest model car his or her income permits—a Cadillac, Mercedes, or BMW. Personal jewelry is significant, too. Many male Self-Compensators own an expensive watch, a pinky or family crest ring, a gold neck chain. A female Self-Compensator might have a mink coat and a diamond bracelet. The house may be decorated in a pseudo-Louis XIV style, with gilded chairs and ornate mirrors.

Politically, Self-Compensators are torn between their liberal roots and their conservative fears. Many Self-Compensators have changed political parties, depending on what seemed in their own best interest. When they were looking for help from economic ruin, the Democratic platform seemed the answer. Now they feel taxes are an imposition, people who don't work are bums, welfare mothers are lazy. "Equal opportunity is fine," they think, "just don't make me pay for it." They are anxious to keep what they have; as a result they are more likely to have become Republicans during the 1970s and 1980s.

Self-Compensators enjoy passive leisure activities; they are more likely to watch sports on TV than run around the block. A man might take up golf, fishing, or duck hunting later in life, to maintain business associates. They like to participate in events that convey status, such as charity balls and award ceremonies. Self-Compensator women enjoy getting their hair done (with the "girls"), watching soap operas, reading gossip magazines, and shopping. They accept their role as their husbands' embellishment, but not without making very clear the rules of the game (what they get for their "cooperation").

Self-Compensators are prone to stress-related diseases like ulcers and high blood pressure. Their tendency to indulge themselves, to refuse to restrict their diet or to exercise, also causes a higher incidence of health problems such as heart disease. The thought of dieting or restricting the kinds of food they eat causes anxiety. Self-Compensators like their meat and potatoes, spaghetti and meat sauce, pot roast and noodles—all the hearty foods that make them feel secure. And they want lots of it, including frequent snacks. As a result, many of them have problems with obesity and associated disorders.

Although Self-Compensators act embarrassed and naive about health issues, they love the attention they get from being sick, and verge on hypochondria. Even more self-centered than the Martyr, Self-Compensators will protest going to the doctor but love being taken care of, and may secretly relish major interventions such as surgery. In fact, they frequently elect to have surgery (i.e., to check for gallstones, ulcers, tumors, or prostate trouble). They dramatize their disorders, for sympathy, but are less likely to follow their doctor's advice, especially about diet and exercise. They are more likely to comply with a drug regimen, since it is easier, and requires few changes in existing behavior. Self-Compensators are self-indulgent; they want it all. They like to buy health technology and gadgets, such as exercise bikes and blood pressure cuffs, but they rarely use them consistently. They like grand gestures rather than hard work and self-control.

When life-threatening disorders strike, Self-Compensators reveal their vulnerability. They fear being out of control, abandoned, and lost. A male Self-Compensator, to protect himself, will bluff and joke at first. He tries to put on a tough show but has a hard time keeping it up. Eventually he will collapse and demand attention in a more primitive way—crying and whining.

When Self-Compensators retire, they do so with enthusiasm. They have no desire to work past 65; they don't want to work past 55, if they can avoid it. Self-Compensators are probably the most likely segment of any generation to feel that they have earned retirement. Most Self-Compensators view their retirement like they view their dinner: just *having* it is important. If they feel any sense of uneasiness or discontentment, they refuse to admit it. They might take a Caribbean or round-the-world cruise immediately upon retiring. They want a "ritzy" life style in their later years, even if it means having things (stereos, video cameras, swimming pools) around them they rarely make use of.

Many Self-Compensators, in keeping with their status-seeking nature, will leave their neighborhoods and move to condominiums or adult communities in Florida or Arizona; many "Sun Birds" are Self-Compensators. They might want to be by the seashore, a lake, or a golf course or country club. Although they want to spend their hard-earned money on themselves, Self-Compensators will still leave something behind for the kids.

Clock Watchers

Clock Watchers are those of the Dream-Deferred Generation who were more immune, psychologically, to the ravages of their era. Clock Watchers have been putting in their time all their lives. For them, the more things seem to change outside their world, the more they tend to stay the same; the Clock Watcher is far more centered on a personal world not controlled by outside forces such as employers, government, and foreign countries. For the Clock Watcher, what cannot be affected isn't important.

Most Clock Watchers were born in homogeneous communities, whether it was an ethnic enclave in a manufacturing city, a small town, or a long-settled Brooklyn neighborhood. They may have stayed in their hometown, or moved to a bigger city. Where Clock Watchers end up isn't relevant, because they bring their world with them.

Clock Watchers' values represent an unusual synthesis of American environments. They entered adulthood at a time when America was rapidly becoming more urban. But their childhood and adolescence were spent in small towns, relatively untouched by the social fads of city kids. Ray Bradbury described a typical Clock Watcher's town— "Greenville, Illinois"—a quiet town of small businesses. There people knew each other, and lived predictable, reliable lives that had continuity. Grandparents, parents, and children enjoyed strong ties, linking them back to preceding generations.

They were not isolated from the cities, however. Adventurous older cousins, returning from schools or businesses in nearby urban areas, brought back tales of adventure and a certain sophisticated style. But a local job was also acceptable, even desirable.

Perhaps because the Clock Watcher experienced both types of environments, adaptivity and continuity are two characteristics of this Birthmark. Underneath the adaptivity is an unusual degree of cultivated passivity uncharacteristic of their parents. Where their parents were stoic, unchanging, hardworking, and repressed, the Clock Watcher is hardy and adaptive.

Early on, Clock Watchers realized that they might not be able to lead the lives they wanted but they could control how they led the lives open to them. They accepted the need to work, although they expected compensation. They were not overly fond of their employers, but they had no yearnings to be the boss, either. They were just putting in their hours. Clock Watchers tend to plow ahead, rather than plan or analyze their situation. Eventually they succeed, through seniority, or simply by outlasting their coworkers.

Many Clock Watchers, unlike farm families in the dust bowl or workers in concentrated manufacturing centers, lived in areas of the country that were only marginally affected by the depression. Clock Watchers' expectations were modest, and thus often realized. Most boys did not plan, or have the chance, to go beyond the 8th grade. Some became apprentices in a trade, or went to a local trade school. Girls, also deprived of higher education but with fewer opportunities, faced a tougher work world and stiff family burdens at home.

Clock Watchers generally were not career-oriented, but since they were adaptable, they had advantages over those who were strictly farmers or factory workers. In a time when labor was reasonably portable, particularly in less skilled occupations, Clock Watchers became tradesmen and factory workers. Clock Watcher men tended to go into a family business, such as house painting, carpentry, plumbing, or running a hardware store. If there was a factory nearby—a textile mill, foundry, appliance assembly, farm implement manufacturer—a Clock Watcher could move in and out of the work force as employment demand shifted. Few people commuted, since there were few roads. When factories closed, the Clock Watcher, instead of leaving to seek work elsewhere, chose other local employment and then signed back on at the factory when and if it opened up again. Although both men and women changed jobs, they rarely changed their economic status.

Family ties were important far past childhood. Clock Watchers often lived near their parents, or even shared a house with them until they married. Those who moved to urban areas suffered the pangs of separation from their family but worked hard to blend in, often creating new family units by marrying someone very much in contrast to what they were raised with—for example, someone younger, or of another ethnic or religious group showing a surprising adaptiveness.

To the Clock Watcher, time is the key. Clock Watchers aspire to the day when their time is their own—not subject to a factory whistle or mid-morning break. For the children of Clock Watchers, upward mobility means to work in a higher paying occupation or self-employed business where your time is your own.

Clock Watchers do not imbue the world with special properties of persecution or reward, as do Martyrs or Self-Compensators. They tend to be more reserved. Many Clock Watchers, some who saw the world while serving in the armed forces, know there's more to life than their narrow scope. But the Clock Watcher believes such things are "not for me." Inside, perhaps, they are frustrated because they lack the tools for change. Like Ralph Cramden and Ed Norton in "The Honeymooners," they may be thinking or scheming about how to break out of their world, but rarely, if ever, do they do anything about it.

The Clock Watcher is fiercely defensive of the rituals and patterns that help make life comfortable, whether it is drinks at the tavern after work, or Sunday dinner at home. They like and need familiar events and surroundings—the local store, movie theater, apartment complex, occasional family outings. When these are upset, they feel anxious and angry. Anything that might diminish their sense of continuity, such as a changing neighborhood, is threatening.

Clock Watchers, indifferent to trendy consumer tastes, prefer known stores and routine purchasing behavior. If a local store closes in town, and a nearby mall opens, a period of adjustment is required to make the transition. But the Clock Watcher is ultimately able to adapt.

Clock Watchers are more likely to suffer from work-related disorders, primarily from stress, such as migraines, but they can develop ulcers or high blood pressure when there are conflicts at work they cannot easily resolve—a supervisor who is unreasonable, or a work mate who is incompetent at work because of problems at home.

Clock Watchers invest very little in caring for themselves, and tend to keep up a strong front, often not willing to discuss intimate domestic or medical matters with family or friends. They do have extended family nearby if they require assistance, but they usually avoid dependent relationships as long as possible.

The Clock Watcher prefers routine health care and would rather be taken care of when the need arises than take the time for preventive health care habits. Clock Watchers are indifferent, if not hostile, to technology, and somewhat intimidated by it.

Clock Watchers are very neighborhood-oriented, and like stability and order. Their social skills, because they lack experience, are not highly developed. This contributes to a fear of authority (or of losing autonomy) and as a result conflicts and confrontations with authority are not handled very well. However, Clock Watchers *can* cope, but they do so more by buckling down and persevering than by creative adaptation. Clock Watchers like old-boy or old-girl networks, whether it is their children's godparents, the Masons' social group, or a regular gang of friends who play cards together. A small core of family and friends provide day-to-day contacts, along with seasonal events with a larger set of relatives.

Clock Watchers look forward to an early retirement. Many were forced into it earlier than they had expected when factories closed. Others were able to make their own retirement plans. They have no problem looking back on their work with pride, but don't feel any serious loss in retirement, as long as they keep busy. Just as their work was never crucial to their self-identity, their retirement patterns also varied. Those who took early retirement tended to have more stereotypical recreational life styles. They attended ballgames, played cards, and spent their weekends hunting and fishing. The Clock Watchers have always been more able to enjoy recreation than others of their generation. They may expand the family collection of recreational vehicles. They have small second homes, rented cabins and campsites by lakes, forests, or deserts. Others may move to trailer parks in more undeveloped communities near their original homes, but most stay in their communities. They help their children set up businesses, look after grandchildren, and continue with their usual activities. For the Clock Watcher, the greatest reward is to finally forget the clock once and for all.

Conservers

Conservers are not only discontented with who they are, they also believe they are wrongly confined to a low station in life. The Conserver's dream is to be of a class he or she does not belong to. They feel their lot in life is due to always being in the wrong place at the wrong time, and they will brood about it. They are angry and bitter, though not to the extent the Self-Compensator is. Self-Compensators *know* what they're angry about; Conservers are not very clear about their own feelings. They confess that they had been better off, but misfortune deprived them of their true position in society. They want to make up this perceived lost status, and try to do so with a vengeance.

Conservers learned about conflict early in life. They saw the difference between the haves and the have-nots and believed those who had were better. That their family didn't fit into the top of the social hierarchy made them uncomfortable. It was because of the vicissitudes of the economy ("We lost a fortune in the crash"), or immigration ("We were landowners in the old country"), or because they were a poorer family of "good breeding" that hadn't managed to live up to its heritage. Whether he or she was from the North or South, the Conserver knew there was a gap between what they were and what they wanted to be. For them, the depression created a disquieting awareness of class differences, exacerbated by external events.

The Conserver often felt self-conscious, and frequently unhappy with ordinary parents and younger, more insensitive siblings. As a teenager, the Conserver worried about clothes, and what the teacher thought of him or her. He or she might try to become the teacher's pet, and blush with embarrassment if seen on the street with shabby or old-fashioned family members. Better educational opportunities only increased this sense of discomfort, as the Conserver was exposed to other people and cultures. Sometimes the Conserver tried to prove that he or she was part of the "in" crowd by affecting their behavior such as style of speech, clothes, and even ill-afforded jewelry or home features (dishes, silver). Family members were often not able to comprehend the Conserver's distress, since they were usually unambitious and unpretentious, with a less sophisticated understanding of the changing society around them.

The young Conservers sought out opportunities to gain favor and status, and often became involved in church activities early on because church membership afforded a measure of status within the community. Later, Conservers made special efforts to be more active leaders in small, social organizations that would afford them a sense of power. Women tended to join the PTA, the Junior League, and coveted membership in the Daughters of the American Revolution.

Conserver men belong to unions, or fraternal groups like the Elks where the hierarchical structure allows them to assume the mantle of power often denied them at work. Conservers look upon such activities as opportunities to rise to a "higher station" in life. At work, Conservers tend to have lower level supervisory managerial jobs. Here they can identify with the power delegated to them.

Conservers not only believe that what they are isn't good enough, but tend to impose this view on others as well. Instead of trying to earn the gratitude of others, like Martyrs, Conservers use their energy to manipulate circumstances to bolster their own self-image, such as being chairman of the planning commission, charity ball, or hospital board. Yet, since they rarely feel sincere or honest in these roles, Conservers typically appear to be social bullies, manipulating others by political maneuvers or social games. Some thrive on "putting people in their place," and are concerned with propriety to such a degree that they intimidate others.

Conservers are not hostile toward others, but feel compelled to exert themselves on behalf of what they believe is right. Strong supporters of authority and law, Conservers enjoy their role and are inclined to act mercifully and generously, as if the power to judge and forgive was truly theirs. Conservers use the rituals and rules of their fraternal or social societies as a screen to sift out others who they feel don't truly belong. Rather than relaxing with peers, they are more likely to head a committee, and campaign to be an elected president or chairperson of their hometown fraternal order. They spend considerable energy maintaining membership in an *imagined* social group—"concerned citizens," "real Americans," "guardians of morality." They have many rules, and obsessive practices that perplex or amuse others. The Conserver thrives on a social network that reinforces his or her identity.

The Conserver is defensive, since he or she often considers others offensive. Underneath, the Conserver fears that others will not respect him or her. The fearsome energy of the Conserver, while alienating many, serves its purpose well. The church lady on "Saturday Night Live" is an exaggerated but accurate caricature.

One favorite activity for Conservers is missionary work and lay preaching on behalf of their faith. Although Conservers are not particularly spiritual, they are extremely dogmatic and enjoy the opportunity to confront people who have diverged from "the truth."

The Conserver's world is built up from the inside, beginning with strong convictions, aspirations, and fears. The home is the stage on which the drama of the Conserver's mission in life is most often acted out.

Despite modest means, the Conserver may insist on items that are rarely used, but immediately trotted out for company—a particular set of china, or a fancy dining room set. At home, the Conserver will observe strict protocol. Children's lunches are laid out in a line. Breakfast, as well as other meals, are pre-planned and served regularly and on time. Cleanliness and order are important. The house is buffed and shined; children's rooms are kept "picked up."

Few Conservers are content with their neighborhoods. They hold their neighbors up to certain standards: that one picked up the morning paper in her nightgown; this family argues too much; those children are juvenile delinquents. Conservers frequently move; their desire to leave often takes precedence over financial good sense. As a result, upward mobility remains an elusive goal.

Conservers believe in conventional male and female roles. Women are encouraged to vote, but only for causes like antiabortion that will strengthen the status quo. Conserver men tend to believe in the right and might of the American military, although they may not have served in the military themselves. Conservers strongly supported the cold war and the anti-communist liturgy that fueled it. By always identifying with authority, Conservers seek to gain stature, and become greater than their meager means allow.

Conservers buy products that reinforce their sense of social order. They love imitation early American furniture, and wall paneling that mimics colonial or antebellum designs. Conservers are attracted to objects that symbolize membership in an elite group, but since they are not really part of such a group, they settle for products such as Franklin Mint limited edition commemorative seals or plates. Those who read like historic biographies (of heroes and generals), Harlequin romances, books with patriotic themes, and leather-bound books that look important. Conservers drive station wagons and sedans. They wear sensible clothes, that is, decent cloth coats and suits that don't go out of style.

Conservers are very family-centered and are anxious to avoid shameful or embarrassing incidents. They discipline their children, invoking the family honor and common decency while threatening them with the belt or hair brush ("This is going to hurt me more than it'll hurt you" or "Don't make me do this, Junior.") Conserver parents want their children to achieve more, but, unlike Clock Watchers or Martyrs, they are convinced they know exactly what defines success and how their children should pursue it. If possible, they enroll their children in private, parochial, military, and Sunday schools to groom them for their future.

Conserver health attitudes focus on selective concerns—that is, compulsive behavior in eating, rest, and exercise—that enable them to make health conditions a theme in their daily lives. Many of these are nervous disorders (psychosomatic), including colitis and constipation, but also asthma and migraine headaches. However, Conservers will also often cover up health problems of their own or family members until they are serious and cannot be handled anymore within the immediate family. This stems from a stoicism about health problems, a feeling of shame about succumbing to "weakness," and a general fear of what might lie below the surface of any problem.

Conservers prefer familiar health care, having had a family physician for most of their lives. However, the Conserver may choose another doctor or hospital because of a prestigious reputation, or because it is affiliated with a desired ethnic or religious group. Conservers are very dramatic; they constantly expect to be stricken with disease, but also expect to survive ("I'll be fine . . . really . . .") if they are not struck down within the next hour by some other expected disaster. In another era they would have had fainting spells to attract attention.

Conservers are generally independent, and remain so as they age, but will make full use of the informal support systems they have or feel entitled to. They have fulfilled their parental obligations and expect attention from their adult children. In crisis they do not hesitate to descend upon married children.

When Conservers retire, they expect a gold watch and all the pomp that goes with it. At first, there is a tremendous letdown, due to the loss of identification and status. This is particularly true if they do not have others to command or oversee at home, that is, a large household to boss around. Once accustomed to retirement, Conservers find other outlets for their prodigious energies. Notorious volunteers, Conservers usually waste little time joining even more social organizations. Deprived of some of the clout so hard-earned in the workplace, the retired Conserver will begin to place more and more energy into these new activities—meetings of fellow retirees and religious and political groups. Conservers tend to become more intense in their values over time. As a result, they rarely fade away, but burn brightly, searing a few along the path of their later years.

CHILDREN OF THE AMERICAN DREAM: 1920–1929

By the end of the first two decades of the 20th century the hyperactive American economy was about to fall. Ironically, the collapse of those years, seemingly an ominous herald of the birth of those born in the 1920s, fell not upon the children, but on those just old enough to be neither well established nor prepared for hardship—children could not know or miss what they had not experienced. In fact, the severity of the collapse brought about a national phenomenon never seen again—the paternalism of the 1930s, the Roosevelt years—followed by World War II and the GI bill. Within this novel national parenting are the seeds of this generation: nurtured by their country and unleashed with their unique spirit on the postwar world. The establishment? Ugly Americans? The powers that be (or were)? The model for the mid-life crisis? These are only a few rough characterizations of the Time Signatures of the Children of the American Dream.

IMMERSION—CHILDHOOD IN THE 1920S

The children of the 1920s were mostly born in towns and suburbs. In general, the lives of these children were improved by the depression. But those born in rural areas led lives that were barely changed from the preceding generation: small schools; limited, homemade entertainment; helping with chores and caring for younger brothers and sisters. City kids spent vacations on the farm—going barefoot, feeding the chickens, eating popcorn with milk and sugar in place of cereal. They got to ride the horse Granddaddy had rented, or swapped for, because there wasn't enough money to get the tractor fixed and fueled for plowing. Families didn't take long motor trips or camping trips for summer vacations anymore. Even for children living in city slums there were settlement houses and recreation programs, book clubs, and trips to the beach.

It was the era of psychological testing. Army test scores from World War I provided psychologists with a bell-shaped intelligence curve for adults, and the Metropolitan Life Insurance Company's height-weight tables provided an analog for body size. These were new measures of normalcy for the middle class, as well as quantified measures of deviance. For children, the Department of Agriculture's pamphlet on infant and child care prescribed what was normal and what wasn't for every aspect of childhood.

In part, this attention to what was "normal" was a reflection of the Americanization of immigrants. Most schools used Stanford-Binet IQ tests, which provided the standards to which children of immigrants could aspire. Since WASP kids were the standard the tests had been normed on, they usually did well. The tests were used to shunt kids to the college track, the business track, or the trades track. The standards tended to encompass small-town values, such as conformity, rather than big-city values, such as individuality. Individuality in terms of above-average scores, however, paid off, and handsomely. But "intellectual" was a pejorative term—someone who set book learning above sociability.

In England eccentricity might be tolerated in small towns. There you were born to your place, but in America you had to convince people you deserved it. Not fitting in meant isolation or ostracism. And because the society was a competitive one as well, not only did you have to fit in, you had to be successful. You chose the highest status group you could; towns were no longer homogeneous. Where once there had been one or two churches—Baptist in the South and Methodist, Presbyterian, Lutheran, or Episcopal in the North—now there were several.

Fitting in now meant being free of complexes. Teachers learned to say "introverted" instead of "naturally shy" and, indicative of common prejudices, "dull" or "slightly mentally deficient" instead of "non–English speaking."

Children of the American Dream were fed on schedule (every four hours and never between meals); weighed and measured by that new specialty doctor, the pediatrician; attended to by nurses in well-baby clinics; and provided with book sets bought when they were infants, such as *The Book of Knowledge* and *Book Trails*, whose stories and articles grew more difficult with each succeeding volume.

They were brought up with music, of all kinds—polkas, symphonies, hymns, violin, jazz, crooning, fiddle—heard daily from birth, first on the Victrola, then on the radio. The Children of the American Dream were the first generation to grow up with radio, and its importance cannot be understated as a force in shaping their view of the world. The programs they heard during their earliest development were entirely in the hands of advertisers. Radio provided the country with a vast cultural arena in which everyone could participate free of charge, but in truth children learned more about toothpaste and soap than history and science.

In 1927 NBC expanded dramatically. New sponsors and programs swamped the airwaves: "The Atwater Kent Hour," "The Ampico Hour," "The Cities Service Orchestra," "The General Motors Family Party," "The Palmolive Hour." Non-music programs included "Great Moments in History," Biblical dramas, and adaptations of classics. By 1928–1929 programs reflecting more rural and ethnic interests (and phobias) appeared, including "Main Street Sketches," "Real Folks," and "Soconyland Sketches." Among the most popular programs of this period were "The Goldbergs" and "Clara, Lu and Em."

CBS became a leader in innovative radio programming, particularly news. Edward R. Murrow, Eric Sevareid, William L. Shirer, and Elmer Davis were household names. CBS was also known for its dramatic programs, featuring the works of Norman Corwin, Archibald MacLeish, Orson Welles (whose famous "War of the Worlds" hoax was broadcast in 1937). For the first time, there were also programs created specifically for children: "Little Orphan Annie," "Jack Armstrong," and "The White Rabbit Bus."

In 1927 *The Jazz Singer* appeared as the first major "talkie." By 1928 Walt Disney's *Steamboat Willie* introduced the world to talking animated films. By 1929 there were over 60 film fan magazines, providing gossip about every nuance of the lives of Hollywood stars.

The emergence of sound in films was accompanied by a rebirth of Broadway musicals. Theme songs became an essential part of every film. Efforts were made to lure Broadway performers like John McCormack, Jeanette MacDonald, and Marilyn Miller to Hollywood. Leaving the stage, Fred Astaire made his first screen appearance in films in 1931. Other popular stars included Bing Crosby, Mae West, Grace Moore, and Dick Powell.

Accompanied by the music of George Gershwin, Rogers and Hammerstein, Cole Porter, Jerome Kern, and Irving Berlin, the stars of stage and screen gave the American public, especially young people, a world to escape into and learn from. The rise of radio and the movies coincided with, and endured through, the depression. Fantasy was a necessity of the hard times. The generation that had missed out on the Roaring Twenties could live footloose and fancy-free, albeit vicariously.

DIVERSION—THE ADOLESCENT EXPERIENCE IN THE 1930S

The 1930s featured musicals with exotic settings and lavish, all-star reviews. Movies were stylish and glamorous. Busby Berkely movies, with their elaborate sets, costumes, and choreography, began in 1931. Movies such as *Public Enemy*, with James Cagney, and *Little Caesar*, with Edward G. Robinson, glamorized recent history. World War II, however, brought changes. New types of film, the "film noir," were produced, representing the darker side of human nature. Musicals continued to be enormously popular, but there were also films about war heroes and about sadistic Nazis. The emphasis on movie stars made parents dream about their children becoming movie stars and relieving them of their deprived lives. Children dutifully toiled away in tap dance classes the way earlier generations had worked hard at school.

Recovery in the mid- to late 1930s was harder on the Children of the American Dream, now in their teen years, than the depression had been. Many had to move, but they could take their culture with them, and still hear their favorite radio show at the same time or go to the movies on Saturday nights.

Those who lived in towns were taught by teachers trained by Normal School teachers who had graduated from such prestigious colleges as Columbia Teachers College, Stanford, University of Iowa, and, later, University of Chicago. In states with decent educational systems, students were tested and measured, "normed" and "streamed." There were Iowa Reading Tests, standardized vocabulary tests, height and weight measured every September, and IQ tests every two years.

The "smart kids" got better teachers and more interesting books. Children, put together in large classes, learned to interact with different kinds of kids and accept diversity. Georgie Velasquez might not be able to do long division but he knew everything about horses and could do percentages in his head. Kimi Kato, who was just learning English, could create magic in her ink-and-brush drawings. Leo, who was slow and whiny, wasn't too bright, but he could play a good game of checkers.

During the depression, families listened to President Roosevelt's "fireside chats." The profound importance of this direct communication to American citizens is easily underestimated by later generations. The accessibility and sense of cohesion provided by these broadcasts did much to stabilize the nation's mood and build support for political programs. The Children of the American Dream grew up trusting in their leaders, and in the media.

Many recall the 1930s not so much in terms of the travails that afflicted the nation, but in terms of popular culture and entertainment. In addition to listening to the radio, children read the Sunday funnies, A. A. Milne's Winnie-the-Pooh books, Nancy Drew mysteries, the adventures of the Hardy Boys, and the Mark Tidd books. At the movies, they watched Tom Mix, Shirley Temple, Tarzan, Roy Rogers and Trigger, Andy Hardy, and Flash Gordon. Talking films transformed the lives of this generation from their early youth.

Toward the end of the 1930s, *Life* magazine and the news broadcasts made Americans aware of the war in Europe. Those in the Girl Scouts, Boy Scouts, and Junior Red Cross tried to participate in relief work. Girls knit scarves and boys made commando knives—a Carborundum steel file, ground down on a wheel, with leather circles slipped down over the hasp to build a leather handle—for unknown friends overseas.

As the war continued, the Children of the American Dream joined the Civil Air Patrol; some, lucky enough to be 16, could enroll in pilot training. Others trained in map or blueprint reading and aerodynamics. They made wooden models for civilian plane spotters, so they could tell P-38s from European planes, and a British Spitfire from a German Messerschmitt. Aviation was very important to this generation. A popular comic strip called "Terry and the Pirates" and, especially for girls, the heroism of Amelia Earhart, helped increase its attraction. Airplanes represented bravery, courage, freedom, and independence. Airports were lined with cars on weekends as families watched planes take off and land the way earlier generations had gathered at the train station to watch the passenger train come through.

The schoolyard was divided into "them" and "us." "Them" might be kids with Polish names whose fathers worked in the asbestos factory, or kids who wore mended overalls. At lunchtime, some kids had fillings in their sandwiches and some had lard. Class differences were sharply visible. In the West, a young girl might look out from her porch and see a tent pitched in the orchard across the way. The tent was made of two pieced quilts overlapped across a clothesline and there was a lantern inside. The light from the lantern was spotty because the quilt batting was lumpy. A man might be bent over, coughing. The young girl may have brought over some old clothes the day before, but found the people didn't speak a kind of English she understood and she couldn't answer the simplest questions ("How's yer kin? You want some clabber?").

As recovery continued, migrants began to enter the mainstream. Hillbillies moved into the automobile plants and tire factories, Canucks moved into the Northeastern shipyards, and Okies moved into the aircraft plants of southern California. Industry had been preparing for war since 1937, creating a new kind of industrial production that passed pre-crash levels in 1939 and 1940 with the Lend Lease Act that made ships and guns for England.

EXPANSION—EARLY ADULTHOOD IN THE 1940S

Like those who remember where they were when Kennedy was assassinated, the Children of the American Dream will never forget the day they heard the news of Pearl Harbor. From 1941 until 1946 war was the central preoccupation for most of the Children of the American Dream. The older generation, unless they had family members in the service, might put it out of their minds, now and then. But young people could not. Not only was it in the media—newsreels, radio, *Life* magazine—it was also in the schools. As teachers left to serve, older, "retread" teachers replaced them. They insisted that children understand the necessity of fighting and winning the war against fascism; children had to have the war interpreted for them. War also had an impact on the mood in school. It was a serious time, and many took their studies seriously.

They also became acutely aware of children in other parts of the world. They saw pictures of kids sitting in the London underground, waiting for the bombing to be over. Some European children were evacuated to America, and tended to be snobbish about how unsophisticated American education was. For some, the war provided opportunities they would not otherwise have had until years later. As in Europe, students as young as 12 went out into the countryside to harvest fruit in the orchards. It was good for morale, and helped fill the labor gap created by escaping Mexican farm workers who sought better wages in war plants.

For the first time, young people had pocket money. The older ones, those born in 1920–1924, were in the service or working full-time. So many had gone into the service or were occupied with the war effort that even young children could earn money for small services. Girls who baby-sat for free a few years earlier now could charge 25–50 cents an hour. Helping out in the family store on Saturday was suddenly a paying job, since there were plenty of other stores willing to hire youngsters. In Fresno, a young boy could deliver telegrams, or promise to look after his cousin's car while he was away. Some kids worked at war plants during school vacations. Those who completed their schoolwork for the year were allowed to leave early for war work.

A large portion of the Children of the American Dream were in their teens during World War II. Becoming an adult was part conspiracy, part accident. Teenagers had to conspire to some extent to escape chaperons (which older teachers and ministers insisted upon) and try out grown-up dancing at roadhouses and dance halls with names like Playland. At the same time, they often found themselves in adult situations by accident. They were substituting for adults but the rules hadn't been adjusted for them. For example, a candy striper (volunteer hospital worker who wore a candy-striped uniform) might find herself alone in the ward with a polio patient in an iron lung and the power goes out. A young boy might come upon a foreman wiping off an inspector's painted "X" that meant a part was no good.

For girls, saddle shoes or penny loafers, plaid skirts, bobby socks, and long men's shirts (not tucked in) were trendy attire. With their pocket money, teenagers bought records, magazines, sodas, ID bracelets, Revlon lipsticks, and war bonds. Boys saved up and bought old cars to fix up. Now teenagers could afford to go to the movies on Friday night, instead of just to Saturday matinees. To help build morale, there were high school football games again, but only between teams in nearby towns, since gas was rationed. In school, girls could excel in sports without being penalized.

Social dancing was taught in school, although parents thought only the foxtrot and the waltz were respectable. Jitterbugging was associated with jazz and criminals, and the conga was for drunks. But young people were often uncomfortable doing the foxtrot and the waltz, unless it was with a steady boyfriend or girlfriend. Jitterbugging, because it was less intimate, seemed safer because of the distance and freedom it offered. Drive-ins and teen soda fountains had jukeboxes, and usually some space for jitterbugging; at home, friends brought records over and rolled up the dining room rug. Going dancing was for teenagers, though. Married folks (he might be 28, she might be 25) rarely went out dancing, a situation so resented by wives that women's magazines carried long columns of advice about it. Women should not complain, they said.

There were Red Cross dances where girls could dance with servicemen. Even girls who were not so adventurous, whose social life was limited to church and the malt shop after school, met and talked to servicemen, and to other girls who dated servicemen, and even to girls who had gotten pregnant.

Dances were important social events; organizing dances and drives was a major pastime. There were war bond drives, as well as local and regional social events, from choir rehearsals to sports meets. Part of growing up was emulating the approved social skills of the time— being part of a team. This meant participating on committees that made posters, prepared food, sold tickets, distributed publicity, and cleaned up afterward.

Popular songs included Glenn Miller's "In the Mood," "Pennsylvania Six Five Thousand," and "Tuxedo Junction"; Artie Shaw's "Stardust," which ended every school dance; Les Brown's "Sentimental Journey"; and Stan Kenton's "Tampico" and "Artistry in Rhythm" as swing began to increase in complexity. In 1946, "To Each His Own" by the Inkspots and "Baby It's Cold Outside" by Esther Williams and Ricardo Montalban signaled a shift toward marriage songs. By the end of the decade, love and marriage had paid off. The big sellers were children's songs like "Frosty the Snowman," "Rudolph the Red-Nosed Reindeer," and "Peter Cottontail."

Some boys got involved in electronics and radio, catching the shortwave transmissions from overseas. Many table radios had police as well as broadcast frequencies. Boys built their own receivers, too. Many listened for mayday calls from downed flyers or torpedoed ships. Some boys drove nitro trucks, worked fishing boats, or got jobs as powder monkeys—not just for the money, but to practice being brave.

Because their parents were busy, with war or volunteer work, many children were unsupervised. Because gas was rationed, they took rides from people their parents didn't know. Before, kids from the slums were seen as criminals while rich kids who misbehaved were considered "spoiled." Now, even middle-class kids, in suburban neighborhoods, could become juvenile delinquents.

Young people saw daily proof of parental inability to enforce private values, due to the exigencies of war. Parents couldn't protect their children from horror stories, rationing, or the black market. Mothers couldn't keep their sons from being drafted, or get sugar for a birthday cake if they'd used their ration, or improve the schools. Fathers had to work overtime, take the bus, and endure numerous indignities on business trips from both the military and profiteers: loud parties in hotels, crowded trains, insolent military officers and their prostitutes commandeering their drawing rooms. Even doctors found themselves having to choose between induction and inspecting the local brothel. (Cut-rate weekly inspection of local brothels in towns near military posts was a task that made doctors "essential to the war industry.") Ministers had to help out, too. In the same day a minister might call on a family that had lost a son on Guadalcanal and a wife whose husband had been caught dealing gasoline or steaks on the black market. These realities of daily life eclipsed the private values a parent would have passed on to a child in ordinary times.

Wartime reality was not reflected in films, however, which still provided an exaggerated view of life. The blonde bombshell had arrived on the silver screen: Sonja Henie, Alice Faye, Betty Grable, June Haver. By the end of the 1940s movie magazines had begun to lose their luster, and movie stars and Broadway actors, living glamorous, exciting lives while ordinary lives were on hold, had begun to fade. People were busy working and raising families. They might go to a drive-in, because of the kids.

This was the first generation of women to wear makeup every day. Eye makeup was used only for the evening, or to "balance" a bright lipstick if you had fair skin and light eyelashes. A girl hid her makeup; she washed her face before she went to parochial school, or before she went home. The use of makeup was due partly to the glamorous Hollywood image. The heavily made up Petty Girl, as seen in *Esquire* and copied on B-19s and torpedo boats, was the epitome of the desirable female. Many men were killed or maimed in the war, and women and girls competed for marriageable men; attention was focused on one's appearance. Wearing makeup was not only a way to look more attractive but to indicate sexuality.

Male perceptions of women, embellished by these images, were idealized and reinforced by their social isolation from normal daily male–female relations. As standards of conduct and relationships changed, understanding the opposite sex became increasingly difficult. Later, new prototypes (the stereotypical "little woman" was disappearing) would often cause disaster in marital relationships. But for now, love was what a girl looked for in a mate—real love, not just making out in the backseat. As boys came back from the war, they seemed really sincere, really in love. They wanted what they had fought for—a home and a family. Now women were plentiful, and there was often a two- to three-year difference in age as men chose younger women. This was a different marriage pattern than before; their parents tended to be even-age couples, perhaps high school sweethearts. In fact, many women in this cohort did not marry until later, as a second wife to a significantly older man.

Young women read *American Girl* and *Seventeen*. Young men typically read comic books, *Esquire*, or special interest magazines such as *Popular Mechanics*. But everyone read *Life* magazine, which showed how lucky we were not to be living in Europe or Japan, and the *Saturday Evening Post*, although it began to decline as television became more popular. The *Reader's Digest*, however, was ubiquitous; if your family didn't subscribe, then you saw it at your doctor's office, at the barbershop, or in school, where it was assigned reading for high school students. The military had arranged it so that civilians could send *Reader's Digest* subscriptions to servicemen overseas, even in combat areas.

The effect of the war was profound. In World War I, the average duration of service was 12 months and total American military deaths were 117,000; in World War II, the average duration was 33 months and there were 291,000 battle deaths alone, and another 671,000 were wounded. Out of 16 million participants, nearly 1 in 15 was killed or wounded.

The distress and pain of the war was a daily concern for those at the front and those at home. So much has been told from the standpoint of the men who were in the war, yet those at home were also traumatized. Young women lost boyfriends, siblings, and classmates; those living in cities such as New York or Los Angeles worked with the Women's Voluntary Corps, going out one evening a week to take coffee and doughnuts to the men who manned the antiaircraft guns. Some worked as aides at local hospitals. Mothers assumed it was a suitable occupation and thought their daughters were delivering flowers and reading to children. In reality, because so many nurses had joined the service or gone to work in military hospitals, young girls changed bed linens, scrubbed surgical instruments, and spoon-fed the elderly.

By the early 1940s, many women and those men not in the military already had jobs in war plants. Young women rode bicycles to factories in slacks and shirts and a snood to keep their hair from getting tangled in machinery. Rosie the Riveter—the competent female factory worker—foreshadowed real changes to come in postwar society, including the restructuring of American households (increasingly single and female-headed), and the emergence of an economy where women were active participants.

The stories of men at war concerned the discovery of the fundamental qualities of comradeship, trust, and a sense of shared purpose. Some, who saw the whole war enterprise as a waste of their lives, developed a cynical view of the workings of the world. They were frustrated and disgusted by the bitter truths of war: incompetent leaders, poor planning, insidious bureaucracies, greedy schemers and cheaters.

A morbid humor emerged as a coping mechanism for those in the war zone, a signature of esprit de corps. Plunged into an alien universe of boredom, fear, and uncertainty, young men in the military formed a temporary social community that could support them until they returned home. For those stationed at home on a weekend pass, or on leave from the fighting overseas, a visceral, almost Dionysian life style of excess was generated. Some indulged incessantly in hobbies and sports, others in sex and alcohol.

Patriotism was sacred. During the war, the needs of the country were uppermost. After the war, the Children of the American Dream returned to a focus on their private lives. Unclear about social norms and ignorant of the historic nature of inequality, they demanded that the promises of freedom and justice for all be kept. Loyalty shifted from government to corporate America, whose manipulation could at least be understood, and therefore accepted and forgiven (just as one could understand and forgive the exaggerations in *Reader's Digest* about cancer). Easier that than to think about how men had been sent ashore on the wrong tide at Tarawa, killed by their own bombers at Anzio, and brutalized by ignorant noncoms (noncommissioned officers); about civil rights (no one talked about the fact that the American Red Cross wouldn't accept blood donations from blacks); about the terror of the atom bomb; or about the possibility that the government was indeed as tyrannical and uncaring as it seemed. However, there *was* a latent awareness of all of these, and that produced a kind of moral uneasiness.

Underneath the pride people felt in the job America had done to win the war was a collective realization that the better world men had fought and died for somehow had not been achieved. The stage was being set for McCarthyism, the cold war, and the Korean War. Someone was to blame. The enemy—now communism—had to be vanquished. People refused to consider that World War II, for which they had sacrificed so much, and which promised so much, had been in any way unfinished or unsuccessful.

On the other hand, the seeds for questioning inequality were sown. A certain section of town was considered off-limits because blacks lived there. An Asian schoolmate might be sent to a concentration camp, and parents offered the ludicrous explanation that she might be a spy. The Daughters of the American Revolution refused to let Marian Anderson sing in the DAR Hall in Washington, D.C., and young people were appalled when their parents tried to justify the discrimination. The toy library young people tried to organize for migrant workers' children was cancelled because of "diseases" the workers might carry. It just wasn't fair.

CONVERSION—ADULTHOOD IN THE 1950S

The 1950s were a time to celebrate getting back to normal, although the Children of the American Dream had no direct experience of what was "normal" to draw on in planning the next stage of their lives. Their models were their parents, popular images from the media, and their own interpretations of what was "right." There was a sense of urgency and zeal with which young people pursued their dreams. Having been taken right out of high school into the military, fed on the glamour of Hollywood war movies, tasted a bit of wild life abroad, and thrust into a live-for-today war mentality, many men had unrealistic, exaggerated, or distorted views of their future. The war era promoted the idea that life was very concrete—go to school on the GI bill, buy a house, get a job. But in many cases, anticipation about the future led to disappointment. GI bill students who flunked out were devastated. Those who thought business would be more conscious of merit and less conscious of rank than the military were crushed when that turned out not to be true. Moreover, some had suffered traumatic psychological damage as a result of their wartime experiences. The only solution was inadequate psychiatric care or to somehow "adjust" to life at home.

Many women had done well in school during the war. Now, with men returning, classes were filled with GIs. Women were told to move over and let the men get good grades so they could get ahead. Colleges were lively places. It was an opportunity to get back into civilian life, and have fun. Veterans anxious to catch up sat side by side with nonveterans five years their junior.

Those who were not totally immersed in family or career were still putting in hours with volunteer organizations. Some worked with the Student Christian Association on their college campus, organizing dinners—cooking spaghetti and garlic bread for 150 people for less than 50 cents a person—for a fund that sent food to displaced persons in Europe.

In the 1950s, immigration increased. A variety of immigrants and refugees from Eastern Europe arrived. In the West and Southwest, Mexicans were increasingly visible, although historically they had been longtime residents in the region. During 1942–1943 Mexicans working the California groves, orchards, and fields had been kept in fenced and patrolled labor camps. First they moved into the Sawtelle district of California, when the Japanese were sent to concentration camps. In 1946, picking crews for the nation's harvest were drafted from the ranks of the unemployed; the Mexicans weren't needed. Many moved to the cities. Later, those who had served in the Army and gotten their citizenship were dissuaded by college counselors from taking technical subjects that would train them to become professionals. College algebra was considered to be beyond a Mexican's ability. It didn't matter that they had already served as navigators and flight engineers.

The music and entertainment of the times vividly illustrated the postwar era's continuing desire to find romance and comfort in a time of difficult economic and emotional adjustment. In the 1950s there were musicals on stage and screen: *Carousel, Oklahoma, The King and I, South Pacific, An American in Paris*. Films such as *West Point Story, Lullaby on Broadway, Calamity Jane*, and *Guys and Dolls* starred Debbie Reynolds, Doris Day, Mary Martin, and Ethel Merman. These represented the spectra of male stereotypes and fantasy—from the good-natured whore to the girl next door—perhaps a reflection of the innocence and optimism of the postwar era. Epic movies like *Samson and Delilah* and *Ben Hur*, expensive and larger-than-life, were in part a response by moviemakers to increasing competition from television. Charlton Heston, Tab Hunter, Kirk Douglas, Marlon Brando, and Tony Curtis were some of the many male movie stars.

During the late 1940s, television had begun to play a role in the lives of the newly maturing generation. In the early 1950s its influence on Americans was increasing. In fact, families were so enamored of it that they would watch test patterns, waiting patiently for the programs to come on. Networks with foreign correspondents such as Bill Shirer and Walter Cronkite began to shift news sources, from the Office of War Information to Fox Movietone and Telenews, which had served the film industry newsreel market before television.

Wholesome family programs, such as "Lassie," "Father Knows Best," and "The Donna Reed Show," and "law-and-order" shows, such as "Martin Kane, Private Eye," "Mr. District Attorney," and "Dragnet," were popular. There was considerable control over plot content by sponsors. For instance, if a tobacco company was the sponsor, only the good guys could smoke—and gracefully, with no coughing—and arson could not be used as a criminal plot device. The national convention for nominating a presidential candidate was aired for the first time in 1952. Dwight D. Eisenhower's use of television to influence voters was to prove even more effective in 1960 for John F. Kennedy. Richard Nixon came across well in his "Checkers" speech, and Adlai Stevenson appeared overly intellectual.

Soon there was a new format, the anthology series, with plays written specifically to be produced on television. The wide variety of programs, which provided substantial evening distraction, included "Philco Television Playhouse," "Kraft Television Theatre," "Studio One," "Revlon Theatre," "Omnibus," and "Playhouse 90." These shows created new opportunities for writers and up-and-coming actors like Paul Newman, Sidney Poitier, Rod Steiger, and Joanne Woodward to show their talents.

In addition to "I Love Lucy" and "The Honeymooners," people watched Bishop Fulton J. Sheen's weekly program, the roller derby, wrestling, Arthur Murray's dance school, and war footage from the many retellings of war stories. But they also listened to Walter Winchell's news flashes and Edward R. Murrow's documentary series, "Hear It Now, See It Now." News programs, faced with increased competition from popular programming, shifted over to what was entertaining, rather than what was newsworthy or controversial. An event not reported on television just did not exist for most people. Were it not for the commitment of individuals such as Edward R. Murrow and Fred Friendly, the nation might not have been effectively exposed to the questionable nature of the anti-communist fervor of Joseph McCarthy. Murrow's exposure of McCarthy and his exploration of government control of research, through his interviews with J. Robert Oppenheimer, helped the country eventually become more open and introspective.

But television in the 1950s suffered from the limitations imposed by the cold war, especially after President Truman introduced Executive Order No. 9835 in 1947 as a measure to ascertain the "loyalty and security" of federal employees through loyalty review boards, assisted by the FBI. The House Committee on Un-American Activities, chaired by Representative J. Parnell Thomas (New Jersey), and assisted by Richard M. Nixon (California), and John McDowel (Pennsylvania), held hearings on communism in the film industry. The refusal of some Hollywood producers and actors to cooperate with this inquiry, particularly to "name names" of supposed Communists in their midst, resulted in their being imprisoned and "blacklisted" from working in their trade. After the film industry, television soon became the target.

The McCarthy witch-hunts of 1948–1952 had an important impact on the media. Erik Barnouw, in *A History of Radio* (Oxford, 1966), described the process: "Evolving from a radio industry born under military influence and reared by big business, it now entered an adolescence traumatized by phobias. It would learn caution and cowardice." The Korean War, and possibly a desire to restrain the media, led the Federal Communications Commission to freeze the issuing of licenses from 1949 through 1951. Senator Joseph McCarthy, self-appointed spokesperson of the paranoia that gripped the country, proved that the media could easily be used to convince people that they had been abused for 20 years by "leftist" Democrats.

The Children of the American Dream were a responsive audience to that message. They had been raised in times when popular issues were often narrowly defined, in terms that evoked fundamental conflicts between right and wrong, success and failure, whether it was depression-era efforts to repair the economy or the war effort. The Children of the American Dream did not protest life in the 1950s. They were too busy concentrating on more important things—carving out their own little piece of American pie.

The Korean War also contributed to the conformist climate of the early 1950s. As the decade began the war made the economy more intricately interconnected and coordinated than ever. Against a background of growing unease and anxiety, President Truman directed a World War II–like mobilization under the direction of Charles Edward Wilson, the head of General Electric, and General Dwight D. Eisenhower, who had been commander of the European theater of operations in World War II. Americans were told that their country, now the undisputed leader of the Western world, was headed for a confrontation with world communism that the atomic bomb might make apocalyptic. The Chinese invasion of South Korea, which led to General MacArthur's attempt to widen the war on his own initiative and President Truman's strong assertion of civilian control, contributed to the atmosphere of tension.

Eisenhower, a World War II hero with no strong political identity, won the 1952 presidential election for the Republicans partly by his pledge to go to Korea in search of a resolution to the conflict. His victory was also due to a campaign as closely coordinated and managed as a modern corporation's marketing operation. The GOP used not only businesslike, detailed planning but mass advertising techniques, including the catchy slogan, "I Like Ike." They also used television; Eisenhower's blandness, in contrast to Adlai Stevenson's challenging intellectuality, was certain not to alienate voters.

An end to the fighting in Korea was negotiated in 1953. The transition back to peacetime production occasioned a brief recession, but Americans generally felt they were safe from another depression. The release from war anxiety further increased Americans' desire for stable, placid times such as they imagined had existed before the depression, two great international wars, and 20 years of Democratic administrations.

But the economy was never completely demilitarized. Before the ideological schism between the Soviet Union and China, international communism loomed as a monolithic enemy. The cold war became an institution, and nuclear weapon production surged ahead. Under these conditions, it was harder than it might otherwise have been to forgo the economic stimulation of continual massive armament. The power of the "military-industrial complex" grew great enough to alarm even the old soldier Eisenhower, as he would reveal in his speech on departing the presidency. Although it stabilized the economy, the continued production of weapons increased, rather than decreased, anxiety.

During the 1950s America was generally self-controlled, wary of risk, self-conscious, and introspective in its arts. It produced a group of anxious artists who asked questions about their own failings and fears. Theater in America went through a tense phase of self-exploration led by playwrights such as Arthur Miller (*Death of a Salesman*), Lillian Hellman (*The Autumn Garden*), Robert Anderson (*Tea and Sympathy*), Edward Albee (*The Zoo Story*), and Tennessee Williams (*Camino Real*). Poets such as Robert Frost (*Swinger of Birches*), Carl Sandburg (*Complete Poems*), and e. e. cummings (*I Thank You God*), were popular, each in his own way looking at the fundamentals of life, not the political or social ramifications of change in America.

The American art scene was filled with a self-exploratory postwar energy, with the likes of Jackson Pollock (unconscious abstracts), Alexander Calder (mobiles), Robert Motherwell (abstract black), and Robert Rauchenberg (early pop art). New York was the cultural center. The Whitney Museum and other "hip" galleries exhibited art by these artists and others.

The 1950s also saw a surge in the popularity of religious books, entertainment, and institutions. Church memberships rose rapidly, providing a sense of community for those frustrated by the tension between family and organization. Many sought community with others of shared values. Bible-inspired movie spectaculars were popular, as were clergymen with mass-audience appeal, such as Dr. Norman Vincent Peale, Bishop Fulton Sheen, Billy Graham, and Peter Marshall, a former chaplain of the U.S. Senate.

Those who wanted to unburden themselves and could afford to sought psychiatric help, and psychoanalysis became very popular. However, psychiatry was often the subject of sneers and snide jokes. People laughed nervously at the notion of letting down their guard, afraid to reveal what was underneath the carefully maintained hairdo, suit-and-tie, or suburban home.

When Jack Kerouac published *On the Road* and Allen Ginsberg wrote "Howl" it seemed, to those who were fed up with the aesthetically lethargic arts, as though the world was energized again, and people could talk about meaningful things.

Women, in particular, often found the 1950s unsatisfying and oppressive. Girls in long, modest dresses—who wouldn't be fickle or have minds of their own—were in. Wives were discouraged from seeking work by husbands and employers, who talked about "a woman who had taken a job just long enough to earn the price of a piano."

The war had disrupted the usual marriage patterns. Single women—a new phenomenon—were particularly discriminated against. Many of the nation's growing research laboratories and universities wouldn't hire a single mother because they claimed that employees' wives would complain. Even if a child's medical record was filed under the mother's name, the doctor's receptionist would inquire what the husband's name was. Many department stores would not open a charge account for a divorced or unmarried woman unless they received a pleading letter explaining that the applicant's parents had had such an account, and that she was steadily employed, had always preferred this store, etc. A woman alone with a child was suspect, and landlords were unwilling to rent to them.

The songs of the period revealed a kind of desperate conformity: Chopin and Rimsky-Korsakov were popularized. By the time Elvis Presley hit the charts in 1955, the Children of the American Dream, older now, were no longer listening. This was a latent, or transitional period of music. The beboppers were a strong undercurrent. Bands had dismantled during the war and were reconfiguring now. Girl singers like Doris Day and Dinah Shore were popular, representative of, like the musicals of the period, a naive mood.

SUBMERSION IN THE 1960S

The Children of the American Dream, now in their late 30s and early 40s, were able to share in a broader, more uniform level of wealth, for the first time in American history. The fear of poverty began to subside. In the 1950s and 1960s, opportunities for increased affluence opened up at the upper end of the middle class. John Kenneth Galbraith's book, *The Affluent Society,* gave the era its name. In place of a society in which workers produce at a subsistence level in order to avoid starvation, Galbraith saw a new society emerging, where workers produced and consumed a superfluity of goods in order to maintain full employment. The new system functioned through the artificial stimulation of consumer demand by advertising and other means of mass conditioning.

Galbraith's analysis is useful in examining many of the trends of the 1950s relating to the Children of the American Dream. One was the extraordinary rise of the suburbs. The population of urban fringe areas increased over 80 percent in 10 years, while the central cities grew by under 20 percent and rural population held steady. The surge of suburban development continued, with diminished momentum, throughout the 1960s; by 1970 the suburbs contained one third of the U.S. population. "Urban sprawl" became the norm, and the suburbs became one of the major life styles of America.

In the suburbs, the basic social and economic unit was the nuclear family: breadwinner husband, homemaker wife, and two or three children in a house owned by the family, with plenty of yard space, and as many added conveniences and luxuries as the family could afford. Because homes, schools, and stores were farther apart, and public transportation scarce, a family had to own at least one car.

For the wife, who had to keep house all by herself, there had to be a complete set of modern laundry and kitchen facilities. Some women also worked outside the home, but there was pressure to stay at home. Women with jobs were characterized as selfish, having abandoned familial duties to earn money so they could spoil themselves with luxuries. In fact, many women worked to make ends meet, but they spoke of work apologetically.

"Leisure" for the newly affluent suburban family included serious work to keep up one's "castle." The 1950s witnessed a "do-it-yourself" boom. Do-it-yourself projects were promoted as hobbies but were in fact often labor-intensive, hard work in the service of an ideal: the household as a self-sufficient unit, like a pioneer homestead or a feudal manor in miniature. The home became a sanctuary of American individualism, for those who could afford it. The work demanded of the suburban family was part of the price they had to pay to maintain the suburban man's dream of himself as lord of the manor, as were the demands on the "lady of the house," who now had to be chauffeur, cook, maid, and social secretary, as well as wife, mother, and hostess.

Suburban homes were also a boon to consumer spending, which provided an outlet for steadily rising productivity, which in turn provided the income for further consumer spending. As their income rose, a family might aspire to a boat, swimming pool, better furniture, a newer and better car, a second car, a newer, and bigger house.

Many homes did, in fact, become significantly more comfortable. But the real price, as Galbraith pointed out, was paid elsewhere. The more exclusively production was directed to private consumer goods, the more public goods were neglected. Public transportation was not developed (although highways were); parks deteriorated; the environment was not maintained against urban sprawl. People became more isolated from each other. Each family did for itself; no one thought to ease the burdens of suburban life through, for instance, cooperative home maintenance or housework arrangements.

In contrast to the individualism of household life was the drastic curtailment of economic and sociopolitical individualism. Not all forms of this were as drastic as the McCarthyite inquisitions that terrorized the liberal intellectual elite. For the first time, a majority of Americans worked for corporations, not for themselves or for proprietors or in partnerships. The Eisenhower era created the "organization man"; and white-collar workers overtook manual workers as the largest single employment category. It was the beginning of the age of bureaucracy in business. Even labor unions, having achieved many of their goals of affluence and security for industrial workers, increasingly cooperated with corporate organizations to maintain stability. Some became like large corporations themselves.

The Organization Man, as described in William H. Whyte, Jr.'s book, and fictionalized in *The Man in the Gray Flannel Suit* by Sloan Wilson, was the middle manager who approached all management as technical problems to be solved. He did not see the value of speculative thought and preferred what was practical. He was fond of supposedly objective measurements such as personality tests. He was a spokesman for an era when many liked to think that all major problems had been solved and that there was no need to analyze, question, or explore. As an enforcer of conformity, however, he was more than a product of his culture. He was a product of a new economic system, where a large organization preferred pursuing stability rather than maximizing profits.

The Children of the American Dream were coming into their own at a time when the New Deal had lost momentum. However, the new conservative administration retained many of the reforms and social-welfare apparatus that Democrats had built into the system. It also did nothing to reverse the ever-tightening interdependency and regulation of the production economy caused by growing defense and public works programs.

Television continued to influence Americans in the 1960s. Lucille Ball, a minor movie glamour girl, became a major television star as Lucy in "I Love Lucy," first aired in 1952. This domestic situation comedy was one people in their own domestic situations could relate to. Ball's wacky, feisty character presented an image of a woman with a strong, imaginative personality, but an incompetent fool beyond the home sphere. It simultaneously created and reinforced the sexist stereotypes of the times.

Television also introduced a constant stream of advertising directly into the homes of consumers. If, as Galbraith argued, the artificial stimulation of demand through advertising was crucial to the working of the affluent consumer society, television became a conduit of that society's lifeblood. The TV commercial was institutionalized as quickly as the cold war.

The winds of change did not sweep down upon the Children of the American Dream as war had. The confirmation of life and the attainment of the deferred—career advancement, family, material possessions—were the priorities of the Children of the American Dream. But gradually the flaws of the American Dream began to be felt. So much had happened in such a dramatic period of history, involving so much effort, that the Children of the American Dream, too settled and set by their mid-30s and 40s, began to feel restless and uncomfortable. Men who had been raised during the longest period of authoritarian, patriarchal government in the nation's history reached 40 without ever having had much of a chance to develop emotionally. It was hard to balance work and home; many men who had worked too much found their home life suffering. Wives were unhappy with the limits of their lives, too. From the depression through high school, the military, GI bill–sponsored education, Veterans Home Loan housing, and a job in corporate America, the Children of the American Dream had been overseen, supervised, guided, and presented with larger-than-life images of success. Family relations came to a boiling point during the mid-1960s, just as other hidden dimensions of America began to crash into daily life with great force.

By the late 1960s, the Gap Generation, now in their late teens and twenties, were in revolt against the exaggerated righteousness of the

Children of the American Dream, the people in power, the inheritors and builders of the postwar system. The carefully controlled world of the Children of the American Dream began to fall apart under the constant challenge of rejection by the Gap Generation, who criticized the enfranchised and flaunted their own experimental life style.

REVERSION TO TRANSITION—1970 AND BEYOND

As they reached the 1970s the Children of the American Dream, now in their late 40s and early 50s, moved into a new phase—the "mid-life crisis." Although this label for a certain stage of life may appear universal, it is particularly relevant to the Children of the American Dream. More than any other generation, they missed out on developing a sense of autonomy and individual identity that prior or later generations acquired while growing up. Their values, acquired during extreme times, were too clearly defined, too strongly believed in to allow for society's failure to meet expectations, and too rigid to change as needed.

The 1970s and beyond provided a profound challenge to the Children of the American Dream. They were often criticized by their children, and many finally had to face up to their own internal inconsistencies. This emotional burden built to a nearly intolerable peak just as their children reached late adolescence. As they watched others around them rebel against the institutions that they had so strongly supported, they felt as if the rug had been pulled out from under them.

Some responded by becoming more rigid. Others, about the time their children left home to go to college or work, found themselves unable to maintain appearances of contentment or acquiescence any longer and had to make room for change. For many, the result was depression; alcoholism and addiction to prescription drugs, such as Valium, Librium, and Seconal, became part of the suburban malaise.

Men and women, after 20 years of marriage, discovered that they had not been "communicating" and were fed up with one another. Much to the shock of family and friends, many couples separated and divorced, often preceded by mutual abuses of various kinds, from brutal indifference to flagrant infidelity. Divorces were often acrimonious, with men and women pitted against one another, and their children caught in the middle.

Few divorced men remained alone for long. Once out of the house, many men indulged in an initial spree of being "young" again, dressing in inappropriate clothes and jewelry, and pursuing a frenetic life style. During this hiatus of being single, however, a particular middle-class single man's culture evolved, consisting of an apartment in a low-cost unit on the fringes of cities and suburbia. Warrens of cheap rooms surrounded a swimming pool; the rooms were cluttered with un-washed clothes and secondhand furniture purchased with an unedu-cated eye—a zebra-skin chair or, in a moment of self-indulgence, a bar set. Few, if any, had done much cooking. Most were accustomed to having someone prepare meals and wait on them. Now they ate out often and purchased vast quantities of frozen dinners.

Women, in particular, suffered from the aftereffects of divorce. Many had few marketable skills, and no personal assets or credit his-tory to enable them to make the transition to independence. Living alone in a very empty nest was neither practical nor heartwarming. Some divorced women remained in the neighborhood, raised their children alone, and then went back to school for training. Those wo-men without a suburban home ended up, like their ex-husbands, liv-ing alone in a community of single adults. But, unlike the men, their standard of living was greatly reduced and many suffered in genteel poverty. Those who were already college-educated were better pre-pared to pursue additional training and a job. But society was ill-equipped and unwilling to respect single women. Some, after a difficult transition, found employment in such fields as real estate and the growing service industry.

The majority of the Children of the American Dream, however, remained married. By the 1980s half had already been retired for five years; the other half are nearing retirement in 1991. If they did not already experience a mid-life crisis, many, particularly men, would face a new, "third quarter" crisis. This crisis represented the conflict, not between their inner and outer lives, but between the society and themselves. For the first time in history, a group of adults reached their 60s with good health and comparative wealth. Now they faced subtle or indirect pressures to quit work. For many, early retirement became available in the 1980s, as corporations tried to trim their work force. Since federal law eliminated the mandatory retirement age and protected workers over 40, companies were hard-pressed to use labor force reduction strategies that emphasized retirement. Big companies provided incentives to retirement, or placed greater pressures on workers to be more productive, hoping that older workers would choose to retire.

For some this meant being able to set up a new business in a dif-ferent field; others became freelance consultants. But for many, who had not planned on retiring, these pressures were felt as an insult and an attack on their integrity as employees.

The Children of the American Dream have grown up believing in a concept they themselves, like their predecessors, helped to perpetuate—the "golden years" of retirement. But as they have gotten older, the members of this generation realize that they do not see themselves as "elderly." These "senior citizens" have second and third careers, often in teaching, politics, and consulting, and are highly active in personal hobbies, sports, and the arts.

By maintaining a level of continuity in their lives not seen in previous generations, they are not complying with the stereotype of "growing old." In fact, they may be the first to change it. But they are a cohort of tremendous preconceptions, so will have to escape their own self-judgments first. Once they do, they may be the first to truly benefit from a society that is less emphatic about judging people according to their age.

BIRTHMARKS

Attainers

Motivated by the need to win and accomplish, the Attainers earned their name from their driving need to make things happen, their highly defined sense of vision, and their exaggerated sense of purpose. Their experiences shaped not only their unique identity but mid-century America as well. For this reason it is important to know how they came to acquire this drive and direction.

The Time Signature of the Attainers was not the depression, an event that was experienced by the Dream-Deferred Generation. The Children of the American Dream were dramatically different, and the Attainers were the pioneers and champions of a new era—a New Deal—not neglected children of a cast-off family. The nation was seen as a strong paternal parent, and, for almost 15 years of their early lives, Attainers were subjected to its strong paternal guidance. From the first 100 days of the Roosevelt administration to their discharge and return home from the armed services in the mid-1940s, Attainers knew their lives and their future were bound up in the fate of the nation. They had to do their part to ensure that that future would be realized. The inspirational messages to "rebuild America," and the knowledge of their parents' suffering, caused the Attainers to internalize strong feelings of ambition and a strong potential for accomplishment.

Not all Attainers were the same. Some were model patriots, ideal organization men; others were more cynical, but equally hungry for achievement. Both men and women believed in the United States, and benefited from wartime training and work opportunities.

The postwar era was a time of big business, huge corporations, and team players. The GI Bill of Rights and Veterans Home Loan program became the launching pad of the Attainer into the large postwar industrial economy. As members of corporations, Attainers had a well-developed sense of self, and high expectations. They believed in a system of reward based on personal merit and earned seniority. Corporations "respected" their worth, even though they often were "relocated" or demoted without much regard. Because Attainers feel threatened by ambiguity, they are strongly task oriented and committed to hierarchical organizational structures. At work, definitions of good and bad, failure and success are clearly defined—by quotas, schedules, and so forth.

Attainers—because they equate achievement with "being loved"—feel good only when they are achieving. But high performance doesn't really satisfy them, and they continue to drive hard. Men Attainers, outside of work, although ambitious and very goal-oriented, often lack a comfortable self-identity, especially when they retire, since their sense of self is so connected to their work. Women Attainers suffered a similar lack of self-identity when they rejected, or questioned, their role as homemaker, tried to re-enter the work force when their children got older, or found themselves single after divorce. Both groups faced a serious life crisis: men when they stopped moving up the corporate ladder or found their suburban life styles to be less fulfilling than they had hoped; women when they had to confront the reality of the empty nest or an unsatisfying marriage.

Many Attainer men married Attainer women, but this union often led to conflicts, due to different expectations after the initial period of family growth. Many Attainer women entered into marriage having already worked and pursued additional education. After channeling energy into raising children, they needed to direct it elsewhere, but their husbands feared the loss of the housewife they depended on and discouraged their wives from college and careers (or agreed with severe doubts and hostility). Many men, who had neglected their wives and children on their climb to the top of the corporate ladder, found a different kind of "empty nest" at home—marriages that seemed devoid of connection and estranged children. The result was a high rate of divorce.

Better educated than many of their peers, Attainers are concerned about what they do to earn a paycheck. They care about the symbolic value of their status. As they got older, they faced the problem of defining themselves in a world where they were confronted with younger competitors, changing corporate organizational structures, and, after retirement, many years to fill in a meaningful life style.

For some, the consequence of early retirement was a loss of identity and direction combined with a feeling of vitality. The Attainer wonders, "Why am I not a part of something?" More and more Attainers try to move on to new roles after retirement. Some become consultants, others start new jobs, particularly retired military professionals. Many Attainers find themselves in positions below what they would hope their experience merits. In a society where age no longer means seniority, this aggressive achievement Birthmark faces a serious loss of stature as they age.

Attainers never thought very much about retirement ahead of time; they expected corporate health insurance and a generous pension. As a result, they face less financial anxiety than their contemporaries.

Attainers have a high degree of health awareness, primarily because they have abused their health considerably. They suffer many stress-related disorders, such as hypertension, ulcers, and heart disease. The incidence of alcoholism and spouse abuse among Attainers rose in the 1950s and 1960s. For women, the role of the self-sacrificing mother who had to repress her own capabilities and aspirations often gave rise to frustration and depression, which, in turn, led to frequent use of tranquilizers. Attainers have more recently become very conscious of the foods they eat and have shifted from meat and potatoes to lighter, more health-conscious fare. Attainers insist on the newest technology and techniques in health care; they are not intimidated about asking for the best care and service.

Performers

Attainers saw institutions, such as the military and corporations, as a means to accomplishment and status. Performers are motivated by a different personal perspective. They are "team players," who believe there is a "right way" to do things. The Performer is very conscious about playing the correct role in life, highly attuned to the values shared by peers and role models. For the Performer, being correct and belonging are the two main themes in life, although "belonging" does not always mean belonging to mainstream institutions. It might mean belonging to local social groups, clubs, and city councils. And "being correct" does not always mean following the letter of the law, but more "local, community values."

Performers make up the largest portion of the Children of the American Dream. They derived their values from lessons learned from parents, school, church, and work. Although institutions are important, underlying the Performer's sense of self is the continuity of relationships from childhood on. Thus the peer group is an important factor in shaping and maintaining values.

The male Performer went to school with neighbors, enlisted with friends, and hoped to be assigned to the same unit. The female Performer worked in war industry, in more traditional, "acceptable" jobs, and dropped out as soon as possible. But the female Performer, since she could not dictate where she would live (or with whom), used church, or Eastern Star, as a way of establishing her peer group.

Performers are self-conscious about conforming to the "normal" stages of life. They are less demanding in the workplace for upward mobility, and don't really believe that there are many legitimate opportunities to change their economic or social status. Yet they are proud of the work they do and are concerned with doing their job right; they take pleasure in doing things right and accept responsibilities and rewards that go along with competence. They like approval but are more concerned that it come from the respect of their peers than from authority figures.

Performers respect and, at the same time, distrust authority. They do not believe that those in power actually deserve the authority they wield. Elitism is disdained, while associations—belonging to a club, for instance—based on shared experiences, are honored. Performers are defenders of hearth and home, and take pride in being like other Americans. Patriotic, caring, and community-conscious, the Performers wish for material improvement, and enjoy the trappings of the "good life" in moderation.

Performers are family-oriented and often rigidly moralistic, with highly defined images of good and bad, tradition and "radicalism." They have high expectations for themselves, as well as for their family. However, high expectations does not necessarily mean high achievement, although this is sometimes the case. Performers want their children to be accepted and to improve their lot in life.

"Belonging" is an important concept for Performers. It defines who and what they are, how they live (e.g., social and behavioral norms). Secret societies provided a sense of belonging, a kind of tribal allegiance, *and* hostility to government (e.g., "We can take care of ourselves"). Performers' fathers belonged to secret societies, such as the Elks, Masons, Shriners, Knights of Pythias, or Knights of Columbus. These had often been created by necessity, as a means of survival for immigrants. Some were able to collect a few cents a week from members to help finance new businesses, provide loans for homes, or scholarships for young men and women. Many were the only social welfare resource available if money was needed for hospitalization, nursing, and burial. Many of these organizations provided life insurance or built retirement housing. Some of the financial institutions they started have become independent companies, hospitals, and service organizations. The traditions established by these organizations continue today, but in a diminished form.

Eventually, the Performer transferred the strong sense of local belonging to the military. The armed forces provided two levels of membership for the Performer. One level was the fellowship of men. The other was the "just cause" they were engaged in. For many Performers, despite all the hardship, their military service was a peak experience. It confirmed their belief in the importance of ties between friends and neighbors, and between citizen and country.

Performers are characteristically sedentary. As adults, very few are physically active, although they may have been active in high school or street sports. They are likely to have encouraged their children to take part in organized games, and may have been active supporters of these and other children's activities. They are likely to enjoy spectator sports and read the sports page and *Sports Illustrated*, but do a little fishing and camping with the family.

Although Performers are very image-conscious, they do not follow through to make their fantasies reality. They prefer to think of themselves as they were, not as they are, and often have trouble facing the consequences of their life style, such as being overweight. Moreover, Performers, who tend not to like to cook, are more apt to eat prepared foods.

Women Performers usually assume the social roles played by their sisters and friends before them—as mothers, grandmothers, and members of local clubs (bridge clubs, garden clubs, the PTA). They also bowl, play golf, and become involved with the Girl Scouts and the Welcome Wagon. They place considerable weight on the advice and experiences of their peer group. They are conscious of popular trends, and enjoy reading *Cosmopolitan*, *Redbook*, and *Good Housekeeping*.

Performers want to reach each milestone of their lives with as little conflict as possible. They think about retirement as a reality earlier in their lives than other groups. Because Performers are more likely to work in union jobs or have management positions in companies that are large enough to provide a pension, they are reasonably well prepared for retirement.

Unlike Attainers, Performers look forward to retirement. They might plan to tour the country in a camper or recreational vehicle, or retreat to a cabin by a lake. Some may try a retirement life style, but often find this too alienating from friends and family.

Often a Performer wife, being younger than her husband, continues to work after he retires. Sometimes the husband will return to work part-time. If he worked in a service capacity as a maintenance man or appliance repairman, he may continue to work for former clients.

Increasingly, Performers are making a gradual transition from their full work life to retirement, rather than taking complete retirement at age 55 or 61, for example. However, most prefer complete early retirement. At first, the freedom from punching the clock is appealing, but the isolation from friends and coworkers may also cause depression, particularly in men. Their wives, accustomed to ruling their domestic domain, may find it irritating having their disgruntled husbands around.

Dreamers

Dreamers wish to be like someone else whom they view as more desirable; Dreamers want to "keep up with the Joneses." They are not motivated by accomplishment, like Attainers, or a sense of a shared mission, like Performers. Dreamers want to belong but don't believe that they do or can. Except for chasing an elusive status, it is difficult for Dreamers to find a satisfying niche for themselves.

Dreamers are driven by their need to identify with qualities they do not comprehend. They surround themselves with products that suggest status, such as expensive scotch, a fancy used car, or complex stereos. Because Dreamers typically cannot afford the best in consumer goods and may not really be sure of what quality is, they frequently end up with cheap or expensive imitations.

Dreamers love fan magazines and gossip rags such as *The National Enquirer*, which cater to readers' naivete and a willingness to suspend disbelief. The Dreamer's ability to judge people and information is often poorly developed, and they frequently make inappropriate personal choices, based on their lack of comprehension and their distorted expectations. Savings are spent on get-rich-quick schemes; long-term investments are not trusted. They sacrifice accomplishment for short-term rewards, even when those are inadequately defined. For example, they might buy cars, jewelry, or furniture on bad financial terms.

Dreamers are perpetually looking for that "one big break" that will make them rich and famous, and they will sometimes buy, or invest in, goods and services that promise status. Unfortunately, they often find themselves stuck in the same casino with other Dreamers, playing the ponies in off-track betting rooms, Lotto, and the slot machines (the "one-armed bandit").

Dreamers believe they are "undiscovered" talents. Although they are frequently talented, they are so shortsighted that they never take advantage of their talents. Many Dreamers have romantic notions about themselves and react enthusiastically to media and government propaganda.

In fact, Dreamers are uncomfortable with who they are. They were often made to feel that way as children, by family and friends. This was usually due to family dysfunction caused by upheavals in family finances, frequent moves, disruptions in school, and so forth. Often they were classified as "dull average" or "underweight," or tests revealed an "inferiority complex." To deny their sense of inadequacy, they compensate by striving for qualities that make them *seem* more glamorous or successful, such as being aggressive, or fast-talking. Dreamers are often the children of salesmen and nonprofessionals, straddling the fence between middle-class comfort and status and working-class discomfort and hardship.

Dreamers approaching their 60s today are bitter, but not chastened. Still seeking success and prestige, they are interested in luxury condominiums and retirement communities but frequently end up moving to those at the low end, or to mobile-home parks or apartments, with little savings to live on.

A well-adjusted Dreamer may have found, over the years, ways to obtain more satisfactory rewards from everyday life by modifying his or her wishes. For example, a Dreamer may take tremendous pleasure from being salesman of the year, or helping to plan the annual company party. While secretly bitter about being unable to break into management, or get promoted, Dreamers will immerse themselves in the routines of life—as a car salesman, for instance, working on commission, making cold calls, and filling up slack time by reading the paper and mass-market paperbacks, doing crossword puzzles, and talking shop with the guys. The male Dreamer excels in selling because he is also selling himself along with the product.

While not essentially spiritual, Dreamers believe in luck and are very superstitious. Religion is practiced as an insurance policy, not out of belief. Dreamers see everyone else in the world as being like themselves—getting away with something. Because their dreams are so elusive, Dreamers live with constant frustration.

Dreamer women finish high school, marry early, and work as sales clerks, beauticians, insurance adjustors, and real estate agents. They are both tough and unrealistic, and tend to rationalize their situation. Gossip magazines and television, particularly soap operas, are means of escape from their frustrating, unglamorous lives. They may wear wigs, like Dolly Parton, and slacks and knit blouses with rhinestones.

Recreation for Dreamers involves associating with success. They go to bars, nightclubs featuring glittery stage acts with suggestive titles (World Famous, Exotic). They love Las Vegas and Atlantic City. Dreamers offer each other a blurred version of a celebrity, imitating that life style as best they can. They may take a discount Hawaii or Caribbean cruise, if the price is right. If they can, they'll play golf at the municipal golf club or as a friend's guest at a private club. Dreamers join bowling teams, traveling to regional competitions. Teams have their own bags, balls, and jackets with team initials and personal monograms. Dreamers like card games, and play gin rummy, poker, and sometimes bridge. They enjoy fishing in nearby lakes and rivers, or at a fishing hole they've frequented for years. They may own a camper. Dreamers prefer music with strong imagery—torch songs, country, and piano bar music.

Cruisers

Distrustful, alone, the Cruiser wants only to "cruise" through life; but life is difficult, an obstacle course of transitions. Childhood and adolescence were difficult, too; parents were noncommunicative, nonnurturing, abusive, unavailable; guidance from extended family was lacking; families moved frequently, looking for work; many were hurt substantially by the depression: displaced dust bowl farmers, unemployed Michigan plant workers. Parents divorced each other, or, suspicious and lacking social skills, ignored or isolated their children. Teenage Cruisers were, like their parents, socially awkward. Foolish pranks and stunts were meant to attract attention ("love"), but rarely endeared them to anyone.

Attainers had the New Deal, Performers their families and peers, and Dreamers their neighbors, but Cruisers had no such outside points of reference. With Cruisers, expectations are low, or unrealistic, and there is no real sense of how the world—school, jobs, even personal relations—works. Cruisers learned early on that status and material comforts were hard, perhaps impossible, to obtain. Survival, rather than a work ethic, is what drives the Cruiser. Getting by is what counts.

Cruisers are unclear about the future and tend to live day to day. Poor relationships—with parents, teachers, the military, on the job— reinforce their poor self-image. Lacking much self-identity, they also lack a sense of empowerment in shaping their own lives. Because Cruisers tend to feel out of control, they resent authority and, in turn, tend to use whatever power they *do* have to bolster their sense of dignity. A bank teller takes her time; a service station attendant finds more and more problems with your car; an assembly-line worker lets a flaw pass by. Unfortunately, since they do not have many avenues for recourse, they frequently turn their power on others, such as customers, weaker family members, and peers.

Cruisers lack confidence in the capacity of social institutions (family, work, government, community) to recognize or satisfy their needs, and so spend considerable energy avoiding complex, new, and different situations (involving social institutions) that might improve their lives. They will use social institutions for advancement, but less by following the rules, which they hate, than by establishing mutually advantageous connections with someone at or near their level who can "pull strings"—to get better rations, a better job, shorter hours, and so on. Cruisers can be good team players when they develop trust, with co-workers, for example, but this is often a long road.

Cruisers often married other Cruisers, who helped replicate a life style they already knew. Marriage relationships are often conflict-laden. Spouses do not have a clear picture of each other as individuals, yet expect to be accepted just as they are. Their lives are often fragmented, with marital discord, separation, and divorce. The song, "Don't Let Your Sons Grow Up to Be Cowboys," conveys a strong message about the difficulties Cruisers have in relationships. It romanticizes the personality of someone who cannot make successful connections, despite powerful feelings. Cruisers often wonder why they do not have better relations with their own children; when conflicts occurred they tended to be authoritarian or distant. They describe their own fathers as quiet and somber, though occasionally loud and raucous when they drank. Their mothers were long-suffering and emotionally repressed.

Followers rather than belongers, Cruisers typically hang at the back of a crowd. Occasionally they get picked on to do the dirty work for others, such as political promotion, boiler room sales jobs, and bouncers. Conspicuous by their reticence, they often do not question the meaning of their situation. They would rather avoid trouble by obeying; but they often *do* get into trouble, by their reluctance, or inability, to assess a situation correctly.

Cruisers frequently lack formal education but may, by virtue of their isolation from the rest of the crowd, acquire substantial skills and capabilities, often self-taught. Cruisers successfully take vocational and technical training, and have strong personal interests, such as practical hobbies.

The difficulty in communicating that characterizes the Cruiser, plus their discomfort with conventional social organizations, rather than any lack of basic intelligence, makes it hard for them to let others know their often wide range of capabilities. For this reason they are often unemployed, or fail to take advantage of promotional opportunities. Cruisers can be found in all types of occupations, particularly service jobs, such as waitresses, technicians, and sales clerks. A Cruiser may also be a mechanic, technical repairman, carpenter, or manufacturing worker, in metal fabrication, machine tool building, or assembly work.

Because Cruisers tend to be introverted, they may in their late years live in a self-sustained isolation. They have a mildly despairing and cynical view of retirement. Unlike Performers, with lifelong affiliations and hobbies, Cruisers have little to fall back on. They are more likely to settle into a dull routine, watching television, working in the garage, sewing, hunting or fishing alone.

Cruisers are not as likely as other members of their age group to be in good health when they reach their mid-60s. In fact, Cruiser men and women both have a peculiarly low level of concern about the causes of health problems. They often smoke, drink a lot, eat meat and potatoes (while watching TV), and rarely exercise, even when fishing or hunting. This disconnection with their body appears almost deliberate, possibly in the hope that someone (typically their wives, but also doctors and hospitals) will then have to wait on them. Many suffer from hernias or serious back trouble. Some have had work-related disorders that resulted in some form of worker's compensation. This may have given them a sense of satisfaction, since they feel they have been denied sustenance from the world for most of their lives.

As they age, Cruisers, if they own a home, are not very likely to move out. They have few savings, small pensions, if any, and they are not very open to change. They may move to a smaller apartment when widowed, but otherwise will live much as they always have, not because they are autonomous but because they are able to live with less.

Cruisers are sporadically self-indulgent, rewarding themselves with presents on rare occasions, often when they can least afford it, then punishing themselves (or their wives and kids) for having treated themselves. Their poor and ambiguous self-image makes them appear too awkward and uncomfortable for close contact. They are the true loners of their generation, separated from others even when joined together in groups, alien even to themselves.

THE BRIDGE GENERATION: 1930–1939

The cohort born between 1930 and 1940 was a bridge—in terms of experience and values—between two major eras of American history—the World War II period of the highly directed and goal-oriented Children of the American Dream and the post–World War II period of the Gap Generation and the Baby Boomers, the generations that were to reshape the second half of America's 20th century. Being neither this generation nor that, the Bridge cohort suffers by comparison.

IMMERSION

The majority of the Bridge Generation was born in the United States. Most of their parents were born around the turn of the century, half of them in Europe, and still had many old-world ties. Families strongly identified with their religion and their roots. Grandparents, especially, born during the Victorian Age, seemed very old-fashioned to the Bridge Generation kids. The parents of the Bridge Generation carried on this conservative outlook on life. Mothers warned against sitting in upholstered armchairs, for example, insisting that straight-backed chairs were healthier and more correct.

In the 1930s times were hard and economic realities could not be overlooked. Few parents were politically active, but everyone cared about politics. Even very young children were often made acutely aware of politics. Many vividly remember the Landon sunflower campaign buttons of the Roosevelt-Landon election of 1936. Sometimes schoolyard fights would break out over politics, and kids got picked on if, say, Papa was a supporter of socialist Norman Thomas. Before the end of this decade everyone had heard of Adolf Hitler, although few could comprehend the darker significance of his rise to power.

Many children started public school when they were at least four and a half years old. Their teachers were affected by the economic and social realities of the depression. It was illegal for married women to teach, although they could substitute. So some young single women teachers decided to forgo marriage in order to stay employed. This created a generation of older single women instructors who exerted a different kind of influence on young people.

Cities were still very ethnocentric—characterized by ethnic enclaves such as Irish, Italian, Jewish—during the 1930s, and small towns were uniform in class and ethnicity. Rural folks still regarded cities with a combination of awe and hostility. In the early part of the decade those who lived in their own homes were very conscious of the security that home ownership represented. There weren't many new buildings typical of the era; often, homes had been built at or before the turn of the century and were highly ornamented with scrollwork and moldings. Many had leaded glass and small, stained glass windows. If finances improved, a family might move to a bigger house, on another street in the same town. A street might have apartments and family homes mixed together in one- or two-family wooden or frame buildings. In the city there were small gardens in back; in smaller towns backyards were quite large. Houses were smaller and simpler in motor car suburbs, built in the 1920s, and there were often several vacant lots per block.

After school, children from one end of the block to the other would play in the streets until it was time to go home for dinner. Street play was active and vigorous. Boys and girls played together—hide-and-seek, stickball, kick-the-can, marbles, ball games, jump rope (with songs like "R-A-T-T-L-E" and "*A* My Name Is . . . Alice"), hopscotch, and action-fantasy games based on popular comic books, *Batman* among them. Kids traded their comic books and Big Little Books such as *Don Winslow and the Submarine Raiders*. These two-inch thick adventure books had more pages and so were considered better than comic books.

Social life was outside—on streets, in yards, and on back porches. Most middle-class mothers did not work outside the home and monitored the play on the street.

There was a real vitality to the streets in the 1930s. There were fewer cars then, and tradesmen and itinerant salesmen, often immigrants, traveled by horse-drawn carts, collecting rags or selling needles and thread door-to-door, or peddling dry goods and notions. The Fuller Brush man sold brushes and brooms from his case. But all that was coming to an end and change was occurring in many ways.

Many remember the first supermarket, perhaps a Piggly Wiggly, or the A&P. In the old-style grocery store you had to ask a clerk to get various items. Those on a top shelf would be retrieved by means of a long pole with a grasper. But at the supermarket you could collect all the items yourself and put them in a shopping basket. Shoppers were thrifty, and price became more important than quality. Many sought out sales and markdowns in department stores. Discount department stores like Filene's Basement in Boston were especially popular. Many children of the Bridge Generation still find it hard to pay full price.

The American diet began to change. Velveeta processed cheese was a big treat. Most families had milk delivery, and ice cream trucks stopped on every block to sell Dixie cups with pictures of movie stars on their lids.

Wages were low, and families had to be careful. Men who still had their jobs after the crash often worked for half the salary they made before. Mother's younger sister might live with the family and pay half her $13-a-week secretary's wage for room and board. The depression was all around them, but Bridge Generation kids were mostly too young to appreciate the hardship.

Fathers who had office jobs worked Saturday mornings, and sometimes an older child would be dressed up to visit Dad's office—to be shown off and maybe to be allowed to press the keys on the adding machine. Sometimes families who were close would get together with Dad at noon and picnic in a nearby park. On Sundays families might get together and go on outings. Fathers silently tried to make ends meet, as best they could.

Cars were considered functional machines, something that families rather than individuals would buy. The first family car might have been a secondhand Essex. Sunday driving was a major source of weekend entertainment. Families would ride to the beach or the lake for a swim, pulling down the shades in the Buick to change their clothes. Others would drive through the open countryside, or go to a WPA museum or swimming pool or an outdoor concert. The CCC had cleared hiking trails and set up public restrooms and picnic grounds. Cities had many affordable treats, like aquariums, where visitors could watch the fish and listen to the echoes, or boats like the swan boats in the Boston Garden or the rowboats at the World's Fair grounds in Saint Louis.

During the 1920s there had been an expansion and institutionalization of medicine. Even during the depression more parents had access to hospitals for their sick children. There were no antibiotics to make surgery unnecessary. But health care was still uneven, especially surgical procedures, which, though necessary, were still risky. Tonsillectomies and appendectomies were common, as were mastoidectomies (an ear infection could result in a fatal case of meningitis). Many Jewish refugees had emigrated from Germany to the eastern United States, and many were doctors, perhaps the source of the common childhood stereotype that all doctors have German accents. In the Midwest a child might, on a typical hospital visit to mend a broken arm, see other children who were suffering from hunger and deprivation due to the depression. A child admitted on July 4th to a pediatric ward might see the victim of a firework accident, which were frequent. Unfortunately, skin grafts were neither easy nor often successful, and many with serious burns died from shock and pain.

Children listened to the radio a lot. Most families had one massive radio, perhaps an Atwater Kent, a Philco, or a Bosch, and by 1939, some children had an older, smaller radio in their bedroom, which they were not supposed to play at night. There were plenty of children's radio shows, like "The Lone Ranger," which often underestimated the sophistication of their audience. Parents listened to Jessica Dragonet, an amateur opera singer. Some remember her terrible screeching on Saturday nights.

Many also remember the screaming voice of Hitler making his inflammatory speeches. At the penny candy store, an icon of the old neighborhoods, you could buy candy, wrapped in a piece of paper that was like a pig's rear. When opened up, it became Hitler's face. By the time children were in 5th grade (9 to 10 years old), Hitler had become the big bogeyman.

Some parents went to Europe to rescue family members, some of whom refused to leave. Having family in Europe made the political drama unfolding far more personal, since relatives were often at great risk. The extermination of the Jews was a horror that was expected by many, denied by others. Many people feared that no Jews would survive.

Children were quite aware of fascism. They heard their parents talk about the big meeting of the German-American Bund that took place in Madison Square Garden in 1938. Gerald L. K. Smith, from Kansas, was an American fascist radio broadcaster who preached "America First" and advocated that we not interfere with Hitler or Mussolini. Charles Lindberg believed in what Hitler was doing and saw America as lacking in moral purity and heroes such as himself. Some supported fascism; others recognized its threat early on while others were indifferent, or barely noticed. Some people wouldn't buy a Ford car because of Henry Ford's anti-Semitic views. At least one southern senator publicly advocated that Jews and blacks be sterilized; no one, publicly, agreed.

There was always a local movie house—the Galaxy, the Elmwood, the Magnet—where you could watch Katharine Hepburn or Bette Davis play a rich heiress, Shirley Temple a temporarily poor one, or Mickey Rooney a spunky kid who managed to make the amateur show a real hit. It only cost a dime before five o'clock. (A wartime tax raised the price to 12 cents.) On Saturday afternoon, older children would take younger ones to see a Gene Autry cowboy movie plus a detective thriller like Boston Blackie or Charlie Chan, a March of Time newsreel, and either a Pete Smith humor short or a serial like Flash Gordon or the Green Hornet.

The movie stars were written about in fan magazines, paper dolls were printed to look like them, and people listened for a scrap of their familiar voices on the radio. Movie stars had made it—they were safe from eviction, hunger, bankruptcy—but unlike other rich people, you could look at them and try to be like them. Mothers would do up their daughters' hair in Shirley Temple curls and send them off to tap class in the hope that somehow, miraculously, a Hollywood talent scout would find them, and "just like in the movies," they'd be rich.

DIVERSION—THE ADOLESCENT EXPERIENCE IN THE 1940S

For the Bridge Generation, now in their teens, growing up took on a new, more serious, and possibly ominous meaning. It was the attack on Pearl Harbor that signaled the turning point. There had been strong doubt about the moral justification of the war, but those whom the massive bombing of London had not convinced stopped arguing after Pearl Harbor—at least in public. The war was clearly perceived as the consummate battle between good and evil. There was more hatred of Hitler, and contempt for the Japanese.

Some parents fought over the ethics of buying black market products. Listening to these fights posed important moral conflicts for children, who were also listening to the moral directives issued by their Commander-in-Chief, President Roosevelt.

There were ration coupons for sugar, meat, and shoes (two pair a year), and gas ration cards, graded A, B, C, depending on how much gas you needed to get to work. Everyone saved tinfoil from cigarettes and brought it in to collection centers. The Red Cross, located in storefront centers, provided yarn and knitting needles and taught girls to knit socks for soldiers and caps that looked like ski masks for the Merchant Marines (a contrast to World War I, when wounded soldiers in military hospitals knitted for their comrades in the trenches overseas). During the early war years there were brownouts and blackouts; everyone had blackout curtains. There were air raid wardens on every block. These men and women took their jobs seriously because even a tiny sliver of light could guide the Germans or the Japanese to bomb your town. Everyone did something—"for the duration"—and everywhere there was a feeling of excitement. It seemed that every male from 18 to 44 was in the service. Older brothers—Children of the American Dream—were drafted in early 1942. Young men thought about going to war, but still made their plans for the future. Girls, particularly those from more educated families, thought they could do whatever they wanted to do. Many opportunities were open to them. They thought about careers, but didn't necessarily map out a plan of action. Self-indulgence was not encouraged; employment, and volunteer and charity work, was. Young women who worked outside the home seemed so much more cheerful and pleasant, and glad to be working.

Not all politics had to do with the war, however. Mayor James Curley was in power in Boston. Curley held court at his house, where people petitioned him for favors and patronage. A man who worked stuffing kapok into cushions for furniture was fired for trying to organize the factory in which he worked. An amateur sculptor now unemployed, he decided to do a bust of Mayor Curley. Finally, after the man had been sculpting him for many weeks, Curley asked him why he had so much time to spend on the project. The sculptor explained the reasons for his dismissal. Curley appointed the man chief (and only) kapok inspector for all of Boston. It was a gesture characteristic of Curley's sense of irony and justice, which endeared him to some, but earned him the hatred and fear of others.

Jazz and swing were popular with young people. They listened to the "Make-Believe Ballroom" or the "9-20" Club on the radio. Several programs were made up of 15-minute segments of several bands, such as Guy Lombardo or the Blue Baron. Hep teenagers read the jazz magazines *Down Beat* and *Metronome*, which came out in the 1930s. Big band music was hep; Glenn Miller's band might not be the hottest, but people lined up for every record he made. The "Lux Radio Theatre" initially attracted many teenagers. They would listen to the Lone Ranger, then the Lux show, then big band music.

Those who were in the right place could watch music history being made in those days. Music was mostly for listening. Big city theaters had new bands every week. Some would arrive at the theater for shows as early as 8:30 a.m.; savvy kids would cut school to get there. Before the movie, there would be an hour music show, then a regular feature movie, then the band would play again. Fans yearned to be the first to hear the bands of Benny Goodman, Harry James, Tommy or Jimmy Dorsey, Glenn Miller (with Tex Benecke and the Modernaires), Count Basie, Duke Ellington, or Charley Spivak. Singers came in also—the Andrews Sisters, Connie Boswell, and entertainers Mary Lou Williams and Jimmy Lunsford.

Many of these bands did not survive the war. In 1947, musicians' union chief James Petrillo said union bands would hold out for higher fees. The strike lasted over a year. This series of labor struggles gave a tremendous boost to the careers of singers Eddie Fisher, Frank Sinatra, Perry Como, and others. It was the death of the dance band, but the birth of massive, adoring, hysterical, teenage fans of handsome singers.

Radio also provided theater: "The Inner Sanctum," "The Lone Ranger," "I Love a Mystery," and "Mr. Keene, Tracer of Lost Persons."

War bonds were the universal investment of the era. Everyone was patriotic and bought bonds for $18.75 that would pay $25.00 in 10 years. There were all kinds of incentives to buy—for example, tickets to the Ice Follies or theatrical events. Rallies were held everywhere, and movie stars urged everyone to buy bonds.

Baseball was *the* game in the 1930s. It was cheap and accessible. Living in a major league city gave kids a strong team spirit—your team *could* win the World Series. For the Boston Red Sox, the Series was always tragic, but the Boston Braves had a feisty, colorful image. The Brooklyn Dodgers (those "bums") were holy icons to several generations. Ted Williams and Joe DiMaggio were among the game's glorious heroes. Baseball cards were a basic medium of exchange, for grade school and high school students alike. First the cards had Indian chiefs pictured on the back, then they began to feature baseball players. Basketball and hockey were also popular. Tennis, golf, and skiing were the country club sports, only for the wealthy.

In the 1940s, the "zoot suit with the reet pleat" was worn by blacks, Hispanics, and a few musicians, but primarily by the Children of the American Dream, not the Bridge Generation. The Bridge Generation wore loafer jackets that had an unfitted boxy cut, with the body one color and sleeves another color. Girls wore bobby sox and sloppy joes (giant sweaters), so that one inch of skirt would show.

High school was the center of life for teenagers. Public school students felt sorry for those who went to sex-segregated schools, and really did not know what teenagers of the other sex thought. High school graduation day was an important event. It signaled the end of childhood—of living at home and being taken care of. After the ceremony, some went to a movie and a Chinese restaurant downtown with their friends. Others had parties at home with their families and peers. The next day, many of the young men enlisted.

After the war, rationing and the black market ended. People were encouraged to consume, after having complied with the wartime savings bond programs for so long. Now there were long, irritating lines to buy tires, stoves, and refrigerators. The housing shortage was a profound problem. Thousands of units were built, often with poor materials and on unreliable schedules. The cheap plumbing, green lumber, and poor carpentry of these houses began to come apart as soon as they were occupied.

The end of the war did not mean a return to normalcy, particularly for the parents of the Bridge Generation. Wartime contracts were being cancelled following Japan's surrender, and unemployment was on the rise. At the same time, prices were also escalating; everything from bus fare to bread was going up. Price controls were more of a sieve than a ceiling by war's end. Inflation was a new phenomenon; kids who worked to help their parents or put themselves through school felt its effects.

EXPANSION—EARLY ADULTHOOD IN THE 1950S

The Bridge Generation, now in their early 20s, were remarkably conservative. The war-induced fear of the foreign, combined with a sense of confusion about social norms that was also established during the war years, encouraged an aversion to "getting involved." Their common features seemed to be caution, suspicion, and a practical self-centeredness. Although they may have had somewhat deprived childhoods and austere adolescences, they had not had to struggle directly with the depression and world war.

What influenced many of this generation was, ironically, a clash between the glory of the war and the unfairness that was rampant around them as they grew into early adulthood. The American Federation of Labor—the craft unions—wouldn't admit blacks, nor (until 1945) would the Coast Guard. At a time when Jackie Robinson was big-league baseball's first black player, second in popularity only to Bing Crosby, the country was not even beginning to face its racial hypocrisy. The problems of civil rights, largely ignored, were festering.

Meanwhile, the Marshall Plan to aid Europe's economic plight was being implemented to protect Europe from what at that time appeared to be the burgeoning threat of communism. The switch from friendship with the Soviet Union to a defensive position became the focus of U.S. domestic and foreign policy. Every month a new source of "Red" anxiety arose in the headlines: Mao's success against Chiang Kai-shek, the Korean War, the fall of the French at Dien Bien Phu. Anything slightly associated with communism, from Alger Hiss to "leftish" writers such as Howard Fast, were targets for the press. As Roosevelt's New Deal turned into Truman's Fair Deal, the mood of the country became distrustful, and turned inward. Many of the Bridge Generation acquired qualities of reticence (how could they compete with the older, larger generation, the Children of the American Dream), cynicism (you often had to make deals under the table to get what you wanted), and suspicion (political views were a risk in the emerging cold war era). Over time, this became a closed or repressed outlook on life, expressed through a concern for material goods, conformity, friendships, and practicality.

Older members of the Bridge Generation fought or would fight in Korea, and some used the GI Bill of Rights to educate themselves. During the early 1950s only about one seventh of the Bridge Generation went to college, which, for most young people, would be their first experience away from home. In college economic differences were obvious: some students were supported entirely by their parents and sported new convertibles and cashmere sweaters; others seemed barely to subsist on peanut butter sandwiches. Many girls had picked out their silver pattern while still in high school and dropped out of college after a year or two to get married.

Regulations regarding separation of the sexes were rigorous, as they had always been. At night girls stayed in the dorm and socialized with each other, holding bull sessions in the halls. A girl might have a number of unrequited crushes, a few relationships, but, for most, intimacy was limited. Boys could go to prostitutes or sleep with "fast" girls.

Many states, such as Massachusetts and Connecticut, had very repressive birth control laws. In most states contraceptives were illegal;

abortion was never spoken of. Doctors could lose their licenses if they performed abortions or gave advice on birth control. Fear of pregnancy kept most women virgins before marriage.

College spirit, the stereotypical Big Man on Campus, and fraternity parties all had their roots in the elitism and shared experience of college, similar to the tradition of soldiers' comradery. In fact, both military and college life had much in common in the 1950s.

Returning GIs were a dramatic new dimension in college life. These serious, mature young men and women (some former WACs, Waves, and Army nurses) did not, however, bring color and comradeship to the campus, but rather a sobering businesslike "got-to-catch-up" attitude reflecting a race to recapture a "normalcy" they never knew.

Living away from home was—for veterans and nonveterans alike— a self-perpetuating ritual of adulthood. It forced young people to make choices, perhaps due to late-night conversations about the future, or a lonely semester spent at school without being able to return home for the holidays. Realizing that choices were not always easy, young people took on the trappings of adulthood to show they weren't afraid of life. Some consumed too much alcohol; some became chain smokers.

For some, living away from home meant entry into reconstructed adult social situations, such as fraternities and sororities. These sponsored a wide range of formal and informal events: picking a "Sweetheart of Sigma Chi," fraternity exchanges, mixers, and collegiate games involving dressing up in Tuxedos and evening gowns and learning the language of flirting, always an awkward art, and seduction. Women students had to deal with 10 p.m. curfews and sign-out sheets, waited for dates, and listened for the switchboard buzzer. Many men and women students sneaked out and back in to the dorm. Some went steady and were a couple. Moving out of a dormitory into a private room or a shared apartment was a major step, typically achieved by seniors, often men, and more likely by graduate students or working adults who had finished or dropped out of college.

Many women were later envious of those able to benefit from the sexual revolution. Ironically, many women of the preceding generation had more of an open view of sexuality because they had reached adulthood during the war. Both men (who were exposed to "worldly matters" in the military) and women (who had less supervised lives) Children of the American Dream were able to explore more, and were surrounded by more unconventional role models.

The Bridge Generation became known as the "Silent Generation." *Fortune* magazine observed that the men of that time "seem to be strangers from another generation, somehow curiously old before their time. Above everything else, security has become their goal. . . . The class of '49 wants to work for somebody else—preferably somebody big." Graduates wanted their place on the corporate ladder. Nonetheless, this generation certainly had its share of beatniks.

While some complained about the apparent intellectual morbidity of campus life, others noted that this generation was actually the freest of the 20th century, liberated from the "moral inflation" of the 1920s and 1930s. While less civic minded on a grand scale, this group was attentive to the value of a life style that was personal and not political.

The Bridge Generation, often characterized by their passivity and indifference, did provide a few magnetic personalities. In only three films James Dean projected a powerful image of a restless rebel. When he died, he had left behind an indelible myth. Marilyn Monroe, born in 1926, became the epitome of female allure, particularly for those just a bit younger. With her immense sex appeal tempered by a waiflike vulnerability, she was the model for young women searching wistfully for some fulfillment they could not clearly define.

In less affluent families, young people exposed to advertising and other propaganda of affluence tended to become frustrated and alienated. As sociologist Paul Goodman has noted, when expectations of living standards rise, as they did throughout the 1950s, then less provision is made for a dignified life of poverty. The result is increased indignity of poverty, which aggravates feelings of frustration and alienation. This is one of several factors that contributed to the rise of what came to be called "juvenile delinquency"—behavior that ranged from petty theft and short-term car theft, to disorderly "acting out" and vandalism, to a violent gang culture. These "problem" kids were just part of a unique postwar youth culture that began to emerge among the younger Bridge Generation (born after 1935) and that would more characterize the Gap Generation. The less extreme forms of alienation were manifested in fads and fashions and, most notably, music—it was the Bridge Generation who were the creative force behind rock and roll. However, youth was not yet a mass consumer phenomenon, nor was it particularly political. Young men did not resist the first prolonged peacetime draft, for instance. (Elvis Presley, born in 1935, cheerfully served in the Army.) In fact, in the 1950s, young people were beginning to settle down. Popular musicians then were Bobby Vinton and Roy Orbison. The twist was the new dance sensation. And rock and roll declined, due to a series of payola scandals.

Payola scandals and bribing public officials were not remote events. They were reminders that the underworld—the "shadow economy"—was not only alive and well but had in fact been spread by the war and the military. It was American entrepreneurship at its least glorious and most aggressive, and one more result of the wartime mixing of peoples and cultures and of the suspension of the rules that kept on surfacing. People from straitlaced backgrounds who had tipped the butcher during the war to get a better cut of meat might tip the building inspector to ignore an expensive code compliance step.

The acceptance of gambling was an interesting aftereffect of the "live-for-today" attitude of the war years, and possibly a holdover from the depression and the 1920s. Men who had been brought up to believe that gambling was evil learned to gamble in the service, where you didn't have to go hungry if you lost your pay. Back home they bet on office football pools and knew where to find a bookie. Almost every bar had its bookie and numbers runners. Poker games were everywhere. A factory worker might win or lose $100 betting on a game, a significant amount when most people made only $60 a week, if they were lucky. Games might start with a quarter to get in; bets might be 50 cents or $1. A man could lose a month's salary in the course of just one night in a floating crap game, on the Jersey flats, perhaps, illuminated by the headlights of 50 or 60 cars.

Men returning from the Korean War tried to position themselves in a world that was led by veterans of World War II, and a new generation of college-educated professionals. Men were able to make a life for themselves whether or not they had a college education. Many men who had professional ambitions and did not have money tried to get into the Army to become eligible for the GI bill. Others, like those who had learned electronics in the service, or radio, didn't really need college. With a bachelor's degree, you could get a white-collar job in a number of different industries. But you could make just as much in the Electrician's Union. You could become an accountant by passing an exam, if you at least had a high school education. Working was considered a means to an end. Some men changed jobs often, but others spent years struggling to rise in the same company. A Korean War veteran might study accounting, business, or machine-tool operation, living with his parents or in-laws. After earning his degree, he might take a local job in an automobile club, a department store, or an insurance company.

Although Rosie the Riveter had been laid off when "the boys" came back, women were still in the job market. Working wives were a significant part of the rapidly increasing female work force. By 1949, three fifths of all persons entering the work force were married women. In the mid-1950s one third of the total work force of 61 million were women (from all age groups). By 1960 40 percent of American women were employed, full or part-time. While many women may have worked to add to the family income, their employment also added to their self-esteem.

While their elders were savoring the expansive consumer society they had struggled to create and taking tours overseas by the thousands, the more well-to-do of the Bridge Generation were spending their money stateside. By 1950, one seventh of the gross national product was being spent on leisure activities. By 1956, air travel was equal to train travel in volume, and not all of it was for business.

In 1954, Eisenhower told Billy Graham that the United States needed a religious revival. In that same year Congress voted to add "under God" to the pledge of allegiance and in the following year made "In God We Trust" mandatory on all U.S. currency. Within a few years Les Paul and Mary Ford's "Vaya con Dios" and Frankie Lane's "I Believe" were among the top 10. The 1950s were filled with admonitions to be conventionally spiritual. There were advertisements on television that proclaimed the virtues of religion: "the family that prays together stays together." Jane Russell, whose sexy image had lured moviegoers during the postwar celebratory period now proclaimed that "I love God, and when you get to know Him, you'll find He's a Livin' Doll." Books such as *The Power of Prayer on Plants* and Norman Vincent Peale's *The Power of Positive Thinking* were enormously popular.

As the Bridge Generation became parents, many still had little familiarity with sexuality and child rearing—due to their more sexually isolated adolescence. Nevertheless, childbearing was a central reality of life, and the focus on babies became a collective learning experience. The word "togetherness" was coined by *McCall's* magazine to describe the family-centered life style that supposedly characterized rapidly expanding urban and suburban America.

In cities, those active in cultural events developed a suspicious view of the world, due to the targeting of young show business people by Senator McCarthy and by the House Committee on Un-American Activities. It was rumored that the FBI photographed everyone who went into New York's Cameo Theatre, which showed Russian and foreign films.

Many of the Bridge Generation were the children of farmers, but few of them went into farming themselves. Most moved off the farm into careers in carpentry, construction, and machinery operation. They tended to maintain many of the same values they shared with their parents. Others, who went away to college, were exposed to other points of view that they incorporated into their background.

CONVERSION—ADULTHOOD IN THE 1960S

In the 1960s, the Bridge Generation were in their late 20s and early 30s. Although often overlooked by sociologists writing about the war generation or the generation that followed, they nevertheless occupy a unique niche in American history. In the 1960s they were exposed to, but not fully absorbed by, the corporation, as described in William H. Whyte, Jr.'s book, *The Organization Man*. Whyte claimed that Americans were group-oriented, and had shifted their allegiance from the individualistic Protestant ethic to an "organization ethic," marked by "a belief in 'belongingness'" as the ultimate need of the individual. The Bridge Generation was also strongly sports-oriented. They had missed out on the action in World War II and had more time to watch ballgames. In many respects they were a spectator cohort.

Psychoanalyst Erich Fromm described an individual with a "marketing orientation" who thought acceptability depended on "how well a person sells himself on the market, how well he gets his personality across, how nice a 'package' he is. Furthermore, although many . . . have fallen into careers that require emotional complicity and repression, this group does not, in any large measure, make up the vast body of people who make up this stereotype of service professional." C. Wright Mills, in *White Collar*, declared that, "When white-collar people get jobs, they sell not only their time and energy, but their personalities as well. They sell by the week or month their smiles and their kindly gestures, and they must practice the prompt repression of resentment and aggression."

Not only were jobs hard to find but most employment growth was in organizations of over 500 employees—manufacturers like GE, public utilities like AT&T, the federal agencies like the Post Office, or state and local government. By the end of the 1950s, 38 percent of the entire work force had jobs in large organizations; only 16 percent were self-employed. The Bridge Generation often appeared naive to their employers. Some found it hard to fit into a culture where payola, kickbacks, and cutting corners were customary. A few refused to try and just kept on surfing or gave everything up for Beat poetry, bongo drums, and scrounging a living in the Bohemian section of large cities (New York's Greenwich Village, San Francisco's North Beach). Those who kept on working often watched TV programs that mocked or punished sharp business practices, such as the British import "The Avengers," or listened to radio comedians like Bob and Ray who made fun of bureaucracy.

For most, however, the stable economy provided new employment opportunities for those with skill and experience, or the chance to stay in a job and gain promotions through seniority. Those who were in unionized jobs had, for the most part, missed the massive labor confrontations of the early 1950s, and settled in as the economy continued to grow. Many blue-collar workers began to make as much money as white-collar workers.

Factory workers, truckers who owned their own rigs, and small store owners were now residents in the same neighborhoods that white-collar professionals lived in. America's class barriers that had been defined solely by income were now beginning to erode, although other barriers (education, skin color, Waspishness) remained. But the inequities faced by blacks were reaching a crisis. Despite court cases that attempted to remedy questions of civil rights, little progress had been made in the complacent 1950s. Most Americans were out of touch with the troubles facing urban blacks who had moved to cities to find jobs and escape rural poverty, or the problems of rural blacks who still faced a lack of educational and economic opportunities. Poverty was not acknowledged by the majority. Too many felt they had succeeded by their own efforts and others were free to do the same; they had little sympathy for those who wouldn't try. Too many were ignorant or uncaring about the cruel realities of discrimination, malnutrition, and hopelessness. After all, the slums were being cleared, weren't they?

Most of the Bridge Generation allied themselves with their elders, but not all. Many straddled two cultural eras. The tension of this precarious position posed challenges for marriages. The increase in the divorce rate in the 1960s included proportionately more members of the Bridge Generation than the Children of the American Dream.

SUBMERSION IN THE 1970S

By the 1970s, the Bridge Generation, now in their late 30s and early 40s, faced the need to redefine their lives. They came to mid-life at the peak of a period of substantial social and political conflict in America. Many read Gail Sheehy's book, *Passages*. As they experienced their own fear and frustration with change, they tried to understand radical notions about marriage, sex, families, and careers.

The preceding cohorts' intense convictions about their values provided a defense against the onslaught of the new generation's views. Because they were a small cohort, much of the Bridge Generation's struggle to sort out their lives was overshadowed by those before them (Children of the American Dream) and those that came after (the Gap Generation and the Baby Boomers).

Women faced the stressful challenge of bridging the gap between their own childhood and the changing world. For those women who had conventional marriages in smaller towns, the new emphasis on careers was baffling. Raising a family had always been the primary priority. Even those with professional training had put their careers second. Nonetheless, more women found that careers were feasible and desirable, especially once their children were in school. More husbands of the Bridge Generation tolerated a spouse's desires to have a career. This acceptance, aided by the upheaval of the economy during the 1970s, resulted in women in rural communities, particularly on farms, as well as urban women, working outside the home.

REVERSION TO REVISION—1980 AND BEYOND

Young enough to be slightly below the "voluntary retirement age" target group in corporations, and old enough to have substantial experience and ambition, the Bridge Generation is still moving ahead with their lives. Many are at risk of displacement from work, however, because they missed much of the training and experience that the new generation of advanced industrial production has brought into industry. As a result, many men in their 50s are facing loss of jobs in rapidly evolving industries such as steel, machine tools, automotive manufacturing, and chemicals.

Many of the Bridge Generation feel nervous and unsettled. They adapted to a world set up for an older generation and have had to cope with the impact of a world being reshaped by a younger one. For the most part, they are slightly in awe of the world before them and working hard to maintain their place. They will push hard to keep their place, socially and economically.

BIRTHMARKS

Good Old Boys and Gals

Good Old Boys and Gals are a transitional group in U.S. history. Their lives are now primarily suburban, but their roots remain rural. They were born in small towns, or in big cities like Dallas that used to be small towns and still have a small-town atmosphere. The children of Good Old Boys and Gals are most likely to have been raised in the suburbs, to be better educated, and to work in industries that are "information intensive."

Good Old Boys and Gals, raised on farms and in small towns, had parents who, for the most part, were farmers or small business owners. Most Good Old Boys and Gals are blue-collar workers: carpenters, plasterers, bricklayers, crane operators, iron workers. Some may be truck drivers, police officers, municipal workers, engineers, and developers. Although what they do to earn a living varies, what Good Old Boys and Gals have in common are their values and how they express them.

Good Old Boys and Gals believe that life is rough and you have to be tough and able to defend yourself—an outlook inherited from parents who suffered through the depression and great-grandparents who struggled as immigrants. Good Old Boys and Gals tend to be somewhat cynical and have acquired their parents' fatalism. Like farmers, their views are often based on hoping against the odds. They do not trust larger institutions and are not very religious in a formal sense, but see religion as a stable reference point in their occasionally chaotic lives. Although patriotic, they did not necessarily think the Vietnam War was a legitimate reason for sending their sons and friends off to battle, but they complied with the law.

Good Old Gals see men as primarily little boys dominated by their desires and vanity. They accept them, as (hopefully) "good men," or at least good-hearted men, who may nonetheless often "break your heart."

Good Old Boys do not "understand" women and therefore do not trust them. They tend to form exaggerated images of women's virtues or failings. As a result, they develop relationships of grudging respect and commitment toward their spouses. Sexuality is considered a basic fact of life, and sexual satisfaction a fundamental need. Divorce, which is high among this group, is accepted. Some people are seen as the "marrying kind" and others are not. Both Good Old Boys and Gals believe in sowing a few wild oats before settling down.

Responsibilities—for family or work—are fulfilled as a serious contractual obligation among Good Old Boys and Gals, not necessarily as a joy. There tend to be different rules for men and women. It is expected, for example, that men will try and slip away from home and household chores, to the local tavern, or to the lake for fishing. Fighting is accepted as a way to solve disputes. Good Old Boys separate the world into "them" and "us" and do not easily tolerate the values of others. Women, on the other hand, are expected to be long-suffering and patient about a husband's behavior. Good Old Gals often have more middle-class values and are more tolerant. Many read more, particularly popular magazines, and watch television shows, such as *Donahue* and *Oprah Winfrey*, that discuss changing values. These sources of information play an important role in preventing isolation from the community, since few Good Old Gals work outside the home, compared to their daughters' age group.

Education among Good Old Boys and Gals has not been generally valued, except perhaps as a means toward getting a job, and even then it is often considered unnecessary. It is just as easy to become an apprentice in a trade if your father, brother, cousin, uncle, or friend sponsors you and serves as your mentor. Training in the military or a trade school is considered sensible and worthwhile. Higher education—liberal arts in a university—is seen as something that might destroy the basic values of Good Old Boys and Gals.

Good Old Boys and Gals believe in being good neighbors and good citizens. They are very willing to help friends and neighbors when in trouble and might give through a collection at a church or a tavern they frequent regularly, or at a project site where they work. For Good Old Boys and Gals, politics is a caricature of the rules of life—good and bad in high contrast; patriotism. Their more rural background combined with the post–World War II era of anti-communism to create in them a political intolerance, primarily associated with a hostility toward the counterculture—anything that threatens their more dogmatic view of life. They are patriotic, but cynical about politicians. Many were attracted to John F. Kennedy in 1960, but were politically passive. They supported Ronald Reagan in 1980. More libertarian than conservative, they want government to leave them alone. They do not like taxes and regulations and reject any politicians who want to spend money on education and resources for others that they did not have when they were young. They are very hostile toward social services for specific groups ("Why should anyone receive special attention? Are they better than us?"), particularly for welfare parents, although they know very little about them. They feel that it is wrong to beget children you can't support and that welfare "only encourages them to have more." However, they understand the need for conservation of natural resources, when what is being conserved is important to them. For instance, a typical Good Old Boy is a hunter who strongly supports wildlife preservation and believes that hunting is an important means of keeping herd populations in balance.

Although Good Old Boys and Gals are not religious, they do go to church regularly because it is the "right" thing to do. Religion is seen as helpful in keeping the ups and downs of life in perspective.

Good Old Boys and Gals distrust professionals such as psychiatrists, lawyers, and elected officials (unless they are true "good old boys"). Their distrust is based on class differences and the belief that many professionals make considerable amounts of money for doing little of constructive value. Professionals, like government in general, are seen as intrusive, and Good Old Boys and Gals pride themselves on resisting them.

Good Old Boys cherish the myth of the "loner" and "rebel," although they rarely engage in really rebellious behavior. Rebellion is symbolic: playing pranks, getting drunk, gambling, and carousing. The loner image, however, remains an important icon in their personal pantheon.

Good Old Boys and Gals are not indifferent to material possessions, but are focused more on acquisitions that give them status among their peers. Women tend to be self-denying or family-centered in their purchasing (e.g., home appliances, sewing machines, furniture). The men are very peer influenced within specific categories, such as recreation vehicles, fishing equipment, and guns. They improve their lives by upgrading things they already own. For instance, they may buy a luxury car, typically American-made, a bigger refrigerator, or color television, or install air conditioning. For recreation they may buy a four-wheel-drive, off-road vehicle, a trailer, a boat, fishing gear, or new rifle. They are practical in their financial outlook, investing in real estate rather than stocks and bonds.

Good Old Boys and Gals have very little anxiety about their parental roles; for wives, their husbands come first, not their children (whether the wives agree or not). They eschew the martyr role, unlike middle-class parents who believe in sacrificing their own needs in favor of their children and who want their children to be "upwardly mobile." Good Old Boys and Gals want their children to pursue their own way of life, regardless of what others may think, but they convey strong messages to them about what "their own way" should be. Because they generally distrust society's institutions—churches, schools, government—they teach their children to survive in these, not adapt, or excel. They often prepare their children to go into blue-collar jobs, and do not push them to become teachers or doctors or bankers. They will work for the power company (remember the Wichita lineman?), insurance companies, and manufacturing concerns at both the line and lower-level supervisory and management positions.

Kinship ties are strong and serve as the primary basis for social activity for the often large families of Good Old Boys and Gals. Thanksgiving dinner with the whole family is an important event. Ties with neighbors and coworkers are also important.

Despite the fact that the families of Good Old Boys and Gals emigrated to the United States many generations ago, there is a strong ethnic consciousness among them. There is also racism. Because Good Old Boys and Gals tend to be established in the labor market, they perceive newcomers as interlopers.

Sports are important to both Good Old Boys and Gals. They provide a reassuring picture of the world, where rules of play are clear, everyone's side is well-defined, and the ability to succeed is based on physical effort and craft rather than intellectual effort. The specificity and continuity of roles and relationships in sports provide a rational, formal, and practical universe which constitutes the idealized view of the world Good Old Boys and Gals like and understand best.

Hunting and fishing—as well as caring for guns or fishing reels—are very important pastimes. These activities were part of their rural background, and have carried through. A Good Old Boy might start in the spring with trout season and fish at several lakes. Other fishing trips during the year may be made for perch or bluegills. Fall is the time for hunting—rabbits, squirrel, pheasant, and geese each have their season. The climax of the year is deer season. This may involve a week-long trip with the same friends to the same place—a farm, lodge, or campground. Deer that are bagged are typically butchered at local shops and made into "summer sausage." During the winter Good Old Boys might go ice fishing.

Good Old Gals like to get out with their husbands, but they also enjoy being in the company of other Gals—at the bridge or canasta table, bowling alley, bingo game, or dance hall. Their hobbies include quilting, crocheting, and cooking. But they also share activities with their spouses, such as gemology (semiprecious stones found, polished, sold, and traded), and home businesses like raising pedigree dogs. They also like to travel together in their RVs to "big events" such as regional "meets" and county fairs.

Weekly recreation for Good Old Boys and Gals will often take place at familiar local settings, at the tavern, a friend's, and possibly at church. Men will go to a tavern for a drink after work every day. On Fridays they bring their wives, go out to dinner, and return later for more drinks, dancing, and conversation. A local tavern is often the site for parties for friends, retirees, and sons returning from military service. St. Patrick's Day is an important holiday. Many Good Old Boys and Gals are Irish; those who aren't are often Catholic but purely Catholic holidays are hard to find.

Good Old Boys look forward to retirement. It is a reward for working, but more important, it represents time and freedom to pursue activities they have always enjoyed. Many Good Old Boys have limited expectations for themselves, so they often find themselves bored and frustrated after retiring. To deal with these pressures they may continue to work part-time in their trade, or perhaps start their own business.

Many Good Old Boys have marriages already stressed by their life style extremes: too much drinking, too little exercise. Their wives, who have friends of their own, may worry about having husbands around full-time. It distracts them from their own, more established routines. Moreover, husbands expect the same attention they used to get when they came home from work.

Many Good Old Boys and Gals have vacation homes in the country where they used to fish or hunt. Others have trailers or recreational vehicles, which they plan someday to tour the country in. Others will move away and resettle in new communities. They may have already purchased land somewhere.

Romantic-Realists

Romantic-Realists are committed to personal life styles that are unconventional and highly individual. Their attitude tends to be tough and self-confident, often covering up feelings of loneliness or bitterness. They have a strong sense of self and do not usually connect themselves to a religion, company, or political party. They may even tend to be somewhat iconoclastic.

While the Bridge Generation took the jobs that were readily available, Romantic-Realists carved out a new place for themselves in traditional corporate structures. They tended to take jobs in cities, and in emerging industries, from advertising to government. They changed jobs often to make the best use of their skills; for them, where they work is essential for doing what they do best. Romantic-Realists are convinced of the value of their own ideas and work hard to see them fulfilled, although they are not necessarily workaholics. Nor are they ideologues. In fact, they tend to avoid politics. Talented and artistic, many have made music, particularly jazz and bebop, an important accompaniment to their lives.

Romantic-Realists were morally moved by the images of social contract and commitment because their families had been affected by the Roosevelt era (WPA, CCC). Also, being more urban (and urbane) and independent-minded, they perhaps worried as much about social equity as they did about the threat of autocracy (having witnessed World War II and its aftermath on young people). Thus the Romantic-Realists tended toward liberalism and idealism. They loved Kennedy with a passion and viewed the challenges of a more just society as a real goal. Nonetheless, they were willing to work with and through the "system" as much as possible.

Romantic-Realists had parents who were emotional, caught up in their own careers and career dilemmas, and intellectual, though not necessarily highly educated. Their parents were often authoritarian and older than average, although more modern than others. Romantic-Realists were encouraged by their parents to look outward for models and teachers, which they did, early on. More so than many others of their generation, this group was willing to consider ideas that were not popular (such as that the poor are victims rather than transgressors, or that women aren't helpless) in order to broaden their understanding. Their independent style made them appear introverted, but they were in fact very social while still being highly individualistic.

Many Romantic-Realists went to college; many never finished. They placed high value on education, but clung to an idealistic view of the utility of knowledge over the value of certificates and diplomas. Their reasons for not finishing school often had to do with their dislike of authority. Not finishing hurt them since they tend to be bright enough to do jobs they cannot be considered for.

Romantic-Realists got married and started families slightly later than many of their peers, usually when they were not economically prepared to do so because they had changed jobs so often and had less seniority in their occupation or profession. Because they value independence, many missed out on early opportunities to develop careers. Instead, they took odd jobs and struggled, often barely getting by. They rented small homes or apartments and stretched paychecks to the limit. Aspiration lived side by side with desperation. They frequently divorced, or maintained marriages with much conflict, inevitably affecting their children's psychological well-being. Romantics lived life hard emotionally, and sometimes had poor health habits, such as drinking and smoking, that are hard to break.

Most Romantic-Realists had to work their way up from the bottom. Many tried artistic careers but ended up in public relations, advertising, civil service, or teaching. Despite these shifts and compromises, Romantic-Realists thrived in these areas, despite complaints about the lack there of true artistic and creative opportunities.

Romantic-Realists value their personal time and tend to pursue hobbies that are more solitary, allowing them to express their basic skills in new areas. An advertising executive might be a highly skilled carpenter; a copy writer an excellent pianist; a city planner a gourmet cook; a teacher a terrific mechanic.

The typical Romantic-Realists seeking their first job might have been placed in a public relations or advertising firm in a big city, among other literate or highly educated people, to perform editorial duties below their capabilities. After several years they may have taken some initiative and been promoted, or moved to another company that offered a better salary and benefits. Many Romantic-Realists just went from one firm to another, not because their needs weren't being met, but because changes in the economy made it necessary. Romantic-Realists are not afraid to change jobs, but have often faced difficulties and disappointments when they did. And, although they try to build in stability for themselves and their family, they are hindered by having moved around so much.

Remarriage and career moves created significant changes in midlife. Typically, many Romantic-Realist women married older men, of a previous cohort, perhaps an Attainer who was attracted to the intellect (but not the assertiveness) of the Romantic-Realist. The values of these two cohorts eventually clashed, as the Romantic-Realist's individuality came into conflict with the Attainer's insecurities. These marriages often ended abruptly and devastatingly, with no financial provisions made for such a breakup.

Romantic-Realist women often reacted against parental advice to "never let them (men) see how smart you are." The men of the Bridge Generation felt threatened by intelligent, competent women (perhaps true of many generations); this has caused many marital problems for Romantic-Realist women, who tend to be smart and achievement-oriented. Many Romantic-Realist women are now divorced, professional women. They do not necessarily like being single, but prefer it to an unhappy marriage.

A painful reality in the lives of Romantic-Realists is resolving difficulties with their children, who were adversely affected by dysfunctional family situations. Teenage and college-age children commonly have problems such as dropping out of school, substance abuse, anger, and jealousy. Romantic-Realists spend considerable time trying to re-build ties and establish real acceptance between them and their children.

Today, Romantic-Realists often live comfortable lives, but not without financial anxieties, due to marital breakups and expensive fi-nancing of children's schooling or therapy. Like others of the Bridge Generation, Romantic-Realists must often care for older family members at a time when they are worried about their own retirement. But whatever problems they face, Romantic-Realists approach them with creativity and wry, acerbic humor, reflecting their efforts to cope without showing their full feelings. Romantic-Realists tend to be pas-sive-aggressive, and verbal, rather than emotional.

Envoys

Envoys are the torchbearers of family aspirations, committed and de-termined to match accomplishment with maintaining traditional fam-ily life virtues. Envoys tend to be the third and fourth children of parents who had arrived in America a decade or two earlier, the last offspring of the Children of the Century.

Unlike their brothers and sisters who, because of the depression or World War II, had their development skewed or altered, Envoys were Americans in every respect, raised without the traumas older family members faced. They did not encounter the obligations and debts first-borns often had to deal with. Their parents expected them to achieve and to be fully integrated into society. Envoys were the best the family could offer, and would bring credit to the family name. Hence, Envoys have highly superego-driven performance goals.

In exchange for the economic opportunities that the investments of others had made possible, Envoys were laden with the obligation to succeed. They took this role to heart, reinforced by their parents' con-tinuing pressure and support. Like the Good Old Boys and Gals, En-voys straddle the old world and the new, a transitional group in a rapidly changing world. But whereas the Good Old Boys and Gals seek to adapt the ways of the past to the present, Envoys are eager to move upward or forward to new people, places, and businesses.

The ghosts of the old world haunted the Envoys as they listened to their grandparents' and parents' stories of struggle. They could not let down those whose lives had been expended to sustain the next generation. Later, as young adults, they heard about the horrors of war, which again emphasized the need for Envoys to succeed and thus affect and shape the world, to make sure oppression and totalitarian-ism were eliminated.

Often not aware of the privileges and attention they were receiving from family members, Envoys sometimes were perceived as vain and self-centered. They were not truly selfish, but they were catered to, drinking fresh orange juice that others did not get, or having better clothing and books.

Half the Envoys entered high school during the later war years; the other half started after the war was over. For both girls and boys, this meant continuing indoctrination of patriotic themes. Girls were encouraged to be supportive of the war effort, and boys prepared to be part of it, although to a lesser extent than their older brothers and sisters. There was also an anticipation of a peacetime environment, and the beginning of the atomic era. There was a curious and often awkward shift in mood toward rebuilding the country, while at the same time an economic uncertainty about how that was to take place.

Envoys were educated as much by their peers as by their parents. They participated in the contemporary culture, passing through all the tests and social rituals—making the high school football or debating team; having a first date and going to the prom; getting good grades.

At the same time, Envoys faced the challenge of maintaining social and emotional connections with their family. Outwardly Envoys would appear to be a generation that was on the verge of losing their family and ethnic identity. Every step they took toward participating in the mainstream society, and in moving up out of their parents' world, forced confrontations with their own identity and that of their family.

Many Envoys were embarrassed to bring friends home from school. They were self-conscious about their parents' accent, lack of sophistication, and social awkwardness. Sometimes they hid or discarded their ethnicity in an effort to fit in with other children.

Those families who were able to inculcate in their children a respect for their ethnic traditions, rather than a fear of being different, were able to help them introduce their friends to the delights of their family's culture. Many Envoys served as cultural ambassadors by bringing friends home for a family meal, a seasonal festivity, or a special event such as a wedding.

But many parents of Envoys had to face the reality of severing their connections to the past in order for their children to move forward. This was often achieved by their going to college, which caused much anxiety and concern. Yet, because parents were committed to their children's efforts to progress, they encouraged them to do so.

Although young people were still gung-ho about doing military service, Envoy boys often looked for ways to finance their college edu-

cation rather than signing up. Envoy girls were able to take advantage
of certain areas of school, such as sports and science, that prior to the
1940s and 1950s had often been closed to women. More important,
Envoy men and women were able to pursue higher education or find
a job just out of high school more easily than previous cohorts. More
Envoys chose higher education than many of their peers because of
their personal conviction that their responsibility for themselves and
their families included making the most of educational opportunities.

Many Envoy women reveled in college education, which was
booming after the war. But they also had anxiety over their own priorities and the pressures from family and competing peers. Envoys were
always torn between having fun and being businesslike in school.
Their sense of duty usually won out. Competition came mainly from
returning GIs. This sometimes created problems in getting into
classes, but once admitted, students were serious and focused on
achievement, just the environment Envoys understood.

Many Envoy women, however, did not finish school, at least not
immediately. Caught up in the emotional fervor of the times, they, as
others, were ready to give up their personal objectives to have children. Many felt they were making up for those who had died in the
war, as well as making up for lost time. Envoy men were less likely
to marry early on in school, but typically married in their last year,
having met their "intended" through friends or family.

Envoys were among the new generation of workers who joined the
booming larger corporations. For their families, this meant migration
to wherever the company needed them. Some Envoy wives of older,
returning GIs settled down in their own hometowns after husbands'
tours of duty at various military bases were over.

Envoy women who were more comfortable accepting their parents'
ethnicity, and perhaps more religious, dedicated themselves to having
children and caring for their parents. This was an unexpected delight
for Envoy parents, who feared losing their daughters to a new city or
town.

For some Envoy women, education was deferred while they raised
their children, but many were later able to pursue training and higher
education, and careers. Others started working early on to enhance
family income. In most cases women worked off and on during the
child-rearing years, extending their working hours as their children
grew up.

Envoy men who stayed near their hometowns often trained locally
for professions such as management, insurance, and banking. Those
who went away to school often returned home and worked as accoun-

tants, doctors, lawyers, engineers, and chemists, reestablishing their contacts with family and family traditions. Today Envoys are actively involved in their communities, assuming more active roles in local business and government.

Bootstrappers

The 1930s produced many men and women who were expatriates of their economic class of origin—the Bootstrappers. What distinguishes Bootstrappers from their families and peers is that they chose to lead a life different from what came before them. Typically they have become accountants, psychologists, scientists, engineers, and bankers. Bootstrappers saw opportunities, and, with a tenacity not often visible to outsiders, plugged away, and achieved their goals.

Bootstrappers were not constrained by either the moral or the class context in which they were raised. Typically born to large families neither rich nor poor, they had parents who were hard-working. Their mothers were caretakers and nurturers, busy caring for many children. Fathers were laborers or professionals. Neither parent had extensive education; formal education was not necessarily required for a professional career.

Taking care of a large family led the parents to pay less attention to the individual child. Discipline was less a personal or moral matter than a practical one of managing the household. While their parents were caring and well-meaning, they were not able, or willing, to provide direction for their children, or at least not the younger children. Left to their own devices, Bootstrappers looked around for other models, but didn't always find them, although older siblings often provided solutions for daily problems.

Bootstrappers saw education as a nuisance, and often were not good students, although they were typically smart intuitively. In fact, surviving in a large household of four or more children gave many Bootstrappers a sense of family politics and group dynamics. They learned early on about how to avoid getting picked on by bigger brothers and neighbors and how to establish alliances with other brothers and sisters to get what they needed. Later they were able to translate these techniques into school and life skills.

Many Bootstrappers grew up with a low sense of anxiety about their status in life. As part of a large family, there were fewer pressures directed specifically at them. The Bootstrapper rarely blames his or her parents, and remembers them as not close, but loving nonetheless. Brothers and sisters, on the other hand, play a particularly important role, as guides, friends, allies, and burdens. Those who had less education ran into problems, both emotional and financial—the "troubled younger brother," for example.

Bootstrappers learned by observing and by keeping their own feelings inside. They may have read books under the bed covers by flashlight at night, or frequented places where interesting events were under way, such as a racetrack or factory. Their curiosity was comfortable for them, and they were not embarrassed by it.

Bootstrappers were never intimidated by large institutions, nor were they scared of authority. They were often externally calm and fearless (while shaking inside) in comparison to their schoolmates. While they had no strong motivation to rebel, they sometimes would align themselves with those who were more rebellious, but not as leaders. They were able to hide within a group, and be cagey about working out survival strategies to advance their own cause from within. Most Bootstrappers just went along with the crowd, not so much as followers as tacticians, learning the ropes of their immediate world and then pulling them.

Bootstrappers are not concerned with titles and symbols as much as they are with feeling comfortable with who they are and what they are doing. They are inner-directed, need-driven, and work (and smoke and drink) hard. Typically, they are their own harshest critics. Bootstrappers, unlike many of their peers, did not have to contend with external pressures or guilt, nor were they easily indoctrinated into accepting or assuming the ways of their parents, since their parents were distant emotionally and not directly involved with their children's lives. Bootstrappers are individualists whose feelings about themselves derive from their own internal values and sense of integrity. Pragmatic but also upwardly mobile, doggedly tenacious, they work very hard—almost to their physical detriment (e.g., stress-related diseases). They are more likely to shape, and be shaped by, the world around them in order to create comfortable solutions.

Many Bootstrappers had to work as youngsters, since they came from homes of modest means. They were ready to take on paper routes as soon as they could ride a bike, and were conscious of the importance of money as a determinant of who gets what in life. Having come from a large family where resources were scarce or unreliable, Bootstrappers were eager to give themselves what others could, or would, not.

Some Bootstrappers dropped out of high school because it did not seem relevant. They were often tough enough to make it by dint of skill and determination, whether in sales or amateur boxing. Others finished high school with mediocre grades, and tried to get into the military so they could get the GI bill benefits afterward. Bootstrappers are very goal-oriented, and willing to do whatever it takes to achieve their objectives.

Bootstrapper women worked as store clerks and YMCA instructors, volunteered as children, and later pursued occupations and professions with management responsibilities; trained as pharmacists, doctors and insurance managers, they were fairly conventional once married. They dropped out of the work force to raise children or follow their husbands' careers, even if they had a profession of higher standing. However, they often returned to their career, or a new version of it, after the children were grown.

Many Bootstrapper men joined the military in the early 1950s to give themselves time to figure out what they would do with their lives. Most had little direction when they entered and might have worked as cooks or administrators. Those who were more aggressive might have made the transition to college after. There they would develop more generally, enjoying school in the usual way. Many of these went on for professional degrees. Others used college to get a sense of business opportunities. Many Bootstrappers viewed the mid-1950s as a time when a man did not have to worry about a career, only about working, since many jobs were available.

Bootstrappers started their families in the early 1950s, usually after whirlwind romances. They were the ones who moved away from the neighborhoods they were raised in and never wanted to go back. At some point they may have broken with their parents, who did not understand their desire to move upward and outward. However, Bootstrappers did not necessarily reject their family's roots and may have settled in a better neighborhood near where they were raised, or in nearby suburbs.

Bootstrappers do not forget their humble beginnings and are not vain about their achievements. They often have a solid appreciation of what their family's meager beginnings provided. Easygoing, they were not hostile to the booming middle-class world but adopted the comfort amenities it had to offer, such as televisions, cars, and vacations. Thus they raised their children in a very different environment from the one they had emerged from.

No matter what their achievements in life, a Bootstrapper can often be identified by the incongruity between his or her mannerisms and professional status. They do not try to rid themselves of such traits, but often use the incongruity as a tool—to put people off, amuse or confuse them, even entice them. They may have a strong accent and use a lot of slang. Bootstrapper men might lean toward hard drinking, rough language, off-color jokes, and sexist attitudes toward women.

Bootstrapper women have only a slightly different approach to how they represent their beginnings to the rest of the world. Many Bootstrapper women struggled harder to hide their past during their careers, since women are less likely to be given credit for pulling themselves up by their own "bootstraps." Instead, they had to blend in more. Women who stood out were often pushed back or overlooked because they were competing with supervisors or husbands who were vigorously pursuing their own careers. As a result, many Bootstrapper women either did not marry or started their careers much later, often when their children were well along in school.

The 1960s were not a difficult time for a Bootstrapper man. He was not struggling with careers and relations with employers the way the Romantic-Realist was. His easygoing personality made it possible to view work as a necessary evil. He sat back, did his job, and enjoyed his life. Essentially pragmatic and self-centered, he knew when he had to put himself on the line and be counted by working hard to deliver a new concept, design, or deal. When this resulted in a major conflict, such as loss of a job, he didn't anguish over the change, but cleaned off his desk and moved on.

Bootstrappers have deep feelings and a stubborn streak of self-preservation which they often keep buried under a calm and mellow demeanor. Their early life experiences did not provide them with well-developed intimacy skills; although they have a strong desire to be loved, and to reciprocate love, they have also been trained to avoid conflict and stress. When wives of Bootstrapper men complain that they are insensitive, they choose divorce instead of working toward resolving marital conflict. They may let relationships slip away because they cannot overcome the burden of emotional distance. For some Bootstrappers, this distant and relaxed style makes them appealing, particularly as managers. They are able to handle office and institutional issues with a friendly, businesslike candor that is often disarming.

Bootstrappers are more likely to contemplate and plan for early retirement than others of the Bridge Generation. Initially, Bootstrappers are likely to react to their retirement like other life style shifts, without too much anguish or introspective thinking. Bootstrappers have little direction, unlike Good Old Boys and Gals, who think about and look forward to retirement, or Romantic-Realists who are committed to working and furthering their careers as long as possible, or Envoys who are anxious to stay on as long as they can to fulfill family obligations. They may continue to work if convenient. However, many may find retirement brings new challenges. They may need to reappraise their style, but find it difficult to learn new ways to express themselves. Their low-key manner may have left a residue of pent-up feelings that have not been expressed through work or family relationships and may cause some difficulties.

THE GAP GENERATION:
1940–1949

Those born in the 1940s were to mature during a peculiarly ambiguous time in American history. It was a period of major conflict and contradictions in American values, one the Gap Generation was to help shape, and in turn be shaped by, in a profound way. Although many, perhaps most, were born post-1946 (the start of the Baby Boom), we cannot call them Baby Boomers, since their upbringing was significantly different from that of their younger siblings, the true Baby Boomers, born in the 1950s. The Gap Generation were, for the most part, the children of a generation of parents who had lived through both the Great Depression and World War II. Overall, this cohort was larger than the previous one, but smaller than the Baby Boomers.

Members of the Gap Generation bridge the two halves of the 20th century, much like a baby delivered by two doctors—a kindly old country doctor on the one hand and Dr. Strangelove on the other. Today, as this group reaches their early 40s and 50s, they are the subject of much attention. The values they express as they go through their Rites of Passage, particularly about aging, will, because they carry with them new views of American social roles, signal a turning point in American social structure.

IMMERSION

The Gap Generation was the last generation to be born mainly in cities and small towns; the cohorts that followed them were mostly suburban. Gap babies from the first half of the decade were wartime babies, living on their father's military allotment checks plus whatever their mother could make working at a war plant, waiting on tables, or filling in for a drafted office worker. Gap babies from the last half of the decade often spent their first few months sleeping in bureau drawers in tiny campus apartments while Daddy tried to study to get into college on the GI bill. They often led improvised lives in their early years—impromptu day care, makeshift father substitutes. Baby was handed off from Mother on her way to work to Daddy on his way back from chem lab, like a baton in a relay race. Even children whose fathers didn't use the GI bill for education had similar infancies— mother and child living with Dad's folks while he was overseas, say, then moving into practically anything when he came back, just to be on their own. That may be one reason why the concept of "owning a home" tends to be so important to this group.

The Gap Generation knew their neighborhoods and felt safe there. Neighborhoods were self-contained, with small grocery stores, candy stores, hardware stores, laundries, and Laundromats. Although middle-class homes had their own washing machines, children growing up in cities remember the sight of billowing sheets on laundry lines stretched across tenement courtyards. Children went unescorted to playgrounds and made their own rules about fairness on the jungle gym, seesaws, and swings. New communities in the 1940s were built with children in mind.

Urban neighborhoods were still ethnic enclaves. Eventually, those who could moved to less densely packed communities, with trees and small houses. Not all of these were suburbs; some were planned communities developed by insurance companies, such as Parkchester, New York, built by Metropolitan Life Insurance. Many had duplexes and small brownstones for families who had known only crowded apartments. Living with a larger, extended family became less common.

Many of the communities were in the midst of other changes. New expressways were blasted through old neighborhoods, cutting off circulation and causing sections of cities to deteriorate. A concrete swath through the Bronx, for example, made it difficult for some children to get to a favorite park or library.

More people had cars, but street life in the cities remained vibrant. There was little air conditioning, so on hot nights city families might still sit out on stoops; children would splash in the water from opened fire hydrants. In the towns and suburbs, however, people sat out in their backyards and visited over the back fence. With so many cars, people felt funny about sitting out on the front porch and being looked at by strangers. Nobody strolled past on summer evenings anymore, stopping to talk a moment—they even drove to the drugstore for their ice-cream cones. Neighborhood organizations were strong; most neighborhoods had churches, and Catholic neighborhoods usually had a church school.

The Gap Generation walked to school, unless they lived on a farm. As their growing numbers reached school age, schools began to expand—not just new teachers and classrooms, but new types of classes as well. The practice of streaming—shunting the slower students to another track—spread to more school districts. Junior high schools spread throughout the country because they solved three problems at once: they kept nearby schools for younger children; increased the number of slots for principal, vice-principal, and guidance counselor; and isolated those afflicted by puberty.

Few children went to racially mixed schools because few neighborhoods were racially mixed. Some city schools had mostly European immigrants, others mostly blacks, whose families had moved north to work in factories. Schools in bedroom communities had mostly white students whose parents were native born. Parent Teacher Associations were active everywhere, but rarely strident.

Children born in the 1940s grew up with fewer toys than those born later. They played Buck Rogers, flying spaceships with consoles of cardboard boxes and old radio tubes. They played war in the few vacant lots that weren't built on and made intricate systems of roads for toy cars from Woolworth's. Girls played jump rope and hopscotch with a potsie; boys played stickball or sandlot ball. Both longed to wear Keds or Spalding saddle shoes (white with a brown mid-section) like the big kids, but most still had to wear slippery leather-soled shoes—"better for your feet, dear."

In the 1940s, radio was the family's main entertainment. Children learned the lyrics of the popular songs; families would try to guess the right answers along with the game show contestants; there were morning and evening newspapers, but few families got both. Mother might belong to a lending library, but her children read comic books about Superman and Wonderwoman. City children were sent to camp during the summer. The camps, organized by churches, political parties, and social organizations, emphasized brotherhood, an important theme in the 1940s. Private camps emphasized nature or sports.

Sports grew in importance during the war and postwar eras. Professional baseball was practically a religion. The Yankees—Joe DiMaggio, Yogi Berra, Phil Rizzuto—were like gods. Children went to ballgames with their parents and boys sent their baseballs to be signed by the players. Going to the game, eating a hot dog and a soda, buying a pennant and a cap, were all rituals. Boys, especially, lived and breathed and dreamed sports.

Television's impact was immediate, hypnotic, and widespread, yet those of the Gap Generation who were older often were less attracted to television than their younger siblings. Children watched film serials such as *Buck Rogers*, *Captain Video*, and *Rocky Jones and the Space Cadets*, as well as "The Milton Berle Show," "Your Show of Shows," and "The Children's Hour." Talent shows for children were popular.

Movies were also popular. Parents took their children to the big downtown movie palaces to see Walt Disney movies such as *Dumbo*, *Fantasia*, and *Pinocchio*, but older brothers and sisters dragged them along to the neighborhood theater on Saturday to see the latest Roy Rogers cowboy movie or a war movie (*Thirty Seconds Over Tokyo*, or anything about submarines or the RAF), even though the neighborhood movie house was getting seedy and was strongly suspected of harboring fleas. During the summer, families might go to the brand-new drive-in movie and bed the kids down in the back seat.

Health care was changing. The kindly doctor who sat beside your bed at home and visited you twice a day until you passed the crisis and your fever broke was replaced by the busy specialist in his office who gave you a shot of penicillin that stopped the fever and bypassed the crisis altogether—but who never quite gave you the same feeling of having been cared for. Because the war mixed so many populations within the United States that had rarely met before, and because it was all right to worry about health but unpatriotic to worry about the strangeness of strangers, there was a strong fear of epidemics and contagion during the 1940s. Polio haunted public swimming pools with images of children in iron lungs who, if they lived, would never walk again.

The parents of the Gap Generation, many of whom fought in World War II, presented their children, quite unintentionally, with a potful of moral dilemmas. They taught them that cheating was wrong, then told anecdotes about getting around rationing by buying black market beef or gasoline. They said gambling was wrong but joined in the office football or baseball pool, bought Irish Sweepstakes tickets, and bragged about how much Grandma won at bingo.

Thus the Gap Generation lacked clear moral guideposts, as well as agreed-on rites of passage into adulthood. The suburbs, where many of them spent their teenage years, mixed cultures, so that families who didn't believe in Hell lived next to families who did; getting along and being nice mattered, which meant don't call your neighbor a bigot when he tells a bigoted joke; the age for leaving school and getting your driver's license, which had been 14, was now 16 in most states, but you still couldn't buy a car on a time payment contract until you were 21. A boy could own a rifle at the same age his father had, but had nowhere to hunt. The adult activities that were available to young people were smoking, drinking, and Not Quite Making Out.

In 1954, when the Gap Generation were entering their teenage years, the Supreme Court decided, in *Brown vs. the Board of Education*, that racially segregated education was inherently unequal and set off the civil rights movement. Also in that year, the hydrogen bomb, the one that could end the world, was tested successfully; the French lost their Indochinese colonies when they were defeated at Dien Bien Phu in what is now Vietnam; and the excesses of Senator McCarthy finally brought an end to the witchhunt against communists, socialists, and "communist sympathizers." Also in that year, a rock and roll record finally hit the Cash Box top 10 list.

Young people need to belong, to be part of their group. For the Gap Generation, to belong might mean being with people who believed in civil rights or who outlawed the atomic bomb the way you did, or it might mean being with people who wore the same clothes you did, knew the same music, and used the same slang.

Their parents, who had worked so hard to make "what we were fighting for" real, found these young people who talked about hypocrisy and were ready to overturn the social order incomprehensible. How could they listen to salacious rock and roll instead of nice, cleancut singers? It was one thing to cheer on Martin Luther King, Jr. in the Montgomery, Alabama, bus boycott, but to join in registering black voters was just asking for trouble. How could a young man refuse to get a neat haircut or say "under God" in the Pledge of Allegiance? The changes seemed to be coming too fast: the Egyptians taking over the Suez Canal, the Cubans throwing out the corrupt old order and installing Castro, the Algerians assassinating their French masters (and being brutally suppressed by the Foreign Legion), the Beatniks talking about corruption that could be dealt with only by withdrawing, and Elvis wiggling in that way.

DIVERSION: THE ADOLESCENT EXPERIENCE IN THE 1950S

Adolescence for the Gap Generation coincided with some major transitions in American culture. At the beginning of the decade, children and adults shared the same sources of music, such as musicals and post–big band music. Big band singers—Frank Sinatra, Doris Day, Jo Stafford, Margaret Whiting—were making their own records now, signaling a broadening of popular music. Then Bill Haley and the Comets recorded "Rock Around the Clock" and suddenly teenagers had their own music. Rock and roll, initially politically neutral, was what really bound this cohort together.

For boys, ducktail haircuts with a curl at the back were popular; crew cuts and butches were abandoned for more sculptured hair styles. Wartime functional clothing became fashionable. Tough kids wore imitations of leather flight jackets, turned-up collars, and garrison belts (black leather with big silver buckles, used in fighting).

For the first time, adolescents did not entirely identify with their parents and other adults. For some, the advent of the atomic bomb created the possibility that there might not be a future to grow up for. The war in Korea and the cold war added to an eerie undercurrent of anxiety and rebellion, as people began to question U.S. foreign policy. The Korean War was not the "good fight" that World War II had been, and people were less comfortable with unbridled patriotism. After World War II, few seriously injured soldiers had survived to rejoin society. During the Korean War, mortality was reduced by improvements in medical technology. Disabled veterans were more visible.

Rules that guided social relations were beginning to change, too. The big brother who had come back from the war told, taught, and encouraged his younger brother about sex. Kids knew that sex was a reality. Although there was still pressure on girls to remain virgins until marriage, some people had sex in cars, and others, without cars, petted at the movies, at the beach, or in the alley or garage, or while baby-sitting.

Science became a new and more fundamental aspect of postwar life. More science courses, as well as physics and calculus, were offered in school. Time was suddenly a major concern for teenagers. A growing sense of uncertainty about the future made teenagers feel they had to live life in a hurry. They took shortcuts: they married young, took jobs quickly to earn a good living, spent fewer years in school, and earned practical degrees.

Unlike the Bridge Generation, the Gap Generation was not ignorant, for the most part, about the realities of American failures. They knew about racism in Little Rock and Birmingham. Some participated in civil rights marches. Folk singers, labor leaders, bohemians, and beatniks took their place in the exotic panoply of youth culture.

Teens who were not part of the mainstream culture generated a culture of their own. Their rebellion was more symbolic than real, however, reflected in clothing, hair styles, music, slang, and fast cars. It was also secretive, and anti-adult (hence the term "generation gap" was coined)—a true social movement. The Bridge Generation had provided the icons and the music with James Dean and Elvis Presley, but it was the Gap Generation that provided the energy and mass. For the first time in history there was a shared culture for and by young people. Originally centered around adolescence, that sense of being different, alienated from the previous culture, would create dramatic conflict for teenagers moving into early adulthood.

Young people, however, appeared to be indifferent to the issues of the day, such as the House Committee on Un-American Activities, political corruption, and the cold war. Older teens seemed concerned only with rock and roll, dates, dances, and a variety of other group-centered activities such as car racing, cruising, slumber parties, playing ball, and just hanging out. However, teenagers were not so much indifferent as they were "confused," a word that gained popularity during this time. Still, indifference and callowness were rampant. For the first time in a long time, the causes that had framed people's lives for so long—the depression, the war, reconstruction—were gone.

America's confidence in its superiority was seriously shaken. Allen Ginsberg's poem *Howl* and Jack Kerouac's book *On the Road* titillated the middle class with a picture of bohemians who deliberately chose to remain outside the mainstream, despite its allure of affluence. Norman Mailer, drawing analogies between culturally dissident whites and insurgent blacks, wrote, rather confusedly, of the "white Negro." There was a wave of panic in 1957 when the communists launched a space satellite called Sputnik, far ahead of the Americans. The quality of American education, and science education in particular, became a topic of urgent discussion. The recession in 1958 and the lengthy steel industry strike in 1959 also diminished the nation's self-confidence. By 1959 world tensions were so strong that the government actively promoted civilian preparation for a nuclear apocalypse in the form of backyard fallout shelters.

EXPANSION—EARLY ADULTHOOD IN THE 1960S

By 1960, there was a spreading sense of unease that America had for a decade only been marking time, getting fat, and falling behind. Liberal intellectuals like John Kenneth Galbraith had pointed out features of the system that could be reformed. Now there were the first stirrings of fundamental political dissension. In many respects the early

1960s were like the late 1950s, only intensified, and in 1961 there was a recession, as there had been in 1958.

In the fall of 1959, *Studies on the Left*, one of the first journals of what would be called the New Left, began publication. Paul Goodman's book, *Growing Up Absurd*, published in 1960, summed up the 1950s and predicted much of what the 1960s would bring.

Whereas Galbraith's criticisms had been relatively mild, Goodman's were searing. Where Galbraith had seen a mistaken misdirection of certain resources, Goodman saw waste of human lives and energies on a large scale. Galbraith had suggested reforms; Goodman called for total transformation. Galbraith had called public management of resources and the environment poorly planned; Goodman declared it radically alienating.

Goodman contended that society denied young people, struggling to grow up, a sense of usefulness and personal dignity. He argued that it had become less usual to adapt "the organized society" to human needs than to do the reverse, and that this procrustean approach to problems did special harm to those still in the process of becoming part of society. He was also one of the first to see that as the poor became relatively fewer, they were becoming more and more firmly caught in their poverty. In fact, he argued that even as the majority became securely entrenched in the middle, America was for the first time developing a rigid class system that would paralyze those at the bottom.

Goodman also saw the educational system as failing to transmit the culture, both humanistic and scientific, that modern Americans had inherited. Partly because of the trend toward the purely "practical and applied" in education (e.g., emphasis on that which is functional or useful), partly because of panic over Sputnik and "defense," some experts were urging that high schools divert all but a small, "academically talented" minority into vocational education. Goodman protested that this not only contributed to class rigidity but also betrayed the very purpose of education.

Goodman insisted that those who did not fit into the organized system, especially "juvenile delinquents" and the Beat Generation, were outsiders because the system had made them so. He did not, however, endorse their methods of rebellion. He saw delinquents as fatalistic and self-destructive, and beatniks as excessively resigned, passive, and even childishly conformist in their attitudes. Finally, he lamented how difficult it was, as he himself had found out, to make any serious criticism of the status quo through the mass media.

Although the majority did not necessarily share Goodman's views, they sensed that new directions were needed. It was no longer enough to be a comfortable, well-fed part of the system. John F. Kennedy most successfully exploited these new yearnings. Kennedy, in his early 40s, looked young for his age. He was handsome, had an attractive, fashionable wife and good-looking young children, and as a family man appealed to Baby Boom parents. For the Gap Generation, who especially lacked leaders and causes, Kennedy, portrayed as a war hero, provided a voice of moral strength and direction. The Gap Generation were Kennedy's major supporters. Youthful and confident, he was the avatar of rediscovered values that were perceived as lacking in society.

Kennedy's campaign speeches spoke of "new frontiers"; he vigorously endorsed that outstanding symbol of challenge and adventure, the manned space program. He projected an image of youth, vigor, and competence in his television debates with Vice-President Nixon. Nixon, who was only a few years older, looked graceless and middle-aged by comparison. Nixon had used television to gain voter sympathy in 1952, but now style was more important. Voters did not want someone out of the Eisenhower era, especially someone whose wife dressed in a drab, "respectable," cloth coat.

International crises continued to escalate. There were East-West confrontations over the status of West Berlin. A summit conference was broken off after a U.S. spy plane was shot down over the Soviet Union. Diplomatic relations with Cuba worsened and finally were broken off, followed by a U.S.-sponsored, then aborted, invasion. President Kennedy committed the first U.S. ground troops to Vietnam in what was as yet only a minor involvement. A confrontation with the Soviet Union over Cuban-based missiles led to what seemed to many of us to be the brink of the long-feared atomic holocaust. More and more novels of political drama and tension appeared on best-seller lists.

In the South, the campaign for civil rights entered a new, more militant, phase—lunch counter sit-ins, Freedom Rides, mass demonstrations, the influx of civil rights workers from the North, the resurgence of the Ku Klux Klan. In 1963 a Sunday morning bombing of a black church school in Birmingham, Alabama, killed four children and shocked the racial conscience of the country. In the same year Rachel Carson's *Silent Spring* was published, waking our environmental conscience as well.

But although the early 1960s extended and escalated the mounting tensions of the late 1950s, they also transformed that anxiety into a sense of excitement and adventure. The invasion of Cuba and the commitment of troops to Vietnam indicated a new, activist, interventionist approach to world affairs, as did the establishment of the Peace Corps. There was a sense that much could be accomplished through such aggressive means.

America had survived the Cuban missile crisis, and after the wave of self-congratulation was over, a direct telephone link was set up between the White House and the Kremlin, and a treaty drawn restricting the testing of nuclear weapons. These negotiations helped to relax international tensions.

The mood became optimistic and forward-looking. The Catholic Church was liberalized by the Second Vatican Council. The Kennedy administration recognized intellect and invited Robert Frost and Pablo Casals, among others, to perform at the White House. If the Russians had a man orbiting in space a year before we did, it was not as alarming as Sputnik had been. We ignored Soviet cosmonaut Yuri Gagarin and focused on the heroism of our own John Glenn. We were on our way.

Television offered new possibilities. The first active communications satellite, launched in 1962, brought images from around the world into American living rooms and made the nation more globally conscious. President Kennedy televised his press conferences, creating a new kind of political propaganda. Leonard Bernstein conducted Young People's Concerts on television and became a new kind of effective and stylish mass educator. Westerns gradually gave way to shows like "Perry Mason" with its strong moralistic flavor, and "The Addams Family," in which it was made clear that family harmony didn't have to be the sort that appeared on "The Donna Reed Show." Television was shaping, not reflecting, the mood of the country, and things were being seen that wouldn't have been seen a decade earlier.

La Dolce Vita and other foreign films brought changes to the film industry. Directors were allowed more creative freedom and dominance. Many symbols of female glamour came from abroad, including Elizabeth Taylor (originally British), Brigitte Bardot, and Sophia Loren. Elizabeth Taylor starred in the film *Cleopatra*, which, although a box office success in 1963, never recovered its costs. Billed as a surefire high-grosser, this last of the giant spectaculars ruined its studio financially.

These were fruitful times for the Gap Generation, who were entering college in ever-increasing numbers. Never a majority, they now numbered enough to be a minority with some influence. College students helped to revive public interest in folk music—at first traditional English ballads, rural blues, and cowboy songs, interpreted by the pure voices of Joan Baez and Judy Collins, and the harmonies of the Lettermen, the Kingston Trio, and Peter, Paul, and Mary.

The British invaded in the 1960s, disguised as the Beatles, the miniskirt, the Nehru jacket, the television series "The Avengers," James Bond books and movies, the model known as Twiggy, and Carnaby Street fashions. The Brits poked fun at the status quo, including British industry, sexual taboos, and the CIA. The Beatles' song "Eleanor Rigby" wasn't about young love but about loneliness as the punishment for being too respectable. Their "Lucy in the Sky with Diamonds" was about the presumed joys of psychedelia. At the same time, we Americans began to take shots at some of the institutions we had been bragging about—mental hospitals in Ken Kesey's *One Flew Over the Cuckoo's Nest* and schools in *Up the Down Staircase*.

The Beatles arrived in America in 1964 to the tumultuous, hysterical adoration of a mass American audience that far surpassed Elvis Presley's, allowing the anxiety of adolescence to be focused and released in a therapeutic way. The youth and difference of the Beatles became a symbol and means to express longing and enthusiasm for change and vitality missing from the contemporary American culture. We needed something literally not-American to allow us to open up again, after Kennedy and despite our urban dilemmas. Accompanied by a host of other British bands—the Dave Clark Five, the Rolling Stones, the Hollies, Herman's Hermits, Freddie and the Dreamers— they stimulated a revival of domestic rock and roll. Among the new sounds that became more popular were "surf" music, typified by the Beach Boys, and Jan and Dean. The Motown sound, promoted from Detroit by Berry Gordy, brought black musicians—the Supremes, the Four Tops, Martha and the Vandellas—to a mass, white audience by repackaging rhythm-and-blues and gospel music in slick productions that whites could readily accept.

Those who were politically active did not reject the American system as such. At most they wanted to force the system to change itself. The goal of the civil rights movement, for instance, was basically a fulfillment of a vision already implicit in the Bill of Rights. When marchers confronted sheriffs in the South, they did so in confidence that they were upholding the nation's highest laws: "We hold these truths to be self-evident, that all men are created equal . . ." They were angry and militant, but not yet rebellious nor nihilistic. Except for a few black leaders such as Martin Luther King, Jr., blacks were not given a forum to speak. They were still regarded by most Americans, even liberals, as merely the object of the struggle.

The assassination of President Kennedy in 1963 is widely taken to be an important, if symbolic, dividing point in American history. Kennedy's death was traumatic for the Gap Generation, because of the intense investment they had made in him and his image. It catapulted into chaos a generation that had been trying to find its place. The underlying reality of this cultural chaos was that the Gap Generation now had proof that America and its institutions were hypocritical and pursued goals without humanity or justice. From 1963 on, with no way to regroup, many of the Gap Generation floundered. Some emulated older siblings or cousins and pursued a traditional route toward success. Others, however, suffered from a sense of alienation that had not been felt by any generation since World War I. Nightclub and college humor (Mort Sahl, Woody Allen) gave voice to their mood.

In practical terms, however, much of the promise of the Kennedy years began to be fulfilled in the mid-1960s. The new president, Lyndon Johnson, was not as glamorous or cultured as Kennedy, but he was as much an activist, and a much more skillful politician. He pushed through Congress the civil and voting rights provisions for blacks, endorsed but not effectively promoted by Kennedy. Johnson announced a "War on Poverty," not to diminish poverty but to abolish it, freeing the underclass. He spoke of building a "Great Society," where education, opportunity, and a comfortable standard of living would be available to everyone. Whether or not the "War on Poverty" was destined to be won, or the "Great Society" headed for true greatness, was not known at that time. The initiative did provide a framework within which the bitterness and fears of the time could be addressed, right or wrong.

President Johnson was to reveal another side of his activism: the Tonkin Gulf resolution committed the U.S. to a full-scale war in Vietnam. Vietnam and the aspirations of the poor, especially blacks, were two elements that would soon explode into national consciousness, further exposing the incongruity of the nation's moral stance—fighting overseas while battling in our own neighborhoods.

As political awareness and activism grew, the "talking blues," union songs, and protest songs of Woody Guthrie, Pete Seeger, and others inspired a new generation of singer-songwriters that included Bob Dylan, Phil Ochs, Tom Paxton, and Buffy St. Marie. Their songs spoke of injustice ("Now That the Buffalo Is Gone"), draft resistance ("I Ain't A-Marching Anymore"), and nuclear war ("A Hard Rain's Gonna Fall"). They performed at coffee houses on dozens of college campuses and small clubs in cities. Novels of espionage and foreign intrigue—combining international adventure, sex, technology, cleverness, and style—continued to grow in popularity. The James Bond novels by Ian Fleming, which had been favorites of Kennedy's, were later made into extremely successful movies. Spy shows were also popular on television.

Black people began to be heard, and not just in pop music. The spokesman of the Black Muslim movement, Malcolm X, called for blacks to reject white society and the restraints of nonviolence urged by Martin Luther King, Jr. Malcolm X's militancy frightened and threatened whites. After he split from the Nation of Islam to seek a more orthodox Islam and a more practical militancy, he was assassinated in 1964. In 1965, the predominantly black Watts section of Los Angeles erupted into riots. Some labeled the disturbances looting and arson; others called it rebellion and revolution.

Now white America became aware of the problems of urban blacks in the North. Black incomes had risen, but still lagged far behind the incomes of whites. In 1965, about 60 percent of nonwhite (predominantly black) families made $5000 a year, compared with 30 percent of the general population. Pervasive economic, housing, school, and social discrimination posed significant barriers to equal opportunity. A report in 1965 by Daniel Patrick Moynihan focused on the disintegration of the black family under the pressures of poverty and the distorting effects of welfare policies, and blamed this as much as poverty itself for the problems of blacks. This report was widely discussed in the news and by social advocacy groups. Many blacks resented being blamed for their own victimization and felt that the realities of economic oppression were being ignored. Meanwhile, white liberals congratulated themselves that Negroes were finally achieving equality.

Cities also suffered. Many areas were becoming ghettos, as blacks moved in from the South in a futile search for jobs and housing, and whites fled to the suburbs. In 1965 President Johnson established the Department of Housing and Urban Development to deal with some of these problems.

The black revolts that began in the mid-1960s made white Americans aware that America was a multiracial society, not one where black people were content to remain on the fringes. Bill Cosby, the hero of "I Spy," a spy-adventure series, became the first major black television star. Sidney Poitier was the top box office star of 1968. The fact that at least selected black faces and voices were reaching a mass market meant that for the first time since the 1930s, America's ideas were coming from not only a privileged intellectual elite but also an articulate underclass.

It was not only blacks who were in revolt. In 1965 students at the University of California at Berkeley demanded an end to limits on political activity on campus. What became known as the Berkeley free speech movement was the first ripple of a flood of student revolts against university policies that had previously gone unchallenged. The founders of the student protest movement were the Gap Generation, extending the activist, reformist spirit of the Kennedy and early Johnson years.

At first students believed change was possible within the system. But the resistance of universities and other institutions to demands for reform radicalized them further. Students protested restrictions on their activities, as well as university involvement (through investments, recruitment facilities, and ROTC) with big business and the military. They demanded changes in policies toward blacks and other minorities, including active recruitment of minorities and new courses and departments for the study of black and other minority cultures. Student protests had a strong intellectual component. The academic founders of the New Left, who attempted to reconstruct political radicalism after the collapse of the communist movement in America, found more and more receptive students. Neo-Marxist philosophers, such as Herbert Marcuse, were widely read and discussed.

As the troop commitment in South Vietnam escalated and the bombings of North Vietnam began, the war became the central focus of protest, particularly since college-age men risked being drafted, although there were still student deferments. For the first time since the Civil War, political resistance to the draft was widespread. The anxiety over the draft continued through 1974.

Not all forms of protest were political. Even those who weren't in college could join in the sexual revolution. Oral contraceptives, controversial since they became available in the 1950s, gained wide acceptance through their distribution in Planned Parenthood Clinics. Premarital sex, no longer hampered by the threat of pregnancy, became more acceptable; cohabitation outside of marriage became more common. Sexual and social rules were just one aspect of the conventional society that the Gap Generation had begun to question.

In the 1950s, college fraternities hosted beer parties, and getting drunk was a common initiation into adulthood. By the mid-1960s, marijuana— long familiar to blacks, musicians, and beatniks—became the recreational drug of choice. It was not only a way to adopt an aspect of black culture, it was the perfect tool for rebellion. The drug experience was antagonistic to the elaborate hierarchical structure of the "organization man" because it focused attention on the immediate, sensory experience and undermined long-range and abstract motivations. In addition, since pot was illegal, the shared sense of being an "outlaw" added to its allure. Psychedelic drugs, such as mescaline and LSD ("acid"), inspired new art forms and a new level of questioning the status quo. They also made "tuning in, turning on, and dropping out" easier.

Colorful and flashy, the practitioners and products of psychedelic culture were quickly picked up by the mass media. The "hip" became the "hippies" of the future, who grew out of the Beats—Ginsberg, Kerouac, and writings from and about the Far East—the *Tao Te Ching*, the "Zen of Archery," and even Kahlil Gibran. You could take a bus to Greenwich Village in New York or the Haight-Ashbury in San Francisco and view these strange new beings, who had long hair (with flowers in it) and dressed in bell-bottoms and tie-dyed shirts and wore sandals.

Even those who did not use drugs or did not drop out were influenced by those who did. Those with conventional life styles and ambitions became defensive. Even the top-40 pop charts featured protest music, although it was sometimes a watered-down version ("The Eve of Destruction"). The music of the Gap Generation was its preeminent Time Signature. Every year, every event had its song. These songs became the oral history of the cohort. In the early 1960s Bob Dylan, Peter, Paul, and Mary, and Joan Baez sang to their own age group. "Masters of War," "Highway 61," "Do You Mr. Jones?" "Where Have All the Flowers Gone?" set the stage for the questioning of the status quo in our own homes and political offices.

By the mid-1960s the drippy pop songs that had dominated ("Donna," "Big Girls Don't Cry") were gone. The teen years of the Gap Generation were being displaced by the British wave, and the folk artists were playing in the background. Motown music was doing better than ever.

The mid- to late 1960s witnessed the expansion of the U.S. side of the rock music scene. The Byrds, the Doors, Buffalo Springfield, Spirit, Grateful Dead, Jimi Hendrix, and Janis Joplin signaled the tumultuous pouring forth of the Gap Generation speaking to one another. The naive hysteria released by the Beatles was replaced by the maturing domestic brew of cynicism and rejection. To wit: Frank Zappa and the Mothers of Invention's *We're Only In It For the Money*, which literally turned *Sgt. Pepper's* inside out. After the cataclysmic 1968 Democratic Convention, the energy of the Gap Generation continued to pulse in frustration. By the eve of Woodstock their dialogue had reached a frenzied pitch.

Yet, it seemed that the critical mass of the Gap Generation had passed. Like moths beating their wings against a light bulb, the Woodstock generation slipped out of "mobilization" and into a new phase, one in which the fire had gone out of the group and retreated into each person's heart.

Changing attitudes among young people toward sex, drugs, politics, and life styles created a "generation gap." The Gap Generation, inspired by Kennedy's spirit of adventure, were now inspired to explore and experiment with how they lived. Some tried communal living arrangements, and rejected the materialism of the corporate culture in favor of more meaningful and satisfying occupations, such as pottery, carpentry, and candle-making. Others moved back to the land, to farms in Vermont or Oregon, casting off what they saw as the artificial, hypocritical culture of the suburbs they had so comfortably grown up in.

The struggle against hypocrisy was partly a struggle for purity and idealism; to the Gap Generation, a mixed motive was an offense. They abandoned families and schools as they would later abandon marriages, on the grounds that the relationships caused some discomfort and to persist would be hypocritical. Drugs, like Eastern religions, offered many young people the illusion that they could reach a higher, magical, reality. They quoted the industrial slogan "Better living through chemistry" and believed it; they told each other that an expanded consciousness, living in that higher magical reality, would change the world, just as putting a flower in a guardsman's rifle barrel in San Francisco would change his attitude. (The National Guardsmen occupying the Haight-Ashbury—clean-cut, short-haired, confused, and often bullying in response to the fear of "the world turned upside down"—remained as obdurate as the rest of the world.)

More and more of the Gap Generation searched for ways to define themselves as something other than what their parents were: loyal worker, patriotic citizen, obedient housewife. The older generation was shocked by the Gap Generation's rejection; they had survived a depression and world war by accepting as a necessity a comprehensive social organization in which everyone behaved, followed the rules, and worked hard without making waves. The fear of many young men that they might be sent to fight in a war the "Establishment" believed in, but they did not, intensified the antagonism.

The last half of the 1960s was a time of mounting frustration. The Vietnam War absorbed more and more of America's energy and attention, and cost more and more lives. The 1968 Tet Offensive destroyed the last hopes of a quick American military victory. Black urban revolts continued, spread, and grew more violent. In 1967, 26 people died in Newark and 43 people died in Detroit; all but nine were black.

The black and minority poor were increasingly frustrated, as antipoverty funds were diverted, first to bureaucrats and administrators, then to the war effort. The lower middle class and the more affluent working class began to feel as threatened as the poor. The steady rise in the gross national product continued as it had since World War II, but began to taper off as the war economy took its toll, with inflation that eroded hard-earned savings. Voters became more receptive to right wing politicians—such as Governor George Wallace of Alabama, a prominent opponent of integration, who blamed the country's troubles on liberals, leftists, hippies, and the now-demanding minorities.

The Democratic party and the Progressive movement were further demoralized by the assassination in 1968 of two of their potentially strongest leaders, Robert F. Kennedy and Martin Luther King, Jr. President Johnson, disheartened by the mounting opposition to his policies in Vietnam, announced that he would not run for another term. Police attacks on young protesters at the 1968 Democratic Convention in Chicago—shown live on television ("the whole world is watching")—generated negative publicity for the Democrats. Vice-President Hubert Humphrey, though popular, could not mobilize the young and progressive middle class, because of his connection to the Johnson administration. In 1968, Richard Nixon and Spiro T. Agnew, appealing to the anxious "silent majority," succeeded in recapturing the White House for the Republicans by promising restoration of law and order. After the disastrous Nixon–Kennedy debates, Nixon was extensively coached on how to present himself on television, including pancake makeup to disguise his five o'clock shadow.

Campus disturbances spread, affecting Columbia, Harvard, and nearly every major school. Hundreds of thousands gathered to demonstrate against the war and university policies. Students for a Democratic Society (SDS), the major New Left campus organization, split into factions. The demonstrations themselves took on a "carnival" atmosphere. Radical leaders such as Abbie Hoffman and Jerry Rubin thought that television should be exploited, and advocated and created media events. Elegant, poetic Eugene McCarthy attracted many Gap Generation supporters, but their rejection of mainstream politics prevented his gaining more support in the 1968 race. He, and his naive supporters, the "effete" liberals, were disdained by Spiro Agnew, the noneffete white-collar criminal. McCarthy's defeat signaled the further withdrawal and rejection of the Gap Generation.

Other aspects of the dissident youth culture became larger and more disorganized. In the summer of 1969, less than a month after an American set the first human footprint on the surface of the moon, a weekend of "peace, love, and music" in upstate New York attracted half a million young people. Although Woodstock was celebrated as the ultimate expression of a new, communal, peaceful generation, it was also condemned as a colossal mess, a weekend filled with rain, mud, spectacular traffic jams, and bad drugs.

In many ways, Woodstock heralded many changes in rock music, which soon became more decadent and less a vehicle for protest. The Beatles, after singing "All You Need Is Love," broke up acrimoniously. Bob Dylan, whose residence near Woodstock had attracted attention there initially, never appeared at the festival. Recovering from a motorcycle accident, he retreated from folk rock and intensely personal poetry to his country music roots. Abbie Hoffman, who would later try to find political significance in the "Woodstock nation," was in fact driven from the stage as a nuisance by an English rocker when he tried to take it over for an impromptu piece of political theater.

Despite the confusion that characterized it, the late 1960s witnessed a last surge of optimism. Because it had become a mass movement, many assumed that the "countercultural" or "revolutionary" trend that influenced many young people would continue to grow and flourish until it fundamentally transformed the country. Professor Charles Reich, who had witnessed the establishment of a hippie-style commune in the Yale Law School quad during one summer, was inspired to write *The Greening of America*. Reich contended that America's view of the world had been influenced by three, radically different forms of consciousness: "Consciousness III," based on community, spontaneity, and connectedness with nature, had replaced "Consciousness II," the highly structured, post–New Deal corporate welfare state, which itself had replaced "Consciousness I," the ruthlessly individualistic, pioneering, entrepreneurial spirit. Reich further contended that this change, from II to III, would cause a social revolution.

Others, such as sociologist Philip Slater, were more sensitive to the tension between communitarianism and individualism among dissident youth. Slater also saw potential contradictions between the impulse to remake society and the impulse to withdraw and create a righteous community. However, people conditioned in an affluent society to seek individual rewards could not simply be preached into abandoning them.

If the "greening of America" took place at all, it did so in isolated, middle-class, garden patches. As the decade neared its end, inflation increased, and the economy became more and more unstable. Working class and lower-middle-class people, fearing loss of economic and social status, became more and more alienated from the new and the experimental. In the 1972 presidential election they proclaimed "Nixon—now more than ever." Only the poor and minorities would retain their political militancy, perhaps less visibly or vocally.

Those of the Gap Generation who had been revolutionaries more by fashion or consciousness than by action would retain more of their individualism and desire for spontaneity than their communal spirit. Liberation would become less a political and social issue and more a personal pursuit. The "me" decade of pop psychology and narcissism, just around the corner, would prove to be a startling reversal of the altruism and social agenda of the 1960s.

CONVERSION—ADULTHOOD IN THE 1970S

The 1970s was the period of conversion for the Gap Generation, now in their late 20s and early 30s. But as such, it was unlike those of previous generations; people did not lose themselves in work but, rather, shifted focus from outside issues to themselves. In the 1960s the Gap Generation had spent a tremendous amount of energy disposing of the trappings of their parents' generation. The 1970s would be a period of identity-building for this cohort, which, in its aggressive rejection of the values of those in power, felt at a loss when it came to defining their own beliefs. Educated as much by television as by school, they turned to the media to see themselves revealed. Basking in their own reflection, catered to by the media through news that monitored their actions over the years, their rebelliousness took on proportions that made it appear to be an organized, national movement. The media had created a shared sense of identity among a generation that would otherwise have been fragmented. Many were convinced that they had to continue the rebellion they had only peripherally participated in or understood. Moral indignation and the desire for a better world were replaced, however, by the search for a better, more fulfilled self—producing a sort of hot-tub hubris.

When the Vietnam War ended and Richard Nixon resigned over Watergate, it appeared that, for the counterculture, the party was over. But the countercultural momentum of the times was strong and the party went on. In the 1970s everyone who had missed out on the 1960s gathered in discos and singles bars, the major social centers of the times.

By the early 1970s, most of the Gap Generation had graduated from college and were entering the world of work. Having now committed themselves to decisions they had postponed during the experimental 1960s, they were concerned with building careers and forming families. They had little confidence in traditional institutions, however, and so entered into an extended adolescence, which, for many, has not ended to this day. The "Human Potential Movement," which, under the guise of self-expression, gave this generation permission to indulge themselves, catered to this sense of prolonged adolescence. Like many movements, groups such as est, Scientology, Transcendental Meditation, and a host of sensitivity and encounter training groups attracted those who hadn't participated earlier. Getting rid of your hang-ups was to become the excuse for giving up existing values. Inducing values confusion was a skill aptly employed by those making a living helping others to clarify their beliefs—the new evangelists of the era. Being born again was not confined to Christianity, but became the business of gurus from India to Indiana. The plethora of self-help books produced during these years aimed at Gap Generation markets were consumed largely by older groups seeking participation in the self-discovery movement. *I'm OK, You're OK* was read by parents of Baby Boomers to better comprehend their kids. This was also true of *Born to Win*, which appealed to many Bridge and American Dream cohort members. The Gap Generation members were more interested in Jung and *The Joy of Cooking*.

This period of experimental narcissism ended when the Gap Generation, worn out, gave up trying to discover the magic cure for alienation. Instead of finding themselves, many were dazed or disillusioned. The painful confusion of this period coincided with the end of an economically stable era. Increasingly focused on career and family objectives, they found that the relatively bountiful economy had begun to recede and that inflation was increasing, until it had in fact replaced all other political issues as the center of personal concerns. People now worried more about making a living than about finding themselves.

One long-term result of the 1970s, however, was the women's movement, which brought significant changes to the lives of both men and women, and their relationships. Far greater in scope and history than any other political issue of the day, such as Vietnam or Watergate, the women's movement came into its third phase of evolution in the 1970s—the growth and acceptance of women in the economy and the beginning of a balancing of male-female social roles. Phase I had been women's suffrage, Phase II the advent of birth control and the legalization of abortion in the 1960s. Now women of the Gap Generation, in partnership with older women, broke out of the "pink-collar ghetto" to become professionals, entrepreneurs, congresswomen, and governors. Single women—unmarried or divorced—were no longer a temporary aberration. A woman's place was no longer at home, nor was her worth determined solely by her marital or parental status. In the course of gaining more education and slightly greater participation in labor markets, women were able to make new inroads in their relations with men. During the 1970s women found that their higher level of education and improved self-image caused new kinds of conflicts with men, including their Gap Generation spouses and lovers. Women found themselves breaking away from unworkable relations more often than before, and sometimes surprising themselves with their strong convictions. Men were occasionally sympathetic or understanding but still more inclined to take advantage of women's desire for greater autonomy. The film *An Unmarried Woman* attempted to portray the moral dilemma of freedom in relationships. With all the progress in public communication during the 1960s and 1970s, the work lives and personal lives of Gap Generation women would remain a "work in progress."

SUBMERSION TO REVERSION—1980 AND BEYOND

The more conventional submersion period of the Gap Generation, now in their late 30s and early 40s, was delayed by the upheaval of the 1960s and early 1970s. Their careers established, the more successful of the Gap Generation became "yuppies," a term now extended to describe upwardly mobile Baby Boomers.

The Gap Generation today is neither more nor less political than it was earlier. The more conservative views of the Gap Generation always existed, although these views were not as popular or interesting to the media as the more dramatic ones. The rise of Ronald Reagan and the Republican party suggests that much of the political fervor of the 1960s and 1970s came not from ideology but from self-interest— fear of the draft, for example. Once the Vietnam War was over, political activity lost much of its impetus. Although (contrary to popular belief) the Gap Generation was not overall any more political than other groups, they were more issues-oriented. Thus, when issues were removed, attention was shifted to other issues.

Environmental issues, for example, have sustained modest interest. Concern about the environment is part of the Gap Generation's world view. However, Gap Generation professionals have ceased to demonstrate and protest their concerns where protest would threaten job security. They prefer to write checks to local advocacy groups that will do the dirty work of cleaning up the environment (such as removing heavy metals deposited in wells by the high-tech companies the Gap Generation professionals work for).

Even the women's movement, accepted as an enduring legacy of the 1960s and 1970s, is more often passive than active. Many middle-class members of this cohort merely tolerate the activist side of the women's movement as a tired issue. Some are embarrassed to endorse or volunteer for women's organizations that remain strong advocates of wage and benefit reform in the workplace. They prefer to read articles about how to stay fit and prevent osteoporosis, or what financial packages to use, than to read about discrimination and equal pay for equal work. Increasingly, as more Gap Generation women have children, they find themselves divided over issues such as abortion, child care, and working.

Civil rights, originally a central concern of the counterculture, has become blurred in its relevance. Many believe equal rights have been attained and do not continue to think about the problems of minorities. The legacy of Vietnam is still carried like a secret scar or embarrassing disease by the Gap Generation. Today issues related to Vietnam are mere metaphors, not the intimate personal realities that this cohort shared. Friends and family may listen to the occasional war story, told by veteran friends, but for most the memories are difficult to translate into meaningful parallels in everyday life. So, the experience of those who fought and witnessed Vietnam is held like a painful dream, worsened by the absence of any way to share it with those who have only seen it in a Stanley Kubrick or Oliver Stone movie. This legacy may in future years yield a new voice from the Gap Generation that will reconcile the war and everyday life. For now, even those who were there are more often mute about the lessons learned, if any. Executives, politicians, and survivors of Vietnam vintage are only starting to be heard from; how they will speak is still not clear.

Today, as adults, the Gap Generation is reaching their stride, and bringing to their early middle age a tremendous amount of authenticity and compassion about life and living. As parents they are eager to provide their children with an environment that is more supportive and "creative" than those they had experienced. Some, having overcompensated, have transformed their children into worried overachievers, or self-conscious anorexics obsessed with appearances. It has been a bewildering time in American history, and this generation, seasoned—and perhaps scarred—by their experiences, is at last closing the gap between themselves and their parents. Having let it all hang out, they are now bringing it all back home.

BIRTHMARKS

Peter Pan and Wendy

Peter Pan and Wendy are opposite sides of the same coin. In each other's eyes, neither one will grow up. One wants to be free; the other wants an unattainable romantic hero. Both have idealized images of themselves and their lives which they strive to achieve or maintain.

Peter Pan and Wendy were raised by the Martyrs and Self-Compensators of the Dream-Deferred Generation. This generation, not so much influenced by global events, paid a great deal of attention to their families. They had fewer children, and had them later in life. Peter Pan and Wendy absorbed a sense of sentimentality—emotionalism and romanticism—from their parents. To some extent this evolved from their parents' feelings of loss and deprivation, a kind of melancholy, arising out of the difficulties of the depression and World War II. Many parents had witnessed or experienced horror and disappointment; their children were now the seeds of the future to be nourished and worshipped. Those parents who were particularly caring protected their children from many of life's harsher realities. They may have been overly protective, but at the same time they instilled in their children high standards and strong feelings about life.

Peter Pans tend to be literate and romantic. As children they had intense imaginations. They were profuse readers, and devoured everything from *Treasure Island* to Tarzan comic books. Their school years were filled with fantasies of being baseball players and war heroes. They were not emotionally close to their fathers, who were often absorbed in work and, while tolerant, were sometimes bitter and distant. They had doting mothers, however, who held up lofty goals. Peter Pans were anxious to be "regular guys"; many were the class clowns and hell-raisers; they wanted to be recognized for all the qualities their parents didn't care about, young Woody Allens in the making.

The inner seriousness of Peter Pans led them to date fewer girls and to settle more quickly with one steady girlfriend. Few had their own car, so "parking" and "necking" were limited. Peter Pans often had sexual fantasies that exceeded opportunity, and this frustration created a foundation for a lifelong ribald sense of humor. Moreover, it helped reinforce their adoption of certain forms of conduct toward women (e.g., being unfaithful) that endured throughout much of their adult lives, despite later efforts to be more sensitive to women.

Peter Pans' attitudes toward women were reinforced in their early adult experiences. College was an opportunity to experience the pleasures of adulthood; many Peter Pans, with coaching from friends, lost their virginity to prostitutes. Peter Pans subscribed to the double standard: good girls didn't do it and bad girls did—and you only married a nice girl.

Peter Pan usually went to college and was serious in his work and idealistic in his pursuits. Major anxiety crises halfway through college were inspired by the conflict between an idealistic vision of the world and what the "establishment" considered acceptable. Peter Pan's ideas were developed initially by a combination of his own readings of philosophers (all of the classic ones, including Kant, Santayana, Marx, and Sartre) and playwrights (Brecht, Ionesco, Miller, and Williams). Later he read contemporary writers (J. D. Salinger, Saul Bellow) on the ills of modern society, including those writing on race and equality (James Baldwin, Franz Fanon). Peter's self-consciousness and anxiety did not lead him to turn away from the world. Instead, an anxiety-driven need to do something caused him to make a lot of noise. He protested, went to rallies, spoke up in class—frequently alienating those who were not as interested as he in rocking the boat. Peter was the earliest of the "counterculture," but usually did not drop out; he was active in the early student protests.

Those who participated in the free speech movement in the early 1960s were not long-haired hippies. Their hair was still fairly short. They wore sweatshirts and perhaps smoked a pipe, but not with marijuana in it. Only a small minority smoked dope; some took Dexedrine to study.

By the time Peter Pan was a junior or senior in college, or out in the world, the revolution was on. Starting with Kennedy's death, life was turned upside down. Peter Pan was more likely to be a sensation seeker and experimental, particularly if it generated attention, which he loved. The civil unrest of the times was a beacon to Peter Pan, who felt discomfort within and distrust without. (Peter Pans tend to have trouble with authority, often undercutting themselves through their irreverence or hostility.)

Peter Pan yearned for something to believe in. Choices that seemed to lead down the path to a new vision of life (a socialist club, a kibbutz, an ashram, a commune) were made and abandoned. Most Peter Pans managed somehow to avoid the draft; those in college got student deferments. More likely, they applied for conscientious objector status, joined the Peace Corps or Vista, burned their draft cards, or moved to Canada. Some got married and had children; some got health or psychiatric deferrals made possible by friendly physicians and family money. Avoiding the draft set Peter Pans free to explore their lives.

Movies such as *The Return of the Secaucus 7* and *The Big Chill*—where former student radicals gather to reminisce and contrast their earlier selves with the present—and, more recently, "thirtysomething" on television, celebrate Peter Pan. But Peter Pan's middle-class roots are strong. Eventually he marries and pursues a career.

Marriages for Peter Pans, however, are often strained by immaturity. Peter Pans are products of a prolonged adolescence that may not yet be over. They have trouble being reliable and consistent. They are less able than others to consciously address and reconcile their feelings about women. Because they had attentive, doting mothers, and because they came of age when the image and role of women were changing, Peter Pans are caught between treating women according to the stereotypes of the 1950s (weak but controlling, dumb, silly, sexy), the stereotypes of the 1960s ("Girls say yes to boys who say no"), and the real women of the 1980s.

The boyishness of Peter Pans is not always a desirable trait. They may try to justify their adulterous behavior as a way to keep their marriage alive. They want to be unencumbered by sexual hang-ups and outdated societal rules, yet they are ethical in their work (refusing work assignments or deal making behind closed doors). They love their children, and will often cling strongly to those relationships.

Peter Pans are often competent professionals, although they may be perceived as eccentric and unreliable. They have helped encourage a more humanistic business approach and greater organizational flexibility. They may put their jobs on the line to take a stand on an issue. Peter Pans often just stand up and say the wrong thing at the wrong time, although they are frequently regarded as very witty and funny.

While committed to issues, Peter Pans tend to have a short attention span and a low tolerance for frustration. Not patient at working out details, Peter Pans are observant and insightful, and can contribute greatly to business and practical problem solving. However, many are unable to see how their adolescent style prevents them from fully realizing their fundamentally creative and talented potential.

Peter Pan tends to work in occupations where his personality is well tolerated. A Peter Pan with a high level of education may work as a lawyer, a civil servant in social service, or a political aide. Many Peter Pans are working as mid-level managers or salesmen in retail businesses such as apparel or automotives, where they can exert their colorful style. Very often Peter Pans need to work alone, and may run their own, usually uneven businesses, getting along, but always having a hard time.

Women, especially Wendys, often fall for the boyish charm of Peter Pans. Some women play the role of the adoring mother; some learn to stay friends, and keep a polite distance. Those who succeed in an intimate relationship with Peter Pans are those who are able to recognize and call them on their immaturities.

Wendy's early schooldays were shaped by her eagerness to make her parents happy. A good student, Wendy was sensitive about her grades and her self-image. She had a strong dialogue with herself, through her diary. Wendy derived her emotional fuel from litera-

ture—whether it was classics such as *Little Women*, which she en-
thused about on her neat, clean, and on-time book report; popular
books such as *Gone with the Wind*, or magazines such as *Seventeen*.
Books helped Wendy build her image of relationships. Wendy became
a romantic at an early age and processed her fantasies collaboratively
with other girls. They shared imaginary, dramatic, romantic adventures, and wrote cryptic entries in their diaries about this lively inner
world. She loved Nat King Cole and romantic ballads as well as musicals.

Wendys were very conscious of how other girls dressed and worked
hard to stay in tune—wearing her hair in a pony tail, like her friends,
and buying angora sweaters when they did, if she could save enough
money from baby-sitting or from gift money from relatives on birthdays. Wendy went out of her way to be pleasant to others. She was
not competitive so much as she was eager to be accepted.

For Wendy, high school was an enduring trauma of passion unful-
filled. Wendy's strong intellect and imagination, combined with her
emotional baggage, made her vulnerable to crushes. Wendy fell in
love with teachers, and with the renegade students whose mystical,
seething anger attracted passionate and maternal sympathy—usually
from afar. Wendy often claimed she was bored by "immature" boys,
and wanted boyfriends who were less obsessed with groping. Nevertheless, Wendy usually had boyfriends, and went to dances, parties,
and proms. But the eager panting of high school boys did not satisfy
Wendy's desires, intellectually or physically. She had high ideals and
passionate notions of what she wanted from life.

Never forgetting the importance of fulfilling her parents' objectives,
Wendy did well in school, and this, in turn, made Wendy's freedom
possible. She went to college—the ultimate accomplishment, since it
was associated with adulthood, mystery, "mature" men, and romance.

Wendy has been a determined person. She would not sacrifice her
education for a man. While she may have had to drop in and out of
college to support herself, she finishes. Work was never a fear for
Wendy. She wanted to work—and usually needed to—from high
school through college. She attended, in any case, the state or city
college out of financial necessity. Sometimes, she had a scholarship.

During her college years Wendy was not politically inclined, but
became aware of issues through her interests in men from her classes.
However, she had strong personal views as to what was appropriate
and would not willingly break rules. As a result, she found herself
emotionally torn when a man she liked wanted her to more actively
support student strikes that would close down school. She balked and

went along passively, helping him rather than the movement. She would type his papers and be a "gofer" for him. Later she would find issues in which she believed more fully, including women's rights. Although she has been very emotional and tended to have ferocious crushes on men, she was able to keep some semblance of balance in her life.

During college Wendy was more likely to study languages and the arts. Her aspirations were to at least be able to teach, but hopefully to find a professional occupation. Wendy was smart, but not very market-oriented. As a result she often had to struggle to find meaningful work. A likely job might have been as a secretary in a commercial graphics firm or trading company. However, with her education she was able to work her way up to become a business manager. A number of Wendys were able to finish graduate school and had a slightly easier time in obtaining a better-paying job.

Wendy took a serious interest in who she was becoming and, despite pressures to conform, explored. She often met the kind of man she had imagined—older, artistic, intense. Yet after a long and passionate relationship, she felt unhappy. Diligently, she worked on their relationship with him, sharing intense intellectual discussions about philosophy and art. They might move in together, try couples counseling, but ultimately separate.

Wendys tend to put career before family, and defer getting married longer than most of their peer group. Although they have long-lasting relationships with men, they—not always the men—put off the final commitment. A Wendy's reasons are not always known to herself. However, her anxieties that the man she has invested so much energy in maintaining a relationship with will not be right cause her to postpone choices for a long time—sometimes too long. Many Wendys remain either unmarried or waiting to marry.

Wendys when they do marry often seem to be disappointed with their choices. Somehow, they develop great expectations, and while making much ado about their realization, cannot take the pleasure they have worked long to earn.

Wendys refuse to accept anything less than their "ideal" man. They have passionate, tempestuous relationships with men who are often unobtainable—a man who is married, lives far away, is from a different culture, or is considerably older or younger. Wendy's search for the perfect partner may, in fact, be because inside she doesn't feel that she is worth being cared about. She may be afraid of being vulnerable and thus closes herself off from others for fear of painful rejection. Despite the many books about self-worth and its impacts, Wendys are a generation-specific example of this type of person. Both Peter Pans and Wendys have a hard time forming intimate relationships that last, due to the stress of trying to live up to their parents' expectations. Yet, given their character, most of their friends can't imagine why they aren't married—it is as if despite their good qualities a barrier stands between them and conventional success in relationships.

Chameleons

Chameleons are the children of the 1940s who saw the world as it was and decided to play along, doing things their way. Chameleons, men or women, have forced the outside world to accept their life style. They live life to meet their personal needs, rather than responding to the pressures of the outside world. In their lives something struck a chord early on that made them part puckish rebel, part conformist. To those who like them, they are smart and individualistic; often, but not always, with a colorful personality. To those who don't, Chameleons are irritating reminders of the past (wild days?). They appear assertive, and sometimes selfish—they always have, and still do, like to party. Ironically, it is not that Chameleons are hard to work with but that they insist on the terms being agreed to in advance.

The male Chameleon and the female Chameleon are, from the outside, very different from each other, and for good reason. The male has had a different set of rules to run with. He is perceived as aggressive or competent, albeit self-centered. The female, on the other hand, who has had to fight the world, is often portrayed by the less informed as being tough, and "feminist" (in a pejorative sense, meant to demean her femininity), when in fact she is pursuing the same personal objectives as her male counterpart.

Chameleons stick out in a crowd. They are quick to smile and scowl, and have a mischievous look in their eyes. The male Chameleon looks young and boyish, smoothing back the shock of hair hanging in his eyes. The female is mature and efficient, dressed in "power" clothes that make a no-nonsense statement.

Chameleons are practical but self-centered and often make choices that seem odd to others. However, they are willing to take responsibility for their actions, even if it makes them appear childish or stubborn.

They are also clever and savvy. When they were children they learned how to play the game. Many come from lower middle-class or working-class, but also nouveau riche families where parents were emotionally distant or had difficulty communicating with their children. As children, whether their families were well-off or not, Chameleons were exposed to the harder realities of life. Their parents taught them about reality. They didn't care so much about whether their daughters were "ladylike" or their sons "gentlemen." They expected their kids to perform.

Growing up, Chameleons soon learned to affect, if not absorb, the rules and style their parents preached. They established their autonomy early on. In school, Chameleons were conscious of whose team they were on, and where they stood in the hierarchy. They knew when they had to prove themselves. Chameleon boys were often troublemakers, even if they were nerds, although they rarely were; Chameleon girls would often hang out with the tough girls, or were loners.

Chameleons were ready to make others jump, too. Although not necessarily bullies, they alternated between assertiveness and shyness. Anger lurking below the surface went unrecognized. They were angry about their childhood, when they always had to do what was right, but weren't taken care of. Their emotionally distant parents, morally and financially pressured (or obsessed), were often quite strict with them. There were rules about bedtime, chores, and going out. You sat down to dinner on time and behaved appropriately at the table or incurred the wrath of their father. When Mother warned, "Wait until your father comes home!" she meant it. She could be severe, as well. Children who misbehaved were grounded, spanked, or whipped.

The Chameleon child wanted affection from the parents but found them generally unapproachable. For Chameleon boys, Father was always trying to run things the way things were in *his* parents' time, with a firm hand. For Chameleon girls, Father seemed distant and indifferent. Their mothers were often preoccupied with coping with the myriad duties of the household.

For Chameleons, friends were a bastion of independence from the family. The need for outside allies led Chameleons to spend more time out of the house with buddies and girlfriends, often not one or two, but many, in a large group. Chameleon girls were often would-be tomboys. They were take-charge kids, often more sexually experimental than boys.

Chameleons knew they had to protect and nurture their own independence, an awareness fostered not only by their parents' lack of funds but specifically by the sense that earning money was the responsible thing to do. It was also the only way to get a tangible reward since their parents didn't really care about them (whatever was given was offered grudgingly, or as an afterthought); as a result, the Chameleon's sense of self-worth was impaired. However, they did believe in themselves, and fought to prove it, primarily through external actions that often made them appear materialistic and selfish. Over the years, such pursuits would eventually prove unsatisfying, because they did not fulfill what had been missing in the early years.

In order to earn the money to free themselves and reward themselves, Chameleons baby-sat, did odd jobs, took summer jobs as soon as they were able, and saved their money. Occasionally they would impulsively spend all their money on themselves—out of need, desire, and anger at their parents and the world.

In high school, Chameleon men sometimes belonged to the wild crowd, the ones with the leather jackets and hot rods, or perhaps the surfer crowd. Even if straightened up late in life, they fondly remember playing hookey, stealing or racing cars, and getting into fights. For some, belonging to an outsider group was fun, a chance to get away from the stifling propriety of the family. Years later, solidly established in careers, some Chameleons still show some of that same cockiness but are more often nostalgic about the past.

Chameleon men, whether or not highly visible in their rebellion, developed a tight circle of friends in high school, some of whom they remain close to today. Chameleon women, however, are more likely to separate themselves from their high school days and form new circles of friends away from home. Many graduated from high school not yet focused on their future. Chameleon women came into their own as they began to recognize the power they had to create and build a career. They were among the earliest of this wave of feminists.

Being in the military, and in Vietnam in particular, intensified the personality of the Chameleon male, most of whom enlisted to avoid being drafted. Having spent so much time adapting to the anonymous yet highly authoritarian environment of the war amplified the skills of the Chameleon, but it also strengthened his determination to make his (or her) own way in life. Chameleons wasted no time in returning to civilian life. In fact, as with their predecessors who had fought in World War II, war experiences energized them. Rather than a sense of urgency or entitlement, they came home with feelings of distrust and cynicism. But instead of complaining, which they had learned early in life was futile, they set about getting an education, going to work, and starting a family.

Chameleon women wrestled with a different set of issues. At least half went to college, where they learned how to translate their rebellion into more self-serving investments. They were fairly aggressive in school and performed well. Those who decided to get married and settle down often felt that marriage was only one option. They raised their children, but itched to get out as soon as they could, back to school, back to work. Many became the entrepreneurs, particularly in technology, of the 1970s and 1980s. Although they were often naive, it was this lack of sophistication and abundance of (post-counterculture) gung-ho spirit that enabled them, in many cases, to succeed.

They were also the first group of career women to make their way up from the bottom, often sacrificing traditional values like home and family to "play hardball" with the men in the business and professional worlds.

By the 1970s, Chameleon career women were making great strides. Reflecting their parents' harsh, businesslike manner, Chameleon women wanted it clear that their success was due to their skills and experience, not preferential treatment as women. Chameleon women want to be treated as "one of the guys." Although supportive of the women's movement in spirit, they feared the stigma attached to it, and resisted identifying with it personally. Often they were not necessarily sympathetic to sisters who complained about sexual discrimination.

Ultimately, dislike of the system makes Chameleons use it to their own ends. They want freedom from supervision and the moralization of others; unlike many of their peers, they do not expect to cure the world's ills or create new corporate life styles. They are entrepreneurs.

Chameleons are, from their own experiences as former rebels, careful about judging one another. Their strategy has always been to be smart, work smart, and make people accept them on their own terms. If they do not fit in naturally, they squeeze in.

The greatest challenge is in personal relationships. Many Chameleons married early, as did many others of their cohort, because they wanted the affection and attention they could not get at home. If they had a high school sweetheart, they kept their promise to marry. Once married, Chameleons try to not be like their parents. They work hard at doing everything differently, but sometimes overcompensate for their parents' failures. If their parents were tough and disciplinarian, they are affectionate and loose. If their parents failed to pay attention to their inner needs, they give their children considerable latitude. By overcompensating, they create the same distance between themselves and their children that they experienced with their own parents.

Because most Chameleons, rejecting their past, stick to their marriages out of duty, many spouses go through difficult times balancing their respective needs. Chameleon women are often rebelling against a constraining marriage; at the same time, difficulties often give her impetus to seek her own path. For example, she may gain work experience by supporting the family while her husband goes to school. Many Chameleon women have not married, and are very cautious concerning men who cannot cope with an independent woman. These women are part of the growing single adult population. They own or rent apartments and are realistic about their prospects of finding a good match. They know that they can live without a husband.

Chameleons are true to both themselves and those they have made alliances with. They may hold to their own priorities, but they deal fairly with others. They are indulgent (male) or workaholics (women), sensation-seeking, and gregarious, propelled by a great simmering anger inside.

Questors

Questors fit many of the stereotypes of the Gap Generation. They've never found a satisfactory social niche and perpetually scan the horizon for the arrival of the Aquarian Age. They have "human growth" experiences; they quit their jobs because work is too oppressive; they break up because they can't give each other enough "space." Questors are into est, Hare Krishna, born-again religion, psychic channeling, tantric yoga, and Zen Buddhism. They believe in synergy, and higher levels of energy and consciousness. Despite their eager search for meaning, they lack a sense of emotional continuity with the world.

Sometimes they convince themselves that they have transcended, but they know they have not really broken any new ground and often get depressed. They can't deal with the intensity of their own (and others') feelings.

Questors work hard to change; they embrace external solutions to life's problems. These solutions are typically larger than the individual (communes, movements), and often beyond the individual's control. Questors were not the casual participants in the counterculture who wore long hair, enjoyed sexual freedom, and then cut their hair and found a mainstream job when it was time to grow up. These relics of the 1960s still yearn to feel "centered," to "take responsibility" for what they're feeling, and to share their "space" with others. Questors tend to be gentle and self-effacing; if part of a proselytizing sect, however, they can become irritatingly didactic.

Some Questor philosophies, essentially humanistic, focus on strengthening democratic institutions; others are fatalistic and emphasize psychic or religious powers. But they all share a peculiar naivete, a lack of historical perspective, and an inadequate comprehension of the realities of business and government.

Questors are a unique product of their time, typically raised in families that were emotionally constrained, full of tensions that were not released, confronted, or resolved. As a child, the Questor, usually the oldest, perceived the unspoken tension, and perhaps an underlying problem such as alcoholism or abuse. The unpredictable, often unexpressed anger that simmered within the house frightened and confused the Questor. Since the Questor's parents insisted that nothing was wrong, or hid unpleasant truths from their children, the Questor learned to deny his or her true feelings as well. Being raised in an authoritarian, dysfunctional family (often with an alcoholic father and a co-dependent mother) left the Questor hungry for emotional nurturance. The technological world failed to provide a solid, emotional foundation for Gap Generation children; this made it hard for Questors to find solace and healing.

Questors also find it difficult to take responsibility for their feelings and actions. They want to feel good about themselves, and they want others to care for them, too. But too often they put up invisible emotional obstacles between themselves and others, and they are unable to relax and express their vulnerabilities in their relationships. These are lifelong barriers to improved feelings of well-being in future relationships. Questors tend to relate well to others who are like themselves and who also accept the inherent limits and often false pretenses of their relationships.

Questor parents were the Clock Watchers and Conservers of the Dream-Deferred Generation. Often intelligent, they thought of themselves as good parents—certainly better than their own parents, who had used physical force to lay down the law. They felt that suppressing their anger made them better parents. Thus the Questor could not establish an alliance with one parent for protection or support. Few Questors came from very religious families where the rules, albeit strict, were clearly spelled out, as was the way to redemption.

Questors, because of their fear and frustration in reading emotional messages at home, often had difficulty joining social groups, yet wanted very much to belong. They were often good students—at least very obedient. The constant need to deny their true feelings, however, often led them to compulsive behaviors, such as tormenting pets, teasing younger siblings, playing doctor with a vengeance, or engaging in violent war play with friends.

The mid-1960s counterculture movement released Questors on a trajectory of searching for answers to questions so long unanswered.

Somewhere buried in the cosmos was a parent who would love, a clarity about one's identity, and a sense of purpose. Many Questors started off on the road to "self-discovery" in the mid- to late 1960s by taking LSD and related psychotropic drugs. While "tripping," many found that the big questions of life could not be easily answered. This often led to an interest in Eastern philosophies and religions as Questors tried to cope with the profound discovery of the uncertainty of life.

The emergence of large-scale national issues of life and death, good and bad, present and future, provided a screen onto which the energy and concern of the Questor could be projected. If they went to college, they took courses in psychology, philosophy, sociology, and political science. This reassured Questors that they were not the only ones rejecting society's values and seeking a new, improved life style.

The Questors were, initially, intellectually committed people who read Fritz Perls, Abraham Maslow, R. D. Laing, Gurdjieff, and Alan Watts. The Questors also explored transcendental and affirmative poets such as Walt Whitman, who had inspired the beatniks, and the existential challenges of European postwar intellectuals such as Jean-Paul Sartre and Albert Camus. Others seized upon the visionaries of earlier times: *The Tibetan Book of the Dead*, the *I Ching*, the *Bhagavad-Gita*, and the *Lotus Sutra*.

Full of new views and old, Questors declared that they were sick of the lack of humanism in society; that they could not conceive of going to work for a corporation; that marriage was an outdated concept.

By the mid-1970s, however, Questors had started to settle into some semblance of a middle-class life style that, despite protests to the contrary, was often only marginally different from that of their parents in its trappings. Their marriages—Questors usually marry other Questors—do tend to be unusual. Emotional problems replicate the problems of the childhood home. Often present is substance abuse, which can be hidden within the Questor life style. Their relationships, typically built on the discoveries of the human potential movement, emphasize giving one another "space"—letting each other pursue their respective interests and trying to be supportive. But despite their goals, many Questor marriages seem to be filled with false pretenses and a lack of communication; many Questors have had affairs to distance themselves and feed their hunger for affection.

Authentic feelings, when they do arise, often come out in the form of self-centered justification. Questors feel they are being "refreshingly honest" when they fail to deal with a situation and just do what they want, offering no explanation. They claim they are being "mellow"; others might say they are insensitive or, in fact, uptight. By their mid- to late 40s they are often in the midst of confrontations with second marriages, career changes, and alcoholism or other substance abuse. Questors, in particular, raise their children according to their own strong values, including sending them to alternative schools. The typical home has little authority—overcompensating for their parents' own rigidity. However, Questors tend to find their own source of structure quickly and, ironically, sometimes become very parental with their passive Mom and Dad.

Entering into the labor market at a time when finding a job was relatively easy, many Questors were able to work their way up from a modest, entry-level position to a higher career position. Questors early on recognized the difficulty of finding a uniquely well suited job. Many Questors would not take jobs in industry or where the job did not reflect ethical and other life style considerations. Frequently, Questors left in search of the next, better job. After many job changes over a prolonged period of time, Questors often accepted the realities of the workplace, although they continued to support opportunities to make the workplace more humane. A few Questors became part of the growing Aquarian Age business world. They became New Age therapists, masseurs, motivation trainers, crafts makers, filmmakers and midwives.

Questors eventually found that having a career was important to them and would link their personal values to career realities. Many Questors have been able to create nonconformist careers which reflect their nonconformist values. There are a few Zen scholars who were once construction workers, homeopathic herbalists who were once accountants, and progressive, nonprofit-organization directors who came from unrelated businesses. Most, however, have settled awkwardly into the world with everyone else. They haven't given up questing: they go to therapy, spiritual courses, aikido, tai chi, and massage; they attend harmonic convergence events and are on the boards of alternative, progressive schools.

Princes and Princesses

Some of the Gap Generation were raised to be special. Valued assets to their parents, they grew up with two very unusual traits: an appreciation of the relationship between material possessions, personal position, and status in life; and an absence of empathy for the human condition. While often intelligent and creative, Princes and Princesses were, like thoroughbred animals, high-strung and had a narrow world view. Whereas Questors had families that did not communicate feelings of anger honestly, Chameleons had aggressive, anxious parents, and Peter Pans and Wendys were catered to in ways that forced them to act out their unrealistic ideals; Princes and Princesses, subjected to an exaggerated external view of their own importance, had no strong sense of their own identity.

Princes and Princesses are often, but not always, only or first-born children. Their parents may view them as ideal, a hero for the family who will achieve what they could not; not by having the child act like an adult and take care of the parents, but by holding out a vision for the child to conform to, a vision of the child as extraordinarily intelligent, gifted, beautiful, handsome, and in every way superior to other children.

Princes and Princesses are caught up in a lifelong drama, acting out the life paths mapped out for them by their parents. The compliant children proceed according to plan; the rebellious ones do exactly what their parents don't want.

The parents drive home the drama on a child who neither comprehends nor truly buys into the image that is being pushed. In other words, such children, even early on, can sense the contrast between who their parents think they are and should be, and who they really are. Since young children do not have strongly defined images of themselves, the parents' unloading of this Prince or Princess role is accepted without any conscious interpretation. "If that is who they think I am, I must be that person, I guess." But the contrast between what is and what should be creates an unusual tension that the child externalizes (acts out) or internalizes. They often do the same thing to their own children years later.

Princes often become highly internalized in their fantasy lives, trying to avoid the sugary pressure of their parents. Often, the Prince turned off the outside world to give himself some room, but frequently the inner world gets turned off as well, as the role is played out for his parents. This introverted prince was known for being absentminded and clumsy, interested in books, averse to playing with other kids, a loner with a vivid imagination. He may have looked to other images to provide an acceptable alternative to his parents, one around which he could build a personal style. He might, for example, have read about and tried to shape himself to resemble some eccentric character in literature, such as Jay Gatsby, and do what he did, dress like he did, and travel to Europe. Even so, Princes find that they are still fulfilling the role dictated to them by their parents.

The role-playing Prince took on the symbols of the parents early on and emulated the style of speech, the gestures, values, and affectations that give the appearance of subscribing to the family image. As prisoners and hostages often do, the introverted young Prince identifies with (rather than fights) his all-powerful "captors." Later, this tactic may cease to work, and the conflict between the Prince's true feelings and his image may surface, causing discomfort and unease.

Fortunately, once in school, other children and teachers provided a healthful reference point for the child. But in this generation, parents held a powerful grip on the information concerning self-image that filtered through to the child. Parents of Anglo-Saxon roots, or Eastern European roots, all were able during this time to use strong images and metaphors to communicate what the child should do and be. The child who could resist was rare, or had important allies.

For Princes and Princesses, the pressure and involvement of the parent was overwhelmingly intrusive and oppressive, without being intentionally hostile. As a result, boys were often reluctant to aggressively compete, although this was repressed by the time they reached high school. The Prince's autonomy was frequently disregarded by his parents, primarily his mother, who cleaned up his room; selected decorations, furnishings, and toys without consulting him; chose his friends and play activities; and talked "at" him, short-circuiting two-way communication. Having no say in decisions concerning himself made it clear to the Prince that who he was was not completely up to him.

Princes and Princesses were frequently subject to the edicts of authoritarian fathers, who expounded on the right path for them to follow, why "they" were not like others, and who "they" were lucky to be like. Boys coped with fathers typically by emulating them, thus avoiding their wrath and obtaining their approval. Girls coped by playing "daddy's little girl." This defensive maneuver was also expressed by rebelliousness, although the father would continue to insist that his little girl could do no wrong. In short, boys emulated and drew in, girls acted out the prescribed roles, both meant to cover up true feelings.

By high school, Princes succeeded in transforming their fears and anxieties into all-American success. Many breezed through college; the more aggressive ones were able to stand out through their activities on the speech team, business club, or student government. Some were more sports-oriented, particularly those who went to Ivy League schools.

Quite a few Princes and Princesses rebelled as they reached college or work age. There were more Princess rebels than Prince rebels, however, and their rebellion was also more visible.

For Princes, rebellion was often far more indirect. While some of the Prince's peers were dramatically romantic (Peter Pans), dramatically sensation seeking (Chameleons), or searching for meaning (Questors), Princes were far less dramatic and far more cautious and pragmatic. Princes could not get tremendous attention by drinking, experimenting with drugs, and chasing girls, partly because everyone else was doing it, too, and because the Prince could virtually do no harm, at least from his parents' standpoint.

Princes could, however, get tremendous attention from their parents by taking steps that were outside of the chosen life path—dropping out of college, quitting jobs without explanation, and marrying the wrong woman. Princes were interested in asserting themselves as individuals on the move, in the development of a career and life, not in causes, making a statement, or finding the truth. They affiliated themselves with activities that had a personal payoff, and demonstrated their rebellion against their parents and, particularly, against the generation in power (whom they held in easy contempt and used as a broader target for their anger over having been prepackaged and programmed by their parents and society).

What did they choose to do? Some did legal service work, others wrote for newspapers, some did draft counseling, or worked in the Great Society programs of the day—on civil rights, housing, or welfare reform. Eventually they abandoned this work to pursue the next steps in their professional careers. They went into business early, sometimes paired with the Chameleons among their friends; they graduated with professional degrees, and generally continued to fulfill the prime directive of their parents—still feeling an itch deep down inside that they could not scratch, no matter how they defined their jobs, relationships, homes, clothes, and food.

For Princes and Princesses alike, rebellion evolved into a personal life style, long before the "me generation" of the 1970s.

The Princess rebels generally went to college. They acted out by sleeping around, not performing well in school, and dropping out, despite feeling guilty and terrified. The Princess rebelled to establish her own identity, sometimes by getting married. This was ironic, because it fulfilled her parents' expectations. However, the choice of husband often conflicted with the hopes of her parents.

When a Princess married, she often chose a man who perhaps was like her father, even if not fulfilling her father's criterion for acceptability. In the early course of her marriage, she often found herself drawing on her own tools for solving problems—the ones she used with her own father and mother. Yet, when these behaviors were acted out in a marriage, they were often far more provocative and challenging to the husband. Very often, the Princess succeeded in either dominating her husband, and in doing so lost respect for him, or in provoking him into acting out and doing what the Princess's father had never, or rarely done—to react in anger. The end result was often the termination of her first marriage, usually fairly early on. Those marriages that survived did so because the couple was able to establish effective common ground for their personalities and their relationship.

Princes tended to marry later. Passive-aggressive in their relationships with women, they treated them with considerable respect and awe, but underneath they expected them to be controlling and overbearing like their mothers, toward whom they bore significant, hidden anger, which was often displaced onto their wives.

A Prince, like a Princess, might also try to rebel in choosing a mate. Typically, he chose a woman as different from his mother as possible—a different race, religion, or personality. The Prince's mother often did not get along with this first wife, who was politely faulted for being uninterested in the family's concerns, or for being cold and self-centered, or hotheaded and hysterical.

A Prince's first marriage started with good intentions, but often deteriorated as the wife tired of being mother, servant, or target. A first marriage would often end after a valiant, possibly lengthy (i.e., 5 to 10 years) time. If a Prince married a Wendy, however, the pairing often worked out well. Wendy, the inverse of the Princess, and the incarnation of the Prince's mother, the Queen, was more willing and eager to cater to the Prince. Conversely, Princesses often chose a Chameleon or Peter Pan, hoping in each case to discover a Prince in disguise but finding instead a prankster who violates class barriers.

As they reach their 30s and 40s Princes and Princesses frequently follow the path their parents had prepared them for all their lives, while feeling some measure of discomfort in doing so as the social messages they receive suggest they are out of touch with social realities. They are caught in a double jeopardy; on the one hand, they want to exert power and choice; on the other, they feel emotionally imprisoned by their successes. Often, in fulfilling their role, they use their position to inflict their underlying hostility toward their parents, and themselves, upon the world. Those who have children carry on the tradition—they want their children to be the best they can. Much attention and funds are lavished on their pampered and adored off-spring. While most Gap Generation parents are concerned with child nutrition, buying the best toys, and providing cultural opportunities, Princes and Princesses excel in setting a high premium on the perfect birth, and then getting their children into the right school—from infancy on—and rush around enrolling their preschoolers in swimming, gym, reading readiness, ballet, French, and other classes. Despite their anger about the pressure they experienced as children, they seem to re-create many of their parents' overzealous and intrusive interventions. Many of the children of the Prince and Princess families suffer from the pressure their parents exert on them. Fortunately, these children have greater recourse to other sources of life style and information that may help them achieve a balanced sense of their own identity.

Now in their 40s, Princes and Princesses are adaptive and aggressive in making their lives meet their own emotional priorities for family and work, fighting the overwhelming inclination to fulfill the mandates imprinted upon them as children. Competent, but not always clear about their own motives, they wield considerable clout in their own families and professional lives and will continue to do so. Surprisingly, many Princes and Princesses are able to find truer expressions of their values because of often forced emotional self-exploration following marital breakups or job changes. Their character can learn and adapt.

THE BABY BOOMERS:
1950–1959

Everyone knows about the Baby Boomers. They are the 76 million babies born between 1946 and 1964 who were to become the most noisily self-conscious group of Americans ever. In this chapter we will take a look at the central mass of Baby Boomers, those born in the decade of the 1950s. These Baby Boomers began as the Spock generation, evolved into the first TV generation, then were to pass through the Now generation, the Woodstock generation, and the Me generation. Today, somewhere between the ages of 31 and 40 they remain the largest cohort in American history, still setting trends, and still the object of an enormous amount of curiosity and analysis. They have been Davy Crockett fans and Sonny Crockett fans. Mouseketeers and Deadheads, dropouts and Daddys, women in hardhats and men in the home. They grew up in the suburbs, dropped out in the Sixties, and found themselves in California T-groups. They have been an advertiser's dream and a government's nightmare—often simultaneously.

IMMERSION

Between 1950 and 1959 just over 40.5 million children were born in America—the mainstream of the Baby Boom. By 1960 11.3 percent of the population was under five years of age, compared to 10.7 in 1950 and a mere 8.4 by 1970.

184

Their parents were the Children of the American Dream, born in the 1920s. They had struggled to provide a safe and secure place to raise their children. For the majority, this meant the suburbs. In the 1950s the suburban population increased by 80 percent.

The Baby Boomers are the first true product of the suburbs. An enormous number of them shared the suburban experience, immortalized in popular culture, particularly television ("Dennis the Menace," "Father Knows Best," "The Donna Reed Show," "Leave It to Beaver," "Lassie Come Home"). Middle-class family life was organized around the children. For many, it was an idyllic time. In fact, it often seemed that the entire society was focused on the family: new schools and playgrounds were built; new businesses flourished (diaper services, powdered formula for bottle feeding, educational toys, magazines for parents); clinics expanded their pediatric departments and drug companies put out baby aspirin and children's cough syrup. Dr. Jonas Salk conquered polio and Dr. Spock was reassuring about colic. Because few Baby Boom parents had easy access to older relatives who had raised a number of children successfully, child guidance clinics spread.

Unless Daddy was still studying on the GI bill, most middle-class mothers stayed home, as housewives and full-time mothers. (In those days, only a third of women were in the work force; by the time the Baby Boomers grew up, over half of America's women would work outside the home.) Many felt isolated or alienated in the neat, boxlike, little houses. Unlike their own mothers, these suburban housewives had no cousin or unmarried sister living with them to help out—or even to talk to during the day. Once the beds were made and the breakfast dishes done, they visited one another for coffee, gossip, and planning, until it was time to fix the children's lunch, bake cookies for the PTA, or pick up the kids from school. Altogether, they invested a significant amount of time, energy, and emotion in their children's lives and development.

Many mothers kept the kitchen radio on all day, to keep from feeling so isolated. Baby Boomers listened to the latest news from Korea, or the account of the latest nuclear test, as they picked Cheerios off their high chair trays. Elvis let them know they weren't "nothin' but a houn' dog, cryin' all th' time," and the Beatles later begged them, "Won't you please love me." And in between, they watched Mommy dabbing her eyes as Loretta Young nobly conquered one more tragic obstacle on television, or a fellow housewife became Queen for a Day.

In the suburbs, married couples had children; those who didn't were an embarrassed and embattled minority. Parents attended PTA meetings, played father-son baseball, and were den mothers. Faith in public institutions was high, and the "organization man" attitude encouraged participation in mass cooperative efforts. Still, nonvolunteer, publicly funded institutions did not fare well. Schools and libraries were often crowded, shabby, and lacked resources. There were too many Baby Boomers, and the trend in the suburbs was toward private, not public, life, and individual, not collective, success.

For many Baby Boomers, entering the overloaded and underfunded public school system was a shock. They were the beneficiaries of "active parenting," child development specialists who focused on children's creativity and need to express themselves, and at-home mothers, and were accustomed to intense and personalized attention. Their parents were always there to answer questions, praise their finger paintings, and indulge all their, even distressing, developmental modes of self-expression. School required them to behave according to strict rules, with little individual attention or positive reinforcement. Suddenly, they had to sit still, be quiet, and listen. The benign neglect and standardized treatment from teachers burdened with too many students and too little of everything else was the first clue that society might not hold them in quite the same high esteem as their parents did. It was often a confusing and alienating experience.

Although not everyone could afford a TV or a new modern, labor-saving appliance, an increasingly large proportion could. The 1960s were the decade of the "affluent society" in America: fewer Americans lived below the poverty line, and there were more opportunities at the upper end of the middle class. Many people were optimistic about American society and its ability to provide a secure and comfortable living for all of its citizens.

As poverty became increasingly less visible, it also became more difficult to regard it as natural or dignified. The depression had made it clear that individuals were not necessarily responsible for their economic situation; many people were poor, regardless of their skills or abilities. By the 1950s poor people were being blamed again for causing their own misery.

No longer a luxury, TVs were standard equipment everywhere, providing a whole generation of children with a shared frame of reference. Television also conveyed an idealized image of modern American life. Ozzie and Harriet never had problems that could not be gracefully solved within a half-hour time slot. Father went to work and appeared on weekends; Mother made cookies and cleaned the house. Sitcom girls dreamed of the perfect boyfriend, and boys considered becoming astronauts. Such alluring images made it pretty hard to see life as it was. Television presented fiction as truth; the newsreels of the 1940s had vanished.

Television also served as a surrogate parent. Baby Boomers spent an average of four hours a day in front of the TV. They knew TV characters as well as they knew their friends and families, and related to situations and attitudes they saw portrayed on the screen. Some claim it was *Howdy Doody* and *The Buster Brown Show*, with Clarabelle and Froggie the Magic Gremlin—the destructive clown and the devilish frog—who taught Baby Boomers the disrespect for authority they so explicitly expressed in the 1960s. In the well-ordered, polite world of the 1950s, suburban children reveled in the intoxicating naughtiness and disrespect that these characters displayed. When Froggie sprayed an eminent professor with an ink bottle, it didn't help anyone understand society or suggest constructive changes. It simply punctured the professor's dignified but overbearing demeanor. Much of the humor was directed at disciplinarian teachers, contrasted against more indulgent parents. Westerns, another popular genre, said conflict was fun, and heroes triumphed over the mediocre masses by virtue of their superior morality and prowess.

Television was also a vehicle for mass marketing and advertising on an unprecedented scale. The 1950s sent the consumer society into full swing, and advertising, now a much more sophisticated and empirically driven industry, expanded to include the world of politics among its consumer products, beginning with the 1952 presidential election.

The zaniness of children's television and cartoons was captured in print by *Mad* magazine, which remains popular today with kids. *Mad*'s irreverent parodies mocked the adult world, filled with repression, rigidity, and hypocrisy. This sense of absurdity for its own sake was reflected in later years in the "yippie happenings" of Jerry Rubin and Abbie Hoffman. Other publications of the 1950s, particularly horror and terror comics, provided kids with a dark side of humor, which allowed them to release the subtle tensions generated by the nuclear age.

The Baby Boom peaked in 1957, when about 4,308,000 babies were born. By the late 1950s the Boom had begun to taper off, as did the optimism of the decade, a trend strongly influenced by the development of the hydrogen bomb. The hydrogen bomb was orders of magnitude more destructive than the atom bomb and capable of destroying all of us; in 1954 the Russians proved they knew how to make it and use it as well as we did. Even as children the Baby Boomers knew that nothing could ever make the world really safe again. The seeds of the social revolution of the 1960s may have been planted then, as children practiced "duck and cover" or "drop drills" under their plywood desks. Monster movies like *Godzilla* incarnated the threat children recognized, and gave them the feeling that in living through the movie, they were conquering their fear.

DIVERSION—THE ADOLESCENT EXPERIENCE IN THE 1960S

The adolescence of the Baby Boomers was special and distinctive. Teenagers, by virtue of their size and influence on music, fashion, politics, and everything else, became a force to be reckoned with, a new separate target for marketers and the media. For most of the previous cohorts, the teenage years were simply an uncomfortable interlude between childhood and adulthood. Suddenly teenagers were trendsetters. The media observed and reported their slang, their fads, and their ever-changing likes and dislikes. Teen-oriented television shows—"American Bandstand," "Hullabaloo," "9th St. West," "Shindig," "Gidget," "The Patty Duke Show"—were on the rise.

Teenage Baby Boomers had several visions of the world to choose from—bland surfer music and beach-blanket movies, motorcycles and the nihilism of James Dean and Peter Fonda, the self-indulgence of the Beatles and *Hard Day's Night*, the jingoism of Sean Connery and his James Bond gadgets, or more exotically, Diana Rigg as the elegantly lethal Emma Peel in "The Avengers" and Patrick McGoohan as the "I'm-too-smart-to-fall-for-that" hero of "Secret Agent" and "The Prisoner." What they didn't have—except perhaps in Salinger's *Catcher in the Rye* and Heller's *Catch 22*—was a clear portrayal of the world as it was. The real world was not on the news, where foreign correspondents filed military press handouts from Vietnam, not in the high schools, where "concerned citizens" battled sex education on the grounds that "if you teach them about sex, they'll think it's all right to do it," and certainly not in local governments, where the business of slum clearance and freeway construction outweighed the distress they produced when homes were razed or cut off. Everywhere, the media were telling Baby Boomers that unhappiness was unnatural and meant that Something Was Wrong.

In true American fashion, Baby Boomers rooted for the underdog—brave West Berlin standing against Soviet aggression, for example. Now the image of the United States as overdog began to haunt the shadows—we risked war to make the Soviets take their missiles out of Cuba and then we hired people to play patriot and invade Cuba (to "free it" from its liberator and give it back to the sugar companies). We let our CIA do terrible things and saw our military advisers pose smilingly with corrupt puppets in Vietnam, Iran, and Central America.

And then one November day, the worst happened: President Kennedy was assassinated and there was a rumor that J. Edgar Hoover had something to do with it—or at least that the CIA did. Many of those who were teenagers in 1963, or about to be teenagers, found the rumor easy to believe. When President Johnson escalated the war in Vietnam, many young people saw it as an attempt to distract the nation—to shift the attention of the young from fighting injustice and wickedness at home to fighting communism abroad. To many Baby Boomers, the assassinations of Martin Luther King, Jr., and Robert Kennedy five years later, although terrible, were merely confirmations of how degraded the nation had become; they caused neither the shock nor the disillusioned anguish of that first assassination. And when young people told each other that the FBI was responsible, more of them shrugged than got angry.

The year 1968 was considered by some to be the emblem of the decade. In that year Baby Boomers ranged from 9 to 18 years of age. The events and mood of the 1960s were an experience that depended on which end of the age range you were at. Those who were of college age by 1972 experienced first-hand the campus upheaval and forged the way for the social revolution; those who were younger, born after 1954, generally missed out on personal involvement in the university-based protest movements and took for granted civil rights, women's rights, experimentation with drugs, long hair, and living together before marriage.

As the superficial sense of the security of the 1950s began to fray, the too-perfect family life portrayed on television was increasingly recognized as a facade. The newly adolescent Baby Boomers were often painfully aware of the reality behind the suburban picture. Throughout the 1960s more and more Baby Boomers were caught in the disintegration of their parents' marriages; from 1960 to 1969 the divorce rate climbed by 46 percent. Many marriages of Children of the American Dream collapsed because of rigid and overly simplistic definitions of marriage and the role of a wife or husband. Many Baby Boomers stared in consternation as Mother began to talk about her rights and "finding herself," and Father openly fretted about the meaninglessness of his job and his wife's discontent. Caught in the cross fire of new definitions of relationships between men and women, many Baby Boomers responded by vowing never to entrap themselves in similar ways. "Dark Shadows," a soap opera that many of them hurried home to watch, gave form to their fears of family as damaging—or at least, painful.

As the Baby Boomers matured and began to realize that many other aspects of middle-class life in the suburbs were also facades, they rebelled. Working class parents saw rebellious kids rejecting their values and attitudes and jeopardizing the advantages their parents had worked so hard for them to have. Worse, many were ridiculing those very dreams and aspirations. Serious conflicts between parents and children caused some kids to leave home. These runaways congregated on street scene corners and around campus protests. Sometimes they were exploited or abused, financially and sexually, by older, disenfranchised, streetwise con artists.

Rock and roll often best expressed the philosophy of rebellion. The sources for rock lyrics ranged from Herman Hesse's Buddhist *Siddhartha*, to the hallucinogenic musings of Carlos Castaneda's Don Juan, to J.R.R. Tolkien's fantasy trilogy, *The Lord of the Rings*, in which good very satisfyingly triumphed over evil. The most accessible works of nearly every Eastern religion formed the basis of impassioned (often stoned) discussions in nearly every dorm room and smoke-filled student union.

While they shared rock and roll, younger male Baby Boomers did not share equally in the harsh reality of the draft. Those born in 1952 were the last to face conscription. Because Vietnam was such a controversial war, and fighting in it was no longer viewed as automatic or patriotic, the draft proved to be a real dividing line among young men, who had to make powerful and profound decisions. Many college students felt guilty about their privileged status; others felt only relief. For most, there was no good solution. The conflict between those who fought willingly in World War II and those who chose not to fight in Vietnam was bitter. The Gap Generation and early Baby Boomers panicked over the draft and how to avoid it: student deferments (not permanent); conscientious objection (rarely granted); health exemption (flat feet, psychiatric instability); escaping to Canada; or going to jail. Holidays and family dinners often disintegrated into bitter arguments as the generations clashed.

Sex posed another arena for debate. Everyone was supposed to be "doing it" with everyone else, with no guilt, no anger, and no expectations. But the freedom of the time, the failures of parental models, and the onslaught of sexually active media characters (e.g., James Bond) and *Playboy* "temptresses" created inner conflicts for Baby Boomers raised to value virginity before marriage, and marriage as the expected state of adulthood.

As the Vietnam War dragged on, the protesters seemed increasingly sympathetic. The violence against youthful protesters by police at the Democratic Convention in Chicago in 1968; the death of four students, killed while demonstrating against the war, at Kent State University in 1970; the death of two more students at Jackson State; the growing concern about the brutality of the military in Vietnam—all these made Americans, old as well as young, question what was going on. Older people said "throw the rascals out," but couldn't agree on replacement rascals. The young said that if the country was morally bankrupt, then there was nothing left except "sex, drugs, and rock and roll." To a great extent, adults, busy with their jobs and their lives, let the young fight the country's battles, here at home as well as in Southeast Asia, and believed what the media told them—that all teenagers thought the way the protesters did, or the hippies did, or the swingers did.

EXPANSION—EARLY ADULTHOOD IN THE 1970S

The 1970s began as the 1960s had ended, with protests, riots, campus unrest, and hostility between those committed to the status quo and those committed to its destruction. Much had changed, however; the Summer of Love in San Francisco Haight-Ashbury had changed to a winter of addiction, petty theft, and increasingly radical acting out. Elementary schools were shutting down, and Ivan Illich's book *Deschooling Society* said we'd be better off without schools altogether. It turned out that Lyndon Johnson had been wrong: you couldn't have both guns and butter, at least, not for long. Nothing had replaced most of the cleared-away slums, and addressing inner city problems of block busting by real estate schemers and redlining by banks meant raising taxes, cutting back on defense and aerospace contracts or new laws. And as for the Beatles' notion that "All You Need Is Love," the most obvious results were long-haired middle-aged men searching for the remnants of the sexual feast the young had indulged in and braless young mothers defiantly nursing their babies in public. The one positive outcome was that blacks, Hispanics, and Asians as well as women had begun to have opportunities society had denied them before.

After the tumult of the 1960s many Baby Boomers were tired. It was time to tread more "reasonable" paths. Individualism and liberation through social change gave way to an internal, private expression. Pop psychology and narcissism flourished. Now the Gap Generation devoted themselves to hot-tub therapy, est, rolfing, and hundreds of other avenues for "personal growth." Baby Boomers followed in the footsteps of older siblings and cousins (the Gap Generation); their parents and grandparents seemed far too distant to be role models.

The Baby Boom culture of the 1970s was noted for its narcissism, but in truth it was also a period of self-consciousness and longing for a better "fit" in the scheme of life. But in either case, the voice that Boomers were hearing was not their own, but that of the Gap Generation. Much of the domestic music, Joni Mitchell, Neil Young, Janis Joplin, Jimi Hendrix, Jackson Browne, James Taylor, as well as Frank Zappa and the Fire Sign Theater spoke of reflections on the awkwardness of life—the purple haze—the necessity of finding out the hard way, the importance of discovery. However, Baby Boomers were more often consumers than active participants in this chorus. They loved the music, but it did not define their lives. For Boomers music was an emotional tie to the world, a substitute for political leadership or religious membership. But it was not a moral mission as closely linked to belief as it had been for the Gap Generation.

Many Boomers were just as ready to dance to the BeeGees and disco music that had its peak during this time as they were to go to rock concerts or buy new albums. What Boomers were really seeking was the pleasure of their own company amidst the dope smoke and booming music. Far out, but not too far from the car.

The self-conscious 1970s were a period of exquisite irony for all Americans, but perhaps more so for Boomers for the simple reason that Boomers' lives—families in particular—were the subject of the jokes. Norman Lear's television shows, for the first time in television's short history, reflected on our failures with a nonpatronizing elegance that was surprisingly easy to digest. Soon after, "Saturday Night Live" provided the Gap Generation with their first direct voice to their own cohort and reached beyond the earlier experiments, such as "That Was the Week That Was," and the more folksy and commercial "Laugh-In" of the 1960s. While the ridiculous continued to coexist with (and was often overwhelmed by) the insipid in television, Boomers, always avid television watchers, found solace in the first honest voices to be heard over the television waves. Nonetheless, this honesty only reinforced a self-consciousness for Boomers, a feeling that they were all dressed up for a party to which they were not invited. Despite the size of their generation, in their early 20s, Boomers, used to following styles, were goofy looking in bell bottoms and long, but not radical, hair styles. They wanted to belong, sensing the size of their own cohort, but did not know where they fit in.

The poor sense of fit was a continuation of the failure of the country to reestablish any national sense of leadership in either politics or business that could engage the imaginations of the Baby Boom cohort. Our presidents were now experiments in style that failed to break the disheartening trend of inadequacy. The 70s began with the moral indignity of the Gap Generation and rolled into the seeming triumph of the Watergate trials, yet these years left Boomers, again, with little in the way of political leadership to which to attach their need for glamour. Prepared for idealism early on, as preadolescents in the Kennedy era, Boomers were left at the altar of great expectations by all-too-human political successors. Ford's self-effacing style and gymnastic gaffes raised a weak laugh among Boomers, who probably did not want another leader to mock but were in search of elusive substance of character.

Carter's perspective, while not "Camelot," seemed a breath of fresh air, but his promises collapsed under the weight of these greater expectations. Carter was only human, no comparison to the ideal president that people, particularly Boomers, seemed to want. His informality and nonroyal presidency was trampled by criticism, primarily because Boomers, and other age groups, did not feel comfortable with reality; they wanted a living legend. With his ship of state swamped by oil price–induced inflation, Carter left office a victim of global trends, his work barely started. As the decade reached its inflation-soaked end, political apathy among Boomers grew. Neither Carter nor candidate Anderson could hold a candle to the intensity of the Reagan image riding the stalking horse of inflation. With Reagan, Boomers went into political hibernation. Liberal idealism, never a centerpiece of Boomer outlook, took a political holiday during the 1980s. Those Boomers who were idealistic and conservative, in contrast, found the Reagan years of the 1980s the dawn of a new era.

For many Baby Boomers, the 1970s were a time of recovery from the social disintegration of the previous decade. But the economy was uncooperative: Baby Boomers attempting to reenter more traditional career paths were hit with a quadruple whammy: inflation, fierce competition for jobs, exorbitant housing costs, and the recession of the 1970s. The job market was unable to expand fast enough to absorb the enormous swell of Baby Boomers. Working-class Baby Boomers from the industrial Northeast were particularly affected. Accustomed to the Affluent Society of the 1950s, they found this an unpleasant and almost unbelievable shock. Despite being twice as likely to have gone to college as their parents, Baby Boomers began to experience downward mobility. The Great Society of their comfortable, suburban childhoods had become unattainable.

Boomers rode out the recession of the late 1970s on a new wave of introspection based largely on material anxiety, achieved through career centeredness and inflation-driven defensive strategies. Keeping up with inflation in an environment rife with layoffs was a continuous fact of life, particularly for those Boomers with less educational skill.

Fortunately, Boomers had the highest educational levels of all working generations, and, having smaller and fewer family responsibilities, were better able to make their way through this difficult period.

For those who did successfully enter the job market, the "organization man" approach to work was no longer viable. One of the great strengths of the Baby Boomers was their focus on interpersonal skills. Interpersonal communication was an integral part of what they fought for socially in the 1960s and what they investigated privately in the 1970s. Although they had rejected the conformity and artificiality of the organization man, Baby Boomers were no longer entirely hostile to corporate America. But the corporate culture itself was increasingly affected by alternative professions, work styles, and life styles.

The burgeoning high technology enterprises of the 1970s were a favorite arena for new work styles. "Japanese style" management, profit-sharing plans, and employee beer blasts on Friday afternoons began to flourish. On the professional level, many Baby Boomers created new specialties and disciplines, from engineering to marketing, in which they became experts, innovators, and, frequently, highly paid consultants. Entrepreneurs came to epitomize the Baby Boomer's compromise between the newly desired material life style and newly articulated needs for autonomy, fulfillment, and flexibility.

For some, however, the gradual disappearance of the 1960s was depressing. Many felt lost, confused, aimless, and unable to substitute personal goals for a communal future vision. Some of these became targets for a growing number of cult religions, many of which began in the 1960s, but solidified in the 1970s. Moonies, Hare Krishnas, and Scientologists all promised their disciples peace, grace, and a life free from alienation. Fundamentalist Christian and Moslem sects also experienced a resurgence, as numerous Baby Boomers sought out something, or someone, that seemed to offer meaning in a meaningless time.

As Baby Boomers became adults, marriage as an institution suffered a decline in popularity. Many Baby Boomers were cynical about marriage, having witnessed their parents' failed relationships. For others, career pressures delayed or prevented marriage decisions. For women especially, the conflict between career and personal goals escalated. Work was now an accepted and expected part of adult life, not secondary or nonexistent, as it had been for their mothers. In 1950, only 24 percent of married men had a wife in the labor force. By the 1970s, 50 percent of all married men had spouses in the labor force, a statistic that continues to rise.

Baby Boomers didn't just have relationships that were different from those of their parents, they thought and talked about relationships in a different way. Motivations, attitudes, and expectations were explored, scrutinized, and investigated. Even the marriages of those 10 years older were not nearly as studied and analyzed as those of the Baby Boomers.

One of the crucial factors in the change in relationships for Baby Boomers was the changing role of women. The women's liberation movement in America evolved throughout the 1960s and 1970s. At first, it attracted attention as much for its emphasis on sexual liberation and bra-burning as anything else. But gradually the movement began to concentrate on political and economic issues, including finding and supporting female candidates for political positions. Women such as Gloria Steinem, Betty Friedan, and Shirley Chisholm publicized the underlying political nature of "women's lib" and helped to increase the visibility and legitimacy of female candidates such as Bella Abzug and Elizabeth Holtzman. Until the late 1970s, the women's movement tended to be mainly middle-class, reflecting concerns with careers and issues such as sharing child rearing and housework. In the late 1970s, however, the "feminization of poverty" began to change the emphasis to such issues as government-supported child care. Whether they identified themselves as "libbers" or not, increasing numbers of women began to benefit from the changes instigated by women working specifically to improve opportunities and ensure equality.

In some ways the 1970s were more intense than the exuberant 1960s, because of the failure or collapse of many ecstatic visions of a new society. Not only was the letdown for the Baby Boomers, when the smoke cleared, greater than it was for the Gap Generation, it was compounded by the economic difficulties that kept them from following in their parents' footsteps. The result was a new pragmatism among many Baby Boomers in early adulthood. They could not maintain the materialistic life style of their parents. In particular, skyrocketing real estate prices made the single-family house, which most suburban Baby Boomers had taken for granted, once again a pipe dream.

A trend toward a new domesticity began to emerge at the end of the 1970s. This was largely due to the interaction of inflationary pressures and maturation of the Boomers. Those who could started to buy houses and condominiums as a hedge against inflation, with their parents' money, if they had it. They were still in the early family stages and, having delayed children (and marriage), were not yet in the heat of the family centeredness that characterized the late 1980s. Not having as many personal financial liabilities, Boomers were able to focus their attention on expression of their identities through purchasing their first generation of high-tech products.

CONVERSION TO SUBMERSION—1980 AND BEYOND

The 1980s dawned with a cynical yawn, a defensive view of job security, and a general abandonment of the exploratory and self-conscious 1970s. Boomers, seasoned from their adventures and misadventures in the 1970s, were now to convert their experiences into a more focused way of life. This was a time of new pragmatism for Boomers. *Fortune* magazine viewed this as a materialistic era, which in terms of consumer activity it may have been. Yet Boomers did not view their interest in career and the accoutrements of achievement as materialism. They saw it as the natural progression of their development.

Consumerism changed direction in the early 1980s. Instead of saving to buy a house, Baby Boomers followed the lead of the slightly older Gap Generation, and insisted on the finest strollers for their babies, and gourmet take-out foods for themselves, as well as Cuisinarts, VCRs, BMWs, and designer jeans. They might not have been able to gather enough financial resources to own a house, but with substantial help from a vast array of credit cards they could spend their disposable income in ways their parents had never imagined. Fashions, technology, and trends changed rapidly; anything shabby or outmoded was discarded and replaced, not mended or saved.

What gave this twist to the Baby Boom lives was the new economic environment and born-again Calvinism of the 1980s—the view that the good do well; it only takes hard work to succeed. The early 1980s witnessed the dawning of the age of the "new venture" (start-up) and the "big deal" (merger or acquisition) rather than any "new deal." Instead of government being the champion, the new privates and corporals of industry emerged as the heroes of the hour. The rapid rise of the Genentech biotechnology stock in the first hour after being issued brought two new concepts into everyday parlance. These were high tech start-ups and venture capitalists (or investment bankers). The turnaround in the economy coincided with a revitalization of the spirit of entrepreneurship and the recognition that our country was made great by high risk takers and innovators.

Why did Boomers so heartily embrace these new icons of success— the yellow investment banker's tie, the BMW, the new preppiness? The reason, the same reason that has plagued Boomers all along, was the absence of any models of leadership, politically, morally, or otherwise. Reagan endorsed a save-your-own-neck approach to life through his new federalism. The conservatism of the 1980s stressed deregulation, letting the markets decide, letting the chips fall where they may. Politics provided support for identifying with those who believe that God helps those who help themselves. In the absence of any social or political models, Boomers could easily attach to post–inflation era possibilities of personal income growth. No wonder Boomers raced for their MBAs and stock options! There didn't seem to be any point in giving a damn about anyone else. But you had to watch out for the evil empire, while you are building your own. So we passively supported the tremendous buildup in defensive armaments to ward off the Evil Empire of the East. We did so well that the Eastern bloc switched rather than compete in the arms buildup that drained their economy (not to mention ours as well). During this time notions of social equity were relegated by Boomers (and others) to the category of losers whining about their failures. The Rainbow Coalition was often confused with the flavor of an ice cream cone, or an environmental movement.

Although much media attention was generated toward this upwardly mobile life style during its peak, only a small portion of the Baby Boomers actually had the income to rank as true "yuppies"; as few as 2.5 percent of the Baby Boomers qualified for that label.

Today many still strive to be yuppies, within the confines of their income, but without quite making it. As many as one third of the Baby Boomers are "New Collars"—post-industrial successors to the traditional blue collar worker. Less affluent than yuppies, they have some of the same life style yearnings for homes, cars, stereos, and vacations in the Caribbean. They tend to be conservative politically, but remain liberal on social issues such as education, child care, and the environment. New Collar workers include "Bright Collars," the technical elite of the growing service society who keep computers and communications systems running.

Certainly the 1980s offered little in the way of spiritual models. The most memorable religious images in the press were the Jonestown suicides, the collapse of various Eastern religious cults, such as Rajneesh's sexual commune, the brainwashing by Moonie-type organizations, manic televangelists, and the corruption in the born-again churches. What was sobering was the fact that Boomers operated with open minds that accepted the variety of spiritual views offered with little criticism or complaint. Spirituality, for most, was just another product in a consumer environment. If anything, it was acceptable to pray before going in for a sales meeting, just to be on the safe side.

Not even the foundations of the counterculture were exempt from the appeal of business, of making money. The phenomenon of recovery from recession and new economic growth that characterized the

1980s was accompanied by the phenomenon of rock and roll becoming big business. Performers were now viewed, from the start, as products. Artists promoted themselves to specific niche markets. The simultaneous promotion of music, videos, clothes, and other "tie-ins" became the hallmark of the modern music industry. Groups such as Kiss, who started out in the 1970s as schoolteachers seeking a way to get rich, became archetypes of a cutthroat industry populated by Baby Boom executives, selling Baby Boom products. Baby Boom music grew into highly defined segments that ranged from classic rock to Aquarian Age ("hot tub") music, new wave, jazz, fusion, heavy metal, reggae, and so on. Rap was yet to make its appearance. Many a Boomer gave up listening to music during this time, jaded, bored, and confused by contemporary music, sticking with the tried and true. Others found inspiration in the wry humor of Talking Heads, Police, and other new wave performers, most of whom were of the same cohort.

The 1980s were propelled by economics and given energy by the new individualism of entrepreneurship. Underlying this emphasis on self-sufficiency was a concomitant focus on the body. Call it the new narcissism. The old narcissism of the 1970s was the search for self-discovery, stressing the senses—psychological and spiritual. Having failed in that search, the new narcissism stressed the next best thing, the discovery of the physical body. Of course, the marketing of the body could not be complete if it did not include a balanced and integrated view of mind and body. The emphasis was generally on the performing self, the competitive self—being all you can be, to quote the Army's ad.

Jane Fonda provided a model combining entrepreneurship, the new businesslike glamour, and health in her workout classes, books, and tapes. But while many women and men were "going for the burn," a vast number of local television and (now commonly available) cable shows broadcasted jiggle-and-bounce shows for the young at heart and heavy of body to watch for reasons extending beyond physical fitness—voyeurism.

Those who found a satisfactory means of expressing themselves in physical activity were not always out on the aerobics floor. The Boomers played soccer, baseball, and basketball with friends and intercompany teams, rode racing or off-road bikes, jogged, and, eventually, walked. Boomers were less afraid of their bodies than older generations to begin with. They were, therefore, more able to play when they wanted to. But in the 1980s, play was still very often connected to physical performance, and, increasingly, to health—stress and weight reduction. Today, the Boomers are still out there bouncing and running around, getting just a bit rounder and slower.

As parents, Baby Boomers seem to replay much of their own childhood, within a different context. They recognize how they were coddled and pressured as children, yet insist on making their own children "right from the start": playing classical music to babies still in utero, sending preschoolers to a Montessori nursery school, sending grade school children to computer camp, ballet classes, gymnastics, and a host of other activities. "Mellow" parenting, briefly prominent in the 1970s, didn't last long.

Nonetheless, many children of the Baby Boomers have a childhood much less dominated by their parents' presence. The high proportion of working mothers and single-parent households means that many are in child care from infancy on, and later on become "latchkey kids"—home alone, without adult supervision after school. Independent and sophisticated, the children of Baby Boomers tend to experiment with sex, drugs, and alcohol at a much younger age.

Boomers finished the 1980s a bit winded, a bit worn out from working so hard at doing their personal best. Now, as they mature, many Baby Boomers find themselves nostalgic for their idealistic youth, especially those who feel they have compromised their dreams of social change and cooperative improvement for self-seeking goals. Much of the popular culture today reflects their yearning for their past; notably, movies such as *The Big Chill*, which, although more accurately a description of the Gap Generation, provided Baby Boomers with a reflection of themselves in the lives of the slightly older cohort who paved the way. The themes of the movie—successful careers based on alternative life styles, music of the 1960s, substance abuse, failed relationships—all hit home.

The second half of the 1980s brought along, as with any experience, some lessons learned. These were reflected in the television programs of the decade, from "Hill Street Blues" to "thirtysomething," and movies, from *Baby Boom* to *Three Men and a Baby*, in which professionals began to recognize the emotional cost of their manic devotion to work. Again, lacking direct models they could share values with, taking little direct guidance from American Dream parents or preceding Gap Generation friends, Boomers had to literally wear themselves out at work, whatever their occupation. They had to wear themselves out in terms of their fatigue with the self-serving nature of the 1980s modus vivendi. They had to tire of the indifference of the past years of self-centeredness. They had to tire of being detached from the political, social, and environmental issues around them. Finally, through their own experience, they could be their own models.

Particularly close to home is the television program "thirtysomething," a weekly drama about Baby Boomers facing the dilemmas of adulthood. The characters must deal with a variety of traumas in career and family decisions, health, the environment, ethics, and relationships. It portrays the typical Baby Boom marriage, based on communication and negotiation, and reflects the difficult consequences of important life choices: remaining single, not having children, juggling careers and children, making a living in a highly competitive economy.

By the end of this decade the Boomers had reached a point where they had to decide, whether they were married or not, to have children or to give up the idea. They also recognized, being working adults, that they would have to adjust their way of thinking, not only to have a decent family life but to maintain their lives as married couples—if they were, indeed, married. The waning of the 1980s saw the older Boomers searching for good schools for their five-year-olds and the younger Boomers reading about the post–Dr. Spock realities of child rearing. Having converted their exploratory 1970s into the can-do-and-do-it-now 1980s, the Boomers are wiser for the wear. They have come a long way without any models, and have had to make themselves in their own images, not any one style—neither as radical as the Gap Generation nor as middle class as their parents. This self-shaping is consistent with their history—being a huge block of followers after the fall of the American Dream, after the revolution of the Gap Generation. The Baby Boomers—looking outward for meaning, inward for answers—want it all NOW. But they're settling for the best they can get and learning how to compromise in everyday life.

BIRTHMARKS

Future Perfects

As the sun set on World War II, and the mushroom cloud exploded on a distant desert horizon, a child was born to Attainer, Dreamer and sometimes Performer Children of the American Dream: Future Perfect, the second half of the 20th century's answer to Tom Swift, a modern "Rambling wreck from Georgia Tech, a heck of an engineer" and Mr. Science rolled into one. The Future Perfect is the first technocrat to be born and raised as one, and believes that any problem can be solved by science. Future Perfects gave us the post-moonshot, space shuttle era systems analysts; rocket engineers; and the information revolution. Future Perfects are disconnected from their personal feelings in ways that complicate their lives. They have set the world on a technological course of rapid change from which we cannot turn back.

As adults, Future Perfects appear to be humanistic and naturalistic, and have a great appreciation of family and wildlife. These Baby Boomers, however, have a style of thinking nurtured by the scientific revolutions of the 20th century, from Albert Einstein to Enrico Fermi; thus they are fraught with contradictions and endorse technologies that can or do consume the very life of the planet. Much of the time they deny these contradictions ("Hey, I just work here"), or reconcile them by not assuming responsibility for the technological problems they have helped cause. They are more likely to embrace a benign or optimistic science fiction fantasy outlook, a la "Star Trek," than a darker futurism, a la *Blade Runner*, "Max Headroom" or *Mad Max*. For Future Perfects, the future is already here, a party we'll all have fun at; we've already conquered it. Underlying this orientation, however, is an inability to get in touch with their feelings.

Future Perfects often had parents who were indirect and emotionally abstract. Typically intelligent and kind, they were not necessarily aware of their own feelings, and often let the realities of everyday life preempt intimacy with their children. The fathers of Future Perfects might have had various careers, from farming to engineering to academia. More significantly, Father usually lost himself in his work and in the minutiae of work-related concerns. Often very family-centered, fathers of Future Perfects believed in family activities such as camping or visiting relatives. He was friendly, eager to please, yet at the same time emotionally distant.

Mother was generally stronger and more grounded. She managed the family and guided her forgetful or absentminded husband through various activities, holidays, and celebrations. She tried to provide more structure and direct support, but in doing so also ended up denying her own needs and feelings. Mother may have appeared to be an efficient and loving parent, impatiently coaching Father on what to do or say. But ultimately her resentment and frustrations made her also unavailable, emotionally. Sometimes she did pursue a career, teaching school or working in some other socially oriented field, such as a nonprofit organization.

Future Perfects emulated their parents by choosing an approach to life that emphasized controlled, systematic behavior and the inner world more than the outer; projecting and developing feelings through work; and taking pleasure from mastery over technical tasks. The two nerds on "Saturday Night Live," Todd and Lisa (played by Bill Murray and Gilda Radner), captured aspects of the Future Perfects in an exaggerated but hilarious caricature.

The early school years for Future Perfects were marginally night-marish. More intellectual than their peers, the Future Perfects were strongly inclined toward math and science, less toward sports and the arts. The race for space, not depression or war, was their childhood theme. As excellent (but not well-rounded) students, Future Perfects suffered quietly. They were often excluded from the mainstream and thus gravitated toward one another. Isolated from their peers, these "smart kids" used their powerful imaginations to entertain themselves. Future Perfects were well-read, particularly in science fiction. Until the 1970s the United States had an intensely loyal but only limited group of science fiction writers, readers, and fans; interest in science fiction was not as widespread as in Europe, nor was it considered respectable here as it was there. U.S. interest broadened in the late 1960s with Heinlein's *Stranger in a Strange Land* and later with Frank Herbert's *Dune*.

Sitting together on the bench at school, chosen last for the team, Future Perfects shared their own versions of dirty jokes, giggling behind their braces and pencil-packed pockets. Puns and rhymes were common. Clad in the least appealing clothes, the Future Perfects trudged through the school day, then returned home, where their universe expanded dramatically. Future Perfects devoted large chunks of time to building models—airplanes, trains, ships, and other objects suggesting the scope of the world—with tremendous attention to detail.

For Future Perfect girls, the experience of being smart was not as traumatic is it was for boys, but it was still hard. Athletics was not an issue for girls in elementary school, but they were expected to compete in other areas. Future Perfect girls tended to be more introverted, less socially adept, and sometimes less able to make themselves up to look attractive than the popular girls. Future Perfects struggled with their shyness and the pain of being outsiders. They were often the teacher's pet, a label that was scorned less by peers in elementary school than in junior high school or high school. Knowing they were good students and could handle school, Future Perfects were able to think more ambitiously about themselves and their future.

High school held a special kind of terror for Future Perfect boys—bullies with muscles and clandestine cigarettes; gym classes where you had to undress in front of other guys; the pressures of dating. Yet despite their fears, Future Perfects often came into their own in their high school years. They did well in most classes and smirked at the "dumber" clods. They honed their barbed wit on each other. They joined various clubs that offered shelter: math and science clubs, the ham radio club, orchestra, or even, in some cases, the marching band (where they could share the glory of sports without the sweat).

But for Future Perfect boys, the glamour of high school was accompanied by the pain of sexual inexperience. Their social awkwardness often denied them the opportunity to experiment with girls and sex, although their vivid imaginations generated tremendous libidinal energy. Parents were often unaware of or unable to acknowledge their teenagers' sexual needs. The threat of parental discovery of sexual activities was a frightening aspect of what was otherwise a healthy adolescent appetite. Yet, because they lacked an easy camaraderie with other boys, Future Perfects often felt that they were inferior and pathetic, lagging far behind the other boys who were no doubt "getting it" all the time; they didn't know that even supposedly sophisticated insiders were also fumbling around in the dark. Although they read the Kinsey Report on American sexual behavior, or a sex manual found hidden in a parent's drawer, Future Perfects had to rely on their older brother's or uncle's *Playboy*, and imaginative improvisation (fantasies about female classmates, teachers, movie starlets; anatomy texts; *National Geographics*) for erotica.

The untapped sexual energy of the teenage Future Perfects became channeled into great mental creativity. Success in school, and the ability to plan for the future, eased the frustration somewhat. College loomed ahead, promising freedom and experimentation.

Future Perfect girls, like their male counterparts, often lacked the comfort of sharing their feelings with other girls. More than one Future Perfect girl, encouraged by her mother to have a party to which she could invite the boy she secretly admired, was either too shy to actually do so, or was so embarrassed when the event took place that she could not face her guests. Future Perfect girls were often outcasts because of their intelligence, and they were teased and bluntly rejected, or ignored by boys.

Although Future Perfect boys and girls were often classmates together, particularly in schools that had a tracking system where the smart kids were placed in advanced classes, they were usually not particularly emotionally interested in one another. They spent more social time with the "nerds," on a Platonic level, often making the best use of each other's company in the absence of more "desirable" options. Despite not being attracted to one another, they did comprise an alliance of sorts. They would sometimes socialize together, even by default (because they couldn't find anyone better), and formed alliances of convenience. Many joined the student government, worked on the student newspaper or yearbook, and were accepted by classmates by virtue of their power and visibility in school. They often were lonely, but took solace in family relations. They bloomed during their college years when they could use their intellect and new freedom to shape relationships with their male classmates.

The Future Perfect often graduated high school earlier and also started college sooner. This early start could initially be a handicap. Less mature than their classmates, they were once again incompatible and thus isolated. Many who went away to college lived in dormitories. Some were free for the first time from parents and the stereotypes of being a good boy or girl which had plagued them throughout public school. These Future Perfects acted out in wild and crazy ways in their early college days. Mischievousness and pranksterism were a hallmark of Future Perfect men in college. Typical pranks included anonymous phone calls at all hours, booby-trapped doors, and throwing clothes out of windows. Future Perfect women were more interested in acting "grown up," and in sexual exploration.

Sometimes Future Perfects experienced a profound depression in their first year of school, during which their built-up emotions, hidden behind a sarcastic, sardonic style, exploded. This common crisis of early adulthood was often suppressed and not talked about. Sometimes it was taken in stride, and didn't last for long. But for some the period was more traumatic, resulting in a disruption of studies or even dropping out for a semester or longer. In most cases, however, their need to be in control was so well developed that they could cope by plunging into work, and thus muddle through the crisis.

The Future Perfects found that the 1960s and 1970s provided exciting prospects for implementing their image of themselves and the world. In addition to the political and sexual rebellions taking place, there was also a technological revolution. Future Perfects planned to be on the front lines; they thought about the future a lot. They envisioned a more humanistic, globally linked world made possible by fabulous advances in science and technology. Other Future Perfects, in pre-law or pre-med tracks, envisioned improvements on a less cosmic scale but were also aglow with the possibilities ahead. Systems analysts, Nobel Prize winners in science, and science fiction writers were the heralds of tomorrow. Thinkers from think tanks such as SRI, Rand, and the Hudson Institute and scientists such as Glenn Seaborg, the codiscoverer of plutonium and the head of the Nuclear Regulatory Commission in the 1960s, provided the images and goals for the year 2000.

Futurists such as Herman Kahn spoke enthusiastically of the technological innovations they expected within the next 30 years: undersea cities; landing on Mars; systematically planned towns, with genetically controlled grass that would grow to only an inch high, for easy maintenance; small, automated farms; and inexpensive and safe nuclear power. The 1962 Seattle Expo and 1964–1965 World's Fair in New York were major sources of excitement to these kids—laying open new vistas of engineering.

Future Perfects were often not aware that these forward-looking institutions were already anticipating the impact of a generation of increasingly independent-minded and often entrepreneurial workers, and the difficulties of adapting to the need for change. A 1966 article in *IBM* magazine foreshadowed these changes by observing that rapid change, temporary work systems, and transitory relationships would all result in social strain and psychological tension. It observed that the tasks of education and the goal of maturity would be to teach people how to live with ambiguity, identify with the adaptive process, make a virtue out of contingency, and be self-directing. Future Perfects were grooming themselves for this Brave New World.

Future Perfect men and women were recruited early by corporations, even though the work force was swollen with the expanding Baby Boom population. Unlike their liberal arts counterparts, both male and female Future Perfects never worried about getting a job. Although those in engineering fields perhaps had the easiest time, those in professions such as medicine, dentistry, accounting, scientific research, data processing, teaching, and law enforcement were also able to find work. They had concentrated on their school performance and had all the right extracurricular credentials.

Many Future Perfects married late, often after college. Wives of Future Perfect men often found that their marriages suffered from their husband's commitment to his work and his lack of emotional responsiveness. Marriages often broke up when wives became unable to cope with their Future Perfect husbands' depressions, brooding, and lack of communication. Future Perfect women married later than their male counterparts, largely due to their pursuit of higher education and professional career development. When they married, their spouses tended to be peers, often older, or more mature, Future Perfects. Nevertheless, many Future Perfect women remained unmarried because they had a strong commitment to their own identity and life style.

The ups and downs of the technology-centered industries often undercut the ability of Future Perfects to achieve a stable life style. Many Future Perfect men and women ended up in singles apartment complexes after the break-up of a 4-, or even 10-year marriage. Frequently, this stage of isolation seemed to recapitulate the rejections and isolation of high school days. Since work was a way to heal the emotional wounds, the workaholic Future Perfects plowed through project after project, leaving little time to dwell on what they were missing.

Those Future Perfects who have strong family ties are fortunate because they have a support network. Others, not close to their families either geographically or emotionally, often live lonely lives. Some become involved in individualistic kinds of activities in which they can nevertheless enjoy the company of others, such as computer networking, bird watching, and even some sports such as bicycling and hiking.

Throughout the 1980s, many Future Perfects found themselves thoroughly immersed in work with computers, and computer paraphernalia, both at the office and at home. As they struggled to create greater balance in their personal lives, they began to think about a family, and a broader life style for themselves. Often living a minimalist home life, not paying much attention to where they lived or how, they began to save for a house and a better car. By the late 1980s most Future men had a strong feeling that they wanted a less stylish, more "normal" life, and they looked harder for women who would accept that life style. Many did not succeed, or they found themselves losing girlfriends they had been living with for some time. Very often, Future men who view women as sexual objects cannot match that view with their need for a partner. As a result, they sometimes end up with women with whom they have little in common. Because of this poor match, they end up unhappy in marriage for reasons that are quite apparent to friends and family.

Future Perfect families that have a better "fit" give rise to children who are very much like their parents; except, being more in the mainstream, the kids are now better accepted and stand out. Now the Future Perfect children can play both soccer and computer games without feeling odd. When Future Perfect families succeed, they are viewed as indicators of what American families actually should be like, relative to technological literacy. Future Perfects are, as they say, having a field day—no longer viewed as nerds with pencils in shirt pockets.

Voyagers

Voyagers were children of Attainers, Performers, Martyrs, and Self-Compensators. They are the warrior-wanderers who, like Ulysses, return home after great battles of questionable meaningfulness and a mysterious and lengthy journey, where they continue to struggle for reconciliation and peace. Voyagers are the Baby Boomers who experienced the Iliad of the 1960s and the Odyssey of the 1970s and survived, older and possibly wiser from their voyage.

Unlike many of their peers, Voyagers were thrust reluctantly into the Vietnam War era—the 20th century analog of the Trojan War. Our Trojan War, waged during the 1960s, was not just the hostilities in Vietnam, but the battle over American culture here at home. The loss of faith in the traditional institutions of their parents' generation, the rejection of the status quo, the violation of America's overblown sense of importance (called imperialism by some) by the resistance of a tiny, underdeveloped country and by America's own citizens, are, metaphorically, replicated in the story of the Trojan War: the abduction of Helen by Paris, her pursuit by Agamemnon's Achaeans (including the great warriors Achilles and Menelaus), and the playful and vindictive attitudes of the gods Zeus, Athena, and Apollo.

For our Ulysses, Mount Olympus was populated by an equally curious pantheon of deities, including television talk show hosts, film cult heroes, and pop avatars of change, from Abbie Hoffman to Maharishi Mahesh Yogi. The playful and vindictive gods were the irrational leaders of the 1960s, from Johnson to Nixon, as well as their secretaries and generals. Comfortable in the affluence of his suburban world, our Ulysses (or his female counterpart) was not the agitator for change but, once convinced, the ferocious warrior committed to the cause. The journey home was an epic voyage through an uncharted sea of changing values and expectations that continually offered tantalizing opportunities and threats.

A stranger in a strange land, perceiving himself (or herself) as alone, Ulysses hoped to find an identity and place for himself that somehow (however faintly) resembled the comfort and affluence of childhood, without its nagging contradictions. Voyagers yearn to achieve, as Ulysses did, the reconciliation of man and woman (Ulysses and Penelope), the reunion of father and child (Ulysses and Telemachus), and the rejoining of man and country (Ulysses and Ithaca).

Both the ancient and the contemporary Ulysses took the long and winding road home. The ancient Ulysses outwitted the Cyclops by putting out its eye; today's Ulysses escaped from the captivity of the TV Cyclops by outgrowing it. The ancient Ulysses avoided the chemical sorcery of Circe and rescued his crew; the contemporary Ulysses experimented with drugs briefly and abandoned them, but did not try to "rescue" others from the same trap. The ancient Ulysses and his crew stuffed their ears with wax to escape the dangerous lure of the Sirens; the contemporary Ulysses avoided the seduction of materialism and searched for meaningful work, often paying a price in a lower wage and slow promotion.

The ancient Ulysses, in order to sail his fleet past the demon of Scylla and the whirlpool of Charybdis, had to permit sacrifice; our Ulysses passed between the rock of loneliness and the hard place of inappropriate marriages by trial and error, giving up relationships that did not work and moving on.

While resting on a forbidden island, Ulysses' hungry men could not resist consuming sacred cattle, and were punished by having their ships broken apart in a stormy sea. Our Ulysses made difficult ethical choices in school and at work—refusing to kill a frog for biology or modify a report to soothe a client—and stood by them despite stormy times with teachers, coworkers, or bosses. Having lost his crew, a depressed Ulysses, marooned on the island of Calypso, was at last allowed to leave—by building a raft and confronting a hostile sea. The gods had taken pity on him. Our Ulysses has had to ride out similar rough seas—divorce, job change, relocation.

Finally, Ulysses returns home, 20 years older. His wife and home are under the assault of aggressive suitors, and his family does not recognize him. Our Ulysses, also 20 years older, is now facing his or her life mid-course; and reconciliation, as it did for Ulysses, requires discovery, negotiation, and action.

While other children were immersed in television, Cub Scouts, Brownies, and Little League, and jazz or tap dance lessons, Voyagers felt at odds with the surrounding world. They were serious, responsible children, prematurely mature, not necessarily wise. The parents of Voyagers treated their children as individuals, encouraging them to examine their beliefs carefully and then act on them. But in doing this they placed considerable stress on their children, who felt compelled to take responsibility for actions that were beyond their ability to comprehend, let alone implement. They listened, with little comprehension, as their parents discussed politics, and were impressed by their seriousness.

Many Voyagers went to church or synagogue, often irregularly. But religion and ethical issues were not emphasized in any dramatic way by their parents. It was their grandparents who exerted an important spiritual influence on Voyagers, giving them a broader, more cosmopolitan, view of the world. These older family members were somewhat mystical; some were elfin or pixie-like, others were ancient and austere, and all were wise. Many Voyagers were treated by their grandparents, especially those who were concentration camp or POW survivors, as the hope of the future. This added to the Voyagers' sense of mission and responsibility.

Voyager boys and girls were proud of both parents, but particularly attuned to their fathers. They would argue with their friends about whose dad was smartest, strongest, richest, most important. Participating in family life and strongly identifying with adult role models were important to them. At about the age of eight they began to take part in family talk at the dinner table. They were encouraged to speak about everyday life. They were also encouraged to become involved in social activities where they could, presumably, learn about the real world: on Halloween, for instance, they didn't just trick or treat, they also collected pennies for Unicef.

Voyagers were creative and had fertile imaginations. Boys and girls both loved to playact, and would include their neighborhood pals in their fantasies. Their homes were often favorite hangouts because they were allowed to play with household appliances and furniture. On a typical Saturday morning the kids might pile up dining room chairs, stools, and couch pillows, draping them with blankets to construct houses or caves or ships at sea. They would dress up in cast-off clothes, create a treasure chest by dumping costume jewelry into a shoe box, leap from bed to chair, and climb on desks to have deadly sword fights with cardboard cutlasses.

As they got older, they constructed tree houses and forts in the nearby woods or empty lots, and created hideaways where they might escape the world of their parents. Boys, in particular, would play more serious games of war, jumping out from behind bushes to machine gun one another with plastic Thompson machine guns. The girls were often relegated to "nurse" status, or the enemy. Their parents, opposed to war games, would not buy their sons the guns they longed for. But they had access to other kids' toys, and acted out World War II and Korean War battles as heroes or martyrs to the cause of democracy. They thought about which branch of the military they would eventually join. Voyager girls were more thoughtful, and read more, and, as was still true of this time, played house, with the occasional boy "guest."

Voyagers had friends who were also Voyagers, and together they would concoct fierce adventures and ongoing stories of drama and intrigue, sharing their dreams and fantasies during playtime and at frequent sleep-overs.

Elementary school was initially unappealing. Voyagers had trouble integrating their highly autonomous view of themselves with the hierarchy and structure of the classroom. They were often at odds with the more conventional, authoritarian teachers. Voyagers were viewed as bright, but not cooperative or easily compatible. Eventually, however, they became more accepting of authority, transferring some of the fear and respect they had for their parents to their teachers. Outbursts and arguments occasionally surfaced.

Voyager boys were often on the fringe of the popular group, perhaps as the best friend of the most popular boy. Voyager girls had a tighter group of friends that studied together and spent time together after school: watching TV dance shows, such as "American Bandstand," "Hullabaloo," and "9th St. West"; washing and setting their hair together; going shopping; going to the movies. Often more attached to their families, Voyager girls tended to be shy, although not unsociable, and less likely to go out. By the 5th and 6th grades, there were parties, which required knowing how to dance. This caused most kids anxiety and anguish, but Voyagers were more awkward than most, having never entered the mainstream. But they muddled through, learning to "slauson" with the other boys on a Saturday afternoon.

Anticipating junior high school was a time of fear and trepidation for Voyagers. They feared the older kids—bullies, rough kids, sophisticated kids, who might tease them or make fun of them. Moreover, schools were often far behind the times. Although there were some outstanding teachers, young and inspired, most had been trained to merely process children from one semester to the next, meeting the minimum standards for educational achievement. They didn't care about making history, science, math, or English relevant or meaningful.

Once in junior high school, however, Voyagers were able to choose new social activities, whether working on the school newspaper or joining a club. Those who had been driven to music lessons (clarinet, piano, violin) could now join the school orchestra or jazz band.

Teenagers were buying more records, singles as well as albums. They were also buying fan magazines, an incredible array of candies, and even more expensive items, such as hair dryers (large, boxy machines with hoses connected to elasticized hats like shower caps), transistor radios, and cheap record players. Voyager boys and girls, however, were typically the last to catch up with the latest craze. Their parents, who emphasized a less frivolous outlook, would advise them to save their allowance to buy their own record player. In the meantime, since they controlled the family hi-fi, they might consent to buying a Beatles album.

Voyagers were precocious readers; they had read Aldous Huxley's *Brave New World* and George Orwell's *1984* long before most of their peers. Voyagers were immersed in a search for self. *The Catcher in the Rye*, by J. D. Salinger, started many on the road of self-discovery; for others it was *The Stranger* by Albert Camus. The impact of these books was profound; reading was as strong an instinct for Voyagers as eating. They were vulnerable to new philosophies, romantic notions, and books that posed troubling questions about the way things were.

Gradually, school began to offer greater challenges. Class projects often made them examine issues such as poverty or capitalism, and helped fuel their developing cynicism about the outside world. Poetry and music began to become more than dreary assignments. By the end of high school, Voyagers were well aware of the contradictions in their safe and secure suburban world, and wondered what would be next.

Preparatory college entrance exams were given; in some schools, courses in choosing careers were mandatory. Students had to decide not only what they wanted to be but precisely what they wanted to be: what kind of an engineer—nuclear, mechanical, industrial, civil, electrical, or electronic? What kind of doctor—surgeon, cardiologist, dentist, psychiatrist, internist? Although Voyagers took these questions far more seriously than most, they were unsure and confused about mapping out their future, complicated by their naivete and unworldliness, and unrealistically high ideals.

Traditional high school events, such as proms and senior picnics, were generally avoided, or treated indifferently. What was happening on college campuses was exciting to Voyagers, although not central to their lives. They saw the hypocrisy of an educational institution that restricted school dress, school newspapers, and other forms of free expression that they had been taught were protected by the Constitution. These conflicts served to motivate Voyagers to go out into the world as soon as possible, but did not necessarily encourage them to become more political. High school had become merely a holding tank for Voyagers, who left as soon as they could, with brief goodbyes to the instructors who had been their allies.

Due to their tendency to treat world issues as personal challenges, Voyagers had, by this time, acquired a load of *weltschmerz* (world pain or weariness), far heavier than that of the average teenager. Under this existential burden, they had acquired a disdainful attitude for institutions, such as school, and wanted to be free of them. Voyagers used their exaggerated mistrust and disgust for existing institutions to separate themselves from the mainstream. Voyager boys were often attractive to girls because they were seen as artistic and philosophical, romantic and eccentric.

Conversely, Voyager women intimidated the boys of their age who were straight and narrow. Voyager women saw themselves as free and strong, which led them to socialize with older men (i.e., college-age).

They frightened their parents by protesting the juvenile qualities of their classmates and hanging out on nearby college campuses, going to poetry readings, concerts, and political events. They also enjoyed platonic relationships with Voyager boys, sometimes forming close friendships that suffered when they decided to go away to college.

Those Voyagers who could went away to college; those who could not moved out of their parents' homes as soon as possible. Voyagers found college to be an initially ecstatic experience, but the ecstasy wore off. In the early 1970s, Voyagers found themselves at the tail end of the revolution. College students had already been through the free speech movement in the mid-1960s, had heard Dr. Martin Luther King, Jr., on campus, saw Dr. Spock run for president, heard Pete Seeger and Arlo Guthrie sing. The tenor of campus life was past the peak of its idealism, and was settling into more serious guerilla warfare between various disaffected factions. Already war weary, the administration was used to sit-ins, strikes, and booths on campus calling for an end to the Vietnam War or to the persecution of Black Panthers, and either was indifferent or reluctantly called in police to break up unauthorized events. The authentic counterculture had collapsed after the Democratic National Convention in Chicago in 1968 and the 1970 murder of students at Ohio's Kent State University. The post-Altamont rock concert student environment was one of acceptance of diversity and an eagerness to just get by comfortably, not one of structured confrontation.

Although the focus had shifted to more practical matters—e.g., the protection of unionized university workers from wage cuts—most undergraduates and graduates were still of the activist Gap Generation, even though there was no longer a clearly defined adversarial relationship between the university and students. The great decade of the 1960s now was something to look back on. Former Black Panthers ran for city council in Oakland, California. Instead of a climate of political intensity, the 1970s were filled with postpartum blues, particularly for Voyager men and women. By the time they had come to college, being hip was not extreme, but average; you were odd if you didn't have long hair and smoke pot. Many young men and women found themselves struggling with their own lives without the momentum of upheaval and a cause to propel them forward. There was more interest in the practical business of making communities work, rather than joining the Peace Corps; more concern with tenant–landlord issues; with food co-ops; with psychological counseling.

The failure of the counterculture to create a totally new society was a major disappointment to Voyagers. Many who did not have to work to put themselves through school took trips to exotic locales such as Nepal, or to communities in the United States where the countercul- ture was supposedly still alive. But most did have to work to get through school, on principle if not because of finances; they wanted moral and psychological independence from their parents. So, grab- bing whatever jobs they could, they sweated away their summers, and worked during the school year, too. For Voyagers, college ceased to be a playground early on. This was also a carryover of the internal pressure to be responsible they had learned when they were young, as well as an honest attempt to define themselves as individuals.

For many Voyagers, eager to embrace new ideas and life styles, college turned out to be a letdown. The exuberance they thought would characterize college life was missing. There were few people to turn to for inspiration. The intellectual environment was confounded by self-doubt. Professors were unsure of their ideas and indifferent to competing concepts. In the looser, less conventional environment, brought about by the demands of students five years earlier to break down the traditional hierarchy of the university, professors saw little need and less reward for encouraging students.

The Baby Boom had arrived too late to be part of the big party, just in time to blunder into an academic system that was worn out, and an economy that could not properly welcome the 42 million new workers arriving at the ebb of economic prosperity. But, being re- sponsible, Voyagers turned their attention not to the failing institu- tions but to the maturation of their own creative capabilities.

During college the Voyager wanted to grow as a person and tried to be open to others but instead found that college life could be incre- dibly lonely and alternatively oppressive. Male and female Voyagers found themselves in a series of long-term relationships; some didn't work out because of incompatibility, but the others broke up as a re- sult of the difficulty Voyagers had in forming deep and lasting bonds with others.

The female Voyager started college with a pseudo-maturity that often led her to an older student as boyfriend. She emotionally dis- engaged from the relationship when she realized that he had little to offer for the future, although he had been a good guide and nice friend. Female Voyagers took advantage of the freedom of college to explore their sexuality, as did male Voyagers. For young men, the novelty wore off fast and left a sense of confusion about the require- ments of relationships and their own self-worth. Many male Voyagers formed stormy relations that lasted a year or two. By their senior year, male and female Voyagers often had found someone they would stay with, although they might not marry until years later. Voyagers tend to be stable in their relationships over time, but have unplumbed depths of emotions that may never be explored unless they are lucky. This emotional distance will cause them problems in the coming years, as their family and friends grow dissatisfied with Voyagers' lack of vulnerability.

Many Voyagers finished college and went on to graduate school or employment. Considering that Voyagers were not top students and tended to take courses that were meaningful (and even then did not compete for high grades) rather than practical, this was an accomplishment. Their professors saw them as intelligent and creative but not necessarily focused or careful in their work. Concentrating on what was meaningful or interesting often hindered them in the real world of jobs.

Despite their dislike for following rules, Voyagers knew when they had to put their noses to the grindstone. Not afraid to work hard, many were determined to go to graduate school, earn a second bachelor's degree, or even go into business for themselves. The career-entry phase of their development proved to be an interesting personal revelation. In graduate school much of the burden was placed on individuals to prove themselves, not by tests or other traditional means. In this new environment, school became a challenge; the work was not for someone else but for themselves.

Their choices for work varied dramatically; many Voyagers ended up in journalism, filmmaking, advertising, law, architecture and landscape architecture, urban design and planning, government, and consulting. Today many Voyagers are self-employed. Whether they have started restaurants or advertising firms, their enterprises reflect their concerns about preserving their autonomy, and their sense of responsibility for their own actions. Although they have changed jobs a few times, they are not only stable in their work styles, they are creative workaholics, given the right tasks.

Voyagers protect themselves from being bruised by the outside world by working at a frenzied pace. In fact, they spend a lot of time pouring out their energy and creativity into their work, and other activities outside of themselves. They invest a great deal in their relationships with their bosses or their clients; each project is a measure of the Voyager's self.

The lives of Voyagers have by no means been "mellow"; partners often suffer through the ups and downs of a Voyager's fervent commitment to work and ideals. Their creative and slightly arms-length style make Voyagers attractive and colorful, but emotionally hard to reach. They are likeable, kind, reliable, and consistent, but not easy to get to know.

Homeboys and Homegirls

Homeboys and homegirls are the backbone of the Baby Boom, more numerous than any of the other Baby Boom Birthmarks. They are much less concerned about the ambiguities and uncertainties of life and more likely to "go for the gusto."

Many Homeboys and Homegirls were the first in their families to go to college, although many did not finish. Those who did earn a degree found jobs in the service industry, as technicians, salespeople, and middle or lower managers. This was an important achievement in a decade where there were fewer opportunities for employment in manufacturing. Many Homeboys became skilled workers, working a standard 40-hour week with overtime options.

A Homeboy or Homegirl was raised in a modest, lower to middle middle-class household, in or near an urban area—from Philadelphia to Houston. Their parents were recent arrivals to the middle class. They had often come from smaller towns or rural communities, or were making their first move up from a poorer part of town. The young Homeboy or Homegirl had little sense of how his or her roots differed from those of the neighbors. Yet he or she could tell that the better-educated families, even those with less money, had different priorities—saving for college, for example.

The parents of Homeboys and Homegirls were Performers, Dreamers, Cruisers, and young Good Old Boys and Gals who benefited from the opportunities of postwar America. Whether they came from Oklahoma farms or Pittsburgh neighborhoods, they had been able to make dramatic improvements in their lives. But despite these new advantages, they brought with them the perspectives of their pasts about difficulty in relationships between men and women, trust of neighbors and distrust of institutions, and the need for self-reliance.

As children, Homeboys and Homegirls were reasonably happy and had a fairly stable family life. Their parents were loving, although they were rarely able to express their feelings and tended to give directions instead: do this, don't do that. Shy about revealing their deeper feelings, the Homeboy/Homegirl family seemed to find anger easier to express than affection, sympathy, or confusion. Homeboys as well as Homegirls were punished by being spanked with their father's belt and were routinely grounded for disobeying instructions, such as when to be home or when to do chores. Parents fought about money, banging up the car after a night out on the town, how to discipline the kids.

Father was the center of attention, often because of his unpredictable temper. Mom and the kids had to figure out how to manage him. Girls, who were much closer to their mothers, learned how to cajole their fathers into giving them what they wanted. In some households, the father smoked a lot and drank in the evenings, particularly on the weekends while he watched golf or baseball on TV. He taught his children what was desirable, whether it was being captain of the bowling team, a lodge member, salesman of the month, or a silent, hard worker.

Homeboys and Homegirls were not student activists in the 1960s; they had neither the conviction nor the desire to speak out. They avoided politics, which only seemed to bring out their anger and defensiveness. Although they were angry with those in power, they also resented "liberals." Instead of being against the Vietnam War, for instance, they felt that America could have won if only the war had been better handled. They were patriotic in the traditional sense and believed that America is a great country and should be a world leader, although it might make a few mistakes now and again. Their defensiveness was often based on their feeling that whatever they acquired was fleeting and vulnerable and could be snatched away at any moment.

Nevertheless, having lived through and survived the 1960s, they have absorbed some of the ideals of the times, in a personal and pragmatic way. Libertarian in outlook, they tend to distrust government and business institutions and are liberal in their attitudes about men and women, and sex. Although they agree with the "live-and-let-live" approach to life, they're likely to add: "As long as how you live doesn't place any demands on me to accept you." Homeboys and Homegirls see themselves as hard-working people who love their family and country, who earn their right to do what they want to do when they want to do it. They are sensitive to any infringement of those rights, such as being told to wear a safety helmet, or not being able to operate a speedboat or off-road vehicle in certain areas.

Homeboys and Homegirls tend to have a dogmatic and defensive view of right and wrong, and are quick to make their views known to others. They prefer not to consider shades of gray. They were able to cheer Rambo as he demolished the "commies," and supported Ronald Reagan's cowboy approach to politics; yet once the cold war was proclaimed over, they have been able to embrace their former enemies as long-lost brothers and sisters. The majority of Homeboys and Homegirls have a broad and tolerant view of religion, although many feign more respect than they actually have. They may go through periods of spiritual redirection that put them back in touch with the church, but they don't last there long.

Homeboys and Homegirls were taught as children that strong beliefs are a defense against the troubling complexities of life. You didn't question your mother and father—you respected them, as you were told to, even if you didn't agree with them or knew they had problems. So what if Mom drank; she still did a decent job in raising her kids. Pop was a good, hard-working man who provided for his family. Sometimes his temper may have gotten out of control, particularly when he was out of work, but you just prayed to the Lord for forgiveness, or got out of the house as fast as you could.

For the Homeboy, real conflict existed at home from the very beginning. He wanted to get away, and wanted to be different. He did not reject his parents' values but was itching to emulate them on his own terms. As a child he thought about ways to become famous and rich. Sometimes his parents were willing and able to help, albeit somewhat indifferently. Many Homeboys wanted to be rock stars; Homegirls dreamed of being dancers or actresses. Most could not afford serious musical or theatrical training. But since the 1960s didn't always require a certificate or a degree, the possibilities of being discovered seemed endless.

Some Homeboys thought sports would be their exit ticket. Playing basketball or baseball became a full-time preoccupation for many Homeboys. This activity was particularly encouraged by their parents, since a star player and winning team accorded them status. Homeboys started in Little League and made their way up through high school teams and the pre-professional Pony League, sometimes even trying out for the minor leagues. Aspirations for a career in sports, however, usually diminished as the limits of one's skills became apparent.

When Homeboys and Homegirls entered into a relationship, they were gratified to finally have a chance to engage in adult behavior. They loved dating, talking on the phone until late at night with their girlfriend or boyfriend. They were the first of their friends to go steady, and treated their relationships seriously, especially compared to other Baby Boomers. Often they put aside schoolwork for romance. They liked the rituals of relationships, and formal rules that defined who was to do what and when. They were jealous and broke up and got back together regularly. They especially liked high school dances, proms, and ballgames. Some Homeboys and Homegirls married their sweethearts (usually another Homeboy or Homegirl) after graduation, although some suffered traumatic breakups. Many who married early found that their marriages did not last long.

Homeboys and Homegirls who had not planned to go to college ended up working as sales clerks in local department stores or as waiters and waitresses in chain restaurants. They viewed their employment as temporary, while they pursued their dreams of being a rock star or an actress. Having played in garages and at school events, some Homeboys were experienced band members. But beyond playing in a local bar or lounge, most never managed to break into the bigger music scene and gave up.

Some went to a community college, others to state colleges. Not wanting to replicate their parents' lives, they resisted the temptation to start a family, although many were already married while in college. They acquired good cars, stereos, furniture, and other possessions. Often they were able to buy a condominium or lease a fashionable car. Money was saved for annual vacations. The Homeboy or Homegirl had his or her hair done at a salon, ate out at restaurants he or she had read about in local magazines, and tried to keep up as consumers.

Typically, a Homeboy's first marriage ends in divorce. He wants children and she does not. She complains that he is still a child himself and she wants to live a more meaningful life. Finding himself single again at 32, he leaves town and moves to a new studio apartment. He likes being single, being on the road as a manufacturer's representative, and meeting a lot of different women, many of whom he seduces because he is, after all, a very good salesman.

Though leery of repeating his mistake (although he doesn't really understand what went wrong with his first marriage, and certainly hasn't considered that his behavior and expectations may have partly contributed to the breakup), he is ready to settle down again. He leaves discos and singles bars behind and attends church and social functions; he takes up ballroom dancing where he meets a woman he likes, a salesperson like himself, also divorced. Eventually they decide to get married and start a family. They move again, to a town that offers business and housing opportunities, and the kind of life style they feel is compatible with their aspirations.

When Homeboy and Homegirl couples are able to consolidate their family goals, they work together as a very successful team, possibly better than other Baby Boomers. Willing and able to set aside personal concerns and needs, their affiliations with family and community are strong and important. They tend to be sociable and extraverted, and enjoy activities such as neighborhood block parties, garage sales, company picnics, church functions, and membership in union or fraternal societies.

Homeboys and Homegirls like simple, "ordinary" food—the hearty ethnic fare (corned beef and cabbage; spaghetti and meatballs) of their Italian, Polish, or Irish families, and "all-American" food such as hamburgers, pizza, and other fast food. Fine food means ample quantities of steak or prime ribs. They prefer franchise or chain restaurants that mimic authentic Italian, Chinese, or Mexican atmospheres. Drinking is an accepted part of life, particularly beer and sometimes wine (chianti for those who choose Italian food, for example).

Although Homeboys and Homegirls face anxieties about meeting financial goals, beyond just getting by, they will load up on discount merchandise—especially food, but other bargains as well. They are not savers, because they have too many financial obligations to put money aside, but they increase the value of their belongings with sweat equity, fixing up a modest, starter home, or purchasing another home in the neighborhood at a bargain price and becoming a landlord.

Underlying their geniality is an almost desperate "can-do" optimism. Fitting in and making a good impression are important. As a result, Homeboys and Homegirls work very hard to "make the grade" in whatever group they're part of, at work or at play. Many Homeboys have developed the ability to be persuasive (a mixture of sweet-talk, hot air, and bravado). They have forced themselves to believe in their own myths and stories, and are thus very convincing to others. A few have even become religious or cult spokespersons, although these are not the norm.

Although they were raised in a comfortable life style, Homeboys and Homegirls often feel that the American Dream has slipped by them. Although they are managing, they cannot partake of the more glamorous yuppie life style they see around them. Some are quite bitter about their inability to improve on their origins the way their parents did. Since it now takes two incomes to make a middle-class household, Homegirls work because they have to, rather than for personal satisfaction or ambition. Many would stay home if they could. Even child care is sometimes unaffordable. Younger children of Homeboys and Homegirls are left with relatives; older children, between 8 and 12, become latchkey kids.

Homeboys and Homegirls are not dependent on the whims of trendsetters although they are aware of them. They are not particularly receptive to change and often have a strong, inner, emotional life that they have trouble expressing, resulting in sometimes idiosyncratic choices, such as suddenly quitting work and moving to a new town. Insensitivity, bullying, and being angry are often the way these feelings come out. Their marriages suffer from a lack of communication and often end in confusion and divorce, particularly painful since neither husband nor wife fully understands the source of their unhappiness. After divorce, Homeboys and Homegirls are even more hard-pressed, financially, and must alter career goals and other dreams, adding to their resentment and frustration.

Homeboys and Homegirls don't expect a lavish life style, but they want at least what their parents had: a home; a late-model car; two weeks at the shore or the lake with the family; an occasional trip (for two) to an exotic locale (preferably the Bahamas or Hawaii, although Las Vegas or Atlantic City will do); and at least some level of college for their kids. Although a majority of Homeboys and Homegirls are able to achieve this dream, for many it is simply out of reach. Caught in the lower middle class, they find even buying a home unattainable.

Lenny the Dharma Bum

Named after Lenny Bruce and Jack Kerouac's novel, *The Dharma Bums*, these Baby Boomers modeled themselves on what these two figures stood for.

Lenny Bruce was a cultural mirror of his time. Controversial because he was brutally honest and authentic, he was arrested for obscenity and tried and harassed for his graphic (judged pornographic) nightclub comedy. Eventually he died, alone, of a drug overdose. Only after his death did he become widely known and admired, although he was often included in the list of older "heroes" of the Gap Generation, along with John F. Kennedy, Robert F. Kennedy, Dr. Martin Luther King, Jr., Marilyn Monroe, and James Dean. His impact on the Baby Boomers was broader and more indirect than these figures. A cultural martyr, Lenny suffered the consequences of choosing a path that searched for and revealed the truth, despite being impractical and self-destructive.

Although written in the 1950s, *The Dharma Bums* and *On the Road* were read by the Baby Boomers when they were teenagers, and became the "seed" literature of the cultural revolution. Restless and fearless, the characters in these books rejected conventional society and its rigid, predictable values. Movies or TV had not yet caught up with the rebellious spirit of the 1960s. Even *Easy Rider* and *Woodstock* didn't provide the kind of road map that *The Dharma Bums* did for how to rethink and reinvent one's life. By high school, Lennies were already well read, embracing Henry David Thoreau's *Walden* and Aldous Huxley's *Doors of Perception* as legitimate critiques of the establishment and a call for rebellion. Their parents had never heard of these books or at least weren't interested in finding out what their kids were learning. Their ability to control their kids dwindled as adolescence approached, and they were often preoccupied by then with their own marital and career problems. The generation gap widened.

The name Dharma Bum implies both the journey and style. Whereas the Voyager, like Ulysses, knew where he was coming from and where he was headed, Lennies did not go directly from point A to point B, following a compass or a map. They recognized the need to survive in society but chose to avoid replicating experiences associated with their parents. Today they may still desire comfort, wealth, and recognition, but don't want to have to follow a traditional path to achieve them.

Lenny the Dharma Bum is the product of the newly emerging and rapidly reproducing American middle-class parents who had enthusiastically welcomed new theories and techniques of child rearing. Their parents had been more distant and formal; ambiguity or self-doubt were not spoken of. Baby Boomer parents looked forward to raising their own children differently, in a more relaxed and affectionate manner. But they had not been trained to be comfortable with their feelings. Self-conscious and reticent, they channeled their anxiety and anger into work, sports, food or drink, and marital spats.

Much of the new focus on an idealized, nuclear family was fragile, superimposed on a more powerful set of emotions that were neither acknowledged nor expressed. Father, trapped in an unsatisfying job, came home from the office needing a few martinis before he could face his family. Mother, trapped at home, any career on hold, poured all of her energies and frustrations into anticipating his arrival. Inevitably, the idyllic family dinner was fraught with tension and unspoken resentment, even hostility. The phony cheerfulness made the tension all the more frightening to children, who sensed their parents' fundamental unhappiness.

Children were encouraged to perform, but were often at a loss as to what their parents wanted. Sensing the gap between the needs of their parents and their inability to satisfy them, children ended up feeling anxious and angry, wanting to please their parents but never feeling as if they had succeeded.

Lennies reacted by rejecting the contradictions of their family life. Although much was left unsaid, their parents argued frequently, oblivious to the effect it had on their children. Lennies felt caught in the middle of what seemed to be an ongoing war. They didn't understand the causes, battles, or weapons, nor did they feel safe or protected. They felt hurt and betrayed by their parents, whose insensitivity often led their children to act rebelliously.

At first Lennies sought attention by being irrepressible class clowns, a bit like Chameleons, but not as street smart. Later, in high school, Lennies got thrown out of class for disagreeing with their teachers. They skipped school. They hung out with other rebels, not just middle-class kids, but working-class kids, black and Asian kids, and anyone who wanted out of the confining cliques of jocks and nerds. They stayed up late, talking, driving around, getting high. Stoned and fed up, they found the neat, orderly world of the suburbs an alien planet. They felt like astronauts, ready to explore strange new worlds.

Lennies want to love and be loved. Strikingly naive at times, they are caught between their rejection of their parents' norms and their failure to establish any clear norms of their own. They are committed to an alternative life style, but have trouble accepting even that level of commitment. They feign contentment, appear easygoing, present a mellow demeanor, and offer "good vibes." Often inertia more than anything else keeps them in relationships. They have trouble identifying and acknowledging their needs, negotiating with others, and resolving conflicts.

Lennies do not, however, avoid conflict entirely. They are and have been a constant source of friction for their family, friends, and lovers. Lennies aggressively pursued counterculture life styles earlier than other Baby Boomers. In high school they shocked their parents by proclaiming their plans to be a farmer, a forest ranger, or a rock musician. Often they refused to pursue any direction at all, and left home or dropped out of college after muddling through a year. Their parents hoped that they were going through a stage that they would outgrow.

Most Lennies finished high school, and were ready for the next big adventure, even if they had no idea what it was. It was at this point that many Lennies became Dharma Bums, as they began the quest for meaning in a meaningless society. Many hitchhiked around the country. Some, who had worked during high school, asserting independence, had enough money to go to Europe for a while, without any elaborate preparation or expectations. They often ended up spending some time living overseas.

Many Lennies dropped in and out of college. They started because their parents figured that it was better to pay for them to be in college than not know where they were. State colleges and even universities were relatively inexpensive; middle-class parents could finance a child's education for two to three thousand a year. Most Lennies did not survive college beyond their first year. Those who managed to stay in often did so because it meant getting their parents' financial support and avoiding the pressure to get a job. Lennies generally chose fields of study that were esoteric and impractical, such as philosophy, medieval studies, obscure languages, or 18th-century English poetry.

Comfortable in small towns in Vermont, Minnesota, New Mexico, or California, some found safe places to indulge their unworldly aspirations. They worked as laborers by day and hung out with like-minded friends, escapees from a civilization seemingly on the brink of collapse. They made their own clothes, drank herbal tea, baked bread, and grew organic vegetables.

Many Lennies did not go to college. They took jobs—as an orderly in a psychiatric hospital, a school bus driver—but their energies were directed toward art, music, or travel. Those who worked at a day job and played music often lived in communes or co-ops, sometimes in rundown buildings. They packed their vans with musical gear and traveled from gig to gig, struggling to make enough money to buy food and clothes.

Today Lenny the Dharma Bum still looks like a hippie, with longish hair and Birkenstock sandals. Somewhat sanctimonious about the materialistic life styles of the 1980s, they nevertheless own a car and perhaps a personal computer for writing poetry or publishing a local arts newspaper. They feel they are superior in their focus on spiritual and moral world issues. They are interested in "whole earth" products and small publishing houses that publish worthy manuscripts. They work for recycling and teach their children to be compassionate toward the homeless. They stock up on herb tea, megadoses of vitamin C, and bee pollen; they drink wine and occasionally smoke a little homegrown pot, but don't use cocaine or other trendy substances. When friends come over for the evening they cook up cracked wheat bread with oat bran and zucchini-eggplant-tofu lasagne from cookbooks such as *Laurel's Kitchen* or the *Enchanted Broccoli Forest*. (Lennies tend to be vegetarians.) To get dressed up, a male Lenny might wear a Costa Rican embroidered shirt, and a female Lenny might put on a funky pair of earrings from the African export shop two blocks from home. They listen to old favorites, from the Grateful Dead to Joni Mitchell, or a new Brazilian jazz group, or Ju Ju music (African Hi-Life music).

As Lennies advance in their professional careers (although they might deny the label "professional" since it implies being mainstream), and acquire more of the trappings of their parents' generation, their success often results in a crisis, since they cannot bear the responsibility of being immersed in the materialistic world. Sometimes their response is to retreat: sell the business, take a sabbatical, or start in a different field. Lennies choose to follow their personal feelings and priorities rather than march along a career path, no matter what sacrifice it calls for or the diminution in material status it produces.

As they get older, Lennies, despite their protests to the contrary, are nevertheless more focused on material possessions. They want to own quality merchandise. They have an increasing appreciation for upscale wilderness clothes, although they may hesitate to buy more than just a few essentials. They have found that they are not truly ascetic by nature but are actually closet epicures. Due to limited resources, however, they may only be able to dream about espresso machines, earth houses, solar heaters, greenhouses, and other purchases they feel are morally justified. If they can afford it they will go on a camping trip to a favorite American region, or maybe embark on a trek to New Zealand.

Materialism is often expressed by taking great pains to remodel their homes. They may introduce Southwestern design themes to a Victorian house, or tear down walls to turn a tract home into a loft studio. Their creativity is unbounded by convention, and they invest tremendous personal energy in each laborious step they take in the process. Over a period of years they may finish one room; some never finish as they move on to the next project. Since they often have few financial resources, they consider their labor as their investment in the world they live in. They take considerable pride in their work, because, lacking other sources of personal reward (professional careers, if they have one, are rarely satisfactory to them), what they can produce is the best measure of achievement.

Lennies tend to be mobile, often choosing, out of necessity and preference, to share with others. They may eventually rent a house or apartment in an underclass or artsy urban neighborhood (often not recognizing they are part of an incipient gentrification process), or in smaller communities surrounding regional arts and education centers (every major college campus has a Lenny neighborhood). They live in integrated neighborhoods if they're urban, and in smaller houses in more working class neighborhoods if they are suburban. Some of them stay in the country, growing vegetables, which sometimes they sell at urban farmer's markets (typically, radicchio, arugula, and other vegetables in vogue). They still bake bread and do their own canning.

Lennies may have received training, albeit circuitously, to become midwives, licensed masseurs/masseuses, restoration contractors (carpenters, painters, craftsmen), cooks/chefs, mechanics, software developers, video technicians and engineers, graphic artists, desktop publishers, and experimental musicians—all part of the growing service industry in the United States. Some Lennies have also realized that they can increase the economic value of their labor by focusing on producing items that reflect their own beliefs. Many companies, such as Woodstock Chimes, started out as small counterculture enterprises and now sell vast quantities of their products at a great profit. Upscale catalogues, such as Smith and Hawken, grew out of the personal tastes and styles of their founders (Paul Hawken preferred high-quality gardening tools).

Being your own boss was popular with Lennies in the 1960s, but usually only in terms of selling your labor as a carpenter or house painter; manufacturing had little appeal and was associated with polluting steel mills, decrepit automobile plants, and an alienated labor force. Just the same, manufactured products with a good value attracted many Lennies to become entrepreneurs (Ben & Jerry's ice cream, for example). Doing business to keep true to your values eventually evolved into running a business to allow production of something valuable to others. Thus Lennies often became entrepreneurs of substantial small businesses over time.

Like most new entrepreneurs, Lennies lacked funds to start their businesses. Moreover, few had experience in planning a business or dealing with financial institutions. However, many Lennies had been involved in running small-scale businesses (their own services), or had played an important role in someone else's business, as a bookkeeper or manager at a restaurant or crafts store. Despite limited funds and experience, their considerable enthusiasm (a Lenny hallmark), and an ability to live frugally (mattress on the floor, shared housing, etc.) allowed Lennies to develop the foundation for the next cycle of their highly individualistic careers. By the 1970s interest in small businesses had grown. Lennies also began to see that their rejection of the corporate life style and insistence on independence and quality was becoming more mainstream.

Many Lennies today work for public service agencies. If they are lucky, they have become civil servants in jobs that do not conflict with their values of respecting individuality and freedom, of doing no harm to people or the environment, and that allow them to go home and let their hair down. Lennies work at women's centers and on fund-raising campaigns for environmental causes. In addition to advocacy groups, they may be found working in small, alternative shops as salesclerks, selling old records and used paperbacks, imported or handmade clothing, and health foods. The less fortunate take any job they can get.

Not all Lennies have found their true niche, however. Many are still stuck in the fundamental dilemma of having to earn a living by day while practicing their true vocation (developing computer software, designing fantasy worlds, playing fiddle music, publishing poetry) at night and on weekends.

Lennies are generally very conscientious about money and give to charity under a sense of obligation, but limitedly, unless it is for a favorite cause, in which case they give far more than the average (they give till it hurts). Some Lennies are interested in organized activities, such as the Sierra Club. However, most Lennies are iconoclastic when it comes to participating in organizations. They are more likely to Save the Whales, which also provides psychologically profound images to which Lennies can attach spiritual import (i.e., whales and dolphins are not only endangered, but are intelligent beings that have messages to give us).

Lennies tend to be highly autonomous, a quality they acquired from their struggle, early in life, to establish themselves with preoccupied, strict, often indifferent, parents. Lennies ignore the American social mainstream, not because they don't care, but because they are still trying to find what will make them happy. They disdain yuppies, who embrace the Republican Party and BMWs with equal fervor.

Lennies are, in comparison with other Baby Boomers, introverted, particularly when it comes to spirituality. They appreciate being on their own and being alone when they need to. They are not afraid of solitude and don't like being dependent on other people. In social relationships, however, they are outgoing and enjoy the company of friends. They are particularly vocal on global issues, such as the environment, foreign policy, and South Africa, and will write letters to editors when sufficiently moved by an issue.

One of Lenny's primary difficulties is relationships. Lenny's easy good fellowship has its limits. Lennies have difficulty establishing and maintaining strong and continuous relationships. They handle stress by denying it, withdrawing from it, or judging the offending person or problem as contrary to cherished values. Infidelities are often excused, or made light of, but underlying these situations are emotional wounds that do not heal easily. Lennies may use good-natured humor to avoid conflict ("Hey, let's not get too heavy about this"). They try to circumvent the tension, hoping, as they did when they were children and overheard their parents fighting, that if they're nice it'll go away. Thus, Lennies prefer to stay in their counterculture world, where there are fewer expectations or traditional pressures to conform or perform. Lennies don't want to be forced to be responsible for the pain of conflict or failure.

TECHNO-KIDS: 1960–1969

$\mathbf{I}$n 1960, over 11 percent of the population was under five; by 1970 only 8 percent was under five. The baby bust had begun and continued throughout the decade. The group that followed the Baby Boomers was smaller, less visible, and less vocal. These are the Techno-Kids, raised in a time when technological development grew exponentially.

The Techno-Kids, now in their twenties, are beginning to emerge as a distinct group; they have their own unique identity and special characteristics. Only recently discovered by the media, they are courted by conservatives, mocked by aging radicals as more conservative than anyone under fifty has ever been, and lectured to by concerned adults about their sexual habits, drug use, and "hurried" childhoods.

IMMERSION

The parents of the Techno-Kids are members of the Bridge Generation, born in the 1930s, straddling the wartime and postwar eras. Young enough to have missed the major impact of the depression, the Bridge Generation remember their childhood primarily in terms of World War II—a time of heroes and national unity.

For the most part, Techno-Kids were born into the conformity of the suburban 1960s. But a few were born into a dizzying array of alternative environments that included communes, converted school buses, and flower-child caravans. They were given, in keeping with the spirit of the times, unusual names such as Sunshine, Amber, and Raven.

The 1960s were a period of rapid social change; much was in flux. Traditional assumptions and understandings about personal relationships and social institutions were being challenged and reexamined. Marriage, in particular, could not withstand the scrutiny: between 1960 and 1970 the divorce rate increased by almost 60 percent, then in the 1970s by another 50 percent. The family stability of the 1950s was, for the most part, gone forever.

Most Techno-Kids' families were intact, but even they felt the impact of the wild and tie-dyed 1960s. Spurred by the women's movement, Moms went off to work. This was one common reverberation of social change in the 1960s, and more Techno-Kids were to grow up with working mothers than kids of any previous generation. Day care became important, and the concept of parenting began to replace that of mothering as more and more fathers got involved in feeding the baby and cooking dinner. Traditional gender-based roles were beginning to relax, although more often by word rather than deed.

Many parents also experimented with more relaxed attitudes toward raising children. As a result, discipline and consistency began to crumble. "Openness"—permissiveness without structure—was "in," and parents and teachers alike believed in "hanging loose" when it came to supervising children. Although Techno-Kids were involved in more real-world activities than many Baby Boomers were, they were much less the center of attention. Lacking clear guidelines and restrictions, younger and younger children emulated and imitated the habits and behaviors of their parents or older siblings in the late 1960s and into the 1970s. Early sexual activity and drug use were common among junior high and even elementary school children.

Raised in what Marshall McLuhan called the "global village," Techno-Kids had unlimited access, through the media, to information and role models; parents were no longer the village gatekeepers. The absence of strong moral leadership meant increased dependence on peers. As more and more social barriers broke down, "anything goes" was often the overriding message.

The most grievous damage done to Techno-Kids was unintentional— or perhaps done with all good intentions. The perpetrator was the public school system, where phonetic reading, new math, bilingual education, integration, and mainstreaming were all introduced simultaneously. Struggles with the community for control added to the chaos. Despite the specific good accomplished for individuals, particularly through the

Head Start Program, Lyndon Johnson's Great Society became a parody of itself under the Nixon administration. The reticent ministrations of a new regime left the nation's education system underfunded and unsupported. Programs were dismantled, or allowed to muddle through to an untimely end. Teacher strikes spread.

All this chaos and uncertainty in the late 1960s and 1970s confused Techno-Kids. Many were turned off, and dropped out in growing numbers (although not to the extent of 1942, when just over half of those entering 5th grade were still in school in 12th grade). What was worse, literacy among graduates declined.

Instead of innovation or transformation of community institutions, the Republican preference for less central government and more decentralized (i.e., local) government gave rise to a plethora of public and community institutions whose lack of standards, quality, and bureaucracy could only be characterized as arthritic. As public schools declined, more parents chose private schools, resulting in an emerging two-tiered educational system that would signify a collapse of the nation's social contract (if ever one existed in education). Techno-Kids felt as though society had lost interest in them, or was determined to pursue alternative ideals destined to fail. Children care less about whether schools are public or private—only that they teach well and provide a supportive environment for their development.

Techno-Kids suffered from being treated as a cultural experiment and ignored as individuals with a point of view. Moreover, parents and other significant adults were often preoccupied with their own ideas and struggles; their kids' lives came second. This lack of nurturance was painful and alienating for many Techno-Kids. In defense, they became pragmatic and realistic: if no one is going to take care of us, they thought, then we'll just have to learn to do it ourselves.

On TV, they observed the conflict between generations, ethnic groups, and classes, and they saw it repeated within their own families. They watched the crises of their grandparents and parents—divorce, job frustration, depression—and wondered if it was normal. They saw the cultural revolution of the Gap Generation on TV and wondered if that was the norm. The insularity of the great suburban experience was much harder to maintain. Kids were exposed to a tremendous amount of unsorted ideas and information at a high velocity. Whether all of this was normal or not, it was the reality they lived in.

For most Techno-Kids it was apparent early on that real-world existence was a fact. Even the inanities of TV sitcoms couldn't quite extinguish the gripping power of the newscast footage of police attacking demonstrators at the Democratic Convention in Chicago, the war in Vietnam, the triumph of Richard Nixon, the debacle of Watergate. Less so than the Baby Boomers, who were older, and also confused, Techno-Kids were unable to decipher which institutions were solid or worthy. Everything seemed to be on the verge of collapse, and television increased the size and speed with which institutions were scrutinized, criticized, and sometimes demolished.

Television was indeed an accepted baby-sitter for Techno-Kids, and educational programs like *Sesame Street* made parents feel less guilty about the number of hours their children spent watching TV. Techno-Kids were Madison Avenue's prime target as advertising became more sophisticated. Children were as adept at singing commercial jingles as they were reciting nursery rhymes. The adventures of Batman and Robin and other comic book–based live action and animated shows became popular. Reading, as a pleasurable activity, had lost its allure.

DIVERSION TO CONVERSION—ADOLESCENCE AND BEYOND POST 1970

The 1970s were a crucial time for the Techno-Kids, now entering their teens. The most profound influence of the period was the ailing economy. The economic turbulence and lack of optimism about the future affected the Techno-Kids deeply. Unlike the two preceding generations, they did not have the leisure to reject the status quo. The liberty their older siblings took in attacking the establishment was granted to them, in part, by the success of that establishment in bringing them up to believe America was plentiful, with truly enough for all. Being able to make a decent living without sacrificing more than 40 hours a week had been assumed by the Gap Generation and the Baby Boomers; Techno-Kids were not so sure that America's bounty could still provide opportunities for them.

By the time they were early teenagers, the drama of Watergate was everywhere, every day. By the time they were mid-adolescents, Richard Nixon had resigned in disgrace and President Gerald Ford tripped down the steps of Air Force I. ("Saturday Night Live," the irreverent, late-night comedy show, had a field day with that one, complete with pratfalls.) In addition to clowns, the country's leaders were portrayed as liars and fools. Jimmy Carter's tenuous presidency, during a time of tremendous inflation and recession, did little to restore the status or image of executive leadership.

The Techno-Kids were to feel the pressures and uncertainties of the free market just as they began to see themselves as potential members. Prosperity was still possible, but it was no longer assured. The changes in the global marketplace began to have strong repercussions, as the structure of the American economy underwent the most profound transition in its postwar history. Years of complacency in industry, combined with inflation, had made traditional American companies no longer competitive. Many were on the verge of collapse; the oil industry and manufacturing were closing plants and reducing their work force. The computer and service industries were just beginning to open up. Like a patron entering a restaurant still under construction, Techno-Kids were about to sit down to an uncertain meal—what was on the menu and who was cooking the food were very unclear.

Many Techno-Kids would find it impossible to emulate their parents' career choices. In Pennsylvania and Ohio mills were shutting down; automobile plants in Michigan, Ohio, and Indiana were also closing, as were their suppliers. Once the pride of American production and innovation, the region was becoming known as the Rust Belt. Jobs in service and construction were also slow; people had little money to spend.

Techno-Kids saw education more as preparation for a specific career than as preparation for life in general. Gap Generation kids had been able to break new ground, explore and define new careers; Baby Boomers had been able to consider their personal values first. Techno-Kids could not afford either luxury.

Social conformity and conservatism was the result. In 1984, Ronald Reagan collected 59 percent of the 18 to 24 year old vote (reflecting Techno-Kids born between 1960 and 1964), the same percentage as in the population at large. In 1986, 40 percent of all 18 to 21 year olds surveyed (those born between 1965 and 1968) labeled themselves Republicans. Only 30 percent considered themselves Democrats, with an equal number calling themselves independents.

Techno-Kids live up to their conservative image more on some issues than on others. On public policies and intensely personal issues such as abortion, the death penalty, and the legalization of marijuana, Techno-Kids are fairly conservative, certainly much more so than the Baby Boomers. On issues that reflect personal life style choices, however, such as cohabitation before marriage or women working, Techno-Kids are quite liberal. For Techno-Kids, working mothers are almost the norm; they, more than any previous group, are children of mothers who worked outside the home. In 1970, 39 percent of all children under 18 years of age had working mothers. In 1975, the percentage increased to 44 percent. By 1980, 53 percent of all children under 18 years, including the majority of Techno-Kids, had mothers in the labor force.

Perhaps because of their troubling experiences as children, Techno-Kids have been more reactive in forming their values. They searched through the institutions their parents knew, and rejected, to find clues for structure and meaning. Many traditions and fads that had been discarded by the Gap Generation and the Baby Boomers were welcomed back. Cotillions and proms began a modest rebirth in the 1980s. Fraternities became popular again. Psychedelic lights, rock music, and marijuana were replaced by beer busts, pop music, and country-rock.

But although the past seems to hold answers for the Techno-Kids, it's a past recast by the changes of the 1960s and 1970s. A girl could ask a boy to the prom. Fraternities are no longer segregated. Many of the advances brought about by the women's movement are taken for granted. Girls assume they will go to college and work afterward. But, given the harsh economic realities of a competitive work force, it remains to be seen whether or not Techno-Kids will be able to uphold these gains, increase them, or just look on while their more conservative members force their generation backward.

One frightening reality for Techno-Kids was the substantial increase in teenage suicide rates. Since 1970, the teen suicide rate has increased by almost 48 percent. This increase reflected a shared sense of alienation, hopelessness, and lack of purpose among Techno-Kids, possibly a result of the failure of parents and public institutions to supply a firm cultural foothold and entry into society.

Cultural orphans, Techno-Kids tend to express their alienation inwardly, against themselves, rather than against the world. Although many Baby Boomers felt aimless and alienated from their families, they found solace in their peers and as part of a generation making changes. A new society seemed imminent, where they would eventually find fulfillment. Each preceding generation had some rite of passage—the march of progress at the turn of the century, the depression, World War II, confrontation with the establishment. But for the Techno-Kids, born into ambiguity and social upheaval, there has been no particular hurdle to get over that would help them define who they are and what they stand for. They have had to establish their own internal morality in the absence of a set of strong values against which to rebel or with which to ally themselves.

Their coming-of-age movie was *Star Wars*, the dizzying, technical tour de force by George Lucas of Joseph Campbell vintage (e.g., about myth and life). Its archetypal themes—the adolescent hero, alone, seeking adventure, finding a mentor (Obie Wan Kenobie), confronting the inner darkness of the self (Darth Vader), mastering the challenge of self-discipline (the Force), and emerging successfully from the rite of purification as a full adult citizen—resonated with the Techno-Kid generation. But beyond the occasionally inspiring allegory, most of their subsequent cultural reference points during the 1980s have been a bewildering and numbing array of violent movies (*Halloween I, II, III*, etc., *Friday the 13th I, II, III*, etc.); adolescent wish-fulfillment fantasies (i.e., *The Revenge of the Nerds, Porkies*); and nihilist social fables (i.e., *Police Academy*). Some films have managed to capture the anxieties and struggles of the Techno-Kids, including *Saturday Night Fever* and, much later, *Fast Times at Ridgemont High*.

Television underwent its mid-life crisis during the 1970s, at about the same time that many Techno-Kids' parents were getting divorced. During the week Techno-Kids watched "The Brady Bunch," "The Partridge Family," "Eight Is Enough," and reruns of "My Three Sons." On the weekends, however, a new kind of program showcased contemporary moral and ethnic conflicts within a humorous context: "All in the Family," "Mary Tyler Moore," "Rhoda," "Maude," "One Day at a Time," "Alice." Shows such as "The Jeffersons" featuring all-black casts increased. "Saturday Night Live" was an important link to the now-coming-of-age counterculture.

But despite a new realism on TV, it was still a glossy and romanticized world, where even bigots like Archie Bunker were portrayed as lovable. Many Techno-Kids, alone in the afternoons and evenings while their parents worked, became addicted to TV, obsessed with superheroes and the neat, 30-minute resolution of problems. The increasingly rapid pace of change has caused Techno-Kids to grow up faster than any previous generation. The mixed message of their childhood was stay in school longer and don't take on adult responsibilities, but be mature sooner since you have unlimited access to information and freedom to experiment. Many Techno-Kids were adultlike children, overly serious and emotionally undernourished. Now they have become childlike adults, who cannot weigh options and decide.

The music of the Techno-Kids during the 1980s, particularly punk and heavy metal, was often explicitly nihilistic and violent, with a conscious lack of reason for its violence. Techno-Kids who were then into heavy metal were both nihilistic and romantic. This romanticism was closely allied with a frustrated desire for rituals and order, from a respected authority. This new nihilism encouraged a desire for battle, and the berserk catharsis of pent-up anger. Its imagery used the glory, mystery, and magical power of the trappings of myths, once satisfied by the armed forces, or a righteous cause. Sporting long hair and wearing leather, the aficionados of heavy metal identified with the physiological intensity of the music, which is loud and concussive.

The lyrics were violent and mystical, full of demons, dragons, and the ravishing of helpless women.

Punk music is more complicated, evolving more explicitly from rebellion and self-destructive anger at family and self. There also has been a strong experimental art culture imbedded in the center of the punk music scene. For Techno-Kids, however, the appeal of punk was very visceral. The lack of direction and the need to express oneself through tantrums and disinhibition channeled through punk music and its attendant seedy night spots in dingy warehouses. The punk life style includes casual and brutal sex and drug use, all intended to push the limits of normality, and somehow break loose of the psychologically grim and grimy emptiness they feel. Although heavy metal and punk rock fans do not dominate their generation to the extent that lovers of more mainstream music do, Techno-Kids are more world-weary than previous cohorts. Their drug of choice is not the benign pot of the 1960s, taken in order to be silly and carefree or expand one's mind, but alcohol and cocaine, to numb the senses.

Although most Techno-Kids scorn the ideas and images of the hippies and flower children, a small and durable group of Techno-Kids wear their hair long, follow the Grateful Dead around the country, and embrace other aspects of the counterculture. They regret missing the protests, be-ins, and love-ins of the 1960s, and eagerly listen to their older siblings and cousins reminisce about the "good old days." But most Techno-Kids are firmly committed to living in the material world. They're interested in fitting in, being successful, achieving goals. They want to re-create, under their own direction, the cohesive family and all the other forms of a stable life style they missed out on as children, that previous generations had taken for granted. In a peculiar fashion, Techno-Kids have hybridized the values of the 1960s and the 1950s to create their own outlook on life.

BIRTHMARKS

Billy Budds

Like Herman Melville's character, Billy Budds are both naive and sincere, always on the verge of a dawning but elusive reality. They are subject to the same moral and spiritual convictions that inspired Billy Budd; Billies have adopted their Bootstrapper and Romantic-Realist parents' conviction that highly defined moral values are the proper inspiration to success. Religious values were important, as was reading; television was an accepted evil. Parents and family friends were highly vocal about their views of the world, and their careers.

During their formative years, Billies' parents provided direct role models and the impetus to seek other role models with the same values. They often watched their own parents struggle for meaning in the face of oppressive circumstances. A Billy Budd's mother may have struggled hard to earn a living after being abandoned by her husband. Father may have been a bitter intellectual, whose creativity turned to sour grapes when real estate supplanted a writing career. Both parents expressed their disappointment in terms of global values. They blamed the conservative government business sector for destroying the education and social service system. Billies imagined a pattern of conspiracy and internalized it; they often combined the idealism and cynicism of their parents.

Loyal children that they were, Billies became their parents' allies in their struggles with the world. They supported their parents by being good—loving, dependable, obedient. They took on their parents' stance: a critic of the system, a religious martyr, committed to the belief that a good person is dedicated to selfless caring for others, or to another social or political cause. A central task for Billies is defining their own authentic values and reconciling them with those of their parents.

The personality of Billies was not easy to detect during elementary or high school, since there was no clear distinction between their parents' values and their own. By college, however, Billies may have searched out ways to express themselves, often in extreme gestures. A boy or girl might become a competitive and active sportsman, devoted above all else to performance. Another might become a punk artist, seeking to make a strong statement. A third might fervently pursue a political career.

For Billies, the personal challenge has always been balancing their desire for a clearer image of themselves with a compulsion to focus on larger social issues. When their own emotional challenges arise, they are frequently poked and prodded by the call of exaggerated moral values, not by their inner needs. The battle to avoid this continual self-martyrdom is what propels them into adulthood.

Cosmopolitans

The Cosmopolitan was fortunate enough to have progressive role models as parents—often Envoys and Romantic-Realists—and friends, and a large family—more than three to five siblings or an extended network of relatives and close family friends. The Cosmo-

politan personality is extraverted, curious, open to change, highly autonomous, and only marginally self-indulgent. Cosmopolitans are
different from other Techno-Kids in being very literate, because of
their family's educational level and commitment to education and because of their tendency to engage in the world, rather than keep to
the neighborhood or backyard.

The Cosmopolitan was born into a household where parents followed a more traditional suburban American life style. One or the
other parent tended to be very close to the Cosmopolitan kid, who
had a firm support group—siblings, aunts and uncles, cousins—that
took an interest in his or her development.

From early on, Cosmopolitans often had to fend for themselves, as
well as do their share of work around the house. However, this early
experience of responsibility was not traumatic and was also reinforced
by having older siblings and parents as models. The Cosmopolitan
became quite autonomous, as a result of parents' high expectations
and the pressure to be grown up. This was, however, acceptable, because parents and family members had positive relationships with one
another.

The mother of a Cosmopolitan was often a professional, whose career had picked up as her children grew up. Sometimes she was an
intelligent person in search of satisfying activities to which to devote
her energies. In either case, her activities were visible to her children,
and a source of pride and status, whether she was a volunteer librarian
or a highly paid doctor.

The Cosmopolitan's mother was a key ally. She also could be pushy,
with expectations that were unrealistic or insensitive to the child's feelings or abilities. Even as adults, Cosmopolitans are often aware of
their mother's judgments and values; she calls and visits them often,
usually in connection with business and professional trips. A Cosmopolitan's father might also have had a profession he valued.

Both parents, however, could be overbearing in their expectations.
Praised early on, paraded around their parents' offices or parties, Cosmopolitans often felt like a showcase for their parents. As a result,
they often behave as if their main responsibility is to be a successful
adult very early in life. This is sometimes balanced by rebellion.

Early childhood for Cosmopolitans tended to be idyllic. Their families were often nature-oriented. They had many pets—two or three
dogs and a gaggle of cats—and, in more rural-suburban neighborhoods, horses or sheep. The family style was interactive, with frequent family gatherings. There was always a grandparent, aunt,
uncle, or cousin who would pay special attention to a fidgety Cos-

mopolitan during a Sunday dinner. Over the years, these family members provided a supplementary, sustaining resource, enabling Cosmopolitans to leave home but always feel connected.

Cosmopolitans blossomed in high school. They tended to take strong positions on social issues during the mid- and late 1970s. They were outspoken about racism, sexism, and birth control, despite their more conventional home life. Because Cosmopolitans were raised in households that placed a strong emphasis on cohesion and respect for the individual, Cosmopolitans were also very active in school events, both curricular and extracurricular, and in sports, theater, or debating.

Both male and female Cosmopolitans tended to experiment sexually in the early years of high school, albeit carefully. They saw their relationships as a demonstration of their autonomy and strength of values. Their families, no matter how tolerant, found their children sometimes exasperating, but not alienating. Cosmos were emotionally loud and reasonably healthy in decrying hypocrisy, but not self-destructive, trying to define the boundaries of their world. Most protests remained within the acceptable parameters of the Cosmopolitan's middle-class world.

Cosmopolitans expected to go to college, and did so. Many had parents who were university alumni and served as a bridge to college for their own children. For Cosmopolitans, college was a time for more radical exploration of their values. The oldest entered college in 1978, the youngest in the late 1980s. Cosmopolitans took their education fairly seriously, pursuing liberal arts degrees with the expectation of going on to get advanced degrees in business, law, or public health schools.

College years were very intense. Cosmopolitans were immersed in schoolwork and hearty partying. They drank, smoked dope, had casual sex, or lived with a lover, much to their parents' chagrin. Every summer was filled with work to finance school. Cosmopolitans were active in sports, mostly intramurally, and were consumers of local culture. They used their scant money to experiment with adult life styles, particularly during their summers, when they shared an apartment with roommates who also worked.

During their undergraduate, and sometimes into their graduate school days, Cosmopolitans' emotional lives were also intense; relationships with lovers and significant others were fraught with high expectations and frequent disappointments. Cosmo men tend to be very serious and emotional. Cosmo women tend to fall in love easily but aren't sure they want to make the commitment. Both men and women tend to have a series of serious relationships. They also place great value on long-term friendships with members of either sex.

Cosmopolitans are sexually very free as young adults. They want a serious mate, but are not initially interested in one who will inconvenience their career or personal interests by making restrictive demands on their lives. Instincts warn them to be careful of commitment because it may lead to a loss of ideals or independence. Still, by their late twenties, most Cosmopolitans are ready to plunge into marriage, and all the family ties, events, and entanglements this entails.

Cosmopolitans also have difficulty committing themselves to jobs. They are hungry for careers in which they can make use of their intellectual strengths, and when opportunities arise will leave college to work. However, their now limited qualifications do not lead them high enough up the corporate ladder, and they leave, sometimes job-hopping for years until just the right niche is found. Some will sacrifice career goals for personal reasons: romance, or continuing a protected life style in a university.

Cosmopolitans are often initially impressed with the trappings of corporate business because it reminds them of their parents' world. They admire institutions and powerful people whom they associate with their own family and friends. Cosmos want to identify with a company or organization. However, they eventually lose faith in power ties, power lunches, and power plays, and leave to try a new direction. Through trial and error, moving from company to company, Cosmos usually find a satisfactory place that is not threatening to their work and family values.

As they reach their late twenties and early thirties, Cosmopolitans are very strong on tradition. They are not religious, but ascribe considerable importance to holidays. They will gather at their parents' home at Christmas or Thanksgiving. Opening presents, eating special foods, and seeing familiar faces are reassuring rituals. They have festive Sunday brunches and New Year's Eve parties. Cosmopolitans can be counted on to be a prime mover in bringing others together.

Throughout their lives, Cosmopolitans tend to be politically strong in their convictions, surprisingly more than other Techno-Kids. Many women reflect feminist views in their relations with men and institutions. They want to be treated with respect, as individuals, in their work. They are still very conscious of discrimination and the tendencies toward sexism among their employers, male or female. Men also tend to have strong views, but are less vocal, unless they discover a niche in the political dialogue—liberal or conservative—where they can place themselves.

Cosmopolitans have evolved a new perception of their identity, specifically where gender roles are concerned. Women have grown up seeing themselves as fully competent with full expectations of careers, not second to men. Men have grown up with fewer expectations of female subservience. Cosmopolitan women are more open about sex, more outspoken, sports-oriented, and athletic, as well as more career-centered than earlier cohorts. Cosmopolitan men are slightly more interested in hearth and home.

Today, Cosmopolitans are struggling with the early stages of their careers, because they spent more years in school than their fellows. Cosmopolitans are now getting married or have been living with someone for several years and are likely to continue a stable life style. Cosmopolitans have been able to establish an improved relationship with their parents as they have become more self-assured and relaxed about their life plans. Their parents, the Bridge Generation, have reached their late 50s and 60s and are contending with their own maturity and developmental crises.

Missing Ingredients

Missing Ingredients are the casualties of their generation. They are the walking wounded, products of any of three of the Bridge Generation groups: Romantic-Realists, Bootstrappers, or Good Old Boys and Gals. Missing Ingredients had troubling experiences growing up in the 1960s. Their parents were preoccupied with their own growing up, emotionally and economically. Some parents had difficult marital relationships; others had to struggle to overcome financial and educational barriers.

Typically, Missing Ingredients' parents went through a period of stormy estrangement before divorcing. Although feigning concern for the children, they were likely to be uninterested or to use their children in an ongoing battle with the former spouse. Even when the battle was not overt, Missing Ingredient children lived with the daily anger of one or both parents, making it part of their personality. They learned to be manipulative, and were likely to act out their anger to attract attention.

Divorce resulted in a more dysfunctional personality for Missing Ingredients than for others, because of the lack of a well-defined self-image. As children, they tried very hard to please one parent, compensate for the loss of the other, and somehow assert independence. As adults, they have been engaged in a lifelong search for love and affection.

Missing Ingredient children needed to take care of themselves more than other Techno-Kids. Parents may have provided daily care, but instilled feelings of guilt and joylessness in the children in return. Many Missing Ingredient children were encouraged to parent their parents, grow up quickly, and abandon their own childhood. As a result, their relationship to family, friends, and significant others has been strained; as adults, they have some friends but rarely align themselves with a group.

The absence of strong parental participation in schools and the growing distrust of more formal teaching and supervisory structures resulted in a highly ambiguous school setting. This led many troubled students to indulge their frustrations without any adult restraints or concern. Students engaging in casual sex or drug use were often ignored. Many of the adults were themselves experimenting with sex and drugs, and were not ready to respond to Techno-Kids' behavior in a consistent way. Not only did this result in poor education, but it allowed a wider range of acting-out behaviors, and increased distress. Many experienced the trauma of early sexual rejection and unwanted pregnancies. The more fortunate were able to channel their needs into activities where they could gain empowerment and approval, such as theater or business.

The desire to receive the love and approval of their parents and their frustration at not getting it often resulted in a kind of emotional paralysis for Missing Ingredients. Out of touch with the reasons for their numbness, they tended toward highly demonstrative and self-destructive acting out. This behavior rarely brought relief; instead, it led to difficulties with parents, school authorities, and the law, as well as generalized depression.

It is not surprising that as Missing Ingredients matured, they abandoned acting out in favor of imitating their parents, although they would probably deny this. Whether they took equivalency exams, got out early, or caught up later by getting a general education diploma, Missing Ingredients were very much set on being on their own by the end of high school. For some, this meant having a baby and living with their parents without any clear view of the future other than job training. For others it meant leaving home to live with relatives and finish school in another town. Many moved in with girlfriend or boyfriend and fended for themselves. Those who were able to go to college were more likely to develop greater skills in finding work and managing their personal relationships.

Frequent confrontations and unsuccessful relationships are the trademarks of Missing Ingredients. They can be tenacious, sometimes abusive, in trying to control their partner in a relationship. This leads to multiple and tempestuous relationships, even though their response to separation and rejection is more dramatic and painful than that of other groups. They struggle between needing to be taken care of—a need not articulated and sometimes unacknowledged—and needing to be on their own. Although they may appear to be socially precocious, it is not unusual for them to choose partners more needy than themselves.

Their explorations are conducted in a more structured and directed manner than those of other Techno-Kids. They look for something, which was lacking at home, to give their lives definition. Learning new skills helps them socially, and they practice new skills and hobbies in a deliberate and intentional way. How Missing Ingredients use their aptitude varies enormously, but tends to be extraverted rather than introverted. Some may dedicate themselves to excelling in sports, learning ballroom dancing, working out, or looking the part of the ultra-fit, smart, stylish person. A Friday night dance provides a way for them to parade their new skills as well as look for potential partners. While other Techno-Kids might go to a local, nondescript bar to socialize, Missing Ingredients will search for the "right" bar to go to so they can fit in, or, more precisely, stand out.

Missing Ingredients have a tremendous amount of inner energy available, for their work and for others. They will often take up the career of professional caretaker because of their need to be cared for. Those whose primary need is to be recognized and loved may choose a business career to gain wealth and power. Many of the aggressive young career people of the 1980s were the talented but emotionally hungry Missing Ingredients, who flourished during the economic recovery that emphasized entrepreneurship and business.

Missing Ingredients were able to transform their emotional hunger into fuel for their careers, as physical therapists, social workers, computer salespeople, caterers, or financial services hotshots. Their feverish investment in their work, and the approval of bosses, clients, and buyers, was a means to prove their worth to themselves.

Keepers of the Flame

Keepers of the Flame were raised in families where there was a strong, autocratic, dogmatic structure. Parents were often older Good Old Boys and Gals, and Bootstrappers. Values were expressed very clearly and briefly, but often without explanation. Many parents of Keepers were distant and authoritarian, emphasizing the importance of family activities even though the emotional message of these activities often contradicted the apparent structure. Parents would bring children to visit family members, then get drunk and fight or have simmering, tense interactions, arguing before, during, and after the visit. Mother or Father might stress how much he or she valued family life when the reality of that life was alcoholism, infidelity, loss of sexual interest, and abusive behavior. A mother might confide in her children about her dissatisfactions with her marriage. Child abuse in such dysfunctional families was common. Sometimes the abuse was verbal, with accusations and threats; other times it was physical.

Other Keeper homes were healthier, but highly structured and restrained. However, children managed to escape much of the day-to-day regulation while absorbing the overriding values of order and control. Parents may or may not have been religious, but came from religious backgrounds. Father may have been somber and formal, running the house by the book in a disciplined and businesslike manner. Mother may have been unhappy, expressing herself through irritability and nagging, through overeating, through poor housekeeping, or immersing herself in life outside the home, with job or relatives.

Regardless of the degree of pathology at home, the Keeper experienced dissonance between the ideal and reality. These contradictions were not easily resolved by young Keepers, who wanted their parents' love but at the same time were angered by their parents' fraud. Coached to conceal their feelings and minimize conflict, Keepers felt the enduring pain of emotional hypocrisy.

The hallmark of Keepers of the Flame is their belief and hope for a wholesome family. They strive to prove themselves different from their parents, and seek to re-create the family in later years as they believed it should have been. For some, the trauma is so great that they may avoid the family altogether.

The early childhood of Keepers was marked by docility and compliance, but with rebellion simmering beneath the surface. During adolescence, a different picture began to emerge. Many Keepers were hell-raisers, on the streets during the 1960s and 1970s. They became smart but not wise about the realities of life. In their early teens, Keepers used drugs, had sex, got drunk, and cut school. Many were particularly indifferent to school and barely got by. Concerned, their parents tried to provide direction, but were often vague and ineffective. Direct confrontation was rare.

Their parents' refusal to deal with their own and their children's problems gave Keepers the more complex task of sorting out their responsibilities for themselves. Their parents might know and like rock music, but disapprove of heavy metal or other 1980s music; they maintain a careful cultural distance from their children. In rebelling,

Keepers, not usually wild and crazy, fit in on the eccentric fringes of their peer group.

The Keeper of the Flame personality grew out of personal frustration and guilt over unsupported independence in young adulthood and the lack of intervention by parents. Keepers rarely, if ever, unburdened themselves freely to their parents about their confusing experiences and were more likely to confide in siblings. Keepers feared disappointing their parents and incurring their displeasure or wrath. The lack of perceived parental concern or support made the contrast between home, where emotions were not shared, and the wide-open outside world, more stark. It also made the exploratory experiences of the world—sex, drugs, etc.—more appealing.

At the end of high school, Keepers typically reformed themselves. They realized the need to focus their lives and reaffirm their belief in the importance of family values, work, and faith. They were honest and friendly but not worldly. To their friends they seemed oddly clean-cut. While other kids were rebelling, Keepers were taking family vacations and appearing to like it. Their compensatory guilt led them to family functions, church, staying close to home, and whatever else they thought the family might appreciate.

Keepers of the Flame are distinguished by a strong emotional facade that rarely crumbles under pressure. They internalize pressure and assume it is their own burden. They seek answers that have a moral clarity and, because they trust others, are often exploited. They are also trusted and assume the burdens of family and friends and others. They work hard and long, ask for little, and build a small world for themselves that they can control.

Most Keepers did not develop strong career images for themselves until college, if then. They might have worked for a year or so in the family business and then settled for a job there. Even those who went off to college might return to a family business such as landscaping or construction, eventually.

When they leave home, they move nearby, frequently into very modest surroundings. They are happy with their local world, experiment little, and travel rarely. When they do travel, it is often to visit family, since it is common for the entire extended family to live within a 100-mile radius. For local entertainment, a baseball or football game would be more appealing than a ski trip; an evening in a familiar restaurant with friends would feel more comfortable than trying a new restaurant in the city. Keepers are slow to change and modest in needs and expectations.

PART

THREE

A REFLECTION ON THE FUTURE: TODAY'S TIME SIGNATURES TOMORROW

In this book a mirror has been held up to America's personality. Reflected in this imperfect mirror are the folks who make up our country. What we see is a kind of "cultural hologram"—that is, a picture that can be examined from many angles. Time Signatures and Birthmarks have given depth and focus to the elastic features of our friends and neighbors, who too often exist without scale or proportion or context, a human blur in the history of our lives, and possibly their own.

In this concluding chapter we offer another type of mirror to reflect back on ourselves, a look at our shared futures; something to think about.

We concluded our survey of the American time traveler with those born in the 1960s. The youngest is now 21, the oldest, born between 1900 and 1909, 91. Those born in the 1970s and 1980s have yet to reach a point where they have concretized their values. But we already know what their Time Signatures are likely to be. After all, we are all part of the same rhythm of history. As for the children of the 1990s, we can only speculate. However, since their Time Signatures will be our Weather Report, we share a strong interest in what these future events might turn out to be.

In this scenario of the future the major theme is the struggle of the U.S. economy. The 1990s will be a difficult period in which we will battle against a decline in overall quality of life. Having absorbed decades of self-praise about America's greatness and goodness, we are uncertain what being an American really means—in the face of a rapidly expanding global economy that includes increased competition and overseas ownership of American business. Profound economic and social change is reshaping the image of America.

The economic reality is that America is up for sale. Everyone owns or wants to own a piece of America's economy. Foreign ownership of U.S. businesses has always existed, but this is different. Some refer to it as "globalization"; others call it the "recolonialization" of America. America is having a taste of its own medicine, it seems.

In technology, geometrically progressing rates of innovation are rapidly making worker skills obsolete, at the same time tantalizing consumers with new products and possibilities. Moreover, a decentralized government has resulted in a new domestic though genteel feudalism among states, resulting in a balkanized nation at a time when a new movement toward restructuring along Western models, combined with ethnocentricity and autonomy, is reshaping Eastern Europe. At the same time cultural changes are being driven by America's new pluralism—a larger nonwhite population and value conflicts between proliferating interest group networks (women, older adults, gays, racists) that cross political boundaries.

This is the story of the 1990s. Where does it leave us on New Year's Eve, 1999, the dawn of the year 2000?

Let's take a look. Remember, everyone is now 10 years older, with 10 years of experiences in adapting or not adapting to the world around them. While our age will be an important factor in how we greet the new century, who we are psychologically may be far more important in determining how well we have weathered or exploited the intervening years. For this reason, we conclude with a profile on each Time Signature group as well as each Birthmark. Whoever we are, the future awaits just the same, but how each of us will greet that future will be as different as night and day.

CHILDREN OF THE CENTURY

On this New Year's Eve, there will be about 2 million Children of the Century 90 years or older, many bridging two centuries of culture. These Americans are in their Transcendence stage, where, if they are successful, they will have achieved a broader vision of their lives and will have come to terms with their mortality. Most of this age group are living in their own homes, or in housing for older adults. A quarter of them have some serious health difficulties, and they are and will be the primary occupants of nursing homes and hospitals. Yet, on New Year's Eve, 1999, this group will be the healthiest group of Time Travelers yet to reach their age.

Economic Outlook

Quality of life for these oldest adults is likely to be affected by the instability in the economy during mid-decade. This age group contains the highest proportion of lower income older adults (70% of this group currently have incomes below $15,000 a year), and with inflation and recession in the mid-1990s, their incomes will take a battering. In the inhospitable, budget-conscious world of the 1990s, these older adults will be forced to pay a greater share of their noncatastrophic health care. They will experience a diminished return from personal assets. Social Security income is likely to be taxed for the wealthier of this group, irrespective of age. Fortunately, a high percentage own their own homes, although these are often valued less than homes of younger age groups. This provides a source of emergency income for those who may need to finance long-term care; however, the trauma of selling a home and moving has a very negative impact on older adults unless handled well.

Technological Conditions

Technological advances are important to Children of the Century (although their cost is less likely to be reimbursed), in particular, less invasive treatments for alleviating the effects of chronic disease and accidents. Prevention of diseases such as arthritis and cataracts will not yet be feasible. New techniques that will be available will include improved laser and ultrasonic cataract surgery, enhanced methods of fostering bone regrowth and healing without surgery, and precision-made ceramic or artificially grown joints (hips) using computer-controlled machining based on three-dimensional imaging, and home health monitoring technology that uses small sensors implanted in the body to send telemetric data on health status to a home computer and from there to a community health monitoring service.

Social and Political Environment

Those with chronic health care problems will be most affected, because of the ongoing battle to reduce health care costs while increasing care. Although by mid-decade catastrophic health care financing will cover more of the inpatient hospital medical costs, and even more long-term care costs (perhaps as much as one year compared to the current half year), Medicare and Medicaid funding for home health care and nursing care will place far more of the financial burden on the individual and family than today. Moreover, even in a positive scenario of the future, some form of rationing of health care is likely by health providers. Within the next decade there will probably be a national policy on long-term care finance, designed to encourage participation in a mixed public-private long-term care insurance that will support in-home and community-based care, in addition to nursing home care.

Cultural Climate

The number of Children of the Century living in 2000 will be very small, relative to the total number of people over 65. Many will have adult children who will provide care or help finance care for their parents, within their means. However, most will still be dependent on public programs for serious health care needs. In a period of growing public concern about budgets and competition for public resources, the very old are likely to be viewed with some hostility, especially if there is an economic crisis. Even if the trend away from hospital and nursing care to outpatient and in-home care continues, the cost of care per person will not drop significantly. Much of the tension will be among care givers who are responsible for older family members but lack adequate financial resources. Their frustration will be, in effect, anger at the health system for failing to provide more satisfactory care finance options.

Preservers

From what we know of our Preserver relatives, we can expect them to have a hard time with the future because, not only will they be very old, but, because they have lived their lives wrapped in the bosom of their families, reluctant to find their own paths, they will be far more likely to be in the care of their adult children. Preservers in their 90s will be grim and often depressed—doubly so because of their fatalistic personalities.

We need to remember that Preservers are typically the last of an era of immigrants; a particular subgroup that has been (unlike their counterparts) inherently dependent people—less educated, less skilled, less open to the world or its changes. As a result they are less self-confident, so as they age they will continue their need for others to care for them. Roughly a third of their age group, Preservers left the work force earlier than others their age. What is worse is that because they are highly introverted, at least outside of the immediate family, they will have few resources that they can count on for help. Helpful neighbors will not be welcomed. Unhappy and bitter, the Preservers' troubled state of mind will go hand in glove with their poor health. Compared to others in their age group, Preservers are significantly less healthy, due to a legacy of old-world diseases, unattended chronic maladies, and the consequences of sweatshop labor in years gone by. As a result we can expect a larger number of Preservers to be in nursing homes or in a personal care home in the year 2000, despite efforts of their children to care for them as long as possible.

They will be surprised to see the new year dawn and not all that happy about it. When asked, or if asked, why they have such a negative outlook, despite their long life, they will respond: "I've had enough, why should I live? Who cares if I don't?"

Adaptors

The Adaptor at age 90 will be a colorful character. An attitude of openness has helped him or her make the most of life even to this late age. This small segment of the Children of the Century has benefited from a style of life that has been relatively responsive to change. Adaptors have made their way through to the future by always learning, rarely shutting out the world. Adaptors are not so much independent as they are extraverted. They are, in fact, needful people and rely on others for help and guidance, but not in a manner that is perceived by family and friends as negative or burdensome. The Adaptor style is constructive. Adaptors have always enjoyed and respected others, and because they relish their engagement with old friends and new, take on the world *con vivace*. Adaptors may have paid the price in more heart disease and diabetes, yet are more able to meet these challenges with a good spirit, as long as they have others to share their lives with.

The children of Adaptors were always inspired by their parents' spirit of engagement and earnestness. Their relations with their parents have always been loving. As their parents have aged, and themselves as well, the physical toll that life has inevitably wrought on the exterior of their parents has not worn away the image that their children carry with them. This has made it easier for them to care for Adaptors in their last decade.

Nonetheless, the realities of family life have created sources of conflict over time, when Adaptor children have had to care for their parents. Daughters and sons-in-law do not always understand the heroic image their spouses maintain of their parent. Just the same, those Adaptors making their way through their ninth decade have had to endure their share of adjustments to family life, not all of them happy. Fortunately, their adaptive nature has empowered them to take the ins and outs of life with good humor and a bit of adventurousness.

Pragmatists

Survival into their late years comes as a continual surprise for Pragmatists, and they are almost apologetic about it. Still, they regale their listeners with tales of grandfathers and uncles who survived to a ripe old age as well. Pragmatists have lived lives of cautious moderation so long they seem eternally old. For Pragmatists, preparation for the transcendent Rite of Passage into "old age" began long ago. With their game but fatalistic view of life, they ordered their cemetery plots, made their wills, and moved into senior housing long before they had to.

Early to retire, and long in retirement, these hardy survivors seem to have worked all their lives, just so they could be old, but not be in the way. They are the ones who always say, when family is gathered round to celebrate a 90th birthday "don't mind me, I don't see what all the fuss is about." Just the same, Pragmatists know what they want, they are just used to saying it in oblique ways. By this point in their lives they have become creatures of extremely refined habit. Unobtrusive, Pragmatists are folksy models of old age, goodnaturedly waving from the front porch, the last of their century's stereotypes of just plain folks.

Their children have always been very affectionate and respectful of their Pragmatist parents' needs; in a sense, many are models of their parents in their practicality. In the year 2000 the children of Pragmatists are in their 60s and 70s themselves, Children of the American Dream and members of the Bridge Generation. Performers and Attainers often make up the Pragmatists' brood. They have in the passing years gone their different ways, the Performers staying near by and the Attainers moving off to new territory. But both make themselves available to their parents.

Explorers

The always surprising Explorers seem to survive out of sheer orneriness. They stand out because of their individuality, in addition to their old age. Ever insular and obstinate, Explorers have always been refining their own style of living, achieving a minimalist art form, such as it is. They are the ones who have always resented authority, whether right or not. In their 90s Explorers will often be poor, living in their self-chosen manner in one or another obscure corner of the country. Yet Explorers have a native wisdom, an inner view that is commensurate with their acceptance and pursuit of independence. One Explorer commented with admiration on how old Eskimos, when reaching a point of frailty where they can no longer contribute to the family, used to go out on an ice floe to die. Another reflects on the stupidity of sentimental adults who don't have a "living will" that says when to "pull the plug" if a catastrophe occurs. Explorers have epitomized autonomy and self-denial all their days.

Explorer children, now in their 60s and 70s, are amazed at their parents' durability. Never close, they have seen them infrequently over the years, and have difficulty discussing personal matters. Occasionally, however, Explorers become the charges of their adult children, a difficult proposition since they are not particularly close and their children are older and worrying about their own needs.

THE DREAM-DEFERRED GENERATION

On the eve of the year 2000 roughly 8.4 million adults belonging to the Dream-Deferred Generation will be 80 to 90 years old. This group, the first to have realized that they would actually live long enough to be entitled to something called retirement, have also lived long enough to see the Social Security system established and mandatory retirement eliminated. On this auspicious New Year's Eve, they are old enough to remember hard times and to fear the possibility of its recurrence. Most are in their Emergence stage, where they are experiencing an inner struggle to allow themselves a rebirth of their self-image, a clarification of their values, and a consolidation of their experiences into what they might call "wisdom" (e.g., "If only I knew then what I know now. . ."). For this age group contemplation of who they are can be both playful and painful. Fortunately, they are better off financially than their elders (Children of the Century), although still cautious.

Economic Outlook

The primary concern of the Dream-Deferred Generation will be the continued threat of new recession or economic decline to their disposable income. This group will have been hurt by the inflation and recession of the mid-1990s and, because they have ridden the ups and downs of the economic roller coaster many times in their lives, they will be extremely cautious, on the whole, about matters financial. They are particularly concerned about the value of their home and neighborhood, their primary and only asset. A large portion of this group live in their own homes and are planning to remain there. During their 70s (in the 1980s) about 20 percent of this population thought about moving out for economic and life style reasons. By New Year's Eve, 1999, about 5 percent of this overall group will have elected to move to older adult housing, including continuing care retirement centers (CCRCs) and older-adult apartments, where they could better manage their personal financial resources and liabilities for health care.

Technological Conditions

Technology will be a major ally of the Dream-Deferred Generation. For them, technology will arrive slightly sooner than for the older cohort. Less invasive treatments and limited prevention and early treatment of health problems will allow a larger portion to live out their lives on their own. Devices that we already take for granted (pacemakers, heart valves, artificial joints) as well as procedures that were not thought practical in the past (reconstructive surgery, angioplasty, laser eye surgery, organ transplants) will be more available to this group while they are young enough to benefit. By the year 1995 devices that use remote measurement of physiological change, such as voice patterns and physical gait (walking), as well as simple sampling of blood, saliva, and urine, will permit ongoing health monitoring and maintenance without necessitating as many visits to doctors' offices—and enable health technicians to provide individuals with more monitoring and maintenance services at lower costs. There will be a substantial move in the mid-1990s by the Social Security Administration to implement a system of "smart cards" that carry individual records—Social Security, medical, insurance, other pertinent personal data—to help the system become more efficient. Unfortunately, although this generation will have more access to health care, they will still be carrying the burden of chronic diseases that could have been prevented earlier, had there been better informed and more aggressive health programs for younger older adults.

Social and Political Environment

Many of the major social and political battles of the Dream-Deferred Generation have already been won—but by no means all. Moreover, some battles will have been lost. While most are not likely to be working at age 80, they will have the right to, and will collect full Social Security. Still, the overall income of wealthier adults will be taxable at a much higher level than today's in order to reduce government expenditures. This will be one of the great battles lost by the advocates of the affluent older adult population. This age group will have Medicare Part A (hospital) and B (physicians' services), including catastrophic health coverage, as well as a new Medicare Part C option that will cover some long-term care benefits financed by insurance payments. However, they will still pay roughly half their total medical bill and will not have coverage for preventive health maintenance or substantial levels of community-based long-term care. Only a very small percentage (5%–10%) will have private long-term care insurance by mid-decade when public policies are shifted to a mixed program of Medicare Part C and incentives for private long-term care insurance.

Cultural Climate

Older adults in the 1990s who are in their 80s will experience far fewer stereotypical remarks and less patronizing treatment by younger people than did their predecessors. Still, the change in social attitude toward older adults will mean little to many in this age group who themselves have subscribed to many of the stereotypes of their own generation. This group will be proving time and again how our age is not a measure of our years, but of our use of them. However, there will be a period of some vague hostility toward older adults on the part of those in their 20s and 30s, as economic pressures mount mid-decade. Generally, the conflicts between health costs and competing interests will put a general strain on intergenerational relations, at least in political forums. However, the movement of many older adults out of their homes and into new communities will have somewhat added to local housing supply, improving opportunities for younger families, and reaffirming the independence of older adults.

Martyrs

Survival into the later stage of life for Martyrs is, if you listen to them, a source of shame. Just the same, you can tell they are pleased to be able to tell you just how little they deserve the pleasures of knowing their grandchildren and great grandchildren. Roughly a third of their generation, Martyrs in their 80s are complaining, irritating their children, yet, despite some serious moments of depression, happy to be here (although hard to tell in many instances). Most Martyrs are content with retirement, and while possibly 15 percent may have worked into their 70s, most have seen retirement as a bonus, not a burden.

Martyrs are economically less well off than many of their generation. Loneliness is a serious problem, caused by inner conflicts that lead them to deny themselves rather than by the absence of others who care. Martyrs who are married are much better off than those who are not. They are an ethnically diverse group—black, Hispanic, Asian, and white, there is no cultural monopoly on the Martyr personality. Martyrs are feisty, and, while subject to depression, they are filled with strong attachments and feelings they want to share, however few new self-discoveries emergence brings. When insight strikes, they are more likely to realize how much they may have alienated children and family through their complaining and how much they need others.

Needless to say, Martyrs are notorious for driving their children up the proverbial wall. A well-beloved stereotype (there is some truth in stereotypes), the Martyr at age 80 is still complaining and fretting as if they were at the brink of death and nobody cared. Their children, who have been henpecked and hounded by alternating praise and guilt all their lives, are now, in the year 2000, in their 50s. While some Peter Pans and Wendys and Princes and Princesses have reconciled themselves to the apparent immortality of their parents, most have not, and, like the good children some of them are, dutifully worry about their aged parents' well-being. All this comes on top of a history of approach-aversion craziness on the part of their Martyr parents: they want attention, then deny that they want anything.

Self-Compensators

Self-Compensators in the year 2000 are wrestling with health problems associated with their self-indulgent life style. But who can blame them? Unlike Martyrs, Self-Compensators, who are about a sixth of their age group, have made a point of making up to themselves with what they think they missed during their adult lives. Naturally, this has led to a life that included a certain amount of excess. Some focused their attention on eating, as if by consuming food and drink frequently and in large quantities they could erase the memories of hunger and deprivation in their earlier lives. Those that have not done themselves in with heart attacks, faulty gall bladders, diabetes, strokes, gout, and related disorders, still insist on their three squares a day, seeing their hefty weight as a reassuring sign of their success.

Tours and hanging out with those of a similar bent continues among Self-Compensators, interrupted by visits to the hospital for minor crises that become more frequent, and, more frightening reminders of the battle they have long been waging with the burden of life (having had most of their major surgery in the preceding decade). This is a time when Self-Compensators often become generous in giving to their children, their grandchildren, and charitable causes. The Self-Compensator is not becoming less materialistic, only more desirous of not losing what they care about.

Children of Self-Compensators have had stormy love-hate relations with their parents, usually maintaining a deep affection over the years, despite the fatiguing obduracy of the male Self-Compensator over matters familial and financial. The children of Self-Compensators, Peter Pans and Wendys, Princes and Princesses, have made their homes a "safe" distance from their parents, and carefully plan and ration their own and their grandchildren's exposure to their gruff and doting grandparents. By the end of the century, the Self-Compensators' comfortable retirement life style is a testament to their now mollified anger. They have showed everyone that they were not to be denied their place in the sun.

Clock Watchers

Clock Watchers will glide into their 8th decade. For this group, which is about a third of their generation, aging is relatively easy because they have not changed their life style very much to accommodate it. Moreover, long before they dropped out of the formal work force, Clock Watchers had already adopted a life style that has not changed much over the years. Clock Watchers may continue to work part-time as the mood, or financial necessity, moves them. But they were never as much a part of the working world as the Self-Compensators and Martyrs. In the 1980s they were for the most part settled into a retirement life where they could do what they had started in childhood—hunt, fish, travel by car or recreational vehicle, pursue a variety of hobbies, and sometimes start businesses based on a hobby or personal interest.

Their children have always found them quiet, very self-sufficient and able to take care of themselves, in their own way. Clock Watchers tended to have few if any children, due to the times in which they lived. They do not ask anything of their children. They resist the notion of depending on them (like their older counterparts, the Explorers), and tend to postpone dealing with their incipient health problems. The children of Clock Watchers, in their 50s in the year 2000, are often neighbors. They sometimes share the same home, as the Clock Watcher may have done with his parents. Clock Watchers have never been demanding, never having much money. They may quietly occupy a guest room in their children's home or an apartment nearby. Clock Watchers view their old age as a package that includes various limits and accept their imposition grudgingly, not trying to retrieve distant youth. Clock Watchers see the world running its course and smile from their off-track vantage point.

Conservers

Conservers have struggled to be the type of person they thought they should be all their lives. Now, as they have passed their God-given threescore and ten, and have reached fourscore, they are quietly wondering what on earth is to become of them, while outwardly putting on a mask of imperturbability. Conservers were never satisfied with who they were when they were younger. In the 1980s they were already retired and over the past decade have gamely done the best they could with what resources they had. Those who were fortunate enough to have more money sought out places to live where they could be with others like themselves ("people of quality . . ."). While some have been living in retirement communities (often religiously sponsored) since their early 70s, a good many (about 60% of their generation) are still at home.

The Conserver emphasizes dignity and self-image above practicality, which tends to give an appearance of aloofness and self-containment in the face of the dramas of life. For the Conserver, the Emergence stage is a profound inner journey.

From their children's perspective, Conserver parents have always been concerned about form, and doing things right. As a result, their children have always felt that their parents were somewhat cold, or stiff. Relationships with their parents have not altered very much during the past decade. Conservers, with their tenacity and narrowness of focus, have always appeared to their children as hard to approach, and so the children have established relatively calm and forthright relations that continue uninterrupted over the years. There are the ritual visits from the head of family every Thanksgiving and Christmas, and visits to the children's homes in spring or summer every year or so. Naturally, Conservers set great store in their grandchildren and were very insistent about keeping up contacts during the 1970s.

We recognize the Conservers in our neighborhoods because they are the older adults who keep their homes crisply maintained, as they do themselves no matter what the changes in the neighborhood might be over the years. They continue to be active in their church and social circles as long as they can, and earn the respect, or awe, of those among their peers less able to endure the abrasion of time. The Conserver will be next to a spouse or neighbor of the same age, seemingly untouched by the terrors of time.

CHILDREN OF THE AMERICAN DREAM

On New Year's Eve, 1999 there will be approximately 15 million Children of the American Dream, age 70 to 80. Of those born this century, this group will be the first to face its 7th decade with little economic trepidation. As their name implies, this cohort is the product of the 1930s childhood of Roosevelt's fireside chats, patriotism, the challenge of young adulthood during war, and an adulthood of the "organization man" society. In a difficult season of American history, Children of the American Dream are likely to be worrying about how the economy is affecting their personal wealth and business plans, but not with the dire concern of the oldest, poorer generations. Given their high degree of financial well-being, many of these Children of the American Dream will be reveling in their retirement, which has been under way, in most instances, for at least 10 to 15 years. But despite their wealth, there will be a segment of this cohort struggling to make sense out of their lives in retirement. All Children of the American Dream will be at the Transition Rite of Passage. At this stage they will be midstream in facing the challenge of reconciling the realities of their work lives and retirement with their previous expectations. For many, the Transition stage will be traumatic, a difficult and ongoing adjustment. For others there will be little pain, and possibly joy as they shed the mantle of responsibility and don the tennis shorts and fishing gear of leisure.

Economic Outlook

The economic environment is troubling to the Children of the American Dream. An optimistic estimate of the number who will be working in the year 2000 places full-time workers at at least 6, possibly 10 percent, of their age group. At least 15 percent of this group, and possibly as many as 20 percent, will still be working part-time in 2000—if conditions permit. Some will be working full-time because they have remained on at their original firms, or have retired and started full-time second careers, as consultants to other companies, or as self-employed entrepreneurs. Many will work part-time because they want the social involvement that work has provided them with for so many years, and some will need the money. They have been particularly troubled by the growth in ownership of U.S. industry by overseas corporations. They feel that somehow America is being sold right out from under them—having labored so loyally as organization men their whole lives through. The companies in which they have owned stock, or who owe them a pension, are unrecognizable. Their favorite vacation hotels have been under foreign management for some time, occupied by people who do not speak English. This generation also has a lot at stake in the economic restructuring that is taking place. This is the first generation with such a high percentage of re-tired workers having company pensions, considerable personal sav-ings, and a valuable home. When they retired between 1985 and 1995, at least 12 percent had incomes over $20,000, not including their pen-sions and Social Security. They are the first generation among whom many will have retired without experiencing any substantial decline in quality of life. Twenty percent of this group, whose retirement income is not high, may need to work to keep their heads above water financially. To do so under the current conditions may be hard. De-spite long experience, restructuring and downsizing and skills obso-lescence could lead to loss of employment.

Technological Conditions

For the Children of the American Dream, advanced technology has been a handy tool during the last quarter of their careers, but they are not at all comfortable with the changes that have taken place. Tech-nology is not new to them, just changing faster and faster. Many of the changes have come at the close of their careers. If they were professionals, they shifted from slide rules to calculators and then to computers; from typewriters to word processors; from machine tools to numeric controlled devices. They are interested in technology-based entertainment and embrace home-based health technology, such as portable "walkman" medical monitor and music systems for use during exercise.

Health technology is particularly appealing to Children of the American Dream because it holds out to them the hope of life at a stage when they are at higher risk. This group has just come through the high health risk period of their lives, and, because of their prior life styles, they are at a higher risk of heart attack, stroke, lung cancer, diabetes, sports-related injuries (arthritis), and other life style–connected disorders. (They are the generation for whom the Royal Canadian Aerobic exercises and the first Surgeon General's report on cholesterol were written.) Children of the American Dream, despite the expense, are major users of the entire spectrum of biosensors, subcutaneous drug delivery systems, and other medical monitoring equipment, including early stage nerve regeneration technology. Whether or not they play golf or tennis with clubs and racket manufactured out of advanced composite materials, this group is demanding new health monitoring and delivery technologies, and they are able, by and large, to afford what they want. Because they are familiar with the workings of the competitive marketplace, this age group is more assertive than others about the products they consume, including the technological capabilities of health care providers.

Social and Political Environment

Many of the Children of the American Dream find themselves frustrated in the year 2000. They are torn between supporting the policies of the previous administrations and recognizing that the U.S. economy has, at least in part, foundered under the debt-load that it has been carrying. For 20 years most of this group had had confidence in the ability of the U.S. economy to shake off bad times—after all, look at the strong comeback the United States made from the recession of the late 1970s and how long its economic winning streak lasted. The recognition that action needs to be taken has placed members of this cohort in an awkward position. First, as part of their shift in attitude, they have accepted (grudgingly) the fact of increased income taxes. Second, they are facing new consumption taxes, along with everyone else. Although they are not too worried about their children, who are now 40 to 50 years old themselves, their fear that the United States will not retain its identity and independence in a global economy has led this generation to make an emotional commitment to investing in rebuilding the country—albeit somewhat late in the game. Now that they have their dream (affluence in retirement), it seems to them that somehow it was purchased at the expense of the nation's foundation. Their well-being is precariously perched on a national economy that is unstable and trending downward due to years of stealing from the future to pay for the present. Now, at least some of this group are ready to bite the bullet and help pull their own weight, as they did as children in the 1930s. This irony is not lost on the Children of the American Dream. They are morally called to duty once again, when they expected to retire in peace.

Cultural Climate

The most important social phenomenon for the Children of the American Dream in the year 2000 is the enduring drama of the third-quarter crisis. One third retired contentedly, pleased to cease full-time work in favor of pastimes long developed and ready to continue. One third were eventually displaced from their jobs, either through efficiency cutbacks or skill obsolescence, or both. But at least a third of the Children of the American Dream worked a full career and are the first generation to face a third-quarter crisis when they reached what is usually traditional retirement age (after an earlier mid-life crisis). At that time, around age 65, many of this group realized they had never developed serious plans for retirement, having been workaholics all their lives. Both men and women in this category (but particularly men) have little sense of what their retirement should be, seeing retirement planning as primarily a financial exercise, not a personal development strategy for the future. As a result, through no small amount of emotional upheaval, a fair number of this age group who had crises decided to seek continued employment. The 1990s find the Children of the American Dream actively engaged in the economy and society—continuing their past activities and, more so than preceding generations–being entrepreneurs. By their mid-70s, at the end of the decade, they are, given the current environment, somewhat uncertain about what to do with what skills they have.

Fortunately, as attitudes toward workers have changed (reflecting a shift toward lifetime renewal of "human capital" at work) and work force growth has slowed, Children of the American Dream are not treated patronizingly in the work force. Particularly if they are working at a company with which they have been affiliated in the past. However, when they make moves horizontally, or to another firm, many experience subtle age bigotry and jealousy, which they have had to overcome through proving themselves, once again.

Attainers

Of all the groups born into the Children of the American Dream, the Attainers are the most visible in their later years. Aged 70 to 80, they are in a difficult transition period at century's end. Compared to other members of their age cohort, they are the most aggressive and autonomous in their world view and life style. Attainers are image conscious, extraverted, and sensation-seeking. Their early upbringing taught them that they will be measured by what they do in life. Their work ethic is strong, and their concern for status is also strong. As a result, they have led lives centered on their careers and on how they are defined by their work. By the year 2000, this part of the generation born between 1920 and 1929 is in the most traumatic stage of their lives. Because of their compulsion to attain, this group will often be jealous of younger workers. For this reason they will not feel as much connection to the workplace as their peers. More isolated than need be, they feel the pressure to retire; it is a pattern that they have anticipated for many years; retirement planning has encouraged them to think about this time; they have saved and invested to make retirement a comfortable transition to a more recreational life style.

The majority of Attainers will retire early, between 62 and 65. Once retired, they will have experienced a year of delightful release from the pressures of their work. Then, a new host of anxieties will begin to emerge. Like conditioned animals Attainers will find themselves compulsively filling their time with activities—gardening, tennis, golf, business associations—trying to accommodate themselves to the rewards they have earned. Many Attainers will succeed in this transition, finding in the full schedule of engagements with fellow retirees a reconstruction of work; drawing from the management of the family portfolio a modicum of seriousness of work responsibilities. Still, there will be Attainers who find themselves increasingly drawn into new business ventures, entrepreneurial activities, and consultancies to their old companies, because they are still vital, still have a strong interest in their work, and need the social linkage that work provides.

Struggling to reconcile their fitter, younger, smarter selves into a world that has yet to define retirement, Attainers will thrash their way through their 6th decade into their 7th. By this point they will have established a *modus vivendi* that is realistic and practical for them. Not necessarily happy, Attainers will have achieved some balance in their lives, perhaps as parents in second families.

Attainers will have had uneasy relations with their children much of their earlier parenting years. Their children, many of whom are Voyagers and Lennies, will simultaneously idolize and resent their parents' career centeredness. Moreover, the strife that characterized so many Attainer households, including divorce, during the 60s and 70s scared many of their children into a more exploratory life style, including delayed marriages, divorce, and delayed childbearing. Now in their 40s, these Baby Boomers have settled down in their own families and have worked out a satisfactory rapport with their parents. The role of grandparent for Attainers was always hard to digest due to their strong self-image as young vital careerists. Just the same, they could not suppress their enthusiasm in their children's long delayed procreation. After all, as archetypes of the Children of the American Dream, Attainers cannot resist passing the torch to the next generation.

Performers

Among the Children of the American Dream, Performers are the most constant in their outlook. Schooled early on in the American Way, they believe in "my country right or wrong." As young men they were eager to sign up for war, dedicated to the cause of freedom. As young women they were ready to go to work to produce the machinery of war and the children of its warriors. Performers were a product of an era when mass communication was new and extraordinarily effective in its single-minded purpose: to shape our views and actions. Performers carried the concept of nationhood and duty close to their hearts: they made suburbia; they worked in companies, whether as machinists, managers, administrators, or engineers.

For Performers, the Rite of Passage of Transition is of little consequence. Their values are firm, although sometimes exaggerated in their rocklike rigor; their clarity not dimmed by the grime of work. Yet, in their 60s, they have viewed the other side of the mountain and are eager to cross over into the promised land of retirement. Retirement is earned; it is right. Not unlike their brothers and sisters, the Attainers, Performers have a tremendous amount of vitality and creative energy. While they may be burnt out from years of work, their inner furnace is still on, providing plenty of energy for new activities. Performers will have an easier time of retirement than Attainers because they view work as a duty that ends, like a shift on the factory floor. But the status of their occupation, what they did, endures, whether they work or not. As a result, by the year 2000 very few Performers are working full-time, and officially, only about 5 percent are officially working part-time. However, possibly as many as 10 to 15 percent are working on various business ventures of their own; self-employed, but not necessarily making money, or reporting it if they do.

In the year 2000 Performer children are about 45 to 55 years old, well-established Baby Boomers on their own, with their own children. These children include Future Perfects and Homeboys and Homegirls who have taken on the world in their own inimitable ways. Performers' relations with their adult children are often good, although somewhat formalized—with rituals of attendance on holidays. These relations are better now than before, although their children are anxious about having to care for their parents in the face of their own financial pressures to put their own kids through college. Sometimes, however, the good-natured and well-meaning children have found their parents' unquestioning acceptance of the American Way a bit too much, and have in their own adulthood reached out for new views and options in life. As a result, earlier on in their lives Performer parents have, on occasion, had to literally rescue their children from cults, or let them come home to roost for a while as they sorted out their divorce, job, or general malaise with the world—even though they had rejected their parents for what they believed was moral hypocrisy.

Performer parents end up caring for their adult children at one stage or another of their lives, more than other groups. They also end up caring for their own parents, who are Children of the Century, or older. Credit this enduring mutual support to their strong belief in family, and their modest affluence, which has given them the time and resources to be more tolerant and supportive. Where Attainers are uneasy with themselves, Performers are less troubled by self-doubt, comfortable with their achievements.

Dreamers

Among the Children of the American Dream, the Dreamers have had a difficult maturation. Dreamers, who are at least a third of their age group, have always been struggling to configure themselves to an image, to grasp the brass ring of life, always just out of reach. In their 60s, Dreamers have been repeatedly hard hit by the changes in the economy during their lives. In the mid- to late 1970s they were bounced from their jobs by factory shutdowns and plant closings. They struggled to find new jobs, losing seniority and wages as they clambered into their next work assignment. Driven by their own internal salesmanship, many Dreamers have moved from job to job over the years, often failing to accumulate much of a pension or retirement savings. The majority, however, found safe harbor in large corporations where they could fill a reasonably successful, though often inglorious niche as salesperson, manager, administrator, or technician.

Despite their lack of success in rising as far up the corporate ladder as they had hoped, they found ways to protect themselves against their own failings. They took advantage of any opportunities they could; many bought small rental properties and became partners in small businesses (which they did not run). They lived modestly, except where their aspirations to greater status led them to squander hard-earned money on cars, appliances, and Las Vegas/Atlantic City vacations. Dreamers often have stormy relations with their children, due in part to their enduring belief in their own ability to increase their status in life but lack of actual ability to implement a scheme often talked about over dinner. Fathers in particular, but frequently joined by mothers, maintain affectations of style and status which the children recognize, usually, as well-meaning but not valid.

The children, still very young, often had to play adult to their parents' naive or immature visions. In their own self-defense, Dreamer children sometimes had to help set their parents' financial matters to rights—through advice, planning, even lending money. By their 60s, many Dreamers are ready to give up the struggle, or at least move into low gear, transferring their energy to more harmless or better directed pursuits.

While Performers have stayed home, or near where they grew up, Dreamers want to leave behind their preretirement life. Dreamers have tremendous vitality, but they were never given the right direction for success, or the right tools to achieve it. Nonetheless, they have earned their retirement through hard, if sometimes misdirected, labor, and take it gladly, saying good-bye and good riddance to work. Dreamers confront their transitional Rite of Passage with one eye closed, hoping to slip by unnoticed. They are rarely ready to confront their excessive, compulsive behaviors, only to modify them for survival purposes. Tenacious as ever, Dreamers dream on.

Cruisers

The achievements of most of the Children of the American Dream have long eluded the struggling Cruisers. A small part of their generation, they are nonetheless an important group because of their failure to benefit from the era in which they lived. In a period of history where government intervention was strong in shaping values, in providing education, in subsidizing housing, Cruisers were only able to take marginal advantage.

Having less formal education and a weaker family support system, Cruisers never were able to grab on to a career; so many worked low level civil servant jobs all their lives—or as mechanics, technicians, clerks, and service workers. They have minimal pensions, meager savings, and modest homes. They often have no health insurance. Although they worked hard, they had no sympathy for their employers or those they served. When they acquired skills, it was from their intuitive senses and direct hands-on experience. Over the years they consumed most of their income. Even with few savings Cruisers left the labor market early.

Cruisers, both men and women, have marriages that just barely survive the times. Getting along with each other is a matter of mutual tolerance in Cruiser families. Love is a gruff expression at best, and expectations are low for exchanges of strong feelings between spouses.

Cruiser men see themselves as unchangeable males and are very resistant to efforts to reform their ways. Cruiser women put up with their men, or leave if they have the strength. The men have few demands from women, but do not give them any serious consideration. The women are often depressed and seek the solace of neighbors and daughters who have not left the neighborhood.

Relations with children are generally cordial. Kids are often emotionally distant, trying to separate themselves from the mire of life in which their parents have sunk; the kids are struggling with their own problems of upward mobility and are embarrassed by their parents' questioning of their careers and social objectives. Cruisers feel that they have been dealt a fairly hard deal in life and want to be left in peace to watch television, hoist a few beers, smoke, tinker in the garage or yard, and occasionally go to a cabin or budget motel for a weekend with friends to play cards, fish, or just get away. As they drift through their transitional Rites of Passage, Cruisers achieve little, and expect little. If anything, time has taught Cruisers to reduce expectations and work with what they have. So they do.

THE BRIDGE GENERATION

On New Year's Eve, 1999 there are about 20 million members of the Bridge Generation aged 60 to 70. This small cohort, born during the 1930s, missing World War II and coming into the adult world in the 1950s, have had a mixed experience of the later part of the 20th century. They were too young to participate directly in the war, and thus did not have to work up the psychological convictions that believing in the war required; they were too comfortably established by the time the 1950s came around to understand, let alone question, the political contradictions of those times (even if they went to Korea). As a result, they moved from the passive 1950s into parenthood in the 1960s, always on the outside of the current wave of social change; but watching it take its toll on their marriages and children, just the same. By 1999, most have succeeded in sliding through the second half of the century in relative innocence and naivete.

While better educated than preceding groups (including the 1920–1930 group with whom they had to compete directly), many in this group lacked sufficient training to adapt to technological changes, and struggled to get on the technology bandwagon of the 1980s. Those who excelled in education had fast-track careers that they have held on to through the 1990s. In the recession years at the middle of the

1990s they were protected from further job loss by their few numbers and age. At the turn of the new century, at age 60–70, they can stay and work if they want, or roll into retirement. Today the Bridge Generation is, for the most part, at the revision Rite of Passage. They are seriously rethinking their life course and worrying about their future, often confronted by their troubled children.

Economic Outlook

The Bridge Generation has had to learn to take the economic prospects of the new century in stride. This is not the first time they have seen decline or restructuring. Many of this generation were the first to be laid off during the major industrial restructuring of the manufacturing sector in the 1970s and 1980s, when millions were displaced first from the steel industry and later from automobiles, heavy equipment, appliances, oil, and chemicals. However, there were a few early retirees from this group in the early 1980s (in their early 50s), as well as workers who just were not able to find employment because of the mismatch in their skills and the emerging advanced manufacturing marketplace. As a result, a large number of the skilled workers in this cohort have had a tough time finding new work. Many shifted to the growing but less well paying service industries, becoming pizza delivery men, car salesmen, insurance claims trainees, real estate agents, and, in some cases, equipment repairmen. Many had to migrate to find work and endured the trauma of resettling their families. In the year 2000 the conditions for at least part of this group are tougher. Those that retired early are working extra service industry jobs to bring up their incomes. Their wives have been working, too, primarily to make ends meet, although this cohort had a fair share of career women (but late starters). It is also in this group that the consequences of corporate cutbacks and downsizing in the 1980s and 1990s have been first felt. Fortunately, more have had a less driven attitude about employment and career than Children of the American Dream. The Bridge Generation will, as they have before, wait out the economic doldrums.

Technological Conditions

What will technological advances mean to the Bridge Generation in the year 2000? The lives of this cohort will be altered primarily in one respect. This is the threat of skills obsolescence. Because of their age during the 1990s, this group will have a high seniority in the workplace, and receive higher wages and benefits (particularly pension contributions) than younger, newer workers who will have relevant skills but will be in short supply. Workers in the Bridge Generation will experience considerable pressure from employers to become more productive, and will often be passed over for promotion, or if part of the staff of a factory or office, may be laid off entirely. Technology, then, will be the nemesis of this age group because they are educationally unprepared to use many of the new tools of business and industry. Those Bridge Generation members who want to stay employed or continue up their career ladder will find themselves pressed to seek out their own retraining, if their employers are not offering it to them. Fortunately, larger companies will be well aware of skills obsolescence and will be spending billions to retrain and upgrade worker skills. As pressures on U.S. firms to become more productive increase in the 1990s, the Bridge Generation will face the challenge of adapting or leaving the work force by defaulting on their own development opportunities.

Social and Political Environment

The turn of the century finds the Bridge Generation lacking a clear sense of identity. For much of their lives they have straddled two eras of American society without belonging to either one. In a sense, the Bridge Generation are the children of the swing era, the parents of rock and roll, the youth of World War II, and the adults of Vietnam. Indicative of their indeterminate status in American history, the Bridge Generation is not acutely concerned with social trends, such as the failure of the education system (because their kids are out of school), but casually take strong positions (they often favor the death penalty). They are not very interested in political causes (economic or health-care policy) except generally to disdain government intervention (less government is best)—except to protect their industry from foreign competition. A few are concerned with environmental issues, primarily those affecting their favorite recreation area. Adolescents and young adults during the passive and paranoid 1950s, they learned astutely how to avoid taking strong political positions. They were, so they thought, continuing the American values of hearth and home, but in fact were never very clear about the underpinnings of those beliefs. They were confused and frightened by the events of the 1960s, overwhelmed by the narcissism of the 1970s, and found false comfort in the new complacency of the 1980s. The economic and political changes of the 1990s forced a surprising reexamination of beliefs among the Bridge Generation as America's stature swung in the balance and East and West renewed their openness to one another.

Cultural Climate

In their 60s, the Bridge Generation are loud, but not active, in criticizing the graphic problems of the day—homelessness, drug use, teenage pregnancy. They are more likely to be against social policy changes, other than supporting local control of schools, hiring more police, strict law enforcement, and parental efforts to encourage celibacy. Many of the Bridge Generation remain indifferent or cynical about social or political issues (sure women should work, if they take care of their families first), until they hit home. Then, typically, when Bridge Generation first and second marriages fail, or their children encounter serious difficulties of their own, they do some serious reexamination of their attitudes. They are, however, highly concerned with the quality of entertainment and recreation opportunities in their lives. In the year 2000, they view the economic environment, with its emphasis on reinvestment, rebuilding, productivity, and innovation, as something to escape from. They ignore the implications, withdraw more, and consume more than most other groups, younger or older. They maintain a normative perspective on life, even while undergoing contradictory life events of their own. These include a higher than average divorce rate and level of single parenting, and more female heads of household, male job displacement, and career change as they muddle their way through their 30s and 40s. Their own children today are a troubled generation, streetwise at an early age and now, often conservative, looking for and pursuing more concrete values in life.

Good Old Boys and Gals

Good Old Boys and Gals had a difficult time in the 1980s, and the 1990s were not much better. Because so many work in industries that are affected by uneven economic cycles and foreign trade, such as construction, automobiles, and oil, they have had to tighten their belts off and on for a good part of their work lives—with peaks and troughs over the last 20 years. Fortunately for these people, their primary ambition has been to put in the requisite years of work and exit the labor force. Unfortunately, this ambition was made more difficult by the collapse of their pension funds in a number of instances (steel workers), and by displacement through plant closings (in the case of auto workers), and slower growth in wages for manufacturing workers (in right-to-work states).

In their early retirement mode Good Old Boys and Gals have the limited respect and admiration of their adult children, who are a mix of Baby Boomers (Homeboys and Homegirls) and Techno-Kids (Missing Ingredients and Keepers of the Flame). Good Old Boys and Gals have always wavered between being pals with their children and being strict authoritarians. Often they combine the two. When Good Old Boys are depressed about their lack of work, they tend to wax sullen and abusive. Avoiding the tension of the home, their children frequently move out early, though typically staying near by. Those Good Old Boys who are more relaxed are often buddies with their sons and daughters, and, during the 1990s, convinced not a few of their kids to join their trade, or enter into business with them. Grandchildren are brought to visit their grandparents but must tread lightly on grandpa Good Old Boy's turf. Those Techno-Kids who went into business with their fathers—including a large number of daughters—have inherited the business already and brought into it other family members.

Good Old Boys and Gals come to their revision Rite of Passage with plenty of regrets but no desire to dwell on them. They know the limits of life, the method of their own personal madness, and accept what they are. For those Good Old Boys who have succeeded in putting in their three decades of time in the plant or on the job, the year 2000 is a release and the beginning of full-time leisure. For the entrepreneurs, the sweat may not be over until their business is handed off to their kids. For those who have neither company job nor their own business, their 6th decade is just more sweat. Game, but less adaptive than others, Good Old Boys and Gals have to grin and bear their tough financial situation, taking what jobs they can get in stores and restaurants (with no great enthusiasm), often suffering a decrease in quality of life—not for the first time, but hopefully for the last.

Romantic-Realists

Plunging into their 60s, Romantic-Realists have achieved a plateau of accomplishment in how they live and in their human relations. In part, they have refined their life styles after two or more decades of experimentation and shifting. During the 1970s they were parenting, often on their own. At the same time they were struggling to establish new careers, having been rocked by the economic upheaval of the times and their own predilection to seek work true to their self-image and personal beliefs. So, whether they were fired or quit, the Romantic-Realists had to define for themselves what they would do for a living and succeeded in doing so.

The 1970s were hard, a period of getting started, all the while trying to keep family together, such as it was. The 1980s were different. Romantic-Realists were beginning to get established in their second careers but were still living frugally—giving up much to their children, while keeping little for themselves. By the close of the decade Romantic-Realists were able to earn enough to buy a new car, possibly a down payment on a condominium, and put some money away for retirement.

The 1980s were troubling for parents because so many of their children (Missing Ingredients, Billy Budds) appeared to be suffering emotionally. Many Romantic-Realist children were not so much troubled as they were eccentric, committed to tremendously difficult and emotional styles defined by lofty ideals. For Romantic-Realists (and other parents) it almost appeared as if they had been particularly afflicted with troubled or difficult children. Their kids were emotionally bruised and overly serious for those in their early 20s. What was going on? Feeling guilt for their past divorces and own commitment to career objectives, some Romantic-Realists found themselves facing children who seemed to have lived too much too soon, who were cynical and unhappy with themselves. Others, in contrast, were astonished by the materialistic, bottom-line personalities that their children had evolved as they matured.

As they pass through their period of revision and then transition in the year 2000, most Romantic-Realists accede to the wisdom of more modest expectations for themselves, but still keep working for their own sake. Creatures of habit, Romantic-Realists enjoy the world they have built around themselves, their friends, their own rooms and objects, and daily pattern of life. For this group, the new century is a curtain drawing back on a play for which the dialogue is to yet to be written. Retirement is a word of little meaning, though its financial implications are fully grasped. Romantic-Realists see their 60s as a period of consolidation and refinement of their personal achievements—achievements that were hard-won and came later in life than for many others of their age group.

Envoys

The Envoy has been a proud contributor to the American economy over the past 30 or so years. Hard workers, whose parents (often immigrants) provided strong encouragement for joining the world of opportunity, Envoys have always balanced their eagerness to achieve with their sense of responsibility to their family. Sometimes more American than their 3rd or 7th generation peers, the Envoys had embraced all things American from the very start, far more intimately than did the Adaptors of the 1900–1909 cohort. (They embraced the concept of America as newcomers, while Envoys, while often children of immigrants, were immersed solidly on U.S. soil; only family members were of the old world.) By the late 1950s Envoys were hard at work building their careers, doing what they had to do to progress, the first of their family to go to college or attain a professional or managerial position. Envoys were willing to leave their home base, like the Adaptors before them. They went away to school, did their military duty (limited as it was in the 50s), and married in their early 20s and had a family. All this was prelude to a long career, with ups and downs, moves forward and back. By the 1980s Envoys had long ago shifted much personal emphasis back to the family and off their own careers and work.

During the 1990s, in their 50s and 60s, Envoys had already scaled down some of their work load and were planning their retirement. By the year 2000, the Envoys are working part-time, or full-time in new careers undertaken after early retirement. Sometimes they will have gone to former jobs and started up again; sometimes trying entirely new work. Envoys believe in active participation in local social organizations, from churches to the Chamber of Commerce, and also volunteer more than most their age. Somehow, their life style seems to synthesize a new Americana, taking from the strong stereotypes of 1950s cheerleaders, clubs, and good business practices, and revitalizing it with an almost hyperbolic enthusiasm, or affection. Envoy children, of the Techno-Kids generation, are, like their parents, adaptive and forward looking but vary between extremes of pragmatic cynicism (Cosmopolitans) and conservative passion (Keepers of the Flame). The Cosmopolitans are more shy and resentful of their parents' overweening enthusiasm for their real (the parents') and putative accomplishments, while Keepers of the Flame exaggerate their response to the moral and cultural values that were their parents' roots. Now in their 30s, the children of Envoys are proving their parents' investment worthwhile, although through their own unique programs of action. Envoys are proud and committed Americans, eager to see the nation blossom, willing to fulfill their part of the social contract that has guided their past choices, whether paying taxes or perhaps teaching local schoolchildren to read as a second career.

Bootstrappers

Bootstrappers have always seen life as a struggle, whatever success they have squeezed out of their experiences. As the century turns, now in the midst of their 6th decade, they are still struggling. This time the struggle is whether or not to let down their guard, to ponder withdrawing from the fray. Bootstrappers have worked so hard at bringing themselves up into the world, and keeping themselves there, that they have conditioned in themselves what might be called an "unfit fitness." They are hell-bent on preserving the status they have gained in their work. They continually discuss retirement from the age of 50 on, yet continually dodge it (longing for it, frightened by it). Like their older counterparts, the Attainers, they do not realize how much they are conditioned to work, how much they need the thrill of the chase. Fortunately for most Bootstrappers they have developed during their lives some broadening hobbies. These offer them a world outside of work on which to focus attention after retirement. The Bootstrapper stays in the fray and takes on all comers, withstanding the demotions, promotions, lateral shifts, and other ignominious sinecures and transitions that corporations, and even new enterprises, inflict upon their senior staff in indirect, if not overt, efforts to shake Envoys loose.

At ages 60 to 70, veterans of 40 years of corporate battlefield strategy, scarred but proud (as they say), Bootstrapper men and women have stressed their health to its limit, and beyond, and have shaken their emotional structure almost off its foundation. Just the same, they carry on, frequently smoking, drinking, and taking drugs (tranquilizers, for the most part) as if they were basic nourishment. Facing tremendous incentives to retire, most Bootstrappers accept the spoils of their war but wait only briefly before turning around and entering into a new venture. Many, who have not lost the taste for the game, will become consultants to their former companies or their competitors', start their own service business to make their skills accessible, or teach in local universities and colleges. The year 2000 will bear witness to a plethora of small firms crowded with the sloughed-off but not forgotten professionals of the preceding decades, 60 and older, yes, but retired? What for?

The children of Bootstrappers will be chips off the old block, to some degree, but, like the original, they will do it their way. They will not have an easy time of it. The Techno-Kids produced by Bootstrappers will likely include Missing Ingredients and Billy Budds. Missing Ingredients will endure great emotional travails of rejection and experimentation in their own lives before sorting themselves out and applying themselves to a meaningful life course. During this time they will have a reconciliation with their Bootstrapper parent who alternates between compassion (remembering earlier days) and anger (at the waste of time and energy). For a long time Billy Budds will impress their parents with their emotional sensitivity and intellectual commitment but distress them with their inability to focus on real-world priorities. By the turn of the century, when his or her Bootstrapper parents are struggling with their own retirement notions, their Billy Budds will become a resource in their own search, helping them to remember their own fundamental beliefs and to stick with them as they make their choices for the new century. Bootstrapper talents enable them to be productive wherever they turn; yet, this inner drive—the fire in their belly—may burn them before they achieve some balance in their emotional lives, possibly jeopardizing their health (physically and emotionally) in the 90s.

THE GAP GENERATION

In the year 2000 there are about 25 million members of the Gap Generation, now age 50 to 60. This generation has been the focus of much of the attention of politicians and advertisers during the 1980s and early 1990s. After all, they were the mass heralds of social change during the 1960s and later settled into being the foundation of a strong consumer society, with children. By the year 2000 we have the opportunity to look into their lives as mid to late career humanists. Where have their values led them? How will they be celebrating New Year's Eve 1999?

Most of the Gap Generation are now facing the reversion Rite of Passage—the time of the late mid-life crisis. Will the Gap Generation fall prey to the same traumas they mocked the Children of the American Dream for? Will they laugh at themselves as they did at the collapse of marriages, the abandoned jobs, the quest for the meaning long lost in the generation they rejected in their own youth? How will the Gap Generation encounter the threshold at mid-life?

Economic Outlook

The relatively small Gap Generation cohort (slightly more than half the size of the 1950s Baby Boom group) will have been put through the wringer by the economic upheavals of the 1990s in which their companies will have changed hands, dropped workers, and scaled up productivity. Gap Generation adults may often have been the managers who had to handle these very problems and were hopefully more a part of the solution than a part of the problem, due to their education, idealism, and rejection of past norms of American industry. At age 50 to 60, this group will be in the throes and afterglow of their mid-life adjustment. They would have had to deal with the failures and successes of their efforts to build a successful career in a time of national trauma, as well as the complexity of contemporary two-career marriages. Economically, most will be doing very well; however, quite a few will be further behind in their career ladder because of the delays along the road in the 1960s and 1970s.

Most likely, they will, by age 50, be on their third career, and possibly second family. Part of their mobility will be due to the adaptiveness they will have acquired as part of their generational experience. Part of their mobility will be a struggle to find satisfactory career niches for themselves as the pace of business change reaches a fevered pitch, with no sign of stopping. Fortunately for this group, their openness to a broader world outlook will enable them to take the lead in establishing beneficial international business relationships with the Pacific Basin, Europe, and struggling Eastern Europe.

Technological Conditions

Technology will be the uncertain ally of the Gap Generation, because they were raised not so much with technology as with the expectation that technology would be fundamental to their lives. On the brink of the year 2000, the members of the Gap Generation will joke about Stanley Kubrick's *2001—A Space Odyssey* and wonder what the intervening decades have actually wrought in the way of improvements in quality of life. The Gap Generation will be quick to admit that they are and have been among the earliest consumers of technology products. While in part due to their affluence and stage of life, it was also due to an acceptance of technological innovation as part of an ever-changing menu of contemporary life. One field of technology rapidly exploited by the Gap Generation is the expanding communications technologies' satellite television, particularly interactive video, now popular adjuncts to cellular telephones. A generation whose watchword has been "the medium is the message," it will be a prime user and advocate for business and home use of all interactive media, from fax machines to "group use software." The technology of health maintenance is also strongly visible for this very health conscious (or health anxious) group. Since the technology was available, they had been users of monoclonal-based fertility testing, home blood pressure, AIDS and insulin testing, and were major endorsers of outpatient medical care, including mammograms and arthroscopic surgery (for knees and elbows injured in sports and hiking), and engineered food products with low salt, fat, cholesterol, and high fiber and vitamin content. Their emotional acceptance of and confidence in biotechnology-based developments is higher than that of older groups and more rapid than younger groups who are less trusting of commercial products. Still more so than any other cohort, the Gap Generation in its 40s and 50s remains more aware and concerned about the technological impacts of industry on everyday life, be it food irradiation, fertilizers and pesticides, or waste in the water or air. Endowed with a healthy skepticism of the intents of business and a highly open attitude (still) toward the "natural" and non-Western, the Gap Generation has helped American consumer markets open to international products and technologies for health and recreation.

Social and Political Environment

The economic troubles of the mid-1990s, and retrenchment through the end of the decade, will be, for this generation, an expected challenge, based on their historic adversarial relation with the powers of the Children of the American Dream (the hated powers that be). We can expect that by 1992 the first signs of this generation's candidates will be visible in the national political arena. By 1996, the first "serious contender" from out of this age group will make an attempt at the presidency.

The Gap Generation may be the steward of the rebuilding of the nation's infrastructure. We can expect the Gap Generation to refuse to walk away from the social, environmental, and economic ills that afflict society, once they have reached a critical point; prior to that, the threshold of pain and indifference will not have been passed. Nihilistic and anti-authority proclivities aside, most Gap Generation people are ready to work for causes that are tangible—not unlike the very generation they initially despised (the Children of the American Dream), and with whom they have never achieved a moral rapprochement (other than grudging respect).

Cultural Climate

The Gap Generation will be, by the year 1999, a more mature and purposeful cohort, focusing their attention beyond life style, and more on life substance. This does not mean that this generation will not have brought to its future the cultural appreciation that it was so apt at cultivating. By no means. Instead, by practicing its values in everyday life, the Gap Generation will have supported, through good years and bad, the enhancement of national culture—and traditional and folk music, classical and modern music, classical and modern dance, theater and cinema. The 1990s will witness strong aesthetic and financial leadership in the arts by the maturing Gap Generation. This will mean, as has been characteristic of this age group, growth in a wealth of eclectic arts, with every individual having their special cluster of favorite recreations and forms of expression, be it pottery, science fiction, writing, or Indonesian textiles.

The cultural environment by the year 2000, however, may easily be overrun by a proliferation of media sources lacking substance. The expansion of cable television and home video will, over the intervening years, create a vast demand for media, from documentaries to dramas. The quality control for this blossoming video market may be negligible, unless a time is reached when consumers exert some critical choice and force improvement in the content of media materials. The Gap Generation, in conjunction with other cohorts concerned with the media, may be able to exert enough potential influence to encourage a growth in quality arts presentations. The more likely attitude, however, will be the phenomenon of "let a thousand flowers bloom"—which means the market will decide.

Peter Pan and Wendy

The coming of middle age will consolidate changes long in the works with Peter Pan and Wendy. Peter, known for his whimsical nature in earlier days, will have settled down in certain respects. He will have had a go at his second marriage somewhere in his mid-40s (around 1980–1985), and will have worked very hard to keep it viable. Because Peter is at heart a child, and a lover of all things childlike, he may very well have started a second family in the 1980s, at the same time his children from his very early marriage to his high school sweetheart were in college. Those Peter Pans who were able to avoid their romantic streak in their college days delayed marriage until their early 40s.

Fortunately, most of Peter's kids are off on their own now. The oldest are Techno-Kids; the others (those born 1970–1979) are what we might call a new generation of Transformers. They—both early edition and new edition—love their parents and have adopted a gently parental attitude toward the Peter Pan parent and his foibles. The relationship is very adult, and, in certain ways somewhat parallel— by starting later in life or starting over again, parent and child have more in common than children of other generations. This makes for interesting dinner conversation, if the children live in the same time zone. The children are 30 or so, possibly with children of their own, and Dad and Mom are sitting at the table with their teenage half brother or sister.

Peter Pan's career path has been a model of flightiness during the last two decades. With few exceptions, Peter has made several job changes, usually horizontal. A few bosses shelter him from the harsher realities of business. Mid-life crisis is not new to Peter; crisis seems to be a part of daily life. Always pondering new ways to strike it rich but rarely taken seriously, Peter makes use of partnerships to make extra money: Peter is the Ideaman. Peter is also an enthusiastic, though often naive consumer of technology products that he does not necessarily understand (but enjoys nonetheless).

Wendy has had a long struggle throughout the 1980s and 1990s. The 1980s saw Wendy frequently as a single woman, after having lived with a number of men for extended periods of time. She and her women friends were, by their early 40s, despairing of finding a mate. About half the Wendys found their man in the mid-1990s—others didn't. They were, in fact, a generation of women against whom the decks were stacked. Born into a smaller cohort, the men had the upper hand when it came to choice. Moreover, the women were, for the first time in recent history, serious about not marrying for the security, but for the meaningful relation. By the year 2000 there were a large number of single women aged 50–60, more than any time in history. Wendys loomed large in this group. They stood on principle and have helped bring about a new culture of single adult women who, despite not fulfilling societal norms of the past, are now, in fact, a benchmark of the future.

Chameleons

The adaptive Chameleons had their mid-life crises earlier than anyone in their age group. Why was this? Chameleons were always emotionally tightly wound under their changeable exterior. Many who had been in Vietnam had been aged by their experience and came out as child-men. They took on the world, working hard to catch up and construct the infrastructure of normal life. They got married, went to school, got jobs, reconnected as best they could with their high school or college classmates. Yet, many of this group took on these healing tasks with few social skills and many underlying anxieties and angers, which had never been, could never be, worked out. By their early 50s many Chameleons had reached a point where they no longer had the zeal or energy they had committed to physically repairing the tear in their social fabric. They began to lose interest and look forward to early retirement. Even the non-Vietnam Chameleons share the trait of being adaptive at the cost of drowning their emotions. They experienced a severe parting of the ways with the material world at least three or four times during their professional lives. The first time may have come with the decision to join the military, to venture into the world of guns and uniforms, tanks and the fellowship of soldiers. Or, it may have come with an early venture into business, maybe a successful enterprise—a restaurant, or a small manufacturing company.

The second time came during the 1970s, in the form of a crisis of marriage. For the Chameleon, leaving spouse and kids was necessary (so they claimed) to be "free" (so what else is new?). The freedom the Chameleons were looking for, of course, was always psychological, not a product of marriage. Many Chameleons returned to the fold, but like many of their generation, they set up life on their own in their 30s (somewhere between 1970 and 1980).

The third time Chameleons had a crisis was in their early 50s, somewhere in the 1990s. At this point in their lives, male and female Chameleons found their skin of many colors beginning to fade. They could no longer change appearance to appease the business world; they were jaded. They lost patience; they burned out. For most Chameleons this burnout was expressed in decreasing enthusiasm with work and less repressed anger with work and coworkers. To cope with burnout, Chameleons contemplated or actually changed jobs or took extended leave, then returned to the old patterns.

Chameleons are, somewhat like the decade-older Bootstrappers, men and women with strongly developed inner lives that rarely see the light of day. Most telling about Chameleons in the 1990s is their growing commitment to their hobbies, in which they have developed not only considerable technical depth, but also social connections. Whether it is restoring cars, mountain climbing, or sailing, Chameleons dream of giving up their work to commit themselves to their hobby. But like most dreams, only the most insightful Chameleons can shake loose the fetters of their career to try an alternative life before their early 60s.

While valuing good fellowship and play, Chameleons need new environments to keep their facades energized. At age 60 Chameleons still need the thrill of performance and playacting to fill out their personal dance card. Work and play, serious and not-so-serious work and hobby continue to blend together as a unique dance for the Chameleon at age 60 and beyond.

Questors

Questors are very aware of their aging, the changes of life. They feel their body and wonder at its shifting sedimentary layers, its tides, and flows. They are, with their seeker's minds, feeling time pass by, and fighting their mystification: is this me, am I really mortal, condemned to this flesh? Questors want to believe (still) that they are transcendent, or will transcend the material weight they are burdened so heavily by. They have not forgotten childhood visions that came to them in a flash at night, or alone on a bluff in, say, Utah. Yet, by the year 2000, the 50- to 60-year-old Questors have come no closer to answering their fundamental questions, save for those who have had years of therapy of some kind.

For Questors, motivation has always been an outgrowth of the failure to solve fundamental inner emotional dilemmas like the rest of us; only in their case, the transposition of the inner needs into mysticism or colorful illusions about the world takes the form of life style. Questors have gone with the flow so many times that they carry emotional inner tubes with them into their relations. Still, their relationships are often emotionally marooned, on a superficial level, with pretense of spirituality and tolerance substituting, involuntarily, for honest feeling. Questors want intimacy that is authentic, but their inner dilemmas keep them from attaining it. Questors need real love, and it is their life struggle to truly feel worthy of it, and to return it.

Questors survive the upheavals of the 1990s economy by adjusting to lower expectations for themselves financially. Most Questors have long since learned to get by with less, emphasizing the nonmaterial, so to speak. They bought their small homes early in their lives (possibly using funds from an earlier, pre–self-discovery career as an engineer or accountant) and have lower expenses, although they typically have few resources set aside for retirement. Their careers, after their initial illumination, have always adhered to the Schumacherian "small is beautiful" principle (fortunately for them), which has enabled them to thrive, if not occasionally prosper, as the U.S. economy shifts to an emphasis on more value-added, custom-designed products. Art and handicrafts, personal services from massage and physical therapy to architecture and landscaping, do very well.

Questors have grown children in their 30s, Techno-Kids, such as Billy Budds and Missing Ingredients, with whom they have been extremely tolerant over the years, and who are, in return, gamely tolerant of their parents' eccentricity. They are comfortably distant from their parents, who seem to their now adult children as odd as an Amish couple in Hollywood (rather than the Beverly Hillbillies): quaint but uncomfortably out of place. Some Questors might cringe on the verge of the new century, but most grin and bear this new harmonic convergence. In fact, many Questors might take credit (in a modest Aquarian Age way) for the melting of the cold war and the warming of East–West relations in the early 1990s.

Princes and Princesses

The year 2000 shows us Princes and Princesses resplendent in their upwardly mobile life styles. Princes, if fate served them well, have been married now since the early 1970s to a Wendy. Assuming neither one was looking carefully, a Prince may have married a Chameleon, and vice versa.

The economy of the mid-1990s did not cause Princes and Princesses undue harm. They were well-educated and early into their careers by the late 1960s. They took for granted, unlike Peter Pans and Wendys, or Questors, what appears to be the established order of life. With a degree of clarity and distance unlike some of their peers, Princes and Princesses pursued the occupational status to which they believed themselves entitled. Princesses, often marrying earlier than their sisters in the same age group, had set up a family and had done most of their duty as parent by the 1990s. Moreover, a good many Princesses divorced their husbands for reasons having to do with incompatibility by the 1970s, when their children were young or before they had any children. But Princesses were very marriage and family oriented compared to their peers, and did not intend to be single and alone, or with a child in their 40s.

The 1990s were a time of mid-life adjustment for Princes and Princesses, but for most this meant tackling serious career changes with new vigor. Neither Princes nor Princesses expect or tolerate setbacks in their lives without a strong compensatory action. As a result, many Princes and Princesses have established their own businesses by 1995, or have reached the next step on their pilgrim's progress up the corporate pathway. For Princes, technological changes affecting work force skill are important, but they do not see the impact on themselves. They make their professional contribution with the confidence that they are certainly not the ones who are being addressed in these industry critiques of the American economy.

Princesses, as well educated as their male counterparts, are even more aggressive in seeking advancement, inasmuch as they have had delays in their career due to early parenting. Unlike some Wendys who delayed child rearing to a later age and faced parenting during the early and mid-point of their careers, Princesses had a slower start, but plunged ahead with more vigor by the time they were in their early 30s. What they had lost in time they made up for in vigor.

By the year 2000 most Princes and Princesses are 50 to 60 and have already achieved most of their priority life objectives (which they had been very good in expressing). They have attained the professional standing they want, are financially secure, and generally comfortable knowing their children are no longer rebelling against their values and are, instead, beginning to buy into their "international citizen" outlook.

THE BABY BOOMERS

On New Year's Eve 1999 there will be approximately 41 million members of the Baby Boom Generation, now age 40 to 50 (born between 1950 and 1959). Baby Boomers will be at a point in their lives where they will have exerted as much impact on the world as they possibly could directly by virtue of their numbers; and now, despite having had fewer children than their parents—in effect indicating that small is indeed beautiful—have started the next baby boomlet. As was inevitable, Baby Boomers are now making their impact as parents—a process they began later than usual, but started nonetheless, during the 1980s. The late 1990s show us the Baby Boomers as proud parents in their 40s, with kids between 10 and 15 years old.

Economic Outlook

Baby Boomers were born into unprecedented affluence and high expectations. They were lucky, or so their parents always told them. Lucky? Maybe. But, unlike the generations before them, this huge group was afflicted with a tremendous amount of anxiety. Anxiety? Yes, an anxiety in which the Baby Boomers' personal expectations for themselves and their future were not 100 percent clear, being, as they were, confused by substantial hypocrisy on the part of many of their role models—parents who showed symptoms of depression, marital conflict, alcoholism, and loss of faith in work and society. All this while at the same time encouraging Boomers to be good Cub Scouts and Brownies, Little Leaguers and paperboys. More uncertain than any generation before or after, the Baby Boomers faced their unique dilemmas as they reached adulthood: a crowded job market with a recession, with most jobs being traditional ones in corporations or government—the very targets their older cousins were burning flags about on TV; later, after they found work, Baby Boomers faced tremendous inflation in wages and in real estate prices at the point in time when they were considering buying a home. If Mom and Dad did not give them the down payment for a home (forming an uncomfortable dependence), most had to wait.

In 1999 the Baby Boom cohort is still the largest single segment of the overall labor market. They have been, in their noncompetitive way, competing with each other to make their way through the first decade of their careers. They are further behind their life schedule than they thought they should be. Still, despite side trips into various educational or career experiments, they have settled into a variation of the life style they knew as children. The Baby Boomers are at heart children of suburbia, whether they live in urban town homes or the countryside.

The economic downturn of the mid-1990s was frustrating to most Baby Boomers, in that it has limited their own family income at a time when they could really use the cash. The reason is that the Baby Boom parents now have children who are in high school (only one or two kids, though, not the 2.85 of their parents). Given the problems with public schools, despite campaigns for improvement during the early 1990s, Baby Boom parents are, with great guilt, increasingly sending their children to private schools—between $6,000 and $12,000 annually. Moreover, because there was a substantial amount of divorce in the Baby Boom cohort, many fathers are paying alimony or sharing child-rearing costs, as well as second families. During the 1990s child rearing has become a major pastime for Baby Boom adults, and the deterioration of public institutions, particularly schools, has led many Baby Boomers to move to newer suburbs surrounding the urban areas where they worked—a flashback to the past.

Technological Conditions

Born into technology, Baby Boomers have always lived with anticipation of discovery. A generation that has taken technology for granted is always pleased and rarely disturbed by technological developments. In the waning years of the 1990s the technologies that stand out are perhaps less important than their ubiquitousness. For Baby Boomers, technology is a metaphor for the evolving shape of the home and work.

At home, satellite dishes and fiber optic cables link the Baby Boom household to commercial service networks worldwide. Many households and offices at home use interactive video, computer software ("groupware"), and even "virtual reality" devices to conduct education and business transactions. The middle-class homes of Baby Boomers are being remodeled into "smart houses" in which extremely powerful computers manage the home—from monitoring and adjusting household heat, light, and security to serving as a computer buddy to Baby

Boom children, who now at century's end grow up with a "house personality" that is like a friend.

Stories of the personalities of homes (how a house was able to monitor a child and save it from eating poison, drowning in the bath, suffocating) begin to grow as technologies intertwine themselves in everyday life. This creates an impetus for popularizing stylishly eccentric homes and home computer systems (built on artificial-intelligence-based expert systems, speech recognition and synthesis, and interactive "virtual reality" devices. People begin to discuss their home personalities as they would their children, parents, or even pets: "We've even given ours a name, she . . . she is like a grandmother, she really seems to care."

Families are able to add more and more diagnostic functions to their home computer systems, many of which are based on artificial intelligence–based expert systems. For example, a home medical system can keep track of personal medical records and use sensors to monitor individual family member growth and health. This trend toward wish fulfillment fantasy in the Baby Boomer generation harkens back to a desire for a benevolent and committed caretaker or older brother (something missing in much of their early adult lives). Affection and bonding with technology become the expression of a need for an adult who can be respected. Home technology ironically substitutes for human guidance, often missing in the Boomers' past.

Office automation will have advanced far earlier than home-based systems, and Baby Boomers will have learned to work with the range of continually changing office technologies. This will be taken in stride over the next decade, although Baby Boomers, in general, will be less quick to learn techniques than their more computer literate younger counterparts. Baby Boomers will be big consumers of continuing education in the office and plant in order to remain abreast of rapid changes in the work environment. Most will have little difficulty (compared to the Gap or Bridge Generation).

All in all, Baby Boomers will be able to take technology in stride, as will most people. Technology, being part of everything, will seem to have less of an overt impact on life than an indirect one. The fact that people will have no inkling of how technologies function will also make technology easier to accept. Designers, by necessity, will have made technology products easy to use so as not to frighten people off.

Social and Political Environment

The social and political environment of the year 2000 will bring out the best in Baby Boomers. While many had predicted that Baby Boomers would arise from the political wasteland of the late 20th century to assume national leadership in the early 1990s, this was not so. The Gap Generation led the way for the 1990s. In fact, the political history of the 1990s was a surprise to those who felt that age alone would change the long-standing political indifference of the Baby Boomers.

By the 1980s the political retardation of all but a few Baby Boomers was quite apparent. What was going on was that the children of affluence were generally not interested in the problems of others. They believed that the years of the Great Society experiments that they had read about in college had run out and were over. They actually subscribed to many of the notions of the Protestant work ethic and thought that anyone who worked hard enough could pull themselves up by their bootstraps and be a success: this was no wonder, given their parents' values. But Baby Boomers also wanted meaningful work. This made their careers more complex than preceding age groups—perhaps with the exception of the Gap Generation.

There was little doubt during the early 1990s that the majority of Baby Boomers were becoming the corpus of the new liberal Republicans. A large part of Baby Boomers were believers in the kinder, more gentle nation, a nation where government had to be leaner to pay off the debt that military spending had saddled the country with. Boomers were a voting population who believed it was ethically right to speak strongly about supporting child care and improving education, and *not* spend federal money to do anything about it. The Baby Boom moved closer and closer to a new Republicanism consistent with their own world view. This new Republicanism of the 1990s was filled with platitudes and little substance: minor cuts in defense; a bit more for the environment. Many Baby Boomers agreed that states could invest in themselves adequately to meet global challenges. But the result was inconsistent policy (read: "state's rights"), a struggling public and private education system, a severely undereducated work force and base for innovation in the economy, and an ever more precariously perched and threatening environment through the mid-1990s.

Baby Boomers, while certainly not bringing any radicalism to their adult political lives, eventually did bring a number of changes to the political world. Slowly, during the early 1990s, the Baby Boomer political agenda began to evolve. The first arena was environmental policy. The agenda began to take shape when the environmental disasters of the 1980s and 1990s began to make Boomers wish they had read Paul Erlich and other environmentalists more closely. ("Sure, I know what an ecosystem is. It's part of my stereo, isn't it?") The rapid escalation of media coverage of toxic waste spills, algal blooms (dead seals, dead whales, and toxic debris such as syringes on beaches), radioactive materials, acid rain, droughts, polluted air, a depleted ozone layer, plus the growing reality of the Greenhouse Effect, began to frighten the now mid-family Boomers.

The fear was magnified by the recognition that today's environmental laws and cleanup programs were both too little and too late to undo damage to some communities. In the early 1990s, with new toxic waste detection equipment, some states were identifying 5 to 10 new toxic or hazardous waste dumps every month.

Baby Boomers, during their mid–child rearing stage of life—about the time their kids were ready for middle school or high school—increasingly began to incorporate environmental priorities into their voting behavior, which affected congressional election outcomes and had some marginal influence on national policy as early as 1992. Unfortunately, although the environmental lobby in Congress had grown measurably during the early 1990s, there was little they could do to significantly influence national policy. The fear of regulation, legal battles over regulations, and the economic consequences of regulation slowed down national environmental policy development. The federal government probably spent more public funds on "safe chemical warfare" than on environmental cleanup technologies during the late 1980s and early 1990s. Clearly (or unclearly, depending on air quality) the mood was changing nationally, and Baby Boomers were increasingly serious and consistent in their awareness of environmental issues.

The second issue that Baby Boomers eventually responded to was an improved education system, one they had initially failed to take serious notice of, except through highly self-interested gestures. While the economy was suffering from an inadequate supply of skilled workers, and even an inadequate supply of labor in many markets, Boomers did not connect this with a historical pattern of voter neglect of the education system by the public sector. To Boomers the problem was school inefficiency and ineffectiveness, not lack of money. The Boomers who had children in the 1970s and 1980s had generally been disdainful of the public school system, and sought out private schools. They did not connect with the fact that their withdrawal from the school system was, in effect, an abandonment of the system to the whims of an educationally indifferent era.

In fact, years of table thumping and business threats about the economic consequences of neglecting the educational system began to take hold in the early 1990s. Support for educational reform started locally, with state support, but became a national question by 1994: Would the national government help states and communities make their schools better? Would they help less economically endowed states? The role of national policy in supporting the increased capability and competitiveness of public schools achieved countrywide prominence by the mid-decade and was an important sign of a reversal in the downward spiral of U.S. communities.

Baby Boomers were not particularly sympathetic to individuals who were homeless in the early 1990s. Coming as they did from a relatively affluent middle-class suburban environment, Baby Boomer politics were always self-centered throughout the 1980s and 1990s. However, when the interests of Boomers became demonstrably the same as those of Americans as a whole a shift in political process began to be achieved. The seeds of this change had been laid down in the days before Baby Boomers were old enough to vote—not during the 1960s, when the world was in a state of self-discovery, but earlier, in the Boomers' childhood experiences of decent public and private schools, school yards, and (reasonably) clean suburban communities during the 1950s.

Baby Boomers began to seriously enter politics in their 30s and 40s, having incubated themselves first in successful business and professional careers. The Baby Boomer political base was not the disaffected voters, nor the extremists at either side, but the new cultural mainstream: the upwardly mobile educated members of their own huge cohort. The Baby Boom political agenda was commonsensical. They wanted sound environmental policy and commitment to action. They wanted stronger and better quality education. And, perhaps most important, they wanted to promote economic innovation and competitiveness. By mid-decade Baby Boomer politicians began to speak to each other seriously about the new foundations, the new basis for America; not merely the country's economic recovery. In the face of dramatic challenges from Europe and Asia, Baby Boomers came to life and began to commit (along with other groups) to the work at hand: rebuild America—not merely roads and bridges, but institutions that teach people and help them become viable participants in our culture.

Cultural Climate

For Baby Boomers, the cultural climate of the end of the century was in dramatic contrast to the world in which they were raised. The turn of the new century arrives on the wings of a decade of internationalism in which Europe consolidated its disparate interests, East Europe was now open and working toward free markets. Japan overseas investment peaks and focuses more on managing a widespread empire of industrial holdings; Hong Kong, China (with Taiwan more indirectly) are now a ferocious economic consortium; and ASEAN nations are also expanding their role in world markets. A new internationalism has been inexorably redefining the world's economic relations but also reshaping the day-to-day lives of Baby Boomers. Culture shock, rather than culture change, better describes what is taking place in 1999 as Boomers—and thus businesses—globe-hop to maintain their place in world markets.

The Baby Boomers, at the peak of their careers, found that the international environment had appeal and had been active in it as much as they could over the decade of the 1990s. Yet, many were not prepared. Countries that were now energetically embracing free market economic pursuits were literally outdoing Americans by the late 1990s, in a few industrial sectors. Baby Boomers found their agemates from other countries frequently better educated, polyglot, and better prepared to play the international game. The Baby Boom advantage in the global economy remained an understanding of modern institutions and the requirements for market-driven operations.

The home culture that is apparent on the eve of the year 2000 is a far cry from that of the Baby Boom neighborhoods in many respects. Few Baby Boomers live in homes as luxurious as their parents'; now 40 to 50, they are not able to buy in, except in the less central housing markets on the fringes of major metropolitan areas or in communities where there has been an outmigration of residents over the past two decades, and the economic tides are now turning (e.g., Philadelphia, St. Louis).

Women's roles change as Boomers enter their 40s and 50s. Boomer women were transitional females in postwar American society, and they still are. Not as reactionary as their older cousins, the Gap Generation, who were really trailblazers, but not as comfortable or sure of their new social roles as their younger cousins, the Techno-Kids, Boomer women are, at this stage, coming to a crisis having to do with their future choices. Now, in the year 2000, most Boomer women are settled into clear career paths and enduring relationships. In fact, quite a high percent, perhaps 80 percent, will have already been married, or had a long-standing living arrangement with a partner well into the early 1990s. But for the most part, as the cultural mood toward sexuality moved into a definitely more cautious phase, women and men of the Baby Boom found comfort in more monogamous relations.

Baby Boomers, followers of the Gap Generation trends in the 1970s and 1980s and practitioners of new liberalism in the 1990s, are now struggling with the impact of their own culture on their lives. Their need for achievement keeps them running hard to keep pace, having taken more time to select careers in the beginning. As a result, now in their 40s, they are not nearly as financially established as their fore-runners were at the same age, in terms of home ownership and personal wealth.

The materialism so much disparaged by the Gap Generation is part and parcel of Baby Boomers, whether or not they are career oriented or link consumption with status and autonomy. The Baby Boom children were taught by their affluent upbringing, inoculated with television fantasy, that consumption is as basic as breathing. To want and to have are natural drives, the expression of which Baby Boomers feel entitled to, whatever their personal wealth. As the clock nears midnight 1999, the Baby Boomers are checking their possessions between video movies just to be on the safe side.

Future Perfects

New Year's Eve, 1999 finds the Future Perfects in a state of excitement. Since they were children reading science fiction they have wanted time to pass so bad they could taste it. What they have yearned for all this time is for their beliefs in the technological possibilities of humankind to come true. They have always known it was possible and expected it would come to pass.

Unlike many other groups who have dropped in and out of careers many times before they reach their mid to late 40s, Future Perfects are models of productivity. Not that they have never changed jobs. By no means. By this stage they have probably moved around two or three times within their industry. This was easy for Future Perfects, who were never wedded to their companies as much as to the work they perform. Whether technologists or professionals in less technologically driven fields, Futures have been able to see their work as play—play with a great deal of fantasy and freedom associated with it. Futures have survived and in the best sense of the word, thrived, in the last decade of the 20th century.

Children of Children of the American Dream, often Performers and sometimes Dreamers, Future Perfects more often than not share their occupational direction with that of one or more of their parents. Dad, typically, was an engineer or technician, or a farmer or mechanic involved with technological tools. Not a product of an economic class as much as a cerebral style, both men and women Futures have wended their way to the future by being a part of its unfurling. Politically naive Future Perfects tend to favor technocratic solutions that ignore the less predictable human realities that undergird social and economic problems. What is more troubling is the fact that this mechanistic way of viewing the world is often applied at home. Too often Futures have not been able to clearly view what is going on in their home lives. Good-natured and not intentionally cruel, Future Perfects are not able to provide the emotional sustenance their spouses and children want. Where families have succeeded in breaking through the layers of intellectual cushioning of emotions that pad the Future Perfect, we witness strong bonds and a folksiness, where children identify well with their parents. Sons and daughters are often clones of their fathers and mothers, going them one better in technologizing the world.

Future Perfects are fairly well adapted to endure and thrive in the decade of the 1990s. Perhaps their disengagement from emotions (less severe in some instances than others), and their concern with problem solving, has given them the tools to persevere and make the most out of the rapidly changing social environment—even if they are less familiar with the world's cultures with whom they increasingly do most business. Because of their productivity and innovativeness, Futures, both men and women, are the type of workers that most companies need and like. Although less entrepreneurial than others of their generation, they are essentially team members in a business world where new product development is a way of life.

Voyagers

The Voyager Ulysses never had any time of extended calm, the wake of his life filled with the ripples of exploration and reaping the harvest thereof. Like Ulysses, Voyagers, children of Attainers and Performers, have moved through lives composed of dramatic personal voyages, but few relaxing cruises. A critical life question challenges them at every pass. The most difficult years were those of the mid- to late 1970s, when they were starting out on first jobs and their most serious (to that point) relationships.

Male or female, Voyagers are dedicated life-crafters. They spent more time in education and experimental careers and worked hard from the ground up. During the 1980s, a Voyager might have become a journalist, having started with copyediting a hometown newspaper on summer vacations, moving to a larger town to get closer to the stories, or to a more remote paper to get more responsibility and control (though little pay). By the late 1980s a Voyager would already be a principal reporter or high level editor, by dint of perseverance and intellectual conviction. He or she might pursue law or politics, at a time when the profession was already overcrowded, working his or her way up through public interest law to broader political issues. Another might have become an entrepreneur, choosing a business that reflected life style priorities, struggling to build a specialty clothing design and manufacturing business from scratch, having first tried a career in graphic design or real estate. Others will have chosen professions that reflect their personal values and aesthetics, whether it is planning, geology, government, public relations, marketing, or restauranteurship. Voyagers will, by their mid-40s, be thoroughly engrossed in their careers, and career survival. Fortunately, by the 1990s they will have passed through their more tempestuous phase of personal development (late 20s and early 30s). Their time of changing relationships, divorce, and high anxiety will have diminished. In fact, these Baby Boomers will have made significant inroads in improving their relations with their parents during the 1980s, helping them face the more difficult transitions of their lives. In the 1990s, their late 30s and 40s will be focused on fairly mature family life and work, particularly helping their children make their way through school with a more sympathetic ally than they themselves had as children.

Homeboys and Homegirls

For Homeboys and Homegirls life has always been a rough ride, but that is what they expected. Raised in families where the value of work was extolled, yet riches held out as a possibility, they struggled with the challenge of achievement and maintaining some level of commitment to their family and personal values. All through their lives they have been seduced by the prospect of accomplishment, while, at the same time, feeling somewhat mystified by how to achieve their fantasies.

Still, Homeboys and Homegirls are financially often better off than many of their counterparts, and have turned out surprisingly well suited to exploit the business opportunities of the 1970s, 1980s, and 1990s. Why is this? One reason is that Voyagers and Lennies were too preoccupied with finding the right career path to take to exploit business opportunities, while Future Perfects were happy to work for others, including the frequently very entrepreneurial Homeboys and Homegirls.

A few were hard hit by the stock market crash of 1987 and had to tighten their belts as they looked for new markets to ply. But, the majority were in the mainstream, not the high-end sales fields but the harder day-to-day jobs of being factory representatives and regional salespeople for struggling national companies. Still, the 1980s were primarily a time of sobering realignment of priorities for Homeboys and Homegirls.

The 1990s presented them with a difficult challenge—adapting to a new, increasingly global environment. Most were good sales and marketing people, good service and technical professionals. Yet, as pressure to compete more aggressively in international markets increased, many were not as prepared as they thought. Never having had much exposure or comprehension of other cultures, European or Asian, they were not sure how to position themselves in sales to overseas clients or represent overseas clients in the United States. They struggled and found themselves facing new competition for their own jobs from a younger and slightly more cosmopolitan cohort that had recognized the importance of foreign languages and cultures in business.

Homeboys and Homegirls, like many of their peers, had married in their early 20s and, often, had divorced in their early 30s. Unlike some of their counterparts, they were more likely to have children, even though they were no more likely to own a home or have substantial income. As a result, when marriages broke up, children were shunted around.

In the 1990s Homeboys and Homegirls were, typically, settling into their second marriages and succeeding better at keeping them together, although they were not without their stormy days. They are more mobile than their age cohort in general, and as a result, while attached to their hometowns, have been ready to move to find better territory and take on new job assignments. During the 1980s, Homeboys and Homegirls and their families moved often, and this was continued in the 1990s, particularly for salespeople.

Homeboys and Homegirls, in their mid-40s, are likely to have continued their close ties to their families, particularly their brothers and sisters, but also to their parents. Their relations with their parents are likely to be good more in deed than in spirit, however. In many respects their parents will not have been content with their own lives or those of their children during much of their lives. They will have had considerable conflict with their spouses and children at one point or another. Despite this they want to maintain close ties, if only because these ties provide a norm in a world that they have never completely understood, and of which they have had a fairly fatalistic view.

At the dawning of the new century, Homeboys and Homegirls will be coping with the impact of the global economy on their lives and outlook on life. At the same time they will be struggling with the desire to improve their family relations, with the children of their first marriage and their current families, and with their own parents, who are becoming more rigid and fatalistic in their outlook on life.

Lenny the Dharma Bum

Most people today would expect Lennies to have disappeared into the woodwork long ago. Yet, the reality is, the Lennies survive on, or just within, the margins of the mainstream. Self-indulgent in ways that would seem to others self-destructive, Lennies express anger at the world in general, and (even at this late date) at their parents in particular.

During the 1980s most Lennies were learning how to use the laws of supply and demand to their advantage. And like Good Old Boys and Gals, they were also learning how to put their streetwise perspectives and countersystem values to work on their own terms. While we might not have recognized Lennies in our day-to-day interactions with shopkeepers, journalists, craftspeople, technicians, and musicians, there they were. Lennies are ultimately not self-destructive as much as they are angry and socially "pouting." They want to live well in terms acceptable to their own view of the world and not subject to the authority of others. To survive, Lennies had to transform their belief system into functional economic parameters. Most of them did this. The late 1980s witnessed the growth of niche markets, into which the Lennie personality (not obvious to everyone, of course) had selected to invest time and energy. Small businesses, started up with loans from family, friends, and fools, came and went, sometimes more than once. They took on a wide range of jobs—desktop publishing, Japanese-style home remodeling, reporting for small magazines, librarian, paralegal, manager of a bookstore or restaurant.

Employers either resented Lennies and had little patience for their lack of team spirit or had a motherly sympathetic view of Lennies and provided an accommodating, tolerant environment in which they could immerse themselves. More than most workers, Lenny got the boot; companies Lenny started were often run according to more idealistic, less realistic objectives than competitors', with obvious results. When self-employed as, say, the proprietor of a bookstore or restaurant, Lennies were able to live on the margin, given their modest life styles (living in a low-rent apartment or shared house, driving a battered old hulk of a car). When Lennies did save money, they often spent it on highly personal purchases, such as a guitar, or personal computer to better express their aesthetic beliefs.

Building on the growth of nonprofit groups during the 1980s, a good many Lennies found positions as underpaid staff providing services to the community. Though somewhat bitter, they at least believed in what they were doing when they worked for community groups. Lennies often managed to find their way into public service as civil servants. Here, as low level bureaucrats, they were able to act out the role of the parent they hated so much, inflicting the pain of interminable scrutiny and administrative constipation upon applicants for government permits or grants, and even on their peers in government. All this in the name of public health and safety.

Since the early 1970s, Lennies have made progress in building relationships with their family. During that period the parents of Lennies found their children to be childlike and unrealistic. Likewise, Lennies were angry at their parents (who may have been Attainers, Performers, or Dreamers), or tried to distance themselves from their strong presence. In the 1980s Lennies began to impress their parents with their capacity to survive and define ways of living that were creative, if not modestly successful. Lennies, in the year 2000, are older, wiser, and, while never wealthy, rich in their own virtue, such as they believe it to be.

TECHNO-KIDS

The future of the young generation just coming of age by 1990 is the hardest one to forecast. Compared to all other generations, they have had less time to define their character and outlook on life. In the year 2000, there will be at least 39.8 million Techno-Kids born between 1960 and 1969, children of the Bridge Generation and the last segment of what most people conceive of as the Baby Boom (1944 to 1960). This group is only two million less in size than the prodigious Baby Boomer group born 1950 to 1959. Yet, as we have seen, despite their size their lives have been and will be substantially different from their older counterparts.

In the year 2000 Techno-Kids will be 30 to 40 years old, having crossed over from their Conversion stage of life, where they made their first real-world trade-offs and started to implement more adult-like priorities. Now they are at the Submersion stage, where they are transferring more of their inner needs to broader personal goals, like career and family. They are between the stage where they firmly choose what they will commit to and a point at which they will be fully immersed in those commitments. What will it be like for

Techno-Kids as they begin to take on the obligations and burdens of full adulthood? Will they be anything like their Baby Boom counterparts, who we see in action so clearly in 1990? Will the life and times of the Techno-Kids' lives make their adulthood different, more difficult, or easier? Let's take a look at what the Time Signatures of the environment in which they will be living may be like, and how their different Birthmarks may respond.

Economic Outlook

The youngest of the Techno-Kids (those born in 1969) will be in their early 20s as the 1990s get started, the oldest (those born in 1960) will be 30 years old. In the 1980s the Techno-Kids finished up their education and started work. The decade of the 1990s will be a time of coming of age, and, for Techno-Kids, these times will actually be good. The economic climate in the early 1990s will still be favorable, primarily due to a slow-growing labor market. Companies riding what is left of the 1980s recovery will continue to need as many skilled workers as they can find. While inflation will have increased and dropped, and realities of recession will be an everyday nuisance, for the first years of the decade the outlook will still seem positive. Those Techno-Kids with less education, and there will be quite a few, will have their choice of service industry jobs, although wages will be low compared to technical and professional jobs.

Many Techno-Kids will have had considerable work experience before they leave school. They learned early (during forays into regional malls) that it takes money to buy clothes, whether neo-punk jeans and leather coats (you can't get those at thrift shops), or post-preppie polo shirts and penny loafers. Their work ethic is not like their parents or the Baby Boomers. Techno-Kids had two experiences that combined to frighten them into being very money oriented and generally cynical about socially oriented ideas, which their slightly flaky and seemingly sentimental ("remember the 1960s?") older cousins seem to care about more.

The first, indirect though it was, was their upbringing during inflationary times (the 1970s), which coincided with a loss of confidence in the country's leadership. Techno-Kids, unlike other age groups, did not have a Camelot Kennedy to revere (Gap Generation), or the workings of a Vietnam-era LBJ Great Society to be confused by or be angry at (Baby Boomers). As they were contemplating what they were going to be when they grew up, they began to acquire a fear of and a grudging respect for the power of the economy and the mystique of enterprise. They learned to fear because they had witnessed the closure of steel mills in Pennsylvania, cutbacks and shutdowns in automobile plants in the Midwest (referred to then as the Rust Belt), and sell-outs of family farms in the Plains states.

Many of their parents, put out of work by the recession of the 1970s, allowed this emotional climate of anxiety over money to bloom. In their 40s, they had been laid off because their plants closed, or had less seniority than older workers. Worse, many were educated in a time when the only skills they had developed were becoming obsolete. While not identical to the 1910–1919 cohort, we see in Techno-Kids some of the same emotional strains. Fortunately, Techno-Kids did not have as intense a loss in their personal development as their older counterparts. Still, the shadow of each depression or recession left its imprint of caution and materialism on the younger generations in each instance.

The economy of the 1990s responded favorably to the energy that the Techno-Kids offered. Despite a prolonged and uneven recessionary period (or "economic adjustment"), young adults in their mid-20s found a demand for their talents. While there were shutdowns in the auto and defense industry in the early 1950s, there were still fewer waiting lines for factory jobs, which were now cleaner and less onerous places to work than they once were. In fact, across the country, beginning in the late 1980s and continuing through the early 1990s, there was limited factory construction and modernization to increase productivity and renew old capital that offered a new generation of technical positions in computerized machinery. The Midwest was now becoming the new industrial frontier. People, who had been leaving the region, were returning to jobs, despite economic confusion at the national level.

Techno-Kids who lived in the well-developed regions fared well, others did not. Plant closures, relocation, and cutbacks began to occur in the mid-1990s as the country further trimmed its resources to respond to competition; a reprise, or perhaps volume two of the earlier economic story of the late 1970s and early 1980s. Fortunately, most Techno-Kids were fairly established in their jobs and careers by midpoint in the 1990s. After all, many were already in their 30s. The burden of the cuts began to fall on the following generation. What was harmful, however, was the consolidation of jobs into leading economic regions away from most rural areas, and the further bifurcation of jobs into the higher level managerial and professional positions and the more work-a-day technical and service positions.

Only those Techno-Kids with a comparative advantage in education would be immune from this economic adjustment process. While the scope of this new round of downsizing may not have been extensive, the population most hurt by it was least able to cope with its impacts. The younger population with poor educational backgrounds joined the ranks of the regionally displaced workers and the large metropolitan underclass—people who had never developed skills to take them beyond service industry jobs in the lowest paying categories.

Technological Conditions

The birth of Techno-Kids, as the name implies, coincided with the birth of the microprocessor. Baby Boomers were children of the transistor era, the Gap Generation children of the vacuum tube. While Baby Boomers were already adults in universities or at work when the first pocket calculators came out, Techno-Kids were elementary school age when electronic pinball games (Pong) came out. Computers were available for course work in many high schools, and students could use affordable pocket calculators in their classes (if teachers let them). Baby Boomers were lucky if their families had an old-fashioned tube hi-fi, or maybe a stereo, when they were in high school, and even luckier if they had a transistor radio of their own. Techno-Kid parents had stereos, and music the kids could understand, even if they were not sure they liked bebop, jazz, or Buddy Holly, the Supremes, and Little Richard. Techno-Kids grew up with microwave ovens and color televisions, inoculations on a sugar cube (Sabin vaccine) that eliminated polio epidemics that put children in iron lungs. Techno-Kids accept and expect technology to be part and parcel of their lives.

Techno-Kids are avid consumers, because of their upbringing in the post-inflation, post-recession, materialistically driven world. Try as they will, even the most ascetic Techno-Kids have a fascination for the products of the era's heroes, whether it is the advanced educational work station produced by Steven Jobs's NeXT Corporation, or home computer networking via modem or fax. Older Techno-Kids with money (e.g., the young business success stories) are not averse to having cellular telephones in their pockets, and facsimile machines at home, and subscriptions to what we might label as technology-focused consumer magazines, particularly the wide range of computer monthlies that discuss the latest trends, or that try to integrate technophile interests with home-centered living (e.g., audiovisual interior design). They also love to attend new-product conventions, whether for computers, skis, boats, or other technologized products.

This is not to say that the majority of the population will not change as technology continues to perfuse our lives, but that change will be easier for Techno-Kids than others. Eating patterns, for example, changed when the Surgeon General's report on heart disease came out in 1968. At that time Children of the American Dream, born in the 1920s, were the ones who slowly began to modify their eating habits, transmitting them by force of market influence and the models they provided to younger and less sophisticated populations. Techno-Kids will have a constant flow of these types of new discoveries and edicts as part of their lives. Techno-Kids have created huge markets in recreational technology—advanced running, skiing, tennis, wind surfing, bicycling, and diving equipment. As principal consumers for new computer-designed, composite, or special-purpose-material sporting equipment, they create an entry point for both older and younger consumers who are more followers and adaptors of new technologies.

This will, no doubt, reinforce the fast pace of product change (e.g., speed up the product life-cycle) and increase anxieties in the corporate sector regarding how to reach this young but maturing consumer group. At least the laugh is on the corporate sector, now running fast to keep apace with the changing demands of this diverse consumer group (although many of the designers of these new techno-products are the Techno-Kids themselves). Fortunately, until the major setback in the economy near mid-decade, Techno-Kid materialism provides considerable compensation to industry for all the gyrations in product development they cause.

Those Techno-Kids who are most connected to computer-based products in their life styles will comprise a substantial part of a rapidly growing cultural phenomenon which did not exist before—the computer network. The use of computer networks, electronic links from individual computer to individual computer or to information data bases, many of which are interactive, will be a norm for most Techno-Kids by the year 2000. Computer networking will be used for many purposes by Techno-Kids and others. The expansion of social ties through computer networking will be well under way by the mid-1990s, and will be fully established as a mode of communication and work by the year 2000. Moreover, the dimensions of network communication will be substantially enhanced for those in the workplace or at home (where service is available) by the development of integrated signal digital networks (ISDN), fiber optic office and home "wiring," proliferating satellite communications up-links, expansion of the integration and high-speed transmission of voice, data, graphics, and video into computer communications, and portability of computers with cellular telephone communications links. In an age of "virtual reality," Techno-Kids will be well connected, even if they are out of touch.

Social and Political Environment

The 1990s open on a world that Techno-Kids find increasingly appealing. Their cynicism about big government (which they have actually never experienced as adults) they feel is well founded, but waning. Somewhat uncomfortable with Gap Generation emotionality and Baby Boom paternalism on various issues, Techno-Kids are generally indifferent to Politics with a capital P, if not hostile to it. As they move into their 30s and vote in the 1992 election, they continue to have a generally passive libertarian to conservative antigovernment point of view, and are part of the reason why the Republican administration is reelected. The new mix of Republican liberalism with no policies or programs appeals to Techno-Kids, who are doing fairly well for themselves (to the early 1990s). They like a person who talks softly and carries a big shtick. After all, they were raised on television's most corroded political viewpoints and anti-communist "top gun" media combined with a mixture of space age science fiction and nouveau-horror images—followed by the "conversion" of the Eastern bloc to Western-style market thinking. Finding a solid reference point for a political perspective in such a mess would be, and was, very hard for Techno-Kids.

Techno-Kids find themselves less able to buy homes and needing two incomes to maintain a middle-class life style, but they don't blame the government; nor do they blame business. They certainly do not place the blame on themselves; in fact, they accept the condition as one into which they have tumbled. They might, in fact, see two-income households not as a problem, but as a natural reflection of the shift in gender roles, reflecting the new equality of the sexes.

Techno-Kid morality is pragmatic and family-focused. It emphasizes marriage, fidelity, and stability to defend against the hazards of single life, rather than as religious sentiment or any sensibilities about the nuclear family. They are family focused in a more progressive way that increasingly integrates more egalitarian roles for women (which Techno-Kid women are insisting upon). The political climate of the United States in the early 1990s seems supportive of new women's roles (since they are driven by economics, which more often than not determines morality), but government has done little to recognize it, other than to pay it lip service. The responsibility for implementing this new morality, such as it is, has been placed in the hands of women and their partners and spouses.

Techno-Kid values are understandably materialistic, despite, and perhaps because of, a new focus on the family. This materialism derives from anxiety and status-driven consumerism, a result of graduating from affluent childhood into economically unstable and uncertain times in which there were few if any of the moral models in politics or religion that existed during the early days of the counterculture. For Techno-Kids, materialism is commensurate with quality of life. Beer commercials, jean commercials, car commercials, hair color commercials, all have been tuned into this equation: "Of course you can have quality of life; we'll sell it to you."

Most Techno-Kids accept the higher-price social norm and work within it to get what they want. In this respect America becomes more like Japan, where prices are high, and attainment of consumer goals are dominant themes of life's reality. However, the larger underclass within this age group (which does not exist in Japan's more homogeneous population) has swollen in ranks because of the inability of increasing numbers of young persons to get the social tools, education, and job experience they need to become economically enfranchised (have a well-paying job and career). The punk syndrome expands within this age group (and gets older), creating an enduring counterculture characterized not by bohemian alternative values, but by nihilism and racism, the feared negativity that evolves when people do not find a place for themselves in the broader scheme of things. This cohort is characterized by a truly schizoid personality, stemming from the expansion of the haves and have-littles in their age group.

While many kept expecting Americans to form and join an American equivalent of the European Green Party, this in fact does not materialize in any substantial way. Why? The Greens in Europe have a long tradition of strong antiestablishment values that were given a more wholesome configuration over the years as European Gap Generation and Baby Boom cohorts became more politically engaged. In the United States, this phenomenon does not take place during the 1980s or 1990s, at least not with any degree of success. Instead of the evolution of an active Green Party, the country experiences the reintroduction of environmental politics more actively across party lines in the early elections of the 1990s and thereafter.

Cultural Climate

The cultural climate of the late 1990s will have two important themes centered on the Techno-Kids. First will be the "twilight" of post–Baby Boom glory, acted out by Techno-Kid consumers—the last gasp of youth-driven consumption. Second will be the crisis of U.S. industrial capacity to meet this consumer demand in the face of international competition. After all, the generation following the Techno-Kids is substantially smaller, foreshadowing a shift to more mature markets, and the business community will struggle to prolong this healthy 50-year-long consumer love affair despite flagging competitiveness. At their economic peak during the decade of the 1990s, Techno-Kids will outshadow their Baby Boom elders in terms of their immediate market impact. Baby Boomers will still be equal in size, but will be at a stage in life when their patterns and priorities are, presumably, more established (though as diverse as any group of 41 million people can be) and focusing on their own children, the new Baby Boom of the 1980s and 1990s. Techno-Kids, however, will be in their 30s at a prime stage of life for shaping the new wave of adult demands for products and life style and for making their contribution to the nation's new harvest of children. All this time U.S. companies will be running as fast as they can to respond to these consumers' needs before losing markets—or their own ownership—to companies from other nations.

Most women in this cohort will work, and most will be competing for and obtaining positions nearly equal in status and pay to men's. The salaries paid to women will probably be the closest to parity with men yet, though not completely on par, still at 80 to 90 percent. However, the participation of women in professions formerly dominated by men will be rapidly changing. While women comprised less than 20 percent of physicians and lawyers in the 1980s, by the year 2000 they have rapidly increased their share to 45 percent. One area where there was a surprising growth was in the sciences and engineering, where women had risen from roughly 10 percent by 1990 to 35 percent by the year 2000. Techno-Kid women are the most actively mainstream career-oriented generation of women to date.

Households of Techno-Kids will depart from the models of the Baby Boom in several ways. First, there will, from the start, be two wage earners. There will be far more structuring of family life style around career priorities, even in the case of workers in lower paying employment. Accommodation, as stated earlier, will be an economic necessity. Because both household heads will need to work (whether they want to or not), children will be born later and will be placed in child care sooner than today. Although Americans may seem to be becoming more domestic, they will have metamorphosed beyond the exaggerated "cocooning" stage claimed to have characterized the 1980s. The 1990s will not witness abandonment of eating out, cinema, and sports activities; rather their gentle revitalization. Techno-Kids are, much more so than Baby Boomers, extraverted and socially active, synthesizing their hybrid of 1950s conformity and 1960s rebelliousness.

Yet, despite their socially engaged way of living that seems to be emerging as they enter into adulthood, there are also shadowy background notes. Perhaps Techno-Kids themselves are not aware of them; possibly, they are projected onto them. Still, they are an interesting highlight to this group's development and future participation in U.S. culture—a darker view of a future technological society produced not by the group's own members but consumed by them, as by others. The evidence of this troubled aspect of 1990s society is in the rapid growth of computer crime and computer security breaches. More and more disaffected Techno-Kids turn this seemingly innocent computer hacking into information piracy. New laws to the contrary, the difficulty of stopping such crime is a reminder of the fragility of the electronic and human infrastructure on which our increasingly paperless society is based.

The new delinquent of the 1990s is the "Cyberpunk": a smart but sociopathic expert at computer system exploitation. The Cyberpunk foreshadows a darker, presumably not-too-distant future that is a grim admixture of anarchy and corporacracy, with an underclass of criminal and counterestablishment guerilla technologists fighting with invisible and omnipresent techno-corporations that gird the planet. Science fiction authors such as William Gibson anticipate this environment in novels in which youth are frequently disaffiliated and jaded riders of the computer networks, "jacked" into their computer consoles, advised by old, burnt-out remnants of recent history. Perhaps these images, while highly entertaining, signal the emergence of a cultural perspective in which the priorities of technology and the economy are out of balance with human values, giving rise to a new counterculture comprising young combatants looking for their place in the intricately wired scheme of things.

Billy Budds

Billy Budds' uniqueness as citizens of the 1990s comes from their mixture of innocence and highly idealized values in contrast to their peers: Keepers of the Flame who are retreating to past models; Missing Ingredients who are making up for a sense of loss; and Cosmopolitans who are more purposeful and in touch with the world. Billies are often the intellectuals and aesthetes of their generation, whether they are formally educated or not. They are an oddity within a cohort that is driven by a retrenchment into practical morality, materialism, and neo-libertarian thinking.

In the 1990s, roughly in their 30s, Billy Budds have recently come through a prolonged period of personal development and experimentation in how to express their value system, finally settling into a comfortable path. Having completed college, or garnered sufficient work experience to have achieved sufficient purchase in their job, they can now say they are starting a career. Prior to this, many Billies lingered long in an employment limbo, devoted to remaining close to their commitment toward social and artistic principles, a commitment and authenticity they felt was generally missing from American life.

At this stage, Billy Budds have worked hard to settle down, taking longer to do so than any of their peers. Billies, while getting started in the world earlier, were guided by their concerns with qualitative matters (how they lived), not the quantitative concerns of career and income. Many Billies are members of a new generation of college graduates who went on to careers that reflected broader, outward-oriented human values. Some, for example, became professors, now that the faculty generation of the 1920s and 1930s was retiring. Others went on to careers in journalism (socially responsible, of course), law (environmental, technology commercialization), administering non-profit organizations, government, and business. Favorite areas in this last category include restaurants, advertising-communications services, sports (emphasizing the personal-ethical nature of this endeavor), and, of course, local politics: with an emphasis on balancing the economic and ecological perspective.

Because they waited, deliberated, and explored their options through trial and error, Billies did have fewer financial resources than their peers by the 1990s. They also live in areas that are consistent with their values, often paying a high economic price to do so. They are not hippies, as they appeared to be earlier but are still driven by the shadow of that original ethic. They carry this theme on, in their own way.

Billy Budds have been motivated by a sense of values that are not so much their own, as a reflection of their internalization of larger scale concerns, a type of superego preoccupation with good and bad and lofty principles. They are, and have been, interested in human, social, and environmental problems, feeling the press of these issues personally. The Billies who rejected mainstream employment, or who did not adequately prepare for a career because of their delays and resistance to complying with social norms, are found in lower paying service industry jobs, such as bookstores, restaurants, and bicycle shops.

Billies, as they move toward their 40s, are a portrait of conviction and unsettling seriousness. On New Year's Eve, 1999, Billy Budds are cautious and, like the rest of their generation, pragmatic about their lives and the prospects for the future. They were philosophical about the economic downturn of the mid-1990s, particularly so since their jobs are the type likely to be hit first by industry and government cutbacks. Yet, being adaptive, they will have pushed through the hard times and focused their attention on their own concept of quality of life and fundamental values. To those who are older, Billies seem to be a reflection of the familiar past of the 1960s with an unfathomable modern twist. That twist is simply that Billies have taken on the symbolic burdens and style of their parents' generation and put their own spin on it. Because many of their parents were themselves frustrated but complacent adults (of the Children of the American Dream and Bridge Generation), Billies somehow are acting out a virtuous model, as if to fulfill some unspoken quest for a metaphysical Holy Grail.

Billies will have married later than their cohort and are more likely to have lived for a longer time with their partner. They treat their relationships very seriously but carry scars from intense but failed past relationships. By the new century Billies will have found partners who understand their intensity, share it to some degree, and provide an ally, as well as a counterbalance, to their lives. Their relationships can sometimes benefit from their tendency to externalize their inner concerns to outside issues.

Billies are less technologically oriented and have always been more reserved about the prospects for technological solutions to social problems than other Techno-Kids. Billies are the last remaining Whole Earth fans, but are equally likely to take an extreme stance against popular trends, eating hamburgers and french fries to protest diet fads. They resent mass phenomena and set themselves above trends.

In their hearts Billy Budds have a strong conviction that people and government can make a stronger and more meaningful commitment to community and the environment, but inside they are also cynical about the prospects for improvement. Part of this labile relation with issues stems from their own internalization of their parents' idealism. It is, as noted, as if their attachment to grand ideas and grand illusions is an ongoing connection with their parents, for whom they carry a torch. Yet, like moths, drawn to the flame inside the window, they beat their wings frantically, without success or ceasing.

Fortunately, there is much creative and constructive action that results from this way of viewing the world. Billies have an endurance, in addition to their emotional intensity, which serves them well as they move into their late 30s within a time of serious economic turmoil. For although they may at times be gruff or disconcertingly intense, they want to—and can—transform this intensity toward issues and caring for others. This ability marks them as people of character and dedication.

Cosmopolitans

Among the generation of Techno-Kids men and women born during the 1960s is a group whose styles are indicative of a new balance between the humanism of the counterculture and the context of old-world values. This group are the young Cosmopolitans. The last decade of this century has witnessed the successful maturation of Cosmopolitans into their adult prime. They are both mainstream members of society and economy and true to their values in ways that neither the more artistic, more conservative, or more material and emotionally need-driven, are.

Cosmopolitans have maintained, as intrinsic to their life styles, two important and related value themes. The first is the priority of justice and equality, particularly with regard to gender roles. The second is a balanced view of the importance of achievement and quality of life. They have developed and consistently incorporated these values into their lives to one degree or another over the past decades, and continue to do so as the century winds up for its close.

The Cosmopolitans' commitment to their values emerged early in their lives. During their childhoods in the 1960s and early 1970s, Cosmopolitans were considered by their parents to be eccentric. This is despite generally good rapport with their children and a fair degree of understanding of their perspectives. Their eccentricity was not because of their sexual or drug excesses, which were very likely to have been part of their lives in any case, but because of their individuality and rapidly emerging commitment to their own views. These views emerged early, and were not necessarily in agreement with the family outlook. In fact, they frequently were at odds with them, although they may have been in agreement with other family members, from grandparents to family friends (so they were not completely alien to the family).

Cosmopolitans evolved early on what might seem a mature outlook, although it was replete with the energy and zeal of youth. Cosmopolitan men and women were less driven by artistic sentiment (Billy Budds) or a moralistic passion (Keepers of the Flame) than by a personal gut-level common sense of right and wrong. They did not preach, or act iconoclastically. They spoke out and then shut up; and when they spoke you heard them. Their sense of justice was learned; they were clear about the differences between honesty and dishonesty, oppression and opportunity. While not missionaries, each Cosmopolitan had one or more beliefs that were important to their world view, something often missing in others.

Among Cosmopolitans, particularly women Cosmopolitans, the sense of justice was often linked to the feeling of identification with the historical continuity of the feminist and civil rights movements. Perhaps their own life experiences strengthened their commitment. For example, some Cosmopolitan women had mothers who were very conventional (being born in the 1930s cohort) and manifested signs of disappointment at having been channeled into a domestic life, despite good education. Other Cosmopolitan women identified with a mother that, while a professional in her own right, had had to struggle against formidable opposition in her family and profession to achieve her position. Both experiences energized a commitment to accomplishing equal opportunity for women in the future.

Cosmopolitan women were very active in defending family planning when they were in their teens and early 20s. Most Cosmopolitan women became sexually active at a very young age, typically reflecting their outrage at the efforts of others to control the lives of women.

Both Cosmopolitan men and women were more committed than their peers to addressing racism, though never at a level of profundity equal to previous decades. Yet, these actions were deliberate and conscious, and exceeded the interest and commitment of their more passive Techno-Kid peers. Many made minor social gestures like attending a traditional (generally "white") social function, such as a cotillion, with a date who was Hispanic or black, and, as students, worked on behalf of affirmative action, for women and minorities. Although usually from middle-class roots, Cosmopolitans practice what they preach and do not run away from issues they confront.

In balancing values of achievement against desire for quality of life, Cosmopolitans were good students of their own families—for better or worse. Their parents were usually reasonably educated and valued education. They also valued the cultural facets of everyday living that filled out life, from art and theater to lectures, concerts, and sports events, as well as religion and celebration of holidays. While the parents often operated in modes that were still characteristic of the nuclear family, with father working and mother at home, even here there were models. Mothers often went back to work or began professional careers when children were adolescents. Father often began a new career after retiring or being laid off the job. Cohesion and adaptation appeared to be successful working models for Cosmopolitan families. Their parents enjoyed family life and knew how to make some of the trade-offs needed to keep both family and work alive.

Fundamental to the outlook of Cosmopolitans is the value they place on education. During the 1980s they pursued it for its intrinsic value as a tool for work as well as a means for enhancing their own character and connection to the world. While not jocks, Cosmopolitans were good at sports and were good sports. Not seduced by the elitism of fraternities and sororities, they later maintained membership in their university's alumni association and helped recruit promising students. Cosmopolitans sometimes fell prey to the aesthetic foibles of college, in their occasional fondness for preppy attire, and fascination with old school ties. They were also realistic about the failures of, and possibilities for, universities to contribute meaningfully to both the educational and economic objectives of the country.

Most Cosmopolitans did go to college. Most finished undergraduate and a large number, but not all, finished graduate degrees by the early 1990s. Although Cosmopolitans were interested in professional careers, they have always valued the concept of family. Many Cosmopolitans came from large families, but some were only children. Whatever their backgrounds, their plans as men or women encompassed the establishment of a family and development of the depth and richness from which they had themselves benefited.

Another facet of Cosmopolitans' depth is their heterogeneous appreciation of others. Cosmopolitans have had no age boundaries in their definition of friends. They liked and were liked by their parents' generation, and the generation before. Their ability to maintain relationships across age and geography is part of their consistency and strong valuation of friendships.

Their commitment to family, equal across men and women, creates an important dilemma for Cosmopolitans of either sex. Nevertheless, Cosmopolitans are strongly committed to working out equitable ways to achieve both family and career objectives. Although they may not provide the optimum solution for each partner, the strategies give the family, as a whole, a stronger footing. The willingness to work out compromises is a critical trait in the resilience of Cosmopolitans throughout the challenging times of the 1990s.

In planning careers and life during the late 1980s and early 1990s, most Cosmopolitans sought partners who would be understanding of the need for compromise. For men, this included facing the reality of supporting the family on one income for a time (which during the 1990s runs counter to economic logic) and playing an active role in child rearing (to preserve quality of life in the family).

For women in the 1990s, this meant getting a career started and then accepting the need for at least a minimum commitment to child rearing before returning to work (this minimum perhaps being from three weeks to three months). When Cosmopolitans are paired together, which would seem to be likely in the 1990s, they demonstrate a flexibility and adaptiveness to the requirements of family. Unlike Keepers of the Flame, who might not pursue their own objectives or only pursue those related to income earning; unlike Missing Ingredients, who would not marry or would return to work without thinking out child-rearing options; Cosmopolitans would craft a realistic, though not necessarily ideal arrangement to ensure family and profession were equally regarded.

Cosmopolitans tended to get married during the early 1990s, or at least make firm commitments to living together. Both partners were good at putting their somewhat exploratory or promiscuous pasts behind them as they began to concentrate on the early stages of their careers. Cosmopolitan careers are likely to cover a very wide field of professional endeavor, including academia (where there will be considerable growth in new faculty positions during the 1990s), law, medicine, government, design and planning, management, engineering and computer software, television and media, public relations and advertising, corporate management, and entrepreneurial ventures of all kinds.

Although Cosmopolitans appear middle class by virtue of their education, their roots are in fact very varied, their parents ranging from rural farmers to steel company executives. What they have in common is that whatever their income or ethnicity, their parents valued education as well as family, and they were able to provide this outlook and access to these opportunities for their children—even if there was no money for financing school. Parents of other Techno-Kid group members may have placed less emphasis on education or family values, and could have been sidetracked in their support of these values by their own social and economic dilemmas (e.g., divorce, unemployment).

By the year 2000 Cosmopolitans will be in their mid-30s, actively pursuing their respective careers. Among the Techno-Kids, we will, by this time, see as many two-career households among the Cosmopolitans as among any of the other groups. While their career development may be slightly less than their peers, given trade-offs made for the family, these differences will become insignificant as the new century proceeds. Cosmopolitans understand the long-term value of their actions and are willing to pay now for future benefits.

Missing Ingredients

Missing Ingredients—who are making up for an emotional hold in their lives—greet the 1990s with a morning run and a rush to the office, which might be the marketing department of a large corporation or a home health care agency. In their 30s, Missing Ingredients are at a stage where they are turning loose the full intensity of their personalities on the business and social world. Unlike Billy Budds, whose career decisions reflect an ideological aesthetic, or Keepers of the Flame, whose choices are more dogmatically driven and focus closer to home, or Cosmopolitans, who are concerned with broader career goals, Missing Ingredients are being driven by their emotional juices, and they are reaching full flow.

During the 1990s, when they were 20 to 30, many Missing Ingredients finished community college, university, or graduate school and are now working. Most found themselves threatened by the authority and structure of school and tried to get through it as fast and as easily as possible, even when they were very good students. Missing Ingredients tend to view jobs much as they did their families. They act out their child–parent relationships with their bosses, attempting to please them and blaming them for indifference to their (the Missing Ingredient's) welfare. While this dynamic is widespread, Missing Ingredients are more dramatic in their workplace psychodrama than many other groups.

Missing Ingredients continued during their 20s and 30s to explore difficult, often one-sided relationships, frequently to the point of emotional exhaustion while denying the pain even to themselves. As a group, they tended to have one marriage during their mid-20s in which, prompted by a strong emotional hunger, they misjudged the quality of their match and often selected a partner whose dependence wreaks havoc on their personal lives. As they enter their mid-30s, they are still dancing with serious relationships more than their counterparts who are more settled.

For better or worse Missing Ingredients construct their own relationships and family life along the lines of their family of origin. They may find themselves in the caretaking role, often to a young and troubled man or woman with a strong personality.

Missing Ingredients tend to be a little (only a little) like Questors in their strong desire to find meaning and happiness, as well as like Lennies in their awkwardness with traditional patterns of personal relations. Questors and Missing Ingredients share a hope for personal salvation through a relationship, someone to quench their thirst for nurturance. While they are each different in the reasons for struggle, both groups have a similar barrier between their inner and outer self.

Missing Ingredients tend to maintain the relationship to their parents that they always had, reluctant to break the pattern, even though their families were often dysfunctional. They may have watched their parents go through more desperation, second and third marriages, or lives of isolated bitterness. When their parents are not legally divorced, but emotionally separated, Missing Ingredients tend to resist going home. They do this to avoid being put in the position of arbitrator, placator, and, sometimes, even parent. The last thing the Missing Ingredient young adults need is to be called back into their childhood role. Yet, few can resist for long when parents repeatedly plead with them to come home.

Some Missing Ingredients will be milking their career opportunities to receive approval and gain empowerment. Others, in a reverse situation, will be equally energetic in pouring out nurturance toward an infinitely hungry world. Both types will reach their late 30s concerned that they have not achieved what they want. Those who have mastered the business world will still find too many emotional raw spots in their life. They will experience more upheavals in job status and career change due to a subtle chip on the shoulder. Unaware of this chip, these Missing Ingredients will wonder why they have not reached a comfortable plateau in their work life, a safe place to reduce the running speed of the emotional engine.

In contrast, the Missing Ingredients who have assumed the giving role will continually feel an undercurrent of dissatisfaction and occasional bitterness sweeping over the experience of accomplishment. The phenomenon of "social worker burnout" will manifest itself here with a strength not found in others, because Missing Ingredients will not have reconciled the motivation to give to others with their need for affirmation and affection.

Despite these painful underpinnings, those Missing Ingredients who have pursued material rewards have been very effective in fighting their way up the ranks of small or large corporations over the years. They have indulged themselves in rewards again and again, trying but finding it difficult to obtain the feelings they want. Still, they continue, and may be effective managers, particularly when reporting to other emotional managers; later, they become executives where they can play out their own parental role. They are viewed by coworkers as competent, eager to smooth the waves of office strife and inclined to deny the emotional elements of conflict.

In the year 1999 Missing Ingredients, now 30 to 40, have been successfully moving through their careers, mostly putting their emotional traits to good use. Still, the damage and pain remain for those Missing Ingredients who have not had an emotional reconciliation with themselves. Those who remained married have found partners who are unlike their parents. Missing Ingredients want their lives to work well and may forbear when they themselves are parents rather than inflict their burden on their children. Those unable to do this will pass the flame of emotional need on to their offspring, putting their children in the position of assuaging their hungers for care and attention.

Missing Ingredient kids from low-income families tended to have a harder time since the streets were so near. Drug use, teenage pregnancy, and marginal literacy were their hallmarks. In the 1990s, a number of these young adults found the emotional and financial resources to upgrade their situations, but the majority did not. By the mid-1990s there will be a large number of people in their 30s who have not found their way out of their deep troubles. These people, living in sprawling but aging suburban enclaves as well as in shrinking rural areas, will become, by the year 2000, part of a dramatic underclass that will remain economically disabled by their lack of resources.

Keepers of the Flame

Keepers of the Flame are the gentle reactionaries at the end of the 20th century. Their image of American life draws heavily from imagined models of the past, most of which never existed but were constructed from family myth or literature, including religious revivalism. Keepers are the children of Envoys and Good Old Boys and Gals born in the 1930s. They may also be the younger children of older Children of the American Dream who had large families.

As Keepers of the Flame slide into their 30s, they are able to maintain an appearance of calm and tranquility; but, as was the case with their parents, there is often a storm brewing beneath the surface. During their 30s, most Keepers settle down into careers, similar to their parents in many respects—more like them than like their peers. Although the fields they enter are more technical, the career characteristics are the same. For example, a Keeper might administer a high tech company, having been promoted after long years of toil, while her mother might have been the administrator of a government office nearby. A young male Keeper may have taken over the family landscaping business after the father's retirement.

In the year 2000 most Keepers of the Flame are far along in their families and careers, both of which evidence the strong influence of Keeper families of origin (stability, conservativeness). They have contributed to the baby boomlet of the late 1980s through the 1990s, often raising two or three children, and actively fostering in them the development of a strong moral outlook. Many Keepers use religion as a buffer between the pain of their experience as children and their desire to preserve peace and reduce overt emotional tension as adults.

Their families are often improvements over their original situations, but, sadly, not always.

Keeper women, while deeply devoted to their sanctified image of family, sought out their own personal development. A good many married in the 1990s, before finishing college. They may have had children in their 20s and struggled with the dilemma of self versus family until their children reached school age. In the 1990s, Keeper families received much media attention as the new traditionalists. A few Keepers kept their domestic impulses at bay while they finished their education. They avoided marriage until their 30s, hoping to find a suitable partner. Some never marry. By the 1990s, however, most Keepers have married, though they have not resolved their inner dilemma about family life. Their anger, guilt, and distrust of intimacy will hamper their relationships. Within marriage, they may experience dark forboding and depression. They struggle with their strongly crafted image of moral right or wrong against their inner needs—holding these needs in check as long as feasible. The personal need for self-acceptance wins out against the desire to fulfill the traditional role model. This may come at great expense—a divorce or major emotional crisis in their 30s.

An alternative Keeper of the Flame family has two educated parents who reinforced each other's convictions and adherence to convention, albeit brought up-to-date and polished. Their spark of anxiety will help them avoid the most blatant errors. If they do not work, unlike their mothers, they will leave. Before this, though, they will work harder than their parents did to improve communication. When they do not try to conceal their discontent, they can raise their children according to their own vision, passing on a new flame rather than the old.

All in all, Keepers may find themselves at odds with their own outlook from time to time as they mature, since their outlook depends on holding back the less consistent and predictable facets of personality. During the 1990s, however, they will be working their hardest to justify their way of life and will use mutual reinforcement to maintain their personal and familial stability. Products of the unstable and volatile 1960s and 1970s, they will only need to look back upon the uncertainty of that time to restore their commitment to hearth and family. Yet, unless Keepers have learned to communicate their authentic feelings to each other and their children, their children are destined to repeat Keeper experiences. Given the stress that the country will experience in the mid-1990s through the year 2000 in adapting to global competition and pressures, Keepers will have to make sense out of these for themselves and for their children.

WE HAVE MET THE DECADES AND THEY ARE US

IN SEARCH OF THE AMERICAN IDENTITY

On New Year's Eve, 1999, Americans will greet the turn of the millennium with eyes that see the prospect from vastly different perspectives. While most of us will still be part of the waiting crowd, having muddled our way through, each Time Signature group will meet the realities of the new setting, the Weather Report, for that first morning of the year 2000 in ways that only the shared history of each cohort can help us comprehend.

Our personal histories, as members of a cohort, are the past, but they are also the prologue to and pattern for the next stage of our life journey. Our shared histories enable us to know ourselves better and understand others better. As adaptable, changeable humans working within the framework of our lives, we cannot ignore our shared past. It is not only where we come from but also the architecture of our present.

Many of us choose to ignore who we have been and where we came from, a characteristic American trait, always focusing on the new. But our values, and to a significant extent, our personalities, will always be shaped by our past, although how we express the events that shaped us will change with time. We carry the accumulated experience of our lives like the spirals of a nautilus's shell, or like a redwood tree, whose rings tell how past drought, rain, and fire have formed

today's living tree. In addition to shaping us, our experience shapes how we interact with others.

Our time-based value differences often lead us into conflict with others, but they also lead us to knowledge of ourselves and where we fit, and to our struggles to improve the fit. This search for a better-fitting world has taken the form of innumerable crusades, each championing a value-based theme: racial and ethnic equality, religious purity and strict observance, sexual parity, generational equity, the new materialism, the new family-centrism and so forth. Whether you join a given crusade, fight it, or ignore it often depends upon your age and how you reached it. Whether or not the sparks of new movements are fanned into flame, they rarely endure, for they are not fueled by any consistent source of American spirit.

These crusading efforts are instead a call for belonging and consensus. The call echoes clearly for a while, then it is altered by the answering voices, growing weaker as the message bounces across the diverse and uneven surface of America. At the heart of the matter is one great question: Is America a country or just a collection of different groups?

IS AMERICA A COUNTRY?

By most criteria of what constitutes a country, the United States of America scores very low. For example, if a country is a geographic area whose residents share a common history of cultural traditions, including language, literature, religion, and food, all we can really claim is movies, TV, the hamburger, and pizza.

A country usually has an ethnically similar population, though some are more similar than others. For example, Japan is fairly homogeneous ethnically, although less homogeneous than the Japanese claim. Most important, a country is distinguished from its neighbors by shared values maintained through social institutions, both formal and informal, such as schools, religious organizations, and the cultural laws we call "mores" or "customs" (unwritten but practiced). These value systems, expressed through cultural norms and expectations, create a country's core identity.

If the criterion for being a country is shared cultural values and traditions, the United States of America does not meet the test. Many would argue that we do indeed have a culture with deep roots in Western Europe. However, a close look at the everyday evidence of our eating, reading, dancing, and recreation shows that this Western European base of culture is no longer a useful benchmark for the commonalities among our identities. Diversity is characteristic of America because the United States was conceived with no unifying social institutions and operates along different cultural models from its cousins anywhere else. Ultimately, as our name implies, we are a union of states, rather than a country.

America may share a language, yet despite the intellectuals and their claims for the unifying function of American English, our daily language has become increasingly loose in its structure and use. Standard American English is virtually a meta-language, used mostly with strangers; our literacy level is low and styles of language are increasingly idiosyncratic. That is why school books are written with oversimplified vocabularies. So yes, we have a language in common, but it is more of a pragmatic lingua franca than a cultural force.

Many non-Americans speak English better than native-born U.S. citizens. Many Americans live in ethnic enclaves where they barely speak English. We have few who fight for the vitality of the language as a cultural factor. Perhaps those who care are more concerned with how well our schools teach how to speak, read, and write than with the aesthetics of the language in America. This is a pragmatic interest, having to do with finding a job and getting ahead, not cultural values.

Education, like language, does not culturally define Americans because we have few unifying "American" concepts to shape common family and community standards in education. The controversy over whether American education should be elitist or egalitarian goes on. We can't even agree on how much formal education is enough or on the extent to which education can be replaced by "street smarts," let alone whose values should be imparted in the process. Because we have no culturally shared values as to what level or type of education an "American" should have, it is difficult to do more than worry. We know that we have to do better in education to cope with a technology-driven, competitive, global economy. But we are beginning to realize that rapid obsolescence—not cultural priorities—is most likely to shape our educational responses.

Religion is often held up as a common denominator for American values, but it is a frail one. Despite the Protestant background of our Founding Fathers, America never had a single religion, although attempts to impose one or another have never ceased. America has more religions than virtually any other place on earth. While we may not be ideally tolerant of one another, diverse religions spring up and co-exist, waxing and waning as the population changes and as young people intermarry or convert. Our various Judeo-Christian, Moslem,

Buddhist, and an increasing number of Eastern faiths and highly idio-syncratic new religions co-exist in an ever more secular environment, where religion is partly a highly personal activity and partly a social weapon rather than a culturally unifying force within and across our communities. The separation of religion from the community, while it causes much anxiety to those who are deeply religious, brings with it a spiritual freedom that has drawn many immigrants, from William Penn's Quakers and the Amish to Soviet Jews.

Despite our reputation for materialism, how much money we have does not define our identity as Americans any more than religion, education, or language. America may be the land of opportunity, but money does not unify Americans. Although some believe that the pursuit of the "almighty dollar" is our primary cultural concern, few would claim wealth as our "true faith."

Wealth has often been used to define social class, since having or not having money once keenly defined shared interests. Today, this is no longer so. We are a nation of people with no money, old money, new money—and today's lottery winners. Money no longer defines social class. An auto worker and a bank manager may earn similar incomes. A schoolteacher may earn as much as a salesclerk (if the teacher is lucky) but hardly ever as much as a plumber.

The forces at work in the United States are not likely to produce a set of social norms out of the values that already exist. Although many would argue that our evolution toward a country with a shared culture is merely a matter of time, that day may never come. Americans have profound values, but they are not the values traditionally associated with a country.

IS AMERICA A NATION?

A nation is a polity, or group of people, who are unified by shared civil laws that are consistently implemented by a system of adminis-tration. A people led by religious sects or by idiosyncratic cultural perspectives can be claimed by its leaders to be a nation. Whether their citizens agree to be led by those in power or not is a different question. America's history and recent trends suggest that we have an ever-changing set of institutions, whose underlying premises vary from one administration to another, from the Great Society to the New Federalism. Our nation may be a very special place, but our lack of national consistency makes it hard to define ourselves as one, except euphemistically.

Those who believe the United States is a nation say that our Constitution and Bill of Rights are the crucial foundations of our national identity, and it is from these basic premises that our system of the executive, judicial, and legislative branches takes shape and in turn gives shape to our democracy. However, as our nation's name implies, we are also a federation of states that each retains a tremendous amount of discretion in governance. While state laws must be subject to interpretation by and operate in compliance with the federal government, states are parallel governmental systems, with a substantial degree of autonomy. In fact, the combined budgets of the states are at least equal to that of the federal government.

The basic criteria for nationhood would seem to be satisfied by our Constitution and Bill of Rights. Our national theme is freedom and noninterference to the extent that free acts do not intrude upon the rights of other citizens. But freedom and noninterference alone are not sufficient to define our people as a nation. What is essential to nationhood is the existence and maintenance of the "social contract," a set of shared values expressed in the mission and legal policies and practices of the national government. The social contract is what all citizens implicitly accept as the purpose of government of the people, by the people, and for the people. Thus, the social contract is the collective, common reason for having a government: we agree to it because we recognize that some things need to be done for everyone, because we cannot do them individually.

This notion of social contract is typically lost in modern dialogue concerning the role of government in the United States. If anything, "the land of the free and home of the brave" is actually pro-individual and antigovernment (particularly "big government"), at least that's what the popular press says it is—"That government governs best that governs least." We have fought long and hard for improvement of those aspects of national law that protect our freedoms as expressed in the Bill of Rights—from freedom of the press to freedom from discrimination.

What is fascinating, and frightening, about our basic credo of freedom is that, perhaps by definition, it inherently minimizes the role of what a nation is and does. Protection of our individual rights is certainly crucial to our national identity. Our primary focus on economic opportunity is a preeminent social priority that makes us a light among nations. But does our concept of the social contract that unifies us as a nation end with the right to succeed financially? If our social contract is limited to a largely defensive "don't tread on me," then we seem almost to have set nationhood aside.

Today, many of us are looking for a popular conviction about the true role of government—what our social contract really is. At the same time, a trend has been under way for well over a decade that seems to be undermining our national identity. The United States has opted for an increasingly modest role for its central government—primarily focusing on defense and social security, if we use the budget as a measure, and on defense of individual rights, deregulation of industry, and limited redistribution of income, if we examine lawmaking and tax policy. This means, for the most part, that we have made our national government into a pragmatic, reactive (and sluggish) agency rather than an affirmative, proactive one. The results are growing increasingly visible: the epidemics of drug abuse, AIDS, homelessness; the trade and budget imbalances; the competitiveness dilemma and energy dependence; the crises of health costs, inadequate child care supply, environmental deterioration, and waste disposal.

While we are not a country in the same sense as France or Japan, we also fail to qualify for nationhood in many other respects. Government in America waxes and wanes in its concept of itself and its intervention in our problems. Over the past century, the United States government has dramatically changed its role with respect to its levels of intervention. This up and down pattern, more dramatic than that of most European governments, tells us that our own principles and values—at least as expressed by different decades of elected representatives—remain in flux. We change and we expect the nation to change as well. We may disagree on what to change, and find ourselves stuck with an unclear or half-formed set of policies, or even with nonpolicies—the default policies that result when government does not act on an issue and de facto condones the status quo. This also means that our nation's continual and unsuccessful search for coherence in policy is a reflection of our fundamental lack of definitive, shared, national values. From the evidence, we just do not all agree on who we are. Our differences mean that compromise is hard and is often an unsatisfactory expression of any point of view—a diluted set of unstable values. There is no public-private agenda in the United States.

IS AMERICA ITS REGIONS?

If the American identity is not consistently reflected by the policies and expressed social contract of our national government, then is the American identity more closely linked to the regions or states from which we hail, or in which we now live? Is America a federation of autonomous "mini-nations" like the republics of the USSR or the European Community? Is this where our identities and allegiances come from? There are some signs that this may be so.

Regions have always been important to defining the American identity. Over the past thirty years in the United States there has been a trend toward increasing regionalization, or decentralizing national government responsibilities to the state government level. States are increasingly being asked by the federal government to pay their own way on issues from education to infrastructure (highways, bridges, public transit).

What does an increasingly segmented and uneven state government role in the United States mean for our identities as a people? Those states with stronger policies and a broad tax base to support them can create a more positive climate for their economies. States with more (and sounder) investment in their "soft" economic infrastructure (schools, technology) and an advanced physical infrastructure (telecommunications, airports, and environmental services) end up with a more competitive economy. States that do not invest in themselves do not adapt to economic cycles as well and become home to "slash and burn" industries—those attracted to low-cost labor who will eventually move on to the next low-cost region or those that come for the low taxes but demand more schools, roads, and airports and threaten to leave if the state refuses.

America is becoming increasingly a nation of regions that are virtual city-states, defined by their economic capabilities—LA, Silicon Valley. People, too, are identifying more with their regions, whether it is the Midwest, Southwest, mid-Atlantic, or West Coast, even though their stay in those regions may be temporary.

It is a region's capacity to change with the evolving needs of the global economy that makes it vital and adaptive, but also, as a result, makes it a less consistent source of identity over time. Regions are changing their historic ways of producing wealth, and people are moving from rural communities to immense suburban metropolitan areas as economies shift from commodities (farm goods) to higher-value-added products (packaged microwavable foods) and services (financial and technical support businesses).

Given the tremendous mobility of our people, are regions a better foundation on which to base our notions of American identity? Within some distinct limits, perhaps; overall, however, they are probably not the best choice.

We live in an era in which, to paraphrase scholar Daniel Bell, the nation state is too large for small tasks and too small for large problems. America has grown too large to equitably and efficiently reflect the wide range of diverse local values in any consensus. At the other extreme, however, America is too small to contend comfortably with the new coordination and collaboration burgeoning among the economic regions—the European community, the Asia-Pacific trading networks, or future trading alliances that may emerge, in Southeast Asia, and eventually in Eastern Europe and South America.

Clearly, the United States is—as a whole and part by part—in a state of change, adapting to new economic and social forces, as are the people. Moreover, regions will never remain the stable cultural or economic environment they may once have been. If Americans cannot be identified easily with their nation, and regions are not a good substitute, where does that leave us?

IS AMERICA ITS "AFFILIATION GROUPS"?

If America is not a country in the same way that European or Asian countries are, and lacks that consistent and well-defined social contract that nationhood seems to require (made manifest by national institutions and policies for education, health, and retirement), and if our burgeoning regions are "dynamic" unstable centers of American values, who are we? Is the American identity so mercurial that we cannot find adequate commonalities above the level of the individual with which to describe it?

In the eyes of foreign companies that now manufacture products in the United States, America often appears to be a huge free market— literally a giant national foreign trade zone, where anyone can come and go about their business, be it enterprise or family matters. To other countries, we appear to be not so much the proverbial "melting pot" as an ever-changing stew or "potpourri" of independent ethnic, religious, and cultural groups, unified primarily by our highest common denominators: our shared belief in freedom and the pursuit of personal wealth.

The most evident shared value of Americans is protection of individual rights. To many Americans, this principle of individuality, so rare in many other nations, is the essence of America. Individuality continues to take center stage in our daily lives as citizens and as consumers. Technologists babble on about how our society is moving toward increased potential for the individual and greater creativity made possible by the ever-growing availability of computer-based technologies. These technologies (cellular telephones, fax machines, voice mail, notebook computers, bulletin boards, networks, interactive video, group-use software, and now "virtual realities") have the potential to give Americans greater freedom of choice in daily life and work. To technologists we seem to gain more and more control over our lives by reducing our dependence on proximity to others.

Many observers see today's movement for greater personal autonomy and control over one's life as a response to decades of depersonalization in work and everyday life. The trend to individuality, however, has buried within it a seemingly contradictory motivation: a race toward belonging so that identity has meaning. As we become more able to choose, and more able to seemingly determine our own views of the world, we are also weakening the connections that give those views meaning. As we become autonomous, we can cut ourselves loose from any of the traditions of geographically based shared values, such as those linking family, neighbor, cities, states, and possibly even nations.

As the world becomes more open, however, our choices broaden while our models for living become fewer and more fleeting (like fashions), and the bases for forming and maintaining values become more tenuous. As a result, many of us are hunting for value systems to connect to that will define the meaning of our actions and prevent us from being outcasts in the lonely crowd. When we abandon traditional value-based reference points, the result can often be disconnection from social norms, the loss of any common social perspective. We cherish our freedom but often suffer the loneliness that goes with that freedom from commitments, obligations, liabilities, rewards, or judgments of any kind. All of us, in our own way—whether we are Preservers or Adaptors, Martyrs or Self-Compensators, Attainers or Performers, Chameleons or Questors, Bootstrappers or Romantic-Realists, Future Perfects or Voyagers, Billy Budds or Missing Ingredients—want to leave the lonely crowd.

The framework of life that once defined shared values in a village cannot withstand the onslaught of new and highly divergent ideas that a multidimensional, multimedia metropolis holds. This flood may be the product of an information society, but it does not signify a knowledge society, and certainly not a wisdom society. Americans who feel that they have lost the reassuring anchor of commonly held values often mourn their absence ("people aren't like they used to be"). We watch expressions of our hopes and values acted out on TV or in the movies. But the historic basis for enduring values is often simply gone, just as small towns fade when the young people move to jobs in expanding suburban areas, just as our grandparents from the "old world" pass on, leaving behind nostalgic reminders of their values, and as our social institutions fail to offer replacements for the sources of meaning that play an important role in our lives.

Today, the trend toward individuality is being balanced by the complementary (or compensatory) pattern of people joining membership groups with highly personal interests in common. "Affiliation groups" have become the new thread linking a highly fragmented culture. Our love of freedom has not overcome our basic hunger for belonging. As the old ways fall by the road—the nuclear family (of legend), the community (once small and safe), the nation (a source of patriotic fervor)—we are attempting to replace them with professional "networks" that reconstruct for us the individual pieces of social fabric that many have missed or never had. These networks include single-parent groups, child-care groups, birth-mother groups, co-dependent groups, political-interest groups, religious groups, self-discovery groups, sports groups, investment groups, sexual-preference groups, caretaker groups, environmental groups, punk groups, museum groups, and a host of hobby and life style groups. There are so many clubs and associations that there is even an association of associations.

We need peers to validate our actions in life, to provide a frame of reference for values of good and bad. Affiliations are a good indicator of our need to reconnect to established comfortable social niches, and maintain who we are. Yet the relationships offered by participation in affiliation groups are rarely deep or broad enough to give us a basis for our identities. At best they reflect a narrow facet of our lives and values, albeit an important one. There must be a simpler, deeper, and more enduring way to find who we are and where we belong in these times.

THE DECADE MATRIX: AMERICA IS ITS TIME TRAVELERS

There is a clue in this pattern, this drive to affiliation by a highly individualistic people: a clue to our identities as a unique culture of American people. Americans, because we lack other unifying qualities, such as a distinct, homogeneous, cultural history and tradition, are a people united by time to a greater extent than other countries and nations. We are perpetually a new country, a new nation, a people whose outlook is being forged by the events through which we have lived. If we want to know who we are, we need to look at who we have been.

We cannot look back generations, across the ocean or deserts to our predecessors; the distance is too great, the distortion of time and space too extreme. We must look at our own selves, and at the times of our lives. Each cohort of Americans has distinctly different experiences that have defined our shared views of the world. Our Time Signatures can give us a reference point for plotting our position in life. Each cohort can discover their bond and the meaning of their own peculiar situation by recognizing that they are time travelers passing through this world together. Further, this lens lets us see more clearly how the times have given unique definition to our personalities, our style of value-expression—our Birthmarks.

Working from this foundation of time—The Decade Matrix—we can begin to recognize that we are not truly free-floating individuals, but are "graduates" of a distinct decade's lessons. We can be embarrassed, or disgusted, or overjoyed at this class membership, but whatever the reaction, the vista is a reflection of what we are and have been—a way to reconstruct who we are. We do not need to necessarily join an affiliation group to find these things out.

America is a culture whose identity is best found in time. Each Time Signature group is a separate, nonrepeating segment of history, almost freestanding, and—in a way—without peers. The Birthmarks of our Time Signature groups are the legitimate personalities of each generation. We can give and take comfort from others when we recognize the importance of our own cohort's story and how each group's Time Signature experiences of the American century have left their own indelible Birthmarks on our identities and our beliefs. However, recognizing that our Time Signatures are the product of our unique times also makes it easier to recognize others of different cohorts. In fact, Time Signatures and Birthmarks of different cohorts may have much in common. History may provide a bond across the decades—between old and young, grandparent and grandchild, friend and neighbor.

Know ourselves, and know others by the roads they have traveled. Our "Rashomon quandary" is to try and see ourselves more clearly through our own life stories and those of our times. In this way we can begin to reconcile ourselves with ourselves and better comprehend the forces that have shaped others of our decade and of decades of this century. Perhaps we Americans need a form of "culture therapy" that will help us recognize the differences in our values across decades, and those foundations which we share across the years.

America is not a country, but we are a people bound by time and geography. We are a nation in flux, but we always have been so. We are not a static culture but are dynamic and rapidly moving voyagers in history who need to reflect on where we have been to know where we are going. Those who do not learn from their own history will most likely trip over their futures. We have met the decades and they are us.

INDEX